Lecture Notes in Computer Sci

Commenced Publication in 1973
Founding and Former Series Editors:
Gerhard Goos, Juris Hartmanis, and Jan van Leeuwen

Andréa W. Richa   Christian Scheideler (Eds.)

Stabilization, Safety, and Security of Distributed Systems

14th International Symposium, SSS 2012
Toronto, Canada, October 1-4, 2012
Proceedings

 Springer

Volume Editors

Andréa W. Richa
Arizona State University
School of Computing, Informatics, and Decision Systems Engineering
699 South Mill Avenue, Tempe, AZ 85281, USA
E-mail: andrea.richa@asu.edu

Christian Scheideler
University of Paderborn
Department of Computer Science
Fürstenallee 11, 33102 Paderborn, Germany
E-mail: scheideler@upb.de

ISSN 0302-9743   e-ISSN 1611-3349
ISBN 978-3-642-33535-8   e-ISBN 978-3-642-33536-5
DOI 10.1007/978-3-642-33536-5
Springer Heidelberg Dordrecht London New York

Library of Congress Control Number: 2012947318

CR Subject Classification (1998): D.4.5, D.4.7, F.3.1, F.1, D.2.13, C.2.4, K.6.5

LNCS Sublibrary: SL 1 – Theoretical Computer Science and General Issues

Typesetting: Camera-ready by author, data conversion by Scientific Publishing Services, Chennai, India

Printed on acid-free paper

Springer is part of Springer Science+Business Media (www.springer.com)

Preface

The papers in this volume were presented at the 14th International Symposium on Stabilization, Safety, and Security of Distributed Systems (SSS), held on October 1–4, 2012 in Toronto, Canada.

SSS is an international forum for researchers and practitioners working on the design and development of distributed systems with self-* properties: (classical) self-stabilizing, self-configuring, self-organizing, self-managing, self-repairing, self-healing, self-optimizing, self-adaptive, and self-protecting. Research in distributed systems is now at a crucial point in its evolution, marked by the importance of dynamic systems such as peer-to-peer networks, large-scale wireless sensor networks, mobile ad hoc networks, cloud computing, robotic networks, etc. Moreover, new applications such as grid and web services, banking and e-commerce, e-health and robotics, aerospace and avionics, automotive, industrial process control, etc. have joined the traditional applications of distributed systems.

The theory of self-stabilization has been enriched in the last 30 years by high-quality research contributions in the areas of algorithmic techniques, formal methodologies, model theoretic issues, and composition techniques. All these areas are essential to the understanding and maintenance of self-* properties in fault-tolerant distributed systems.

This year the program was organized into several tracks reflecting most topics related to self-* systems. The tracks were: (i) Self-Stabilization, (ii) Ad-Hoc and Sensor Networks, (iii) Fault-Tolerant and Dependable Systems, (iv) Safety and Security, (v) Cloud Computing, (vi) Formal Methods, (vii) Social Networks, and (viii) Peer-to-Peer, Self-Organizing, and Autonomic Systems.

We received 75 submissions from 29 countries. Each submission was reviewed by at least three Program Committee members with the help of external reviewers. Out of the 75 submissions, 21 papers were selected as regular papers, and 10 papers were accepted as brief announcements. Among the 21 regular papers, we considered 2 papers for special awards. The best paper award was given to Tomoya Takimoto, Fukuhito Ooshita, Hirotsugu Kakugawa, and Toshimitsu Masuzawa for "Communication-Efficient Self-stabilization in Wireless Networks", and the best student paper award was given to Yanhong A. Liu, Scott D. Stoller, and Bo Lin for "High-Level Executable Specifications of Distributed Algorithms". This year, we were very fortunate to have three distinguished keynote speakers: Dahlia Malkhi, Boaz Patt-Shamir, and Nitin Vaidya.

On behalf of the Program Committee, we would like to thank all the authors that submitted their work to SSS. We sincerely acknowledge the tremendous time and effort the Program Track Chairs and the Program Committee members invested in the symposium. We are also grateful to the external reviewers for their valuable and insightful comments and to Easychair for tremendously simplifying the review process and the generation of the proceedings. Finally, we also thank

the Steering Committee members for their valuable advice and the Organizing
Committee members for their time and effort to ensure a successful meeting.

Organizing this event would not have been possible without the financial
support of the Fields Institute for Research in Mathematical Sciences and the
National Science Foundation of the United States.

October 2012   Andrea Richa
                                                       Christian Scheideler

Organization

Program Committee

Ittai Abraham	Microsoft Research
Marcos Aguilera	Microsoft Research
Lorenzo Alvisi	University of Texas at Austin
Frederik Armknecht	Universität Mannheim
Anish Arora	The Ohio State University
Jim Aspnes	Yale University
Paul Attie	University of Texas at Austin
Rida Bazzi	Arizona State University
Fabricio Benevenuto	Federal University of Ouro Preto (UFOP)
Marina Blanton	University of Notre Dame
Erik-Oliver Blass	EURECOM
Borzoo Bonakdarpour	University of Waterloo
Marius Bozga	Verimag/CNRS
Sonja Buchegger	Royal Institute of Technology (KTH)
Antonio Carzaniga	University of Lugano
Bernadette Charron-Bost	Ecole Polytechnique
Richard Chow	Palo Alto Research Center
Antonio Cutillo	EURECOM
Anwitaman Datta	NTU Singapore
Sylvie Delaet	LRI, Université Paris-Sud 11
Murat Demirbas	SUNY Buffalo
Shlomi Dolev	Ben-Gurion University of the Negev
Pierre Fraigniaud	CNRS and University of Paris 7
Felix Freiling	University of Erlangen-Nuremberg
Davide Frey	INRIA
Jie Gao	Stony Brook University
Sukumar Ghosh	University of Iowa
Seth Gilbert	EPFL Lausanne
Jan Goebel	Siemens AG
Mohamed Gouda	NSF and University of Texas at Austin
Maria Gradinariu Potop-Butucaru	University of Paris 6
Guofei Gu	Texas A&M University
Artur Hecker	Télécom ParisTech
Maurice Herlihy	Brown University
Ted Herman	University of Iowa
Jaap-Henk Hoepman	Radboud University Nijmegen
Shing-Tsaan Huang	National Central University, Taiwan

Adriana Iamnitchi	University of South Florida
Taisuke Izumi	Nagoya Institute of Technology
Henric Johnson	Blekinge Institution of Technology
Sayaka Kamei	Hiroshima University
Anne-Marie Kermarrec	INRIA
Abdelmajid Khelil	TU Darmstadt
Adrian Kosowski	INRIA - Bordeaux Sud-Ouest
Gunnar Kreitz	Royal Institute of Technology (KTH)
Balachander Krishnamurthy	AT&T Research Labs
Ioannis Krontiris	Goethe University Frankfurt
Fabian Kuhn	University of Lugano
Vinod Kulathumani	West Virginia University
Sandeep Kulkarni	Michigan State University
Shay Kutten	Technion
Mikel Larrea	The University of the Basque Country
Insup Lee	University of Pennsylvania
Martin Leucker	University of Lübeck
Heather Lipford	UNC Charlotte
Zvi Lotker	Ben Gurion University of the Negev
John C.S. Lui	Chinese Univ. of Hong Kong
Nancy Lynch	MIT CSAIL
Leonardo Martucci	TU Darmstadt
Toshimitsu Masuzawa	Osaka University
Sayan Mitra	University of Illinois at Urbana-Champaign
Neeraj Mittal	The University of Texas at Dallas
Achour Mostefaoui	IRISA, Université de Rennes
Mirco Musolesi	University of Birmingham
Mikhail Nesterenko	Kent State University
Calvin Newport	Georgetown University
Guevara Noubir	Northeastern University
Marina Papatriantafilou	Chalmers University of Technology
Andrzej Pelc	Université du Quebec en Outaouais
Doron Peled	Bar Ilan University
Franck Petit	LiP6 CNRS-INRIA UPMC Sorbonne Universités
Yvonne-Anne Pignolet	ABB Corporate Research
Alexander Pretschner	Karlsruhe Institute of Technology (KIT)
Daniele Quercia	University of Cambridge
Rajmohan Rajaraman	Northeastern University
Hans Reiser	University of Passau
Andrea Richa	Arizona State University
Konrad Rieck	TU Berlin
Peter Ryan	University of Luxembourg
Jared Saia	University of New Mexico
Stefan Saroiu	Microsoft Research

Christian Scheideler   University of Paderborn
Elad Schiller   Chalmers University of Technology
Christian Schindelhauer   University of Freiburg
Stefan Schmid   TU Berlin / Deutsche Telekom Lab
Ulrich Schmid   Vienna University of Technology
Alexander Shraer   Yahoo! Research
Scott Smolka   Stony Brook Universtiy
Thorsten Strufe   TU Darmstadt
Neeraj Suri   TU Darmstadt
Sébastien Tixeuil   LIP6, Université Paris 6
Stavros Tripakis   University of California, Berkeley
Tatsuhiro Tsuchiya   Osaka University
Volker Turau   Hamburg University of Technology
Max Walter   Siemens AG
Jennifer Welch   Texas A&M University
Josef Widder   Vienna University of Technology
Yuan Xue   Vanderbilt University
Yukiko Yamauchi   Kyushu University
Wang Yi   Uppsala University
Hongwei Zhang   Wayne State University
Lenore Zuck   University of Illinois in Chicago

Additional Reviewers

Brukman, Olga   Larmore, Lawrence
Chen, Yu   Le Merrer, Erwan
Cornejo, Alex   Leal, William
D'Souza, Deepak   Li, Jing
Deuker, André   Markin, Grigory
Devismes, Stéphane   McGill, Stephen
Dubois, Swan   Mekhaldi, Fouzi
Duggirala, Parasara Sridhar   Nowak, Thomas
Erlandsson, Fredrik   Outa, Rami
Hatem, George   Park, Junkil
Herman, Ted   Roy, Dhrubojyoti
Izumi, Tomoko   Subotic, Pavle
Johnson, Taylor   Yamauchi, Yukiko
Khader, Dalia   Zhang, Yihua

Resilient Distributed Consensus

Nitin H. Vaidya

Dept. of Electrical and Computer Engineering
University of Illinois at Urbana-Champaign
Urbana, IL 61801, USA

Abstract. Consensus algorithms allow a set of nodes to reach an agreement on a quantity of interest. For instance, a consensus algorithm may be used to allow a network of sensors to determine the average value of samples collected by the different sensors. Similarly, a consensus algorithm can also be used by the nodes to synchronize their clocks. Research on consensus algorithms has a long history, with contributions from different research communities, including distributed computing, control systems, and social science.

In this talk, we will discuss two resilient consensus algorithms that can perform correctly despite the following two types of adversities: (i) In wireless networks, transmissions are subject to transmission errors, resulting in packet losses. We will discuss how "average consensus" can be achieved over such lossy links, without explicitly making the links reliable, for instance, via retransmissions. (ii) In a distributed setting, some of the nodes in the network may fail or may be compromised. We will discuss a consensus algorithm that can tolerate "Byzantine" failures in partially connected networks.

Low-Congestion Distributed Algorithms

Boaz Patt-Shamir[*]

School of Electrical Engineering, Tel Aviv University, Tel Aviv 69978, Israel
boaz@eng.tau.ac.il

The traditional model for computing over a communication network (called LO-CAL) allows sending a message of arbitrary size in a single time step. This way, the time complexity is a measure of the locality of algorithms: saying that an algorithm runs in time T is equivalent, under the LOCAL model, to saying that the problem can be solved if each node learns all information the nodes which are reachable within T hops. Therefore, in this model any problem can be solved in time linear in the network diameter.

While work on the LOCAL model has produced many interesting results, it is widely accepted that this model does not capture the true complexity of distributed computing: it is mainly useful in understanding what *cannot* be done distributively, i.e., lower bounds. A better approximation of reality is the CON-GEST model, where a link can carry only a bounded number of bits in a time step. Usually, it is assumed that message size is $O(\log n)$ bits, so that each message can carry a constant number of reasonably-sized pieces of information, such as node identifiers, or values of polynomial magnitude. It turned out that in this model, many problems cannot be solved in $o(\sqrt{n})$ time, even in networks of diameter, say, $O(\log n)$ hops. On the other hand, letting D denote the network diameter in hops, there are some problems in which the $O(D + \sqrt{n})$ time upper bound is nearly achievable in the CONGEST model (to within a polylogarithmic factor).

In this talk we review some known results in the CONGEST model, as well as some new progress directions. In particular, we will consider approximate all-pairs shortest-paths in *weighted* graphs, namely we assume that each link has a positive weight, and the task is to find, for each possible source and destination nodes a route that connects them, whose total weight is not much larger than the minimum possible. The best known distributed algorithm for this problem to date in the CONGEST model in the classical Bellman-Ford algorithm [1, 2], whose time complexity is proportional to the maximal number of hops in a weighted shortest path, which could be $\Omega(n)$ even in graphs of constant hop-diameter.

References

1. Bellman, R.E.: On a routing problem. Quart. Appl. Math. 16, 87–90 (1958)
2. Ford, L.R.: Network flow theory. Report P-923, The Rand Corp. (1956)

---

[*] Supported in part by the Israel Science Foundation (grant 1372/09) and by Israel Ministry of Science and Technology.

What Happens When Systems Go Elastic?

Dahlia Malkhi

Microsoft Research, Silicon Valley
1288 Pear Ave
Mountain View, CA 94043, USA

Abstract. A *reconfiguration* operation allows systems to deploy new hardware, remove failed components, and change various configuration properties like node roles and weights.

This talk is titled 'what happens when systems go elastic?' because the foundations of dynamic distributed systems are weird. For example, the classic theory of replication indicates that you need 2F+1 machines to tolerate F failures, but the entire engineering world uses primary-back (two-way) replication with $F = 1$; until recently, there was no existing liveness model of the type 'F-out-of-N crashes' for dynamic systems; and when you examine Paxos, the flagship consensus protocol for state-machine-replication, you find that dynamic Paxos reconfiguration causes unintended violation of causal ordering.

In this talk, we cover progress on several fundamental issues regarding dynamically reconfigurable systems.

- We tackle the question of liveness, and overview a pioneering straw-man failure model in which a dynamic system is guaranteed to make progress. Our model is cast as a dynamic interplay between an adversary and system events.
- We explain precisely the above claim on Paxos, implying a foundational distinction between the popular State-Machine-Replication paradigm and Virtual Synchrony (a.k.a. group communication).
- Accordingly, We give a recipe for *virtually-synchronous* reconfiguration of replicated services.
- We demystify the $F + 1$ vs. $2F + 1$ seeming gap, by rigorously integrating into the execution model an auxiliary configuration service (e.g., industry solutions like Chubby and ZooKeeper).
- We overview our successful efforts to extend the ZooKeeper coordination service itself to be elastic.
- We demonstrate that no source of agreement is actually necessary for dynamism per se, breaking the popular gospel that dynamic systems must maintain agreement on system views.

Acknowledgements: Marcos Aguilera, Ken Birman, Flaviu Junqueira, Idit Keidar, Leslie Lamport, JP Martin, Ben Reed, Alex Shraer, Robbert VanRenesse, Lidong Zhou

Table of Contents

Communication-Efficient Self-stabilization in Wireless Networks*

Tomoya Takimoto, Fukuhito Ooshita,
Hirotsugu Kakugawa, and Toshimitsu Masuzawa

Graduate School of Information Science and Technology, Osaka University, Japan
{t-takimt,f-oosita,kakugawa,masuzawa}@ist.osaka-u.ac.jp

Abstract. A self-stabilizing protocol is guaranteed to eventually reach a safe (or legitimate) configuration even when started from an arbitrary configuration. Most of self-stabilizing protocols require each process to keep communicating with all of its neighbors forever even after reaching a safe configuration. Such permanent communication impairs efficiency, but is necessary in nature of self-stabilization.

The concept of communication-efficiency was introduced to reduce communication after reaching a safe configuration. The previous concept targets the point-to-point communication model, and is not appropriate to the wireless network model where a process can locally broadcast a message to its neighbors all at once.

In this paper, we refine the concept of the communication-efficiency for the wireless network model, and investigate its possibility in self-stabilization for some fundamental problems; the minimal (connected) dominating set problem, the maximal independent set problem, and the spanning tree construction problem.

1 Introduction

A *self-stabilizing* protocol [1] is guaranteed to eventually reach a safe (or legitimate) configuration even when started from an arbitrary configuration. This property enables self-stabilizing protocols to autonomously adapt to transient faults and dynamical topology changes of networks. A main concern in efficiency of self-stabilizing protocols is efficiency *in convergence* after faults, i.e., the *convergence time* required to reach a safe configuration from any configuration. The convergence time is a natural efficiency measure of self-stabilizing protocols since it is very similar to the time complexity measure of ordinary (non-self-stabilizing) protocols. However, a crucial difference in communication cost between self-stabilizing and ordinary protocols lies in the cost of communication *after convergence* to a safe configuration; self-stabilizing protocols cannot allow any process to terminate its communication even after reaching a safe configuration, while ordinary ones can eventually allow every process to terminate all the

---

* This work is supported in part by Grant-in-Aid for Scientific Research ((B)20300012, (B)22300009, (B)23700056, (C)24500039) of JSPS.

A.W. Richa and C. Scheideler (Eds.): SSS 2012, LNCS 7596, pp. 1–15, 2012.
© Springer-Verlag Berlin Heidelberg 2012

activity. Especially, in practical applications, communication efficiency is more important *after* convergence than *during* convergence: self-stabilizing protocols are expected to stay at safe configurations most of the time since deviations from the safe configurations caused by transient faults or topology changes occur infrequently. Nevertheless, most of self-stabilizing protocols require each process to keep communicating with all the neighbors forever.

To circumvent the inefficiency after reaching a safe configuration, the concept of *communication-efficiency* was introduced [2,3]. The concept is targeting the *point-to-point* communication model in the sense that the communication efficiency is achieved by reducing the number of process pairs that keep communicating with each other after reaching a safe configuration. Thus, the concept is not appropriate to the wireless network model where a process can locally *broadcast* a message to its neighbors all at once.

Contribution of this paper: The contribution of this paper is threefold.

1. We introduce new communication efficiency measures for the wireless network model, *k-broadcast-stability* and *k(-average)-broadcast-efficiency* [1]. Informally, the *k*-broadcast-stability guarantees that at most *k* processes keep (locally) broadcasting after reaching a safe configuration. On the other hand, the *k(-average)-broadcast-efficiency* guarantees that at most *k* processes broadcast messages every step (on average) after reaching a safe configuration (the broadcasting processes can differ at different steps). Notice that these concepts are derived from the *k*-stability and the *k*-efficiency in [2] as refinements for the wireless network model.

2. Concerning the broadcast-stability, we show the following results.
   - For the the *minimal connected dominating set* (MCDS) problem and the *spanning tree construction* (ST) problem, the $(n-1)$-broadcast-stability is *impossible* to attain, where n is the number of processes in the network. This result implies that any self-stabilizing protocol for the problems requires all the processes to keep broadcasting forever.
   - For the *minimal dominating set* (MDS) problem and the *maximal independent set* (MIS) problem, $(I_G^{min}-1)$-broadcast-stability is *impossible* to attain but I_G^{Max}-broadcast-stability is *attainable*, where I_G^{min} and I_G^{Max} are respectively the minimum and the maximum sizes of the maximal independent set of the network.

   An interesting observation from these results is that the connectivity requirement of the minimal dominating set makes an essential difference in possibility of the broadcast-stability.

3. Concerning the average-broadcast-efficiency, we show the following results.
   - For the MCDS, the MDS, the MIS and the ST problems, $o(n)$-average-broadcast-efficiency is *practically impossible* to attain if processes know no upper bound of n. More precisely, the convergence time of any $o(n)$-average-broadcast-efficient protocol cannot be bounded.

---

[1] These measures are also summarized in a brief survey paper [4].

- When every process knows an upper bound N of n, there exists a *universal* 1-average-broadcast-efficient protocol with the convergence time $O(N)$ for *all the static problems*. The strong result is obtained by presenting a transformer from a silent self-stabilizing protocol with a known convergence time T to a 1-average-broadcast-efficient self-stabilizing protocol with the convergence time $O(T + N)$.

Related works: Aguilera et al. [5] introduced the concept of *communication-efficiency* in implementation of failure detector Ω. Following the work, some papers investigated communication-efficiency in failure detector implementation [6,7,8,9]. The implementations in [5,6,9] can tolerate any number of crash processes and require only $n - 1$ unidirectional links to carry messages forever.

Some works [2,3] discussed communication-efficiency of self-stabilizing protocols in the point-to-point communication model. The communication-efficiency is achieved by reducing the number of process pairs that keep communicating with each other after convergence to a safe configuration. They introduced two concepts, *stability* and *efficiency*, as quantitative measures of communication-efficiency. Informally, the stability guarantees that the number of process pairs that keep communicating with each other is limited. On the other hand, the efficiency guarantees that the number of process pairs that communicate with each other is limited at every step (the pairs can differ at different steps). They investigated the stability and the efficiency for the vertex coloring problem, the MIS problem, the maximal matching problem [2], and the ST problem [3]. Another challenge, *communication adaptability*, to reduce communication complexity after reaching a safe configuration is presented in [10].

Kutten et al. [11] pointed out that reducing the communication overhead after convergence leads longer convergence time, and results in increasing the communication overhead during convergence. They presented a randomized self-stabilizing protocol that succeeds to reduce the communication overhead both during and after convergence for the ST problem.

The rest of the paper is organized as follows. Section 2 presents definitions of the wireless network model, self-stabilizing protocols, and the communication-efficiency. Sections 3 and 4 investigate possibility of the broadcast-stability, and Sections 5 and 6 investigate possibility of the broadcast-efficiency. Section 7 concludes this paper.

2   Preliminaries

2.1   System Model

We consider distributed systems with a (local) broadcast communication primitive such as wireless communication. The system model is defined as follows.

A *distributed system* is modeled by an undirected labeled graph $G = (P(G), L(G))$, where $P(G)$ is the set of n processes and $L(G)$ is the set of bidirectional communication links. Each process $v \in P(G)$ has a unique ID denoted by ID_v. A link connecting processes v and w is denoted by (v, w). We say w is a *neighbor* of v if $(v, w) \in L(G)$, and the set of neighbors of v is denoted by $N_G(v)$ (or simply by $N(v)$ when G is apparent). We consider only connected distributed systems and denote the set of such systems by $\mathcal{G}$.

A process can communicate with its neighbors by (local) *broadcast*: when a process v broadcasts a message, each neighbor $w \in N(v)$ of v receives the message. We assume that the broadcast is reliable and all the neighbors correctly receive the message.

An important feature of wireless networks such as ad hoc ones is that a process is unaware of its neighbors until it receives messages from them. Thus, we assume each process v has no knowledge of $N(v)$ or $|N(v)|$. Also, when v receives a message, it cannot identify its sender unless the message contains the sender's ID.

A process is modeled by a state machine and a *configuration* of a distributed system G is specified by an n-tuple $c = (s_0, s_1, \ldots, s_{n-1})$, where s_i stands for the state of process v_i $(0 \leq i \leq n - 1)$. We consider only a *synchronous* distributed system where all processes execute actions in a lockstep fashion. In each synchronous step, every process executes the following three operations.

1. Broadcast a message (depending on its state) to all the neighbors.
2. Receive messages from neighbors that are sent in the beginning of the step.
3. Update its state (depending on its state and the received messages).

When the configuration changes from c to c' in a step, we denote the transition by $c \mapsto c'$. *Execution* of a distributed system is an infinite sequence $E = c_0, c_1, c_2, \ldots$ satisfying $c_j \mapsto c_{j+1}$ $(j \geq 0)$, where c_0 is called the *initial configuration*. In this paper, we consider only deterministic protocols, and thus, execution starting from the initial configuration c_0 is uniquely determined.

2.2   Self-stabilizing Protocol

A *problem* is defined on the *output variables* of processes and specifies the requirement that the output variables should satisfy. A problem is called *static* when the output variables should be eventually stable with satisfying the problem requirement. All the problems considered in this paper are static.

A configuration c is called *safe* for a static problem when it satisfies the problem requirement and the output variables of all processes remain unchanged in the execution starting from c. A protocol is called *self-stabilizing* for a static problem if it eventually reaches a safe configuration even when starting from any initial configuration.

2.3   Communication Efficiency

The previous concept of communication efficiency [2,3] aims to reduce the number of communicating process pairs. But it is not adequate to a distributed system with a broadcast communication primitive, where a process can send a message to all the neighbors by a single broadcast operation. We introduce an alternative concept of communication efficiency for distributed systems with a broadcast communication primitive. Intuitively, communication-efficiency in such a system should aim to reduce the number of broadcasts after convergence.

In the following definitions, $k : \mathcal{G} \to \mathbb{N}$ denotes a function from a distributed system to a positive integer, and $S_{A,G}(c)$ denotes the set of processes that broadcast messages in the step starting at configuration c of a protocol A .

Definition 1 ($k(G)$-broadcast-stability). *A self-stabilizing protocol A is $k(G)$-broadcast-stable if, for any execution $c_0, c_1, \dots$ of A in any distributed system $G \in \mathcal{G}$, there exists i such that a suffix $c_i, c_{i+1}, \dots$ satisfies*

$$\left| \bigcup_{j \geq i} S_{A,G}(c_j) \right| \leq k(G).$$ □

The $k(G)$-broadcast-stability guarantees that eventually at most $k(G)$ processes keep broadcasting, and thus, at least $n - k(G)$ processes eventually stop broadcasting.

Definition 2 ($k(G)$-broadcast-efficiency). *A self-stabilizing protocol A is $k(G)$-broadcast-efficient if, for any execution $c_0, c_1, \dots$ of A in any distributed system $G \in \mathcal{G}$, there exists i such that a suffix $c_i, c_{i+1}, \dots$ satisfies*

$$\forall j \geq i, \ |S_{A,G}(c_j)| \leq k(G).$$ □

The $k(G)$-broadcast-efficiency guarantees that eventually at most $k(G)$ processes broadcast messages in every step. Note that the broadcasting processes can differ at different steps. It is clear that $k(G)$-broadcast-stability implies $k(G)$-broadcast-efficiency, but the converse does not hold.

A relaxed variation of the $k(G)$-broadcast-efficiency is to allow at most $k(G)$ processes to broadcast messages in every step *on average*, which attains communication-efficiency practically equivalent to the $k(G)$-broadcast-efficiency. The variation is defined as follows.

Definition 3 ($k(G)$-average-broadcast-efficiency). *A self-stabilizing protocol A is $k(G)$-average-broadcast-efficient if, for any execution $c_0, c_1, \dots$ of A in any distributed system $G \in \mathcal{G}$, there exists i such that a suffix $c_i, c_{i+1}, \dots$ satisfies*

$$\lim_{j \to \infty} \tfrac{1}{j-i+1} \sum_{k=i}^{j} |S_{A,G}(c_k)| \leq k(G).$$ □

3 Impossibility of Broadcast-Stability

This section presents impossibility results concerning the broadcast-stability. The impossibility proofs are based on the simple observations that any process cannot become aware of changes of the processes that never broadcast messages. The details of the observations are as follows.

Observation 1: Let G be a distributed system, $E = c_0, c_1, \dots$ be an execution of a protocol A in G, and U be a set of processes that never broadcast messages in E. Consider any distributed system G' obtained from G by removing some processes in U, removing some links between remaining processes in

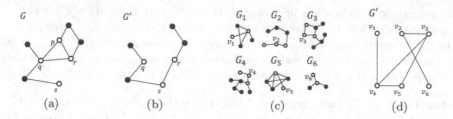

Fig. 1. Construction of G' in Observations. (a) G and $U = \{p, q, r, s\}$ in Observation 1. (b) An example of G' in Observation 1. (c) $G_1, G_2, \ldots, G_6$ in Observation 2. (d) An example of G' in Observation 2.

U, and adding some links between remaining processes in U (Fig. 1(a),(b)). (When G' obtained by the above modification is disconnected, any of its connected components is considered as G'.) Then, $E' = c'_0, c'_1, \ldots$ is an execution of A in G' such that the state of every process at c'_i is the same as that at c_i for every i ($i \geq 0$).

Observation 2: Let $G_1, G_2, \ldots, G_n$ be distributed systems such that the process sets are mutually disjoint, $E_x = c_{x,0}, c_{x,1}, \ldots$ be an execution of a protocol A in G_x, and v_x be a process (if exists) that never broadcasts or receives messages in E_x ($1 \leq x \leq n$). Consider any distributed system G' consisting of processes $\{v_1, v_2, \ldots, v_n\}$ and arbitrarily added links (Fig. 1(c),(d)). Then, $E' = c'_0, c'_1, \ldots$ is an execution of A in G' such that the state of every process v_x at c'_i is the same as that at $c_{x,i}$ for every x ($1 \leq x \leq n$) and i ($i \geq 0$).

3.1   Spanning Tree Construction

The *spanning tree construction (ST) problem* requires each process to select a neighbor as its parent so that the parent relations of all processes form a spanning tree of the distributed system. Each process has an output variable *prnt* to store the ID of its parent. In the process selected as the root of the spanning tree, *prnt* stores its own ID.

The broadcast-stability is impossible to attain for the ST problem:

Theorem 1. *Let $k(G)$ be any function satisfying $k(G) < n(= |P(G)|)$ for any distributed system $G \in \mathcal{G}$. There is no $k(G)$-broadcast-stable self-stabilizing protocol for the spanning tree construction problem.*

Proof. Assume, for contradiction, that there exists a $k(G)$-broadcast-stable self-stabilizing protocol A for the ST problem. Then, any execution of A in G has a suffix $E = c_i, c_{i+1}, \ldots$ in which a spanning tree is constructed (and remains unchanged) and at least one process never broadcasts messages.

(a) Case that there exists a non-leaf process, say v, of the spanning tree that never broadcasts messages in E: Let G' be the distributed system obtained from G by removing v, and $E' = c'_i, c'_{i+1}, \ldots$ be the execution of A in G' described in Observation 1. In E', the output variable $prnt$ of every process remains unchanged. However, the variables of all the processes do not form a spanning tree, since there is a neighbor $w \in N_G(v)$ of v that selects v as its parent but v does not exist in G'. This implies that protocol A cannot reach a safe configuration in E', which is a contradiction.

(b) Case that only leaf processes of the spanning tree never broadcast messages in E: Let G' be the distributed system obtained from G by removing all the processes that never broadcast in E, and $E' = c'_i, c'_{i+1}, \ldots$ be the execution of A in G' described in Observation 1. No process stops broadcasting in E', which contradicts $k(G')$-broadcast-stability for $k(G') < |P(G')|$. □

3.2 Minimal Connected Dominating Set

A *dominating set* of G is a subset $D \subseteq P(G)$ of processes such that each process $v \in P(G) - D$ has a neighbor in D. If the subgraph $G[D]$ of G induced by a dominating set D is connected, D is a *connected* dominating set of G. If no proper subset of (connected) dominating set D is a (connected) dominating set, D is a *minimal* (connected) dominating set.

The *minimal connected dominating set (MCDS) problem* requires us to choose processes so that they should form a MCDS of the distributed system. Each process has a boolean output variable $mcds$ and stores true when it is a member of the MCDS.

Theorem 2. *Let $k(G)$ be any function satisfying $k(G) < n(= |P(G)|)$ for any distributed system $G \in \mathcal{G}$. There is no $k(G)$-broadcast-stable self-stabilizing protocol for the minimal connected dominating set problem.*

Proof. We can prove this theorem by similar argument to the proof of Theorem 1, with restricting our attention to distributed systems of line topology ($n \geq 6$). Notice that the MCDS of such a system is uniquely determined as the set of all the processes except for the two end processes. □

3.3 Minimal Dominating Set and Maximal Independent Set Problems

For the minimal dominating set (MDS) problem, we can prove the following impossibility result, which is weaker than Theorem 2 for the MCDS problem. Actually, we can present a broadcast-stable self-stabilizing protocol for the MDS problem in Section 4. These results show that the connectivity requirement of the minimal dominating set brings an essential difference in possibility of the broadcast-stability.

Theorem 3. *Let $k(G)$ be any function satisfying $k(G) < I_G^{min}$ for any distributed system $G \in \mathcal{G}$ where I_G^{min} is the minimum size of the maximal independent set of G. There is no $k(G)$-broadcast-stable self-stabilizing protocol for the minimal dominating set problem.*

Proof. We restrict our attention to distributed systems of line topology, and assume, for contradiction, that there exists a $k(G)$-broadcast-stable self-stabilizing protocol A for the MDS problem.

Let $\mathcal{P}_n$ be the set of n-process distributed systems of line topology. Since $I_G^{min} = \lceil n/3 \rceil$ holds for any $G \in \mathcal{P}_n$, at least $n - \lceil n/3 \rceil + 1$ processes eventually stop broadcasting in any execution of A. In case of $n = 3\ell$ for a positive integer ℓ, this implies that there exist, in any execution of A, three consecutive processes that eventually stop broadcasting. Notice that the process in the middle of the three never broadcasts or receives messages after some configuration in the execution. Thus, Observation 2 allows us to construct a distributed system of line topology by choosing such a process from each of some distributed systems.

More concretely, we consider n distributed systems $P_1, P_2, \ldots, P_n$ ($P_i \in \mathcal{P}_n$) such that their ID sets are mutually disjoint. We choose, from each P_i, a process v_i that never broadcasts or receives messages after some configuration in an execution. Following Observation 2, we can arbitrarily add links, and thus, we can construct a line that does not satisfy the MDS specification. This is a contradiction.   □

An *independent set* of G is a subset $I \subseteq P(G)$ such that no processes in I are neighboring. If no proper superset of an independent set I is an independent set, I is a *maximal* independent set (MIS). The following theorem on impossibility of the MIS problem is derived from Theorem 3 since any MIS is a MDS.

Theorem 4. *Let $k(G)$ be any function satisfying $k(G) < I_G^{min}$ for any distributed system $G \in \mathcal{G}$. There is no $k(G)$-broadcast-stable self-stabilizing protocol for the maximal independent set problem.*   □

4   Broadcast-Stable Self-stabilizing Protocol

Theorems 1 and 2 imply that all processes have to keep broadcasting forever in any self-stabilizing protocol for the ST and the MCDS problems. Thus the broadcast-stability is impossible to attain for these problems. In this section, we show possibility of the broadcast-stability for the other two problems, the MDS and the MIS problems.

A broadcast-stable self-stabilizing protocol, *stable-MIS*, for the MIS problem is presented in Protocol 1. Each process v has a boolean output variable ind_v to denote whether v is a member of the constructed MIS: v is a member of the MIS iff $ind_v = \mathtt{true}$.

The main idea to achieve the broadcast-stability is that only the processes in the constructed MIS are allowed to keep broadcasting. The assumption of synchronous distributed systems guarantees that a process v has a neighbor in the MIS if and only if v receives a message. To break symmetry, the message contains the sender's ID and a process with a larger ID has higher priority to become a member of the MIS.

The following two lemmas obviously hold.

Protocol 1. *stable-MIS* : actions of process v in each step.

Output Variables:
1: ind_v : boolean;
Internal Variables:
2: M_v : set of messages;
Actions:
3: **if** $ind_v = $ **true then**
4:    Broadcast($\{ID_v\}$);
5: **end if**
6: $M_v \leftarrow$ received messages;
7: **if** $\exists m \in M_v[m.ID > ID_v]$ **then**
8:    $ind_v \leftarrow$ **false**;
9: **else**
10:    $ind_v \leftarrow$ **true**;
11: **end if**

Lemma 1 (Safe configuration). *A configuration c of protocol stable-MIS is safe if c satisfies the following conditions:*

1. $\forall v \in P(G)$, $[(ind_v = $ true$) \Rightarrow (\forall w \in N(v)$, $ind_w = $ false$)]$.
2. $\forall v \in P(G)$, $[(ind_v = $ false$) \Rightarrow \exists w \in N(v)$ $(ID_w > ID_v \land ind_w = $ true$)]$. $\square$

Lemma 2 (Convergence). *Starting from any initial configuration, protocol stable-MIS reaches a safe configuration in at most n steps.* $\square$

The following theorem is derived from Lemmas 1, 2, and the fact that only processes in the constructed MIS keep broadcasting. The theorem also holds for the MDS, since protocol *stable-MIS* is also a solution to the MDS problem (Recall any MIS is a MDS). In the theorem, I_G^{Max} denotes the size of the *maximum* independent set of $G \in \mathcal{G}$.

Theorem 5. *Protocol stable-MIS is a I_G^{Max}-broadcast-stable self-stabilizing protocol for the maximal independent set problem and the minimal dominating set problem. It reaches a safe configuration in at most n steps in any distributed system $G \in \mathcal{G}$.* $\square$

5   Impossibility of Broadcast-Efficiency

The average-broadcast-efficiency can be improved by prohibiting each process from broadcasting a message *every step* and, instead, by allowing each process to broadcast a message only *every k steps* for some positive integer k. This reduces the average-broadcast-efficiency by a factor of k (e.g., from n to n/k), but may increase the convergence time by a factor of k. Actually, we can show a negative result when no upper bound of the number of processes n is available at any process: $o(n)$-average-broadcast-efficiency is *practically* impossible to attain in the sense that any protocol with such efficiency has no upper bound (even depending on n) on the convergence time.

The negative result is obtained by the argument based on the following observation, which is similar to Observation 2. Observation 2 was used to show existence of an infinite execution in which no process broadcasts messages. On the other hand, the following observation is used to show existence of a sufficiently (but finite) long fragment of execution in which no process broadcasts messages.

Observation 3: Let $G_1, G_2, \ldots, G_n$ be distributed systems such that the process sets are mutually disjoint, $E_x = c_{x,0}, c_{x,1}, \ldots$ be an execution of a protocol A in G_x, and v_x be a process (if exists) that never broadcasts or receives messages in an execution prefix $E_x^t = c_{x,0}, c_{x,1}, \ldots, c_{x,t}$ $(1 \leq x \leq n)$. Consider any distributed system G' consisting of n processes $\{v_1, v_2, \ldots, v_n\}$ and arbitrarily added links. Then, $E' = c'_0, c'_1, \ldots, c'_t$ is an execution prefix of A in G' such that the state of every process v_x at c'_i is the same as that at $c_{x,i}$ for every x $(1 \leq x \leq n)$ and i $(0 \leq i \leq t)$.

The following lemma holds for distributed systems of line topology.

Lemma 3. *Consider any execution E of any $k(G)$-average-broadcast-efficient protocol A in a distributed system $G \in \mathcal{P}_m$ for any $m > 3$. There exist three consecutive processes and an execution fragment composed of $\lfloor \frac{m-3}{3k(G)} \rfloor$ steps such that the three processes never broadcast messages during the execution fragment.*

$\square$

The following theorem can be obtained by argument similar to the proof of Theorem 3.

Theorem 6. *Assume no upper bound of the number of processes n is available at any process, and consider any $o(n)$-average-broadcast-efficient protocol A for the maximal independent set problem, the minimal dominating set problem, the minimal connected dominating set problem, or the spanning tree construction problem. Then, the convergence time of A cannot be bounded by any T (which may depend on n).*

Proof. We restrict our attention to distributed systems of line topology, and assume, for contradiction, that there exists a $k(G)$-average-broadcast-efficient self-stabilizing protocol A for the problem, where $k(G) = o(n)$, with the convergence time bounded by T (which may depend on n).

Let $G_1, G_2, \ldots, G_n$ $(G_i \in \mathcal{P}_m)$ be n distributed systems of m-process line topology such that the process sets are mutually disjoint. Each G_i contains a process, say v_i, that is the middle of the three consecutive processes in Lemma 3. Note that v_i never broadcasts or receives messages during the execution fragment of length $\lfloor \frac{m-3}{3k(G_i)} \rfloor$ in G_i. Observation 3 allows us to construct a distributed system G of line topology consisting of $v_1, v_2, \ldots, v_n$ so that its initial configuration is not safe and no process broadcasts messages in the first $\lfloor \frac{m-3}{3k(G_j)} \rfloor$ steps, where

$k(G_j) = \max_{1 \leq i \leq n} k(G_i)$. By setting m to satisfy $\lfloor \frac{m-3}{3k(G_j)} \rfloor > T$ $(k(G_j) = o(m)$ guarantees existence of such m), we can show that the convergence time of A is longer than T, which is a contradiction. □

6   Broadcast-Efficient Self-stabilizing Protocol

In Section 5, we showed that the $o(n)$-average-broadcast-efficiency is impossible to attain without greatly sacrificing the convergence time if no upper bound of n is available. However, the situation drastically changes if an upper bound N of n is available. In this section, we show that knowledge of N allows the 1-average-broadcast-efficiency without paying high penalty on the convergence time: we present a method for transforming any silent self-stabilizing protocol with a known (upper bound of) convergence time T to a 1-average-broadcast-efficient self-stabilizing protocol with the convergence time $O(T + N)$.

We assume that an upper bound N of n is known to each process. We also assume that a self-stabilizing protocol A given as an *input* of the transformation satisfies the following conditions (called *input conditions*).

(a) A is *silent*, that is, no process changes its state after reaching a safe configuration.
(b) In any execution, every process broadcasts a message every step.
(c) In any unsafe configuration c, there exists at least one process that changes its state in the step from c.
(d) An upper bound T of the convergence time is known.

Protocol 2 presents the transformation method by showing the protocol *Eff(A)* resulting from the input protocol A. The main idea for attaining the 1-average-broadcast-efficiency is to allow each process to broadcast a message *only every N steps* after reaching a safe configuration of A. It is obvious that such *slow-down* in activity brings the 1-average-broadcast-efficiency to A. However it is impossible for a self-stabilizing protocol to correctly detect a safe configuration. Especially, the fault positive in the detection may increase the convergence time of A from T to NT: when processes prematurely slow down before reaching a safe configuration, the convergence time may become N times longer.

The idea for overcoming this difficulty comes from the following observations.

1. Even when every process prematurely detects a safe configuration and restricts it to broadcast a message only every N steps, each process can acquire the states of all the neighbors in N steps. Thus, from the input condition (c), there exists a process that changes its state in N steps. This implies that the premature slowdown can be detected in N steps.
2. When a process detects the premature slowdown, it can signal, in n steps, all processes to stop the slowdown and come back to *ordinary execution* of A that allows all processes to broadcast messages every step.
3. Once all processes execute ordinary execution of A during T steps, the protocol reaches and remains at a safe configuration.

To realize a method inspired from the above observations, we use a *local clock* of each process and *clock synchronization*. Each process v has variable $clock_v$: $\{0, \ldots, T + 2N\}$ as a local clock, and uses it as follows.

1. The local clocks of all the processes become synchronized by executing
$$clock_v \leftarrow \min\{\min\{clock_w | w \in N_G(v) \cup \{v\}\} + 1, T + 2N\}.$$
   The intuition is that processes try to adjust their clocks to that with the lowest clock value, and the clock value is bounded by $T + 2N$. As long as $clock_v$ is synchronized with those of the neighbors, the clock value increases by one every step until it reaches $T + 2N$.

2. Any clock value less than $T + 2N$ suggests that a safe configuration is not reached yet (though the suggestion may not be correct). Thus, it makes process v execute ordinary execution of protocol A.

3. Clock value $T + 2N$ suggests that the configuration is safe (though the suggestion may not be correct). Thus, it makes process v slowdown and broadcast a message only every N steps.
   Even when $clock_v = T + 2N$ holds, process v executes actions of A on receipt of messages. If the configuration is safe, v never changes its state. Thus, a change of v's state implies detection of an unsafe configuration. In this case, v also executes $clock_v \leftarrow 0$ to come back to ordinary execution of A. The clock synchronization mechanism brings, in n steps, all processes back to ordinary execution of A. We call the process v that executes $clock_v \leftarrow 0$ an *initiator*.

As we show later, if a safe configuration is not reached sufficiently long time, the clocks of all processes become synchronized before the clock value of any process reaches $2N$. Once the clocks become synchronized, all processes execute ordinary execution of A. The ordinary execution lasts during at least T steps (until the clock value reaches $T + 2N$), which guarantees that protocol A reaches a safe configuration.

In Protocol 2, each process v has variable $state_v$ to store its current state of A, and executes protocol A using the variable. Each process also has variable $cache_v$ to store the set of messages: for each neighbor $w \in N(v)$, the latest message from w is stored in $cache_v$. Process v uses the stored messages to execute actions of A, when v receives no message from a neighbor, say w. This situation occurs when w slows down. Notice that $cache_v$ may store false messages from non-neighbors (that may not exist in the system) in the initial configuration. To eliminate such false messages, v removes the stored message from w if v receives no message during $N + 1$ steps (for simplicity, this action is omitted in Protocol 2).

Lemma 4 (Safe configuration). *A configuration of Eff(A) is safe if the following conditions are satisfied.*

- $\forall v \in P(G)$, $clock_v = T + 2N$.
- $\forall v \in P(G)$, $cache_v$ *stores the latest message from each neighbor* $w \in N(v)$.
- *Letting c' be an n-tuple $(state_{v_0}, \ldots, state_{v_{n-1}})$ where $\{v_0, \ldots, v_{n-1}\} = P(G)$, c' is a safe configuration of A.* $\square$

Protocol 2. *Eff(A)* : Actions of process v in each step.

Constants:
1: N : upper bound on n
2: T : upper bound on the convergence time of the input protocol A
Variables:
3: $state_v$: a state of v in protocol A
4: $cache_v$: a set of messages received from neighbors
5: $clock_v$: $\{0, ..., T + 2N\}$
6: $count_v$: $\{0, ..., N - 1\}$
Actions:
7: **if** $clock_v < T + 2N$ **then** // process v executes ordinary execution of A
8:      Broadcast($(ID_v, msg_v, clock_v)$); //msg_v is the message sent by A
9:      $M_v \leftarrow$ received messages;
10:     Update $cache_v$ using M_v to store the latest message from each neighbor;
11:     Update $state_v$ using $cache_v$ by actions of A;
12:     $clock_v \leftarrow \min(\{m.clock | m \in M_v\} \cup \{clock_v\}) + 1$;
13:     $count_v \leftarrow 0$;
14: **else** // process v executes slowdown execution of A
15:     **if** $count_v = 0$ **then**
16:         Broadcast($(ID_v, msg_v, clock_v)$); //msg_v is the message sent by A
17:     **end if**
18:     $M_v \leftarrow$ received messages;
19:     Update $cache_v$ using M_v to store the latest message from each neighbor;
20:     Update $state_v$ using $cache_v$ by actions of A;
21:     **if** $state_v$ changed **then** // an unsafe configuration is detected
22:         $clock_v \leftarrow 0$;
23:     **else if** $\exists m \in M_v [m.clock < T + 2N - 1]$ **then**
24:         $clock_v \leftarrow \min\{m.clock | m \in M_v\} + 1$;
25:     **end if**
26:     $count_v \leftarrow (count_v + 1) \bmod N$;
27: **end if**

Lemma 5 (Convergence). *Starting from any initial configuration, protocol Eff(A) reaches a safe configuration within $2T + 4N$ steps.*

Proof. We consider any execution $E = c_0, c_1, \ldots$ of *Eff(A)*.

(a) For the case that no initiator appears by c_{T+N} (in the first $T + N$ steps), we show that *Eff(A)* reaches a safe configuration by c_{T+2N}: It is clear that the clocks of all processes become synchronized by c_{n-1} (although they may already reach $T + 2N$). Consider the following T steps (from c_{n-1} to c_{T+n-1}). If the clock value does not reach $T + 2N$ by c_{T+n-1}, all processes execute ordinary execution of A during the T steps, and thus, $(state_{v_0}, \ldots, state_{v_{n-1}})$ reaches a safe configuration of A by c_{T+n-1} and remains unchanged after. Then, the clock value reaches $T + 2N$ by c_{T+2N}, and thus, *Eff(A)* reaches a safe configuration by c_{T+2N}. On the other hand, consider the case that the clock value reaches $T + 2N$ by c_{T+n-1}. Let c_g $(g \leq T + n - 1)$ be the configuration at which the clock value reaches $T + 2N$. If c_g is unsafe, there appears an initiator in the next step. Thus, c_g is safe, since we are considering the case that no initiator appears by c_{T+N}. Consequently, *Eff(A)* reaches a safe configuration by c_{T+2N}.

(b) For the case that an initiator appears by c_{T+N}, we show that *Eff(A)* reaches a safe configuration by c_{2T+4N}: Let c_f ($f \leq T + N$) be the configuration such that the first initiator, say v, appears in the step from c_{f-1} to c_f. Since $clock_v \leftarrow 0$ is executed in the step, the clock synchronization mechanism spreads the effect to all the processes in the following $n - 1$ steps. Thus, the values of all clocks are no greater than $n - 1$ at c_{f+n-1}, whether other initiators appear in the period from c_f to c_{f+n-1} or not. This implies that the clocks of all processes become synchronized by c_{f+2n-2} since no initiator appears in the period from c_{f+n-1} to c_{f+2n-2}. Since the clock value at c_{f+2n-2} is no greater than $2n$, all processes execute ordinary execution during T steps from c_{f+2n-2} to $c_{T+f+2n-2}$, and $(state_{v_0}, \ldots, state_{v_{n-1}})$ becomes a safe configuration of A by $c_{T+f+2n-2}$. The clock value reaches $T + 2N$ by $c_{T+2N+f+n-1}$. Consequently, *Eff(A)* reaches a safe configuration by c_{2T+4N}. □

It is clear that Protocol *Eff(A)* is 1-average-broadcast-efficient. Thus, the following theorem is obtained from Lemmas 4 and 5.

Theorem 7. *Protocol Eff(A) is a self-stabilizing protocol for the problem that the input self-stabilizing protocol A is targeting. It is also 1-average-broadcast-efficient and its convergence time is $O(T + N)$, where T is the convergence time of A and N is a known upper bound of the number of processes n.* □

Many self-stabilizing protocols proposed so far satisfy the input conditions: for example, self-stabilizing protocols for the MIS problem (also for the MDS problem) with the convergence time $O(n)$ [12], and for the ST problem with the convergence time $O(N)$ [13]. Application of the transformer to these protocols provides 1-average-broadcast-efficient self-stabilizing protocols with the convergence time $O(N)$ for these problems. More interestingly, we can obtain a much more general result: the 1-average-broadcast-efficiency is attainable for *any static problem* without paying high penalty on the convergence time.

Theorem 8. *When an upper bound N of the number of processes n is available at every process, there exists a 1-average-broadcast-efficient self-stabilizing protocol with the convergence time $O(N)$ for any static problem.* □

To prove Theorem 8, we consider a *universal static problem* Π on any distributed system G: each process has an *input*, and is required to compute an *output* that is (deterministically) computable from the *complete information of G* (i.e., a graph G where each node v is labeled with ID_v and the input of v).

The core of a self-stabilizing protocol for Π is to construct the complete information of G at each process, and it can be achieved by letting all processes know the tuple $(ID_v, NID_v, Input_v)$ of every process v, where NID_v is the set of IDs of v's neighbors and $Input_v$ is the input given at v. There exists a self-stabilizing protocol for constructing the complete information of G at each process with the convergence time $O(N)$, and it satisfies the input conditions of the transformer. Thus, we can obtain Theorem 8.

7   Conclusion

In this paper, we introduced and investigated communication-efficiency of self-stabilizing protocols in the distributed system model with the (local) broadcast primitive. A wireless network is a typical example of the system model, and the communication-efficiency may play an important role in reducing energy-consumption, which is a critical issue in the wireless networks. As the first step, we considered only the *reliable* broadcast primitive. However, to consider a *lossy* broadcast primitive is practically important and is one of our future works.

Another future work is to introduce the *sleep* mode in which a process stop broadcasting and receiving messages to save energy consumption, while we assume, in this paper, a process is allowed to receive messages all the time.

References

1. Dolev, S.: Self-stabilization. The MIT press (2000)
2. Devismes, S., Masuzawa, T., Tixeuil, S.: Communication efficiency in self-stabilizing silent protocols. In: Proc. of IEEE ICDCS, pp. 474–481 (2009)
3. Masuzawa, T., Izumi, T., Katayama, Y., Wada, K.: Brief Announcement: Communication-Efficient Self-stabilizing Protocols for Spanning-Tree Construction. In: Abdelzaher, T., Raynal, M., Santoro, N. (eds.) OPODIS 2009. LNCS, vol. 5923, pp. 219–224. Springer, Heidelberg (2009)
4. Masuzawa, T.: Silence Is Golden: Self-stabilizing Protocols Communication-Efficient after Convergence. In: Défago, X., Petit, F., Villain, V. (eds.) SSS 2011. LNCS, vol. 6976, pp. 1–3. Springer, Heidelberg (2011)
5. Aguilera, M.K., Delporte-Gallet, C., Fauconnier, H., Toueg, S.: Stable Leader Election. In: Welch, J.L. (ed.) DISC 2001. LNCS, vol. 2180, pp. 108–122. Springer, Heidelberg (2001)
6. Aguilera, M.K., Delporte-Gallet, C., Fauconnier, H., Toueg, S.: On implementing omega with weak reliability and synchrony assumptions. In: Proc. of PODC, pp. 306–314 (2003)
7. Aguilera, M.K., Delporte-Gallet, C., Fauconnier, H., Toueg, S.: Communication-efficient leader election and consensus with limited link synchrony. In: Proc. of PODC, pp. 328–337 (2004)
8. Biely, M., Widder, J.: Optimal message-driven implementations of omega with mute processes. ACM TAAS 4(1), 4:1–4:22 (2009)
9. Larrea, M., Fernández, A., Arévalo, S.: Optimal implementation of the weakest failure detector for solving consensus. In: Proc. of SRDS, pp. 52–59 (2000)
10. Dolev, S., Schiller, E.: Communication adaptive self-stabilizing group membership service. IEEE TPDS 14(7), 709–720 (2003)
11. Kutten, S., Zinenko, D.: Low Communication Self-stabilization through Randomization. In: Lynch, N.A., Shvartsman, A.A. (eds.) DISC 2010. LNCS, vol. 6343, pp. 465–479. Springer, Heidelberg (2010)
12. Ikeda, M., Kamei, S., Kakugawa, H.: A space-optimal self-stabilizing algorithm for the maximal independent set problem. In: Proc. of PDCAT, pp. 70–74 (2002)
13. Arora, A., Gouda, M.G.: Distributed Reset. IEEE Trans. Comp. 43(9), 1026–1038 (1994)

Self-stabilizing Local k-Placement of Replicas with Minimal Variance

Sven Köhler, Volker Turau, and Gerhard Mentges

Institute of Telematics
Hamburg University of Technology, Hamburg, Germany
{sven.koehler,turau,gerhard.mentges}@tu-harburg.de

Abstract. Large scale distributed systems require replication of resources to amplify availability and to provide fault tolerance. The placement of replicated resources significantly impacts performance. This paper considers local k-placements: Each node of a network has to place k replicas of a resource among its direct neighbors. The load of a node in a given local k-placement is the number of replicas it stores. The local k-placement problem is to achieve a preferably homogeneous distribution of the loads. We present a novel self-stabilizing, distributed, asynchronous, scalable algorithm for the k-placement problem such that the standard deviation of the distribution of the loads assumes a local minimum.

1 Introduction

Large scale distributed systems such as cloud computing networks, peer-to-peer file sharing systems, or sensor networks, often require replication of resources. Replicas are placed on other nodes of the network. There are different reasons to create replicas: reduction of retrieval time (e.g. caching systems), better utilization of computing devices (e.g. load balancing), or the increase of fault tolerance resp. availability (e.g. backup systems). The placement strategy for the replicated resources significantly impacts performance in all these cases.

This paper considers distributed systems where each node wants to place replicas of a resource on k different neighbors. The nature of the resource is of no importance for the following. As an example consider the case where each node wants to replicate its own state on k neighbors. We pursue the goal to achieve a preferably homogeneous distribution of the replicas assuming that all replicas induce the same load. This is called the local k-placement problem. There are different measures for the homogeneity of a distribution, e.g. the Gini coefficient, the standard deviation, or the discrepancy which is the difference between the maximum and the minimum load among all nodes. In many cases the network topology will not allow to have a complete homogeneous distribution, i.e. the same load for every node resp. standard deviation 0. Therefore, finding a distributed algorithm for this placement problem is a real challenge.

The main contribution of this paper is a distributed, asynchronous, self-stabilizing algorithm that performs placement of k replicated resources on direct neighbors of each node such that the standard deviation of the distribution

A.W. Richa and C. Scheideler (Eds.): SSS 2012, LNCS 7596, pp. 16–30, 2012.

assumes a local minimum. The basic idea of the algorithm is that each node periodically checks whether the shifting of one of the node's replicas from one neighbor to another would lower the standard deviation of the load of its neighbors. If such a case is detected, the shift of the replica is initiated. The challenge is to coordinate these movements such that no livelocks will occur and that after a finite number of moves the homogeneity of the distribution is optimized. The proposed algorithm is self-stabilizing, i.e. the system provably converges to a legitimate state in finite time, without any external intervention, and regardless of its initial configuration. The system remains legitimate until a fault occurs.

The motivation for the proposed algorithm stems from the work on fault-containment in dynamic networks based on a transformation adding fault-containment to any silent self-stabilizing protocol [9]. Fault-containment is achieved by maintaining backups of each node's local state on a constant number of nodes in the neighborhood.

The main result of this paper is a self-stabilizing algorithm to determine a local k-placement that has local minimum variance. The algorithm terminates after $O(n\Delta^2)$ moves respectively $O(n\Delta)$ rounds under the distributed scheduler.

2   Related Work

Since the early days of distributed computing load distribution received a lot of attention and many schemes have been devised. In general the term refers to algorithms improving the overall system performance by transferring some form of load (e.g. a task or a resource) from heavily to lightly loaded nodes. In the following we review only work with strong links to this work. Gärtner et al. present a method to provide load balancing for replicated servers on a per access basis [3]. In this case the replicated resources are servers, i.e. processes and data. But instead of moving resources between nodes, accesses to the resources are redirected to achieve a homogeneous access distribution. The self-stabilization property of the algorithm is achieved by a composition of two distributed algorithms.

Ko et al. present a distributed algorithm that places replicated resources in a network among all nodes such that the furthest distance to a particular replica of a resource is minimized [7]. The algorithm guarantees an approximation of ratio 3. No analysis of the time complexity is given. A similar problem is tackled by Kangasharju et al. They consider techniques for optimally replicating objects in content distribution networks [4]. The goal is to replicate objects on servers with finite storage so that when clients fetch objects from the nearest server holding the requested object, the average number of nodes traversed is minimized. They show that this optimization problem is NP-complete and present heuristics.

Two self-stabilizing algorithms for migrating the job load around the network are presented by Flatebo et al. [1]. In the first algorithm each node compares its own load with the load of its neighbors. In case a neighbor momentarily has a lower load, the node migrates a job to this neighbor. The second algorithm aims at migrating jobs globally to lightly loaded nodes. The run-time complexity of the algorithms is not considered.

Sauerwald and Sun consider the problem of balancing load items on networks [11]. Starting with an arbitrary load distribution, in each round nodes exchange tokens with their neighbors. The goal is to achieve a distribution where all nodes have nearly the same number of tokens. The authors present a detailed analysis of their randomized algorithms. Lenzen and Wattenhofer recently determined tight bounds for a related task the so-called balls-into-bins problem [10].

Load balancing received a lot of attention in the field of peer-to-peer networks. The problem arises in two flavors: balancing the distribution of the key address space to nodes (in DHT-based systems) and balancing the distribution of items among the nodes. Karger and Ruhl address both problems in the context of a Chord DHT [5]. Serbu et al. present a solution that aims to equilibrate the request load and routing load of the nodes in DHT-based peer-to-peer systems where requests follow a Zipf-like distribution [12]. Instead of changing the placement of objects the routing tables are reorganized.

In contrast to the above reviewed literature, in our work the items to be distributed are replicas of a node's state and they are only distributed in the direct neighborhood of the node and not at arbitrary places in the network. To the best of our knowledge, this problem has not been tackled yet.

3   Notation

3.1   The Problem

A distributed system is described by an undirected graph $G = (V, E)$. Let $n = |V|$, $m = |E|$, and Δ denote the maximal degree of G. The set of neighbors of $v \in V$ in G is denoted by $N(v)$. Let $k > 0$. For each $v \in V$ let $k(v) = \min(k, |N(v)|)$ and $B_k(v) = \{B \subseteq N(v) \mid |B| = k(v)\}$. A *local k-placement* is a function β that assigns to each $v \in V$ an element of $B_k(v)$. Denote by $L_\beta(v) = |\{w \in V \mid v \in \beta(w)\}|$ the *load* of β on v. There are several expressions to measure the homogeneity of a local k-placement β. In this paper we consider the standard deviation, or equivalently the variance:

$$var(\beta) = \frac{1}{n} \sum_{v \in V} (L_\beta(v) - \mu_\beta)^2 \quad \text{with} \quad \mu_\beta = \frac{1}{n} \sum_{v \in V} L_\beta(v).$$

The lower the value of $var(\beta)$ the more homogeneous is β. Figure 1 depicts two different local 1-placements of the same graph (arrows indicate the placement of the replica of each node). The local 1-placement on the left has a variance of $1/2$ while that on the right has variance $1/4$.

Distributedly computing a local k-placement with the globally minimum variance seems to be a difficult task. Therefore, we content ourselves with computing local minima. A local k-placement has *local minimum variance*, if the reassignment of a single replica from one neighbor to another does not lower the variance. The local 1-placement on the left of Figure 1 does not have local minimum variance. If node f shifts its replica from node e to g the variance is decreased and result in the 1-load balancing shown on the right. This balancing has local minimum variance. Note that an optimal local k-placement of this graph has variance 0. Not all graphs have a local k-placement with variance 0.

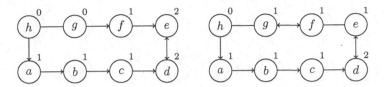

Fig. 1. Two local 1-placements of the same graph

3.2 Model of Computation

The notation we use for describing the self-stabilizing algorithm is based on the multi-protocol model as described in [8]. In particular the concepts algorithm, protocol, instance, rule, move, configuration, execution, round, and the different scheduler models are used as defined there. This section stresses some aspects of the model of computation. The algorithm is described in the shared memory model. Globally unique identifiers, e.g. for symmetry breaking, are not required. But in order for a node to keep references to neighboring nodes, neighbors must be distinguishable. Thus, locally unique identifiers are assumed. The self-stabilization property is first proved for the central scheduler and then for the distributed scheduler using a variation of the concept of serialization from [8]. The time-complexity is expressed in both moves and rounds.

4 The Algorithm

This section describes the implementation of an algorithm for the local k-placement problem. Each node intends to place k replicas on k distinct neighbors. k is assumed to be an integer constant. The goal of the algorithm is to minimize the standard deviation or equivalently the variance of the number of replicas stored by each node. Let β be a k-placement and $u \in \beta(v)$. If node v moves its replica from node u to some neighbor $w \notin \beta(v)$, then we obtain another k-placement β' for which $\beta'(v) = (\beta(v) \setminus \{u\}) \cup \{w\}$ holds. It satisfies $L_{\beta'}(u) = L_\beta(u) - 1$, $L_{\beta'}(w) = L_\beta(w) + 1$, and $\mu_{\beta'} = \mu_\beta$. This yields

$$var(\beta) - var(\beta') = \frac{2}{n}(L_\beta(u) - 1 - L_\beta(w)) \qquad (1)$$

Thus, the variance of β' is lower than the one of β if and only if $L_\beta(u) > L_\beta(w) + 1$. This yields the basic strategy of the proposed algorithm: Once a node v detects such a pair $u, w \in N(v)$, it moves a replica on u to w.

Each node $v \in V$ maintains a variable $v.\beta$ which is a set of up to k pointers to neighboring nodes. Once the algorithm has stabilized, $v.\beta$ represents the value of $\beta(v)$ of the computed local k-placement. Based on variable $v.\beta$, the current load of a node, i.e. the number of replicas placed at the node, is defined as follows:

$$L(v) := |\{w \in N(v) \mid v \in w.\beta\}|$$

However, with distance-1 knowledge only, it is impossible for v to determine the value of L for a neighbor. Hence, each node $v \in V$ maintains the so-called *load variable* $v.l$ which is updated with the current value of $L(v)$ whenever possible.

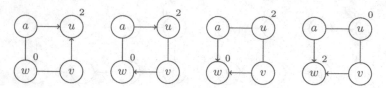

Fig. 2. Example for oscillation, $k = 1$

The variable $v.l$ can be out-of-date and that can potentially lead to oscillation, even under the central scheduler. An example is illustrated in Figure 2. The numbers next to u and w denote the values of $u.l$ and $w.l$. The arrows represent the values of $v.\beta$ and $a.\beta$. The scheduler selects v first and afterwards a. Both move their replica from u to w. However, the decision of a to do so is based on outdated values of $u.l$ and $w.l$. Thus, after updating the values of $u.l$ and $w.l$, the situation is symmetric to the initial configuration. Even under a fair central scheduler, this may result in a livelock.

To prevent a livelock, the algorithm uses a synchronization mechanism. Before node $v \in V$ moves a replica from u to w, it will lock u with regards to removal and w with regards to addition of replicas. While u and w are locked, it is not allowed for other nodes to move their replica away from u or towards w. Also, during the locking procedure, both $u.l$ and $w.l$ will be updated. Hence, at the time v has successfully locked u and w it is safe to assume the following:

$$u.l > w.l + 1 \Rightarrow L(u) > L(w) + 1 \qquad (2)$$

It is, however, still possible for nodes other than v to move their replicas towards u or away from w. Hence, $L(u)$ may grow larger than $u.l$ and $L(w)$ may become less than $w.l$. This has no impact on Equation (2). The two locking mechanisms, one for removal and one for addition of replicas, are implemented using two pointer variables each, called *query* and *ack*. In order for node v to lock a neighboring node u with respect to replica additions, v first sets its query $v.q_a := u$. It then waits until u changes its ack to $u.a_a = v$. Once v and u point at each other, u is said to be locked by v. Thus, a node can be locked for addition by at most one neighbor at a time. If no query is made or there is no query to acknowledge, then $v.q_a$ and $u.a_a$ assume the special value $\perp$. In order to lock a neighbor u with respect to replica removal instead of addition, the variables $v.q_r$ and $u.a_r$ are used instead of $v.q_a$ and $u.a_a$.

The proposed algorithm $\mathcal{A} = \{P_L, P_{A_r}, P_{A_a}, P_Q\}$ consists of four protocols. Their implementation is shown in Figure 3. Protocol P_L updates the variable $v.l$ whenever the instance (v, P_L) is selected by the scheduler. Protocols P_{A_r} and P_{A_a} provide the acknowledgments for the locking mechanisms. Note, that instances (v, P_{A_r}) and (v, P_{A_a}) only acknowledge queries if the load-variable $v.l$ is up-to-date. The value of $v.a_r$ and $v.a_a$ is controlled via the sets $A_r(v)$ and $A_a(v)$. They contain all neighbors waiting for an acknowledgment by v. (v, P_{A_r}) updates $v.a_r$ such that $v.a_r \in A_r(v)$ or $v.a_r = \perp$ if $A_r(v) = \emptyset$. (v, P_{A_a}) implements the same for $v.a_a$ and $A_a(v)$. Note, that no assumption about the function $choose(X)$ are being made in case that X contains multiple elements. $choose(X)$ may return

$$validLoad(v) \equiv v.l = L(v)$$
$$validPlacement(v) \equiv |v.\beta| = k(v) \land v.\beta \subseteq N(v)$$
$$ackNeedsUpdate_x(v) \equiv v.a_x \notin A_x(v) \land (A_x(v) \neq \emptyset \lor v.a_x \neq \bot) \quad \text{for } x \in \{a,r\}$$
$$queryNeedsUpdate_x(v) \equiv v.q_x \notin Q_x(v) \land (Q_x'(v) \neq \emptyset \lor v.q_x \neq \bot) \quad \text{for } x \in \{a,r\}$$
$$queryValidAndAcked_x(v) \equiv v.q_x \in Q_x(v) \land (v.q_x).a_x = v \quad \text{for } x \in \{a,r\}$$
$$choose(X) := \begin{cases} \bot & \text{if } X = \emptyset \\ \text{element of } X & \text{otherwise} \end{cases}$$

Protocol P_L: $\neg validLoad(v) \longrightarrow v.l := L(v)$
Protocol P_{A_r}: $validLoad(v) \land ackNeedsUpdate_r(v) \longrightarrow v.a_r := choose(A_r(v))$
Protocol P_{A_a}: $validLoad(v) \land ackNeedsUpdate_a(v) \longrightarrow v.a_a := choose(A_a(v))$
Protocol P_Q:
  Rule Q_1: $\neg validPlacement(v) \longrightarrow$
            $v.\beta := v.\beta \cap N(v)$; add $k(v) - |v.\beta|$ pointers to $v.\beta$
  Precondition for Rules Q_2–Q_5: $validPlacement(v)$
  Rule Q_2: $queryNeedsUpdate_r(v) \longrightarrow v.q_r := choose(Q_r'(v))$; $v.q_a := \bot$
  Rule Q_3: $\neg(queryNeedsUpdate_r(v) \lor queryValidAndAcked_r(v)) \land v.q_a \neq \bot \longrightarrow$
            $v.q_a := \bot$
  Rule Q_4: $queryValidAndAcked_r(v) \land queryNeedsUpdate_a(v) \longrightarrow$
            $v.q_a := choose(Q_a'(v))$
  Rule Q_5: $queryValidAndAcked_r(v) \land queryValidAndAcked_a(v) \longrightarrow$
            $v.\beta := (v.\beta \setminus \{v.q_r\}) \cup \{v.q_a\}$; $v.q_r := \bot$; $v.q_a := \bot$

Fig. 3. Algorithm $\mathcal{A}$

any non-deterministically chosen element of X. The definition of the sets $A_r(v)$ and $A_a(v)$ is as follows:

$$A_r(v) = \{w \in N(v) \mid w.q_r = v \land v \in w.\beta\}$$
$$A_a(v) = \{w \in N(v) \mid w.q_a = v \land v \notin w.\beta\}$$

Protocol P_Q controls the queries and the current placement. Rule Q_1 of (v, P_Q) is responsible for removing all invalid pointers from $v.\beta$, i.e. pointers that do not refer to a neighbor of v, and adding valid pointers until $v.\beta$ has reached the desired cardinality $k(v)$. Rules Q_2 to Q_4 of (v, P_Q) are responsible for setting the queries $v.q_r$ and $v.q_a$. The values of the variable $v.q_r$ is controlled via the sets $Q_r(v)$ and $Q_r'(v)$. The former contains those neighbors $w \in N(v)$ with maximal $w.l$ at which v currently places a replica and for which a neighbor $u \in N(v)$ exists which currently does not store a replica and satisfies $u.l < w.l - 1$. $Q_r'(v)$ contains only those $w \in Q_r(v)$ which do not already acknowledge a query by v such that it is save to assume that (w, P_{A_r}) will update $w.l$ before providing an acknowledgment. The query $v.q_r$ is said to be *valid*, if $v.q_r \in Q_r(v)$. If $v.q_r$ is not valid, Rule Q_2 updates $v.q_r$ such that $v.q_r \in Q_r'(v)$ or $v.q_r = \bot$ if $Q_r'(v) = \emptyset$. Note that Rule Q_2 also resets $v.q_a$ to $\bot$. As long as the query $v.q_r$ is either invalid or not acknowledged, $v.q_a$ must remain $\bot$ such that locks with respect to addition of replicas are not established before the removal lock. This is essential for deadlock-free operation. Rule Q_3 makes sure that $v.q_a$ is reset to $\bot$ to avoid any premature queries, e.g. due to transient faults or initial inconsistencies. If $v.q_r$ is valid and acknowledged, then Rule Q_4 controls the value of $v.q_a$ via $Q_a(v)$ and $Q'_a(v)$. The former contains all neighbors $w \in N(v)$ that currently do not hold replicas of v and have minimal $w.l$. Again $Q'_a(v)$ contains only those neighbors $w \in Q_a(v)$ which do not already acknowledge in order to ensure an update of $w.l$ before the lock is being established.

$$Q_r(v) = \{w \in N(v) \cap v.\beta \mid w.l = \max\{u.l \mid u \in N(v) \cap v.\beta\} \wedge$$
$$\exists u \in N(v) \setminus v.\beta : u.l < w.l - 1\}$$
$$Q_a(v) = \{w \in N(v) \setminus v.\beta \mid w.l = \min\{u.l \mid u \in N(v) \setminus v.\beta\}\}$$
$$Q'_r(v) = \{w \in Q_r(v) \mid w.a_r \neq v.id\}$$
$$Q'_a(v) = \{w \in Q_a(v) \mid w.a_a \neq v.id\}$$

If both $v.q_r$ and $v.q_a$ are valid and acknowledged, then Rule Q_5 is enabled and will move one replica of v from $v.q_r$ to $v.q_a$ by changing $v.\beta$. Note, that both queries might be reset via Rules Q_2 or Q_4 multiple times as $Q_r(v)$ and $Q_a(v)$ change whenever a neighbor executes a move of protocol P_L. The following Boolean predicate identifies all legitimate configurations of $\mathcal{A}$:

$$Legit_A \equiv \forall v \in V : validLoad(v) \wedge validPlacement(v)$$
$$\wedge \; v.q_r = v.a_r = v.q_a = v.a_a = \perp \wedge Q_r(v) = \emptyset$$

5   Potential Function for the Central Scheduler

Potential functions were used as a tool to prove self-stabilization for the first time in [6]. Kessels defines a potential function as a function mapping the set of configurations Σ to an ordered set without an infinitely decreasing sequence. The aim is to find a potential function whose value is strictly decreasing with every step of $\mathcal{A}$. In this section we will present the potential function $potvec$ that maps Σ to the lexicographically sorted $\mathbb{N}_0^6$. Furthermore, this section will present a technique to transform $potvec$ into the potential function pot whose co-domain is merely $\mathbb{N}_0$. For the construction of pot, the central scheduler is assumed. Hence, the maximum value of pot is an upper bound the move-complexity of $\mathcal{A}$ under the central scheduler. The distributed scheduler is discussed in Section 6.

$$potvec(c) := \begin{pmatrix} \#_{v \in V} \; \neg validPlacement(v) \\ \#_{v \in V} \; malicious(v) \\ \sigma(c) \\ \#_{v \in V} \; \neg validLoad(v) \\ \sum_{v \in V} progress_Q(v) \\ \sum_{v \in V} progress_A(v) \end{pmatrix} \qquad \text{with } \sigma(c) := \sum_{v \in V} L(v)^2$$

For a Boolean predicate $X(v)$ the term $\#_{v \in V} X(v)$ denotes the number of nodes for which $X(v)$ is satisfied. The key component of $potvec$ is posed by $\sigma(c)$. Very similar to the variance, $\sigma(v)$ decreases by $L(u) - 1 - L(w)$ if a replica is moved from node u to w (cf. Equation (1)). Since algorithm $\mathcal{A}$ is based on the idea to move a replica from u to w whenever $L(u) > 1 + L(w)$, it can be expected that

$\sigma(c)$ decreases regularly, namely due to the execution of Rule Q_5. However, two scenarios exist, in which $\sigma(c)$ actually increases.

The first scenario is a node v executing Rule Q_5, but in spite having locked neighbors u and w, either $L(u)$ is less than $u.l$ or $L(w)$ is larger than $w.l$. such that $L(u) > L(w) + 1$ does not hold. Hence, Equation (2) is violated. Still, v moves a replica from u to w based on the outdated values of $u.l$ and $w.l$. Such situations can only arise from inconsistencies in the initial configuration and executions of Rule Q_1. Nodes, which will (depending on the schedule) be able to execute Rule Q_5 under such circumstances at some future point in the execution are called *malicious* (see the corresponding predicate below). The number of malicious nodes constitutes another component of *potvec*. Depending on the choices of the scheduler, a node may become non-malicious if either $u.l$ or $w.l$ is updated before v executes Rule Q_5. Also note, that a node becomes non-malicious by executing Rule Q_5 and that the locking mechanism ensures that no malicious nodes are created. The only exception is Rule Q_1 which bypasses the locking mechanism and thereby may increase the number of (potentially) malicious nodes. An execution of Rule Q_1 also poses the second scenario in which the variance actually increases. To reflect that, the first component of *potvec* denotes the number of nodes enabled with respect to Rule Q_1. It decreases whenever a node executes Rule Q_1 which happens at most once per node during an execution.

$$malicious(v) \equiv queryValidAndAcked_r(v) \wedge (L(v.q_r) < (v.q_r).l$$
$$\vee \, (queryValidAndAcked_a(v) \wedge L(v.q_a) > (v.q_a)\,l))$$

$$progress_Q(v) := \begin{cases} 0 & \text{if } queryValidAndAcked_r(v) \wedge v.q_a \in Q_a(v) \\ 1 & \text{if } v.q_r \in Q_r(v) \wedge v.q_a = \bot \\ 2 & \text{if } v.q_r = \bot \wedge v.q_a = \bot \\ 3 & \text{otherwise} \end{cases}$$

$$progress_A(v) := \begin{cases} 0 & \text{if } \neg ackNeedsUpdate_r(v) \wedge \neg ackNeedsUpdate_a(v) \\ 1 & \text{if } ackNeedsUpdate_r(v) \neq ackNeedsUpdate_a(v) \\ 2 & \text{if } ackNeedsUpdate_r(v) \wedge ackNeedsUpdate_a(v) \end{cases}$$

The remaining components of *potvec* are the number of nodes with an out-of-date load variable, and the functions $progress_Q$ and $progress_A$ reflecting the progress of the locking procedures.

Function *potvec* has been designed such that with every step of $\mathcal{A}$, at least one component of the potential vector decreases. If components of *potvec* increase, then there is at least one decreasing component with a smaller index. Hence, with every step of $\mathcal{A}$, *potvec* decreases with respect to the lexicographical order. To obtain an upper bound on the move-complexity of $\mathcal{A}$ under the central scheduler, we construct a potential function with a scalar value using a weighted sum of the components of *potvec*:

$$pot(c) := \sum_{i=1}^{6} w_i \cdot potvec_i(c)$$

where $w_6 = 1$. The other weights are determined iteratively from w_5 to w_1 as follows: In order to determine w_j, $1 \leq j \leq 5$, we consider all transitions $c_0 \to c_1$ which are the result of a single move of a single instance and for which $potvec_j$ is the left-most component that changes. Let d_j denote the minimal amount by which $potvec_j$ decreases. Then chose w_j such that the following holds for all such transitions $c_0 \to c_1$:

$$d_j \cdot w_j \geq 1 + \sum_{i=j+1}^{6} w_i (potvec_i(c_1) - potvec_i(c_0))$$

If necessary, w_j is modified such that $w_j \geq 1$ for all $\Delta \geq 1$ and $k \geq 1$. Using this technique, we obtained the values as given below. The reasoning for obtaining each individual weight is contained in the proof of Lemma 1.

$$w_6 = 1 \qquad\qquad w_5 = 4 \qquad\qquad w_4 = 12\Delta + 1$$
$$w_3 = 12\Delta + 7 \qquad w_2 = 24\Delta^2 - 22\Delta \qquad w_1 = 48k\Delta^2 - 8k\Delta - 6k + 13$$

Lemma 1. *Under the central scheduler, pot decreases with every step of $\mathcal{A}$.*

Proof. Let $(v, p) \in V \times \mathcal{A}$ denote an enabled instance of $\mathcal{A}$ and let r denote the rule of (v, p) that is enabled. In the following it is shown that $pot(c)$ decreases under an execution of Rule r of (v, p). In the following, a case-by-case analysis is conducted.

$p = P_L$: The number of nodes with invalid pointer as well as $\sigma(c)$ do not change. Also, $progress_A$ will not increase for any node, since A_a and A_r do not depend on the value of load variables. The number of malicious nodes may decrease, however it cannot grow. The number of nodes with an invalid load variable will decrease by at least 1. $progress_Q$ may increase from 0 to 3 for up to Δ neighbors of v since Q_r or Q_a change for them. For all other nodes, $progress_Q$ does not change. Hence, pot decreases by at least $(12\Delta + 1) - 3\Delta \cdot 4 = 1$.

$p \in \{P_{A_r}, P_{A_a}\}$: (v, P_{A_r}) and (v, P_{A_a}) do not modify $v.\beta$. Hence the number of nodes with an invalid placement does not increase. The number of malicious nodes does not increase since the rule is only enabled if $v.l = L(v)$. Also, $\sigma(c)$ does not change. The number of nodes with an invalid load variable does not increase as well. $progress_Q$ does not change for any node. $progress_A$ remains unchanged for all nodes except v, for which it decreases by 1. So pot decreases by at least 1.

$p = P_Q \wedge r = Q_1$: The number of nodes with invalid placement decreases by 1. The number of malicious nodes can increase by at most k. $\sigma(c)$ increases by at most $k(2\Delta - 1)$. The number of nodes with invalid load variable increases by at most k. $progress_Q$ does not change for all nodes except v, for which it may increase from 0 to 3. $progress_A$ does not change for any node. Hence, pot decreases by at least $(48k\Delta^2 - 8k\Delta - 6k + 13) - k \cdot (24\Delta^2 - 22\Delta) - k(2\Delta - 1) \cdot (12\Delta + 7) - k \cdot (12\Delta + 1) - 3 \cdot 4 = 1$.

$p = P_Q \wedge r = Q_2$: $progress_Q(v)$ is either 3 or 2 before the move of v. After executing Rule Q_2, $progress_Q(v)$ is equal to 1. So $progress_Q(v)$ decreases by at least 1. Rule Q_2 resets $v.q_r$ and $v.q_a$. In the worst case, it holds $v.q_r \in N(v)$ both before and after the move. So $progress_A$ increases by 1 for two neighbors of v.

Also, $v.q_a \in N(v)$ might hold prior to the reset of $v.q_a$ to $\bot$. Hence, $progress_A$ increases by 1 for a third node in the worst case. For all other nodes, $progress_A$ remains unchanged. The number of nodes with invalid placement or load variable does not increase. $\sigma(c)$ does not change. Also, the number of malicious nodes cannot not increase, since $Q'_r(v)$ only contains nodes u with $u.a_r \neq v$. So pot decreases by at least $4 - 3 = 1$.

$p = P_Q \wedge r = Q_3$: $progress_Q(v)$ is 3 if Rule Q_3 is enabled. After the execution of Rule Q_2, $progress_Q(v)$ is either 2 or 1. Hence $progress_Q(v)$ decreases by at least 1. $progress_A$ increases by 1 for at most one node. For all other nodes, $progress_A$ remains unchanged. All other components of the potential function remain unchanged. So pot decreases by at least $4 - 1 = 3$

$p = P_Q \wedge r = Q_4$: If Rule Q_4 is enabled, then $progress_Q(v)$ is either 3 or 1. If 3, then it decreases to either 1 or 0. If 1, then it decreases to 0. So $progress_Q(v)$ decreases by at least 1. $progress_A$ increases by 1 for at most one node. For all other nodes, $progress_A$ remains unchanged. All other components of the potential function remain unchanged. So pot decreases by at least $4 - 1 = 3$.

$p = P_Q \wedge r = Q_5 \wedge \neg malicious(v)$: From $\neg malicious(v)$ it follows that $L(v.q_r) > (v.q_r).l$ and $L(v.q_a) < (v.q_a).l$. From the guard of Rule Q_5 it follows that $v.q_r \in Q_r(v)$ and $v.q_a \in Q_a(v)$ yielding $(v.q_r).l > (v.q_a).l + 1$ and $L(v.q_r) > L(v.q_a) + 1$. Hence the $\sigma(c)$ decreases by at least 2. Also, the number of nodes with invalid load variables increases by 2. $progress_Q$ does increase for v from 0 to 2. For all other nodes $progress_Q$ remains unchanged, since $v.l$ is not updated. However, since $v.q_r$ and $v.q_a$ are set to $\bot$, $progress_A$ increases by 1 for two neighbors of v. For all other nodes, $progress_A$ remains unchanged. Also, the number of malicious nodes and the number of nodes with invalid placement does not increase. Hence, pot decreases by at least $2 \cdot (12\Delta+7) - 2 \cdot (12\Delta+1) - 2 \cdot 4 - 2 = 2$.

$p = P_Q \wedge r = Q_5 \wedge malicious(v)$: The number of nodes with invalid placement does not increase. However, the number of malicious nodes decreases by at least 1, since both $v.q_r$ and $v.q_a$ are reset to $\bot$. $\sigma(c)$ may increase by at most $2\Delta - 4$. The number of invalid load variables grows by at most 1, since one load variable must already be outdated for v to be malicious. $progress_Q(v)$ increases from 0 to 2 and $progress_A$ increases by 1 for two nodes. For all other nodes, $progress_Q$ and $progress_A$ remain unchanged. Hence, pot decreases by at least $(24\Delta^2 - 22\Delta) - (2\Delta - 4) \cdot (12\Delta + 7) - 1 \cdot (12\Delta + 1) - 2 \cdot 4 - 2 = 17$. $\qquad\square$

6   Potential Function for the Distributed Scheduler

In the previous section, a potential function for the central scheduler was presented. The distributed scheduler selects a set $S \subseteq V \times \mathcal{A}$ of enabled instances in each step. The instances execute their moves in parallel. Composite atomicity is assumed. Due to the parallel execution of moves, a single step under the distributed scheduler can result in an increase of pot when using the weights as defined in Section 5. This section shows that pot is strictly decreasing and thus is a valid potential function under the distributed scheduler, if the weights w_3,

w_2, and w_1 are increased. The value of *pot* will decrease by at least $|S|$ for every step S under the distributed scheduler. Thus, *pot* is suitable for obtaining an upper bound on the move complexity of $\mathcal{A}$ under the distributed scheduler.

In [8] we proposed a new technique for proving self-stabilization under the distributed scheduler. The idea is to substitute a step S under the distributed scheduler with a sequence of steps $\langle m_1, m_2, \ldots, m_x \rangle$ under the central scheduler such that $(c : m_1 : m_2 : \ldots : m_x) = (c : S)$ with $m_i \in S$. The notations $(c : m_1)$ and $(c : S)$ are defined in [8]. The sequence $\langle m_1, m_2, \ldots, m_x \rangle$ is called *serialization* of S. For algorithm $\mathcal{A}$ such serializations do not always exist. However, in this section a so-called *partial serialization* of the steps of $\mathcal{A}$ is constructed. A partial serialization of a step $S \subseteq V \times \mathcal{A}$ under the distributed scheduler consists of the sequence $\langle m_1, m_2, \ldots, m_x, S', m_{x+1}, m_{x+2}, \ldots, m_y \rangle$ where each $m_i \in S$ denotes a step under the central scheduler and $S' \subseteq S$ denotes as step under the distributed scheduler such that

$$(c : m_1 : m_2 : \ldots : m_x : S' : m_{x+1} : m_{x+2} : \ldots : m_y) = (c : S)$$

The intention is that S' is is less complex than S. The partial serialization for a step $S \subseteq V \times \mathcal{A}$ is constructed via a so-called *ranking* r, which assigns a value of the lexicographically sorted $\mathbb{Z}^2$ to each instance. The partial serialization $\langle m_1, m_2, \ldots, m_x, S', m_{x+1}, m_{x+2}, \ldots, m_y \rangle$ consists of all instances $m_i \in S$ sorted by their rank $r(m_i)$ in ascending order. The set S' consists of all instances $m_i \in S$ with rank $r(m_i) = (3, 0)$.

$$r(v, p) := \begin{cases} \bot & \text{if } (v, p) \text{ is disabled, otherwise:} \\ (0, 1 - 2v.l) & \text{if } p = P_{A_a} \\ (0, \min\{-2u.l \mid u \in Q_a(v) \wedge u.a_a = v\}) & \text{if } p = P_Q \wedge e(Q_4) \\ (1, 0) & \text{if } p = P_Q \wedge e(Q_3) \\ (2, 1 + 2v.l) & \text{if } p = P_{A_r} \\ (2, \min\{2u.l \mid u \in Q_r(v) \wedge u.a_r = v\}) & \text{if } p = P_Q \wedge e(Q_2) \\ (3, 0) & \text{if } (p = P_Q \wedge e(Q_5)) \vee p = P_L \\ (4, 0) & \text{if } p = P_Q \wedge e(Q_1) \end{cases}$$

where $\min \emptyset = \infty$ and the Boolean predicate $e(Q_x)$ is true if and only if (v, P_Q) is enabled with respect to Rule Q_x.

Lemma 2. *The sequence* $\langle m_1, m_2, \ldots, m_x, S', m_{x+1}, m_{x+2}, \ldots, m_y \rangle$ *as induced by r is a valid partial serialization of S.*

Proof. The proof shows that r is a valid invariancy-ranking (as defined in [8]) considering the parallel execution of all moves with rank $(3, 0)$. Due to space constraints, the proof has been omitted. □

Lemma 3. *Under the distributed scheduler, pot decreases by at least $|S|$ with every step S of $\mathcal{A}$ under the distributed scheduler if*

$$w_3 = 12\Delta + 21 \qquad w_2 = 48\Delta^2 - 18\Delta \qquad w_1 = 96k\Delta^2 + 12k\Delta - 20k + 13$$

Proof. Let $S \subseteq V \times \mathcal{A}$ be a step under the distributed scheduler. By Lemma 2, $\langle m_1, m_2, \ldots, m_x, S', m_{x+1}, m_{x+2}, \ldots, m_y \rangle$ is a valid partial serialization. Let c_0

denote the configuration prior to the step S. Let c_1 denote configuration $(c :$ $m_1 : m_2 : \ldots : m_x)$, c_3 configuration $(c_1 : S')$, and c_4 configuration $(c_3 :$ $m_{x+1} : m_{x+2} : \ldots : m_y)$. Then $c_4 = (c_0 : S)$ holds. It is easy to verify that Lemma 1 still holds for the adjusted values of w_1 to w_3. Lemma 1 then yields that $pot(c_1) \leq pot(c_0) - x$ and $pot(c_4) \leq pot(c_3) - (y - x)$. To prove the claim it remains to show that $pot(c_3) \leq pot(c_1) - |S'|$.

S' only contains instances of P_Q which are enabled with respect to Rule Q_5 since r is a valid invariancy ranking. Note that the sequential execution of all (v, P_Q) yields the same result as their parallel execution in a single step, since Rule Q_5 only changes $v.\beta$, $v.q_r$, and $v.q_a$, all of which do not impact any the execution of Rule Q_5 on a neighboring node $u \in N(v)$ in any way. Hence, S' can be replaced by a sequential execution of Rule Q_5 for all instances $(v, P_Q) \in S'$ under the central scheduler followed by sequence of moves that set the load variable $v.l$ to the value of $L(v)$ in c_1 for each $(v, P_L) \in S'$. Let c_2 denote the configuration after all execution of Rule Q_5 and prior to the moves that set the load variables.

Note, that pot decreases from c_1 to c_2 by Lemma 1. However, from c_2 to c_3, the value of pot may increase due to the moves which change load variables. We distinguish three types of nodes $v \in V$. Type A: The value of $L(v)$ is identical in c_1 and c_2. Type B: The value of $L(v)$ differs in c_1 and c_2 and $L(v) \neq v.l$ in c_2. Type C: The value of $L(c)$ differs in c_1 and c_2 and $L(v) = v.l$ holds in c_2.

If v is of type A then the update of $v.l$ is identical to a regular execution of protocol P_L and pot decreases by Lemma 1. If v is of type B, the number of nodes with an invalid load variable does not increase. However, replacing one invalid counter value with another may invalidate queries of at most two $u \in N(v)$. For them, $progress_Q(u)$ increases by at most 3. If v being of type C, $\#_{v \in V} \neg validLoad(v)$ increases by one in addition to the increase of $progress_Q$ as described for type B. In total, the update of $v.l$ increases pot by at most $1 \cdot (12\Delta + 1) + 3 \cdot 4 = 12\Delta + 13$.

For all three types, $progress_A$ nor $validPlacement$ do not change for any node. Also, the number of malicious nodes does not increase from c_2 to c_3. Assume $\neg malicious(v)$ in c_2. If $(v, P_Q) \in S'$ then $v.q_r = v.q_a = \bot$ in c_2 and thus in c_3. Hence v is not malicious in c_3. If $(v, P_Q) \notin S'$, v and $(u, P_L) \in S'$ with $v.q_r = u$ and $u.a_r = v$, then $L(u) \geq u.l$ in c_2. From $u.a_r = v$ it follows that $L(u)$ cannot decrease from c_1 to c_2. Hence, $L(u) \geq u.l$ still holds in c_3 and v is not malicious in c_3. The case $v.q_a = u$ and $u.a_a = v$ is analogous.

An execution of Rule Q_5 by each $(v, P_Q) \in S'$ results in at most two type B/C nodes (namely $v.q_r$ and $v.q_a$). All other nodes are of type A. In the following, we show that each $(v, P_Q) \in S'$ compensates the increase of pot for at least 2 type C nodes. Following the same reasoning as in the proof of Lemma 1, a move (v, P_Q) decreases pot by at least $2 \cdot (12\Delta + 21) - 2 \cdot (12\Delta + 1) - 2 \cdot 4 - 2 = 24\Delta + 30$ if $\neg malicious(v)$ and $(48\Delta^2 - 18\Delta) - (2\Delta - 4) \cdot (12\Delta + 21) - 1 \cdot (12\Delta + 1) - 2 \cdot 4 - 2 = 24\Delta + 73$ otherwise. It follows that $pot(c_3) \leq pot(c_1) - |S'|$.   □

7   Analysis

Lemma 4 (Correctness). *If $\mathcal{A}$ has terminated, then $Legit_{\mathcal{A}}$ is satisfied.*

Proof. $validLoad(v)$, $validPlacement(v)$, and $\neg queryNeedsUpdate_r(v)$ hold for all nodes $v \in V$ (Protocol P_L and Rules Q_1, Q_2). Assume there exists a node $v \in V$ such that $w = v.a_a \neq \bot$. Protocol P_{A_a} implies that $w \in A_a(v)$, hence $w.q_a = v$ and $(w.q_a).a_a = w$. Rule Q_3 implies $queryValidAndAcked_r(w)$. This yields that $w.q_a \in Q_a(w)$ (Rule Q_4). Furthermore, by Rule Q_5, $queryValidAndAcked_a(w)$ is false, hence $(w.q_a).a_a \neq w$. This contradiction proves that all $v \in V$ satisfy $v.a_a = \bot$ and $A_a(v) = \emptyset$.

Assume there exists $v \in V$ such that $w = v.q_a \neq \bot$. Then $w \notin v.\beta$ since $A_a(w) = \emptyset$. This implies $w \notin Q_a(v)$ and hence $queryNeedsUpdate_a(v)$ is true. By Rule Q_4 $queryValidAndAcked_r(w)$ is false, therefore $v.q_a = \bot$ by Rule Q_3. This contradiction proves that all $v \in V$ satisfy $v.q_a = \bot$.

Assume there exists $v \in V$ such that $w = v.q_r \neq \bot$. $\neg queryNeedsUpdate_r(v)$ implies $v.q_r \in Q_r(v)$, hence $Q_a(v) \neq \emptyset$. Protocol P_{A_r} and $A_r(w) \neq \emptyset$ imply that $w.a_r \neq \bot$. W.l.o.g. assume $v = w.a_r$. Hence $queryValidAndAcked_r(v)$ and thus $v.q_a \neq \bot$ by Rule Q_4. This contradicts the result of the last paragraph. Hence $v.q_r = \bot$ for all $v \in V$. This yields $A_r(v) = \emptyset$ for all $v \in V$ and thus $v.a_r = \bot$ by Protocol P_{A_r}. Furthermore, $Q_r(v) = Q'_r(v)$ for all $v \in V$. Thus, $Q_r(v) = \emptyset$ by Rule Q_2. This proves that $Legit_{\mathcal{A}}$ is satisfied.   □

Lemma 5 (Closure). *If $Legit_{\mathcal{A}}$ is satisfied, then $\mathcal{A}$ has terminated.*

Proof. Let v denote a node and consider a legitimate configuration. (v, P_L) and Rule Q_1 are disabled for v since $validLoad(v)$ and $validPlacement(v)$. It also holds $v.a_r = v.a_a = \bot$ and $u.q_r = u.q_a = \bot$ for all neighbors $u \in N(v)$. Hence, (v, P_{A_r}) and (v, P_{A_a}) are disabled for v since $A_r(v) = A_a(v) = \emptyset$. From $Q_r(v) = \emptyset$ it follows that $Q'_r(v) = \emptyset$. Since $v.q_r = \bot$, Rule Q_2 is disabled. Rule Q_3 is disabled since $v.q_a = \bot$. Rule Q_4 and Q_5 are disabled since the query $v.q_r = \bot$ is not valid.   □

Theorem 6. *Algorithm $\mathcal{A}$ is self-stabilizing under the distributed scheduler*

Proof. Correctness and Closure follow from Lemmas 4 and 5 and Termination from Lemmas 1 and 3.   □

Theorem 7. *In a legitimate configuration, the variables $v.\beta$ of all $v \in V$ induce a local k-placement with local minimum variance.*

Proof. For each $v \in V$ let $\beta(v) = v.\beta$. $Legit_{\mathcal{A}}$ implies $validPlacement(v)$ and therefore $\beta(v) \subseteq N(v)$ and $|\beta(v)| = k(v)$ for all $v \in V$. Hence, β is a local k-placement. From $Q_r(v) = \emptyset$ for all $v \in V$ it follows that no node can lower the variance by moving a replica from one of its neighbors to another.   □

Theorem 8. *Algorithm $\mathcal{A}$ terminates after at most $\mathcal{O}(n\Delta^2)$ moves under the distributed scheduler.*

Proof. For each node $v \in V$, $L(v)$ can not be larger than Δ. The value of σ reaches its maximum if the $k \cdot n$ replicas are concentrated on as few nodes as possible. Hence, $\sigma(c)$ can not become larger than $\lceil \frac{kn}{\Delta} \rceil \Delta^2 \in \mathcal{O}(n\Delta)$ and $w_3\sigma(c) \in \mathcal{O}(n\Delta^2)$. All other components of *potvec* are $\mathcal{O}(n)$ and the w_j are $\mathcal{O}(\Delta^2)$. Hence $pot(c) \in \mathcal{O}(n\Delta^2)$. The claim follows from Lemmas 1 and 3. $\square$

Theorem 9. *Algorithm $\mathcal{A}$ terminates after at most $\mathcal{O}(n\Delta)$ rounds under the distributed scheduler.*

Proof. Let c_0 be the initial configuration of an execution and c_i denote the configuration at the end of round i. Note that c_{i-1} is the first configuration of round i. Within the first round, each node that is enabled with respect to Rule Q_1 in c_0 executes Rule Q_1. Note that $\#_{v \in V}$ *validPlacement*(v) never increases. Hence in c_1 all nodes $v \in V$ satisfy *validPlacement*(v) and any execution starting in a configuration such as c_1 never contains any moves of Rule Q_1.

During the second round, all malicious nodes become non-malicious either by executing Rule Q_5 or due to a move of Protocol P_L of neighboring nodes. Hence in c_2, all nodes $v \in V$ satisfy $\neg$*malicious*(v) and *validPlacement*(v).

Let c_2 denote any configuration in which all nodes satisfy $\neg$*malicious*(v) and *validPlacement*(v). In the following it is shown that any execution e starting in c_2 that does not contain a move of Rule Q_5 is at most 5 rounds in length. Since e does not contain an execution of Rule Q_5, it must hold that in c_3 and all subsequent configurations of e, all nodes $v \in V$ satisfy *validLoad*(v). Hence, $Q_r(v)$ and $Q_a(v)$ are constant in the suffix of e starting with c_3. Let $v \in V$ with $Q_r(v) \neq \emptyset$ and let $v.q_r$ and $v.q_a$ be invalid or equal to $\perp$. In c_4, $v.q_r$ is valid. In c_5, the node $u = v.q_r$ acknowledges a removal query. W.l.o.g. let $u.a_r = v$. In c_6, $v.q_a$ is a valid query. In c_7, the node $w = v.q_a$ acknowledges an additional query. W.l.o.g. let $w.a_a = v$. Starting with c_7, v is enabled with respect to Rule Q_5. If the execution would continue for another round, then v would execute Rule Q_5. If $Q_r(v) = \emptyset$ for all nodes $v \in V$ in c_2, then all nodes reset their queries to $\perp$ and all nodes have updated their load variable in c_3. In c_4, all nodes have reset their acknowledgments to $\perp$. The algorithm then terminates in c_4. The claim follows from the fact that the maximum of σ is $\mathcal{O}(n\Delta)$ (cf. the proof of Theorem 8). $\square$

8   Concluding Remarks

This paper presented a novel self-stabilizing algorithm for the k-placement problem that stabilizes in $\mathcal{O}(n\Delta^2)$ moves respectively $\mathcal{O}(n\Delta)$ rounds under the distributed scheduler. The produced k-placements have the property that the standard deviation of the distribution of the loads assumes a local minimum. The algorithm can be applied in different areas of distributed computing. In particular it complements the work on a transformer to achieve fault-containment as described in [9].

Another approach to solve the k-placement problem is to design an algorithm in the distance-2 model. Note that under the distributed scheduler, a naive algorithm (merely consisting of the equivalent of Rule Q_5) would be vulnerable to a livelock resembling the one shown in Figure 2. Also, transforming the algorithm to the distance-1 model as described in [13,2] leads to an increase of the move-complexity by a factor of $\mathcal{O}(m)$. The resulting algorithm would not achieve the efficiency of the proposed algorithm. Furthermore, the transformations require unique node identifiers which is not the case for this work.

We are aware of scenarios, in which algorithm $\mathcal{A}$ requires $\mathcal{O}(\Delta)$ rounds. In particular, for a complete graph, $\mathcal{A}$ requires $\mathcal{O}(n) = \mathcal{O}(\Delta)$ rounds. We are not aware of an example where algorithm $\mathcal{A}$ actually requires $\mathcal{O}(n\Delta)$ rounds. The proof of Theorem 9 does not consider that multiple nodes can move their replicas simultaneously. However, how many nodes can do so heavily depends on the topology and the initial local k-placement. However, it seems difficult to account for this in the analysis. Nevertheless, we conjecture that $\mathcal{A}$ always stabilizes in $O(n)$ rounds.

References

1. Flatebo, M., Datta, A.K., Bourgon, B.: Self-stabilizing load balancing algorithms. In: Proc. IEEE 13th Annual Int. Phoenix Conf. on Computers and Communications, p. 303 (1994)
2. Gairing, M., Goddard, W., Hedetniemi, S., Kristiansen, P., McRae, A.: Distance-two information in self-stabilizing algorithms. Parallel Processing Letters 14(3-4), 387–398 (2004)
3. Gärtner, F.C., Pagnia, H.: Self-stabilizing load distribution for replicated servers on a per-access basis. In: Proc. 19th IEEE Int. Conf. on Distributed Computing Systems, Workshop on Self-Stabilizing Systems, Austin, Texas, pp. 102–109 (1999)
4. Kangasharju, J., Roberts, J.W., Ross, K.W.: Object replication strategies in content distribution networks. Computer Communications 25(4), 376–383 (2002)
5. Karger, D.R., Ruhl, M.: Simple efficient load-balancing algorithms for peer-to-peer systems. Theory Comput. Syst. 39(6), 787–804 (2006)
6. Kessels, J.L.W.: An exercise in proving self-stabilization with a variant function. Information Processing Letters 29(1), 39–42 (1988)
7. Ko, B.-J., Rubenstein, D.: Distributed self-stabilizing placement of replicated resources in emerging networks. IEEE/ACM Trans. Networking 13, 476–487 (2005)
8. Köhler, S., Turau, V.: A New Technique for Proving Self-stabilizing under the Distributed Scheduler. In: Dolev, S., Cobb, J., Fischer, M., Yung, M. (eds.) SSS 2010. LNCS, vol. 6366, pp. 65–79. Springer, Heidelberg (2010)
9. Köhler, S., Turau, V.: Space-Efficient Fault-Containment in Dynamic Networks. In: Défago, X., Petit, F., Villain, V. (eds.) SSS 2011. LNCS, vol. 6976, pp. 311–325. Springer, Heidelberg (2011)
10. Lenzen, C., Wattenhofer, R.: Tight bounds for parallel randomized load balancing: extended abstract. In: Proc. 43rd ACM Symp. on Theory of Computing, pp. 11–20. ACM (2011)
11. Sauerwald, T., Sun, H.: Tight bounds for randomized load balancing on arbitrary network topologies. CoRR abs/1201.2715 (2012)
12. Serbu, S., Bianchi, S., Kropf, P., Felber, P.: Dynamic load sharing in peer-to-peer systems: When some peers are more equal than others. IEEE Internet Computing 11, 53–61 (2007)
13. Turau, V.: Efficient transformation of distance-2 self-stabilizing algorithms. Journal of Parallel and Distributed Computing 72(4), 603–612 (2012)

Self-stabilizing Algorithm for Maximal Graph Partitioning into Triangles

Brahim Neggazi, Mohammed Haddad, and Hamamache Kheddouci

GAMA Lab., University of Lyon, Claude Bernard Lyon 1 University
43 Bd du 11 Novembre 1918, F-69622, Villeurbanne, France

Abstract. The graph partitioning problem consists of dividing a graph into parts, patterns or partitions which satisfy some specifications. Graph partitioning problems are known to be NP-complete. In this paper, we focus on the particular pattern of triangles and present the first Self-stabilizing algorithm for Maximal Partitioning of arbitrary graphs into Triangles (MPT). Then, we give the correctness and convergence proofs of the proposed algorithm.

Keywords: Graph partitioning, Independent triangles, Self-stabilization.

1 Introduction

The notion of self-stabilization was introduced by Dijkstra [8]. The distributed system is self-stabilizing if it can start from any possible configuration and converge to a desired configuration in finite time by itself without any external intervention. Convergence is also guaranteed when the system is affected by transient faults. This makes self-stabilization an elegant approach for non-masking fault-tolerance [9]. Each node has only a partial view of the system, called the *local state*. The node's local state includes the state of the node itself and the state of its neighborhood. The union of the local states of all the nodes gives the *global state* of the system. Based on its local state, a node can decide to make *a move*. Therefore, self-stabilizing algorithms are given as a set of rules of the form [**If** $p(i)$ **Then** M], where $p(i)$ is a predicate and M is a move. $p(i)$ is true when the state of the node i is locally illegitimate. In this case, the node i is called a *privileged/active* node. If all nodes of the system are not active, we say that this configuration is *safe*.

Many self-stabilizing algorithms were proposed in the graph theory such self-stabilizing algorithms for finding graph parameters including a minimal dominating set, a maximal matching, an independent set [16], a spanning tree [6]. The graph partitioning problem is defined on a *graph* $G = (V, E)$, where V is the set of nodes and E is the set of edges, such that it is possible to partition the graph G into smaller components with some specific properties. These properties are often defined on the size of the partitions (clusters), on their shape (subgraphs) or both (patterns).

A.W. Richa and C. Scheideler (Eds.): SSS 2012, LNCS 7596, pp. 31–42, 2012.

The problem of graph partitioning has several applications including scientific computing, scheduling, load balancing and parallel computing [2,25], clustering and detection of cliques and communities in social networks [26].

In the literature, some works were proposed for graph partitioning problems according to self-stabilization paradigm. Graph partitioning into clusters was considered by *E. Caron et al.* in [7] and by *D. Bein et al.* in [4]. In [5], *F. Belkouch et al.* considered a particular graph partitioning problem that consists in decomposing the graph into k partitions of order k. Their algorithm relies on self-stabilizing spanning tree construction then it converges within $3(h + 1)$ steps where h is the height of the spanning tree. *H. Ishii et al.* considered the partitioning of the graph into maximal cliques [22]. They proved the impossibility of finding maximal cliques in anonymous networks, and they proposed a self-stabilizing algorithm that finds maximal cliques in ID-based networks within $O(n^4)$ under central daemon. In [17], *R. Hadid and M. H. Karaata* proposed a self-stabilizing algorithms that finds all the disjoint paths in anonymous mesh networks. Briefs announcements were also proposed in [23] and [1] for both disjoint paths and edge-disjoint paths in arbitrary graphs.

All algorithms cited above consider graph partitioning into some particular subgraphs where at most either particular shape (e.g. clique, path, ...) is needed or particular number of nodes is needed in each partition. In this paper, we give interest to graph partitioning problem into particular patterns where both shape and number of nodes in partitions are imposed. One famous problem strongly related to graph partitioning into particular patterns is the problem of finding maximal matching in graphs. This problem consists in finding maximal partitioning of the graphs into independent edges. The first self-stabilizing algorithm considering this problem was proposed by *S. Hsu et al.* [21]. The algorithm stabilizes within $O(n^4)$ under a centralized daemon. The complexity of the solution was first improved by G. Tel [27], who proposed a proof for a complexity of $O(n^2)$. This value was later improved by *S. T. Hedetniemi et al.* who proved a stabilization within $O(m)$ under the central daemon [20]. They also proposed a generalization of the problem called Maximal b-Matching where each node could be connected to at most b matched edges [13]. The generalized algorithm also runs within $O(m)$ under central daemon. In [14], *W. Goddard et al.* considered the maximal matching problem under the synchronous daemon. However, the work of *F. Manne et al.* [24] seems to be the most elaborated for the self-stabilizing maximal matching problem. Indeed, it proves that the problem could not be considered in anonymous networks and proposes an algorithm that stabilizes within $O(m)$ even under unfair distributed daemon. While all of these cited works gave interest to provide approximative solutions (maximal matchings), work of *R. Hadid et al.* [18] proposed a self-stabilizing solution for finding optimal matching (maximum matching) but only on bipartite graphs.

The purpose of this paper is to develop a self-stabilizing algorithm for graph partitioning into particular patterns that are triangles. The perfect partitioning into triangles is one of the classical NP-complete problems [11]. Hence, the perfect partitioning into triangles does not always exist for an arbitrary graph, so, we consider maximal graph partitioning into triangles such that there exists a local maximization criterium (no new triangle can be added using only nodes not already in a triangle). To the best of our knowledge, this is the first work that considers this problem.

The rest of this paper is organized as follows: the next section defines the used model and some definitions. In Section 3, we give a self-stabilizing algorithm for graph partitioning into triangles. We then present the correctness proof of our algorithm in Section 4, and the convergence and the complexity proof by using variant function in Section 5. Finally, Section 6 gives the conclusion of this work.

2   System Model and Definitions

In this paper, we mean by *graph* an undirected connected graph. So, the system is represented by a graph $G = (V, E)$, such that V is a set of nodes and E is a set of edges. We assume that each node has an unique *id* which is locally distinct (radius 2 is sufficient). We denote by Δ the maximum node degree in the graph G. Assuming that each node knows his neighbors, we denote by $N(i)$ and $N[i]$ the open and the closed neighborhoods of the node i, respectively, such that $N[i] = N(i) \cup \{i\}$.

The problem of graph partitioning into triangles is defined as follows [11].

Given q such that $n = 3.q$ where q is a positive integer and n is the number of nodes in the graph G, the Partition into triangles is q disjoint sets $V_1, V_2, \ldots, V_q$ of the three nodes each such that, for each $V_i = \{v_{i[1]}, v_{i[2]}, v_{i[3]}\}$, the three edges $\{v_{i[1]}, v_{i[2]}\}$, $\{v_{i[1]}, v_{i[3]}\}$, $\{v_{i[2]}, v_{i[3]}\}$ belong to E. For example, in Figure 1, $\{1,2,3\}$ and $\{4,5,6\}$ form triangle partitions. The NP-complete proof was presented in [11].

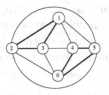

Fig. 1. Partition into triangles

Self-stabilizing algorithms can be designed according to different daemons, also called schedulers. There are two types of daemons which are often assumed in the literature of self-stabilizing algorithms: (*i*) Centralized type. At each step, the centralized daemon selects only one privileged node arbitrarily, and a selected node makes a move. (*ii*) Distributed type. At each step, the distributed daemon selects an arbitrary non-empty set of privileged nodes, and the selected nodes make their moves simultaneously. A special case of distributed daemon is called synchronous daemon, where all privileged nodes are selected by the daemon for making their moves simultaneously at each step. A good taxonomy of existing daemons was presented in [10].

We find also the notion of fairness, the demons can be fair (weakly) or unfair (adversarial). Fair daemon means that every node that is continuously enabled is eventually selected but for the unfair demon, there is no such restriction on the fairness, so the daemon may execute any enabled node at every step.

Generally, algorithms are designed assuming a specific daemon. An algorithm designed for one daemon may not work with another daemon. Thus, in order to simplify algorithm development, some mechanisms, called Transformers of self-stabilizing algorithms from some daemons into other daemons have been proposed in the literature [3,15,19,12].

In this paper, we assume unfair central daemon, meaning that, there is no restriction on the fairness. This kind of daemon can be considered as an adversary against the stabilization of our algorithm.

3   Maximal Graph Partitioning into Triangles (MPT)

Sine perfect partitioning, as defined in the previous section, does not always exist for an arbitrary graph, so, we consider the partitioning of an arbitrary graph G into triangles as a set of disjoint subsets T_i of nodes such each subset T_i forms a triangle and $1 \leqslant i \leqslant \lfloor \frac{n}{3} \rfloor$. Since, the subsets T_i are disjoint, we say the formed triangles are independent. A partitioning into triangles MPT of G is called maximal iff there are no $u, v, w \in V : \{u, v, w\} \nsubseteq$ MPT and $(u, v), (v, w), (u, w) \in E$.

The main idea of the proposed algorithm can be summarized as follows: each node i, in the graph G, maintains a list of pointers $L(i)$ that defines to which triangle i may belong. We say $L(i)$ is valid, if $|L(i)| = 0$ or $|L(i)| = 2$; $L(i)$ contains only pointers (id) to neighbors of i $(L(i) \subseteq N(i))$ and doesn't contain duplicate id. So, it is possible that at the starting of the system, the list is not valid, however, it is easy to add a rule that forces it to become valid. For this raison, and to simplify the description of the algorithm, we assume that the lists are valid. The nodes try to coordinate between them in order to belong to exactly one triangle. To do this, we have three rules:

- The invitation Rule (R1) : when the pointer list of the node i is empty $(L(i) = \phi)$ and there are two neighbors (say, j and k) forming a triangle with i and their lists are empty, then node i invites/points the two neighbors j, k by executing the Rule R1.
- The Withdrawal rule (R2) : when i points on two nodes to form a triangle and one of these two nodes points another adjacent triangle. In this situation, we say that i is chaining. Hence, node i withdraws its invitation by executing the Rule R2. R2 is also executed when the pointer list does not form a triangle in the graph G.
- The acceptation Rule (R3) : if the pointer list of the node i is empty and there is at least a node belonging to the same triangle $\{i, j, k\}$ which pointes it, then the node i accepts the invitation. We added another condition in the

Rule R3 imposing to a node to agree the belonging to a triangle as quickly as possible in order to achieve it. For example, in Figure 2, the node i accepts to belong to the triangle $\{i, j, k\}$ instead of the triangle $\{i, j_1, j_2\}$.

This last condition reduces the complexity of the stabilization of the system and provides a local stabilization (in radius 3) and avoids the wave stabilization that affects the entire system (diameter max).

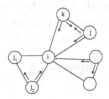

Fig. 2. When i execute R3

The proposed algorithm MPT needs two predicates. The first predicate is $Is\_triangle_i(j, k)$, means that the set $\{i, j, k\}$ forms a triangle in the graph G. We assume that this predicate uses distance-2 information for the node i knows if it belongs to a triangle or not. The second predicate, $Is\_pointed_i(j, k)$ means that it exists at least one node j or k which points the node i and the second node remained such as $Is\_triangle_i(j, k)$ is true. Formally the two predicates are defined as follows:

- $Is\_triangle_i(j, k) :: \{i, j, k\} \subseteq N[j] \bigcap N[k]$ and $i \neq j \neq k$.
- $Is\_pointed_i(j, k) :: (L(j) = \{i, k\} \vee L(k) = \{i, j\}) \wedge Is\_triangle_i(j, k)$.

The proposed algorithm is composed from the three following rules:

Algorithm 1. Algorithm MPT

Require: input arbitrary Graph G

Ensure: output Graph partitioning into triangles MPT

    R1 [Invitation]:

    IF $L(i) = \phi \wedge (\forall j, k \in N(i) : \neg Is\_pointed_i(j, k)) \wedge (\exists j, k \in N(i) : L(j) = L(k) = \phi \wedge Is\_triangle_i(j, k))$ **THEN** $L(i) = \{j, k\}$;

    R2 [Withdrawal]:

    IF $L(i) = \{j, k\} \wedge (\neg Is\_triangle_i(j, k) \vee |\{i\} \cup L(i) \cup L(j) \cup L(k)| > 3)$ **THEN** $L(i) = \phi$;

    R3 [Acceptation]:

    IF $L(i) = \phi \wedge (\exists j, k \in N(i) : Is\_pointed_i(j, k) \wedge |L(j) \cup L(k)| \leq 3) \wedge (\nexists j_1, j_2 \in N(i) : Is\_pointed_i(j_1, j_2) \wedge |L(j) \cup L(k)| < |L(j_1) \cup L(j_2)| \leq 3 \wedge j_1 \neq j)$ **THEN** $L(i) = \{j, k\}$;

---

4   Correctness Proof

Lemma 1: When the algorithm MPT stabilizes, if a node i has $L(i) = \{j, k\}$ then $\{i, j, k\}$ forms a triangle.

Proof: we prove this Lemma by contradiction. Suppose that the algorithm MPT stabilizes and $\exists i \in V$ such that $L(i) = \{j, k\}$ and $\{i, j, k\}$ is not a triangle. The algorithm MPT stabilizes, means that all rules are not enabled and by assumption $L(i) = \{j, k\}$ and $\{i, j, k\}$ is not a triangle. In this case, the Rule R2 is enabled for the node i. So, contradiction with assumption.

Lemma 2: When the algorithm MPT stabilizes, $\forall i \in V$, if $L(i) = \{j, k\}$ then $L(j) = \{i, k\} \wedge L(k) = \{i, j\}$.

Proof: we prove this Lemma by contradiction, the algorithm MPT stabilizes and $\exists i : L(i) = \{j, k\}$ such $L(j) \neq \{i, k\} \vee L(k) \neq \{i, j\}$.

As the reasoning is symmetric for j and k, so, we assume that $L(i) = \{j, k\} \wedge L(j) \neq \{i, k\}$. In this situation, we have : $L(j) \neq \{i, k\} \Leftrightarrow L(j) = \phi \vee L(j) = \{i, x\} \vee L(j) = \{x, y\} \vee L(j) = \{k, x\}$.

- **Assumption 1:** $L(i) = \{j, k\} \wedge L(j) = \phi$.
  By Lemma 1, $L(i) = \{j, k\} \Rightarrow \{i, j, k\}$ forms a triangle. We have two cases for the node k. If $L(k) = \phi$ then the node j has to execute the Rule R3, contradiction with Assumption 1. The second case, $L(k) \neq \phi$, we will have then two situations: The first one, if the node k points another triangle else $\{i, j, k\}$, it means that $|\{i\} \cup L(i) \cup L(j) \cup L(k)| > 3$ then the node i executes R2 to withdraw the invitation, implying contradiction with Assumption 1. For the second situation, if the node k points the same triangle $\{i, j, k\}$ then the node j has to execute the Rule R3 in order to accept the invitation for forming the triangle $\{i, j, k\}$ else the node j has to accept another triangle than $\{i, j, k\}$, implying $|\{i\} \cup L(i) \cup L(j) \cup L(k)| > 3$. This pushes the node i to execute the Rule R2 for the removal, implying also contraction with Assumption 1.
- **Assumption 2:** $L(i) = \{j, k\} \wedge L(j) = \{i, x\}$ such $x \neq k$.
  By Lemma 1, if $L(i) = \{j, k\} \wedge L(j) = \{i, x\}$ then $\{i,j,k\}$ and $\{i,j,x\}$ forms two adjacent triangles, with common edge (i, j). This implies $|\{i\} \cup L(i) \cup L(j) \cup L(k)| > 3$ and $|\{i\} \cup L(i) \cup L(j) \cup L(x)| > 3$, so, at least, the two nodes are activated by the Rule R2. Contradiction with Assumption 2.
- **Assumption 3:** $L(i) = \{j, k\} \wedge L(j) = \{x, y\}$ such $i \neq k \neq x \neq y$.
  By Lemma 1, if $L(i) = \{j, k\} \wedge L(j) = \{x, y\}$ then $\{i, j, k\}$ and $\{i, x, y\}$ forms two adjacent triangles, with common node j. This implies $|\{i\} \cup L(i) \cup L(j) \cup L(k)| > 3$, so, at least, the node j is activated by the Rule R2. Contradiction with Assumption 3.

– **Assumption 4:** $L(i) = \{j, k\} \wedge L(j) = \{k, x\}$ such $i \neq j \neq k \neq x$.
 The proof is similar to that of Assumption 2, but with considering the common edge to be (j, k).

Lemma 3: When the algorithm MPT stabilizes, $\forall i \in V$, if $L(i) = \{j, k\}$ then $\{i, j, k\}$ forms an independent triangle.

Proof: By Lemma 1, $L(i) = \{j, k\} \Rightarrow \{i, j, k\}$ forms a triangle and by Lemma 2, $L(i) = \{j, k\} \Rightarrow L(j) = \{i, k\} \wedge L(k) = \{i, j\}$, so, each node in the graph can belong to only one triangle.

Lemma 4: When the system is stable, the algorithm MPT always gives maximal triangle partitions.

Proof: System is stable and the algorithm is not maximal partition triangles, means that we can find three nodes which belong to the same triangle and their pointer lists are empty.

It is obvious that when the system is stable, every node i in the graph has $L(i) = \{j, k\} \vee L(i) = \phi$. If $L(i) = \{j, k\}$, by Lemmas 3 and 4, $\{i, j, k\}$ forms an independent triangle (partition) composed of three nodes. The rest of nodes, which their pointers list $L(i) = \phi$, cannot be activated by R1 or R2, are called in the next section the single nodes.

We assume that the system is stable and $\exists i, j, k \in V : L(i) - L(j) = L(k) = \phi \wedge Is\_triangle_i(j, k)$. Given a node i, if i is not pointed, then it will execute the Rule R1 in order to invite j and k else i executes R2 in order to accept the invitation. So, this is in contradiction with our assumption.

Theorem 1: When the system is stable, the algorithm MPT finds always maximal partitioning graph into triangles.

Proof: Theorem 1 is a direct consequence of Lemmas 1 to 4.

5   Convergence and Complexity

In a configuration c, the node i could be in one of the following states: (see Figure 3)

– Agree$(i) \equiv L(i) = \{j, k\} \wedge L(j) = \{i, k\} \wedge L(k) = \{i, j\}$.
– Single$(i) \equiv L(i) = \phi \wedge (\forall j, k \in N(i) : Is\_triangle_i(j, k) \Rightarrow Agree(j) \vee Agree(k))$.
– Waiting$(i) \equiv L(i) = \{j, k\} \wedge L(j) = \{i, k\} \wedge L(k) = \phi$.
– Free$(i) \equiv L(i) = \phi \wedge (\exists j, k \in N(i) : Is\_triangle_i(j, k) \wedge \neg Agree(j) \wedge \neg Agree(k))$.
– Chaining$(i) \equiv L(i) = \{j, k\} \wedge (|\{i\} \cup L(i) \cup L(j) \cup L(k)| > 3) \vee \neg Is\_triangle_i(j, k))$.
– Proposing$(i) \equiv L(i) = \{j, k\} \wedge (j, k \in N(i) : L(j) = L(k) = \phi)$.

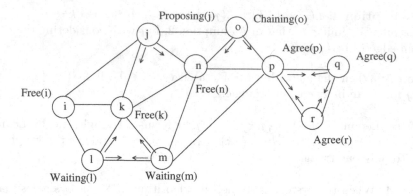

Fig. 3. States of nodes

Lemma 5: If Agree(i) or Single(i) then the node i will never make a move again.

Proof: If Agree(i) $\Rightarrow L(i) = \{j, k\} \wedge L(j) = \{i, k\} \wedge L(k) = \{i, j\}$, this implies $|\{i\} \cup L(i) \cup L(j) \cup L(k)| = 3$ and by Lemma 3, $\{i, j, k\}$ forms independent triangle. In this case, the three rules are not enabled. So, neither i nor j nor k will make a move again. If Single(i), means that $L(i) = \phi$ and $\forall j, k \in N(i) : Is\_triangle_i(j, k) \Rightarrow Agree(j) \vee Agree(k))$ then i has not available pair of nodes which can form a triangle with them, because j or k is agree and can never make a move, so the node i is dead and it can never execute any rule.

Lemma 6: If $\exists i$ such that $Waiting(i) \vee Free(i) \vee Chaining(i) \vee Proposing(i)$ then there exists at least one enabled node in the system.

Proof: we prove that in each State, we have at least one enabled node: State 1: if proposing(i), meaning that $L(i) = \{j, k\}$ and $L(j) = L(k) = \phi$, then the node j and k are enabled by the Rule R3. State 2: if waiting(i), meaning that $L(i) = \{j, k\}$ and $L(j) = \{i, k\}$ and $L(k) = \phi$ then the node k is enabled by the Rule R3. State 3: if chaining(i), means that $L(i) = \{j, k\}$ and (i, j, k) is not a triangle, so, the node i is enabled by R2. If $L(i) = \{j, k\}$ and $|\{i\} \cup L(i) \cup L(j) \cup L(k)| > 3$ then the node i is also enabled by R2. State 4: free (i), meaning that $L(i) = \phi$ and $(\exists j, k \in N(i) : Is\_triangle_i(j, k)$ and $\neg Agree(j) \wedge \neg Agree(k)$. If Free($j$) and Free($k$) then the node i is enabled by R1. Else, the nodes j and k can be proposing, waiting or chaining states, and we prove in States 1, 2, 3 and 4 that in each situation, there are at least one node that is enabled. So, we prove that in each node State (proposing, waiting, chaining and free) there are at least one node that is enabled. So, there exists a node in these States, the configuration of the system is not safe.

Lemma 7: The system converges in $O(n^4)$ moves.

Proof: We define A, S, W, F, P and C as total number of agree, single, waiting, free, proposing and chaining nodes, respectively, in the c configuration.

We use variant function method to prove the convergence of the algorithm MPT. For this, we define the function $VF(c)$ which returns a vector (A+S, W, P, F, C). We define lexicographical order between these vectors, for example (3,2,1,4,4) is greater than (3,2,1,3,5).

Note that every c configuration for which $VF(c)=(n,0,0,0,0)$ is a safe configuration, once the system reaches a safe configuration, no node moves. Whereas, by Lemma 6, in every non-safe configuration, there exists at least one node that can make move when it is selected by the unfair central daemon. So, in this section, we show that every rule increases the value of our function VF.

1. **Invitation Rule [R1]**

   If the node i executes the Rule R1 then the node i is not pointed by any neighbor with whom i could form a triangle and $L(i) = \phi$ (i.e i is a free node). So, after the execution of the Rule R1, the number of proposing nodes increases by one and the number of free nodes decreases by 1.

2. **Withdrawal Rule [R2]**

   If the node i is chaining, so it is activated by the Rule R2. In this situation, we have three cases for activating R2:

   (a) **Case 1:** when i is not pointed by another neighbor with whom i could form a triangle.

   In this case, when the node i executes R2, the number of chaining nodes decreases by 1 and the number of free or single nodes increases by 1. Note, that the node i becomes a single node if all triangles to which it can belong are not available anymore (Formally, $\nexists j, k \in N(i) : Is\_triangle_i(j, k) \land \neg Agree(j) \land \neg Agree(k)$).

   (b) **Case 2:** when i is pointed by another neighbor with whom i could form a triangle.

   In such configuration, since i is pointed and $L(i) \neq \phi$, and all nodes pointing i are chaining. Let x be the number of these nodes. Since i is enabled by R2, means that i is also chaining, then, we have $x + 1$ chaining nodes. Once i executes R2, a node that was pointing to i will become either proposing or waiting node. Let y be the number of nodes that become waiting and let z be the number of nodes that become proposing. We have $x = y + z$. Hence, when i executes R2, the number of free nodes increases by 1, the number of chaining nodes decreases by $x+1$, the number of proposing and waiting nodes increases, respectively, by y and z.

(c) **Case 3:** when i points two neighbors that not form a triangle (Formally, $L(i) = \{j, k\} \wedge \neg Is\_triangle_i(j, k)$).

In this case, when the node executes R2, the number of chaining nodes decreases by 1 and the number of free or single node increases by 1.

3. **Acceptation Rule [R3]**

If a node i is enabled by R3 then free(i). In this situation, we have two cases:

(a) **Case 1:** when the node i is pointed by at least 2 waiting nodes j, k which belong to the same triangle. (see Figure 4(a))

In this case, when the node i executes the R3, the number of agree nodes increases by 3, the number of free nodes and waiting nodes decreases, respectively, by 1 and 2. Note, that in this case, we can have another proposing or waiting nodes pointing the node i which they will be chaining after the move of node i by accepting the node j and k. Even in these situations the VF increases.

(b) **Case 2:** when the node i is pointed by x proposing nodes.(see Figure 4(b))

We have x triangles to which i may belong. So, when it executes the Rule R3, it will arbitrary chose one triangle among x. In this configuration, the number of proposing nodes reduces by x, the number of free node reduces by 1, and the number of chaining and waiting nodes increase, respectively, by $x - 1$ and 2.

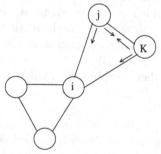

(a) When the node i is pointed by at least 2 waiting nodes.

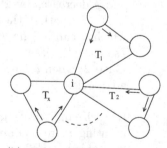

(b) When the node i is pointed by x proposing nodes.

Fig. 4. Case when i is activated by R3.

Brief Announcement: Self-stabilizing Synchronization of Arbitrary Digraphs in Presence of Faults

Mahyar R. Malekpour

NASA Langley Research Center, Hampton, Virginia
Mahyar.R.Malekpour@nasa.gov

1   Introduction

This brief announcement presents a fault-tolerant self-stabilizing distributed clock synchronization protocol for an arbitrary, non-partitioned digraph. Synchronization algorithms are essential for managing the use of resources and controlling communication in a distributed system. **Synchronization** of a distributed system is the process of **achieving** and **maintaining** a bounded skew among independent local time clocks. A distributed system is said to be self-stabilizing if, from an arbitrary state, it is guaranteed to reach a legitimate state in a finite amount of time and remain in a legitimate state. For clock synchronization, a legitimate state is a state where all parts in the system are in synchrony. The self-stabilizing distributed-system clock synchronization problem is, therefore, to develop an algorithm (i.e., a protocol) to *achieve* and *maintain* synchrony of local clocks in a distributed system after experiencing system-wide disruptions in the presence of network element imperfections. The **convergence** and **closure** properties address achieving and maintaining network synchrony, respectively.

The main challenge associated with distributed synchronization is the complexity of developing a correct and verifiable solution. It is possible to have a solution that is hard to prove or refute. Such a solution, however, is not likely to be accepted or used in practical systems. Thus, a proposed solution must be proven to be correct. The proposed solution must restore synchrony and coordinated operations after experiencing system-wide disruptions in the presence of network element imperfections and, for ultra-reliable distributed systems, in the presence of various faults. A fault is a defect or flaw in a system component resulting in an incorrect state [1]. Furthermore, addressing network element imperfections, e.g., oscillators drift with respect to real time and differences in the lengths of the physical communication media, is necessary to make a solution applicable to realizable systems.

There exist many clock synchronization algorithms for special cases and restricted conditions. There are many solutions that are based on randomization and, therefore, are non-deterministic, e.g., the second protocol in [2]. There are many solutions that deal with the closure property [3] but either do not address convergence or provide an ad hoc solution [4] for initialization and integration, separately. Typically, the assumed topology is a regular graph such as a fully connected graph or a ring. These topologies do not necessarily correspond to practical applications or biological, social,

A.W. Richa and C. Scheideler (Eds.): SSS 2012, LNCS 7596, pp. 43–45, 2012.

DISJ has five actions, as follows.

Reset: A process which detects that it is an erroneous state, or needs to decrease its level, executes this action, setting $x.out$ to 0 and $x.parent$ to $\perp$, becoming a *free* process.

Initialize: A free process whose output bit is zero becomes the root of a new BFS tree.

Join: A free process x whose output bit and input bits are both 0, but which has a neighbor whose output bit is 1, joins a BFS tree by linking to a neighbor.

Change Color: A process x which is a member of a BFS tree changes color, from 0 to 1 or from 1 to 0. In order to change color, all children of x (in its BFS tree) must have color opposite to x, while either the color of $x.parent$ equals $x.color$, or x is the root of a BFS tree. When a root changes color, a color wave is deleted, as we explain below.

Finish: In the case that $Output = 1$, the network eventually consists of the disjoint union of one or more BFS trees, one rooted at each process whose input bit is 1. In order for DISJ to be silent, we must freeze the color waves. This action enables a convergecast *finishing wave* to move up each BFS tree; when that wave reaches the root, that root will no longer execute the change color action. Eventually, DISJ will halt.

Normal Growth. A true tree grows by processes executing the Join action. Only a process of color 1 can recruit a neighbor, and the new recruit is given the color 0. That new recruit may wait two rounds before it can recruit new processes itself. If there are no fictitious trees, color waves move up the tree, and the new recruit will eventually be enabled to be the recruiter.

Fictitious Trees. A fictitious tree recruits as a true tree, but the color waves are unable to move up indefinitely; thus its growth eventually stops. After a fictitious tree becomes "color locked," it deletes itself by repeated execution of the Reset action. Within $O(n)$ rounds, there will be no more fictitious trees; within $O(d)$ additional rounds, a legitimate configuration will be reached.

References

1. Dijkstra, E.: Self stabilizing systems in spite of distributed control. Communications of the Association of Computing Machinery 17, 643–644 (1974)
2. Dolev, S.: Self-Stabilization. The MIT Press (2000)
3. Datta, A.K., Larmore, L.L., Vemula, P.: Self-stabilizing leader election in optimal space under an arbitrary scheduler. Theoretical Computer Science 412(40), 5541–5561 (2011)

On the Self-stabilization of Mobile Oblivious Robots in Uniform Rings

Fukuhito Ooshita[1] and Sébastien Tixeuil[2]

[1] Graduate School of Information Science and Technology, Osaka University, Japan
f-oosita@ist.osaka-u.ac.jp
[2] Université Pierre et Marie Curie - Paris 6, LIP6-CNRS 7606, France
Sebastien.Tixeuil@lip6.fr

Abstract. We investigate self-stabilizing algorithms for anonymous and oblivious robots in uniform ring networks, that is, we focus on algorithms that can start from any initial configuration (including those with multiplicity points). First, we show that there exists no probabilistic self-stabilizing gathering algorithm in the non-atomic CORDA model or if only global-weak and local-strong multiplicity detection is available. This impossibility result implies that a common assumption about initial configurations (no two robots share a node initially) is a very strong one.

On the positive side, we give a probabilistic self-stabilizing algorithm for the gathering and orientation problems in the atomic ATOM model with global-strong multiplicity detection. With respect to impossibility results, those are the weakest system hypotheses. In addition, as an application of the previous algorithm, we provide a self-stabilizing algorithm for the set formation problem. Our results imply that any static set formation can be realized in a self-stabilizing manner in this model.

1 Introduction

Background and Motivation. Studies for mobile robot networks have emerged recently in the field of distributed computing. Their goal is to achieve some tasks by a team of mobile robots with weak capabilities. Most studies assume that robots are identical (robots execute the same algorithm and cannot be distinguished by their appearance) and oblivious (robots have no memory and cannot remember the history of their execution). In addition, it is assumed that robots cannot communicate with other robots directly. The communication among robots is done in an implicit way having each robot observe the positions of others.

Since Suzuki and Yamashita presented a pioneering work [12], many results about such robots have been published. Some works consider problem solvability in a two-dimensional Euclidean space [5, 6, 12], while others consider it in graphs [4, 7, 9–11]. In this paper, we focus on an unoriented anonymous ring network since algorithms for ring networks give solutions for the essential difficulties that arise in robot networks such as symmetry breaking. The most fundamental problems in ring networks are the gathering problem and the exploration problem. The goal of the gathering problem is to make all the robots gather at a

A.W. Richa and C. Scheideler (Eds.): SSS 2012, LNCS 7596, pp. 49–63, 2012.
© Springer-Verlag Berlin Heidelberg 2012

non-predetermined single node, and the goal of the exploration problem is to make every node visited by at least one robot. There are many algorithms under various settings for gathering [7, 9, 10] and exploration [4, 11]. The main interest of the works on a ring network is to characterize the minimum assumptions that allow deterministic algorithms. Klasing et al. [9, 10] propose deterministic gathering algorithms in the asynchronous model. They assume the global-weak multiplicity detection, that is, each robot can detect whether the number of robots on every node is one or more than one (it cannot detect the number of robots exactly). In [7, 8], the assumption is weakened to the local-weak multiplicity detection, that is, each robot can detect whether the number of robots on its current node is one or more than one.

All aforementioned works in the discrete (aka graph) model for robots makes the assumption that initial robot positions are *unique*, that is, in the initial configuration, no two robots share the same node. Still, it is generally accepted that robot algorithms, due to the obliviousness of the robots, are "almost" self-stabilizing, that is, they can recover from an arbitrary initial global state. Characterizing what "almost" means in this context is the topic of this paper, and our goal is to clarify the set of problems that can be solved in a self-stabilizing setting, considering classical hypotheses in robot networks (deterministic vs. probabilistic, non-atomic CORDA vs atomic ATOM model, global vs local multiplicity detection, strong vs weak multiplicity detection, etc.). Obviously, in an arbitrary initial configuration where occupied nodes host the same number of robots and are symmetric, no deterministic protocol can break the symmetry, which is needed for solving *e.g.* gathering or orienting a ring. Hence, only probabilistic algorithms may be self-stabilizing.

Our Contribution. In the first part of this paper, we investigate the difficulty of probabilistic self-stabilizing algorithms using weak assumptions. In more details, we show that there exists no probabilistic self-stabilizing algorithm that achieves gathering in the non-atomic CORDA model or if only local-strong and global-weak multiplicity detection is available. Remind that the local-strong multiplicity detection permits to obtain the number of robots on the current hosting node. This impossibility means that the assumption about initial configurations made in previous works is very strong: removing it requires many additional assumptions. Simply put, robot algorithms on graphs are *not* "almost" self-stabilizing.

In the second part, we investigate which problems can be solved in a self-stabilizing manner, and we focus on the gathering and orientation problems. Those two problems are essential to solve most tasks in mobile robot networks. In fact, the difficulty of most problems comes from the lack of agreement on robots' views, *i.e.*, no origin and no orientation in the network. For example, consider the problem that deploys a minimal independent set (MIS) of robots in the network. It is easy for robots to recognize the same form of a MIS from the number of nodes in the ring network. If the network has some origin and orientation, robots can easily recognize the corresponding nodes that construct a MIS. However, if the network has no origin or no orientation, robots cannot uniquely recognize the same nodes due to symmetry of the network configuration even though they know the exact shape of a MIS for a particular number of robots and ring size. Construction of a global origin and orientation is realized by the gathering and orientation problem.

We give probabilistic self-stabilizing algorithms for the gathering and orientation problems. We assume the weakest possible model with respect to impossibility results: we assume the semi-synchronous ATOM model and global-strong multiplicity detection. Remind that the global-strong multiplicity detection can return the number of robots on every node. First, we give a self-stabilizing gathering algorithm that achieves gathering in $O(n \log k)$ expected asynchronous rounds and $O(kn)$ expected moves, where k is the number of robots and n is the number of nodes. Since the gathering requires $\Omega(kn)$ moves from initial configurations where robots are evenly scattered, the proposed algorithm is asymptotically optimal for the number of moves. Second, we give a self-stabilizing orientation algorithm using the gathering algorithm. This algorithm not only provides an orientation of the ring but also extracts ℓ robots from the robot pool created by the gathering algorithm, where ℓ is the number of robots required to solve an application problem. This algorithm works if $k \geq \ell + 2$, and requires $O((\log k + \ell)n)$ expected asynchronous rounds and $O(kn)$ expected moves. Finally, as an application of the proposed algorithms, we provide a self-stabilizing algorithm for the set formation problem. The set formation problem can form any static set such as a uniform distribution and a MIS. For the set of size s such that $s \leq k - 1$, this algorithm requires $O((\log k + s)n)$ expected asynchronous rounds and $O(kn)$ expected moves.

Related Works. Many results about a network of mobile robots have been published since Suzuki and Yamashita presented the pioneering work [12]. They formalize a network of mobile robots in two-dimensional Euclidean space. They give possibility and impossibility results of the gathering and convergence problem, and characterize the class of geometric patterns that robots can form. Note that they prove that two robots cannot achieve gathering deterministically in a two-dimensional Euclidean space. Consequently any deterministic gathering algorithm assumes some conditions on the number of robots or the initial positions. Dieudonné and Petit [2] show that with the global-strong multiplicity detection, there exists a deterministic self-stabilizing gathering algorithm if and only if the number of robots is odd. Probabilistic self-stabilizing gathering algorithms in the continuous model are proposed in [1, 6].

On the other hand, algorithms for mobile robots in graph networks are considered in [4, 7, 9–11]. For ring networks, Klasing et al. [9, 10] propose deterministic gathering algorithms in the asynchronous model with the global-weak multiplicity detection. They also show that there exist some initial configurations where any deterministic algorithm cannot achieve gathering. Izumi et al. [7] provide a deterministic gathering algorithm with local-weak multiplicity detection. The algorithm assumes that initial configurations are non-symmetric and non-periodic, and the number of robots is less than half number of nodes. For odd number of robots in the same model, Kamei et al. [8] propose the gathering algorithm that also works in symmetric configurations. Note that all of the above works assume some initial configurations and thus they are not self-stabilizing.

Many algorithms for pattern formation problems in two-dimensional Euclidean space are proposed, however algorithms for set formation problems in rings are scarcely proposed. To the best of our knowledge, the work in [3] is only the one that considers the uniform distribution on a ring. The work proposes deterministic algorithms in a weaker model but they also assume that each node is occupied by at most one robot in the initial configuration.

2 Model

System Models. The system consists of n nodes and k mobile robots. The nodes $v_0, v_1, \ldots, v_{n-1}$ construct an unoriented and undirected ring in this order. For simplicity we consider mathematical operations to indices of nodes as operations modulo n. Neither nodes nor links have any identifiers and labels, and consequently robots cannot distinguish nodes and links. Robots occupy some nodes of the ring.

Robots considered here have the following characteristics and capabilities. Robots are *identical*, that is, robots execute the same algorithm and cannot be distinguished by their appearance. Robots are *oblivious*, that is, robots have no memory and cannot remember the history of its execution. Robots cannot communicate with other robots directly, however they can observe the positions of other robots. This means robots can communicate implicitly by their positions. We assume each robot has some multiplicity detection. We consider two types of multiplicity detection: the global-strong multiplicity detection, and the local-strong and global-weak multiplicity detection. When each robot has a *global-strong multiplicity detection*, each robot can detect the number of robots on each node. When each robot has a *local-strong and global-weak multiplicity detection*, each robot can detect the number of robots only on its current node and detect whether the number of robots is one or more than one for every node.

Each robot executes the algorithm by repeating cycles. At the beginning of each cycle, the robot observes the environment and the positions of other robots (look phase). According to the observation, the robot computes whether it moves to its adjacent node or stays idle (compute phase). If the robot decides to move, it moves to the node by the end of the cycle (move phase). We consider two types of the synchronous models: the ATOM model and the CORDA model. In the *ATOM model*, a set of activated robots is selected by the *scheduler*, and cycles of the activated robots are executed synchronously. In the *CORDA model*, cycles of robots are executed asynchronously. Note that in the CORDA model each robot can move based on the outdated view, which the robot observed before. On the other hand, robots can move based on the latest view in the ATOM model. For both models, the scheduler is *fair*, which guarantees that each robot is activated infinitely often. When we analyze the worst-case performance of algorithms, we consider the scheduler as an adversary. That is, we assume that the scheduler knows every information, such as positions and decisions of all robots, and activates cycles to degrade the performance of algorithms as much as possible.

A *configuration* of the system is defined as the number of robots on each node. If a node is occupied by some robots, the node is called a *robot node*. If a node is occupied by exactly m robots, the node is called a *m-robot node*. When $m \geq 2$ holds, a m-robot node is also called a *tower node*. If a node is occupied by no robots, the node is called a *free node*. In addition, we define a *1-robot block* as a maximal set of consecutive 1-robot nodes. We define the size of a 1-robot block as the number of nodes in the 1-robot block. A 1-robot node with size 1 is also called an *isolated* 1-robot node. If there exists an axis of symmetry of the ring in configuration C, C is called *symmetric*. If configuration C is symmetric, some robots may recognize the ring in different direction from other robots.

When a robot observes the environment, it gets a *view* of the system. Consider a configuration such that nodes $v_{i_0}, v_{i_1}, \ldots, v_{i_{w-1}}$ ($i_0 < i_1 < \cdots < i_{w-1}$) are robot nodes and each robot node v_{i_x} is occupied by m_{i_x} robots. Then, when we assume a global-strong multiplicity detection, the view of a robot on node v_{i_x} is defined as a sequence $\max\{(M_0, D_0, M_1, D_1, \ldots, M_{w-1}, D_{w-1}), (M_0, D_{w-1}, M_{w-1}, \ldots, M_1, D_0)\}$, where $M_y = m_{i_{(x+y) \bmod w}}$, $D_y = (i_{(x+y+1) \bmod w} - i_{(x+y) \bmod w}) \bmod n$, and two sequences are compared by lexicographical order. When we assume a local-strong and global-weak multiplicity detection, the view of a robot on node v_{i_x} is defined similarly except that M_y ($0 < y < w$) is one or two: $M_y = 1$ implies $m_{i_{(x+y) \bmod w}} = 1$ and $M_y = 2$ implies $m_{i_{(x+y) \bmod w}} > 1$. When $(M_0, D_0, M_1, D_1, \ldots, M_{w-1}, D_{w-1}) = (M_0, D_{w-1}, M_{w-1}, \ldots, M_1, D_0)$ holds, we say that the view on v_{i_x} is symmetric. In this case the robot on v_{i_x} cannot distinguish two directions when it moves. In such cases, we assume the scheduler decides which direction each robot moves to. This means that, even if a robot moves to a direction with probability $1/2$ and to the opposite with probability $1/2$, the scheduler makes it move in the same direction at all times.

We evaluate the algorithm with the number of expected asynchronous rounds and expected total number of moves. A *round* is defined as the shortest fragment of an execution in which each robot executes at least one complete cycle. The total number of moves is the sum of moves each agent makes.

The Problems to Be Solved. We give the definition of the problems to be solved in this paper. First, we define the gathering problem, which aims to collect all the robots at a single node.

Definition 1. *An algorithm A solves the gathering problem if and only if the system reaches the configuration where all robots stay at a single node and do not move.*

Next, we define the orientation problem, which aims to make an orientation in a ring. In this paper, we construct a configuration such that applications can easily use the orientation. To be concrete, we construct a configuration such that there exist exactly one tower node and exactly one 1-robot block with size ℓ neighboring to the tower node, where ℓ is the given input for the application

Fig. 1. The goal of the orientation problem

(See Fig. 1). As we show later, the configuration is useful because each robot in 1-robot block can easily recognize its role from the position.

Definition 2. *An algorithm A solves the orientation problem (and 1-robot block creation) for given input ℓ if and only if the system reaches the configuration satisfying the following conditions: 1) All robots do not move, 2) there exists exactly one tower node, and 3) there exists exactly one 1-robot block with size ℓ that is neighboring to the tower node.*

Next, we give the definition of the set formation problem. The aim of the set formation problem is to construct the target set by robot nodes. However, since the ring is unoriented and nodes have no identifiers, it is impossible to exactly indicate nodes by the target set. Instead we indicate the target set by the relative set $SET \subset \{0, 1, \ldots, n-1\}$. From the set SET, the family of terminal sets $\mathcal{F}(SET)$ is defined as follows:

$$\mathcal{F}(SET) = \bigcup_{0 \leq i \leq n-1} \left\{ \bigcup_{j \in SET} \left\{ v_{(i+j) \bmod n} \right\}, \bigcup_{j \in SET} \left\{ v_{(i-j) \bmod n} \right\} \right\}.$$

For example, to realize a uniform distribution for 12-node rings, we can define $SET = \{0, 3, 6, 9\}$. Then, node sets such as $\{v_0, v_3, v_6, v_9\}$ and $\{v_1, v_4, v_7, v_{10}\}$ are included in $\mathcal{F}(SET)$. We define the set formation problem as follows.

Definition 3. *An algorithm A solves the set formation problem for a given set $SET \subset \{0, 1, \ldots, n-1\}$ if and only if the system reaches the configuration satisfying the following conditions: 1)All robots do not move, and 2) letting S_t be the set of robot nodes, $S_t \in \mathcal{F}(SET)$ holds.*

Lastly, we give the definition of probabilistic self-stabilizing algorithms.

Definition 4. *An algorithm A is a probabilistic self-stabilizing algorithm for problem $\mathcal{P}$ if and only if, for some function $p : N \times N \to (0, 1]$, algorithm A solves $\mathcal{P}$ with probability at least $p(k, n)$ from any initial configuration for n-node and k-robot rings.*

3 Impossibility of Probabilistic Self-stabilizing Gathering Algorithms in Weak Models

In this section, we show the impossibility of probabilistic self-stabilizing gathering algorithms on weak models. As we described in Section 1, we assume the

ATOM model and the global-strong multiplicity detection to propose algorithms. In this section we show that such strong assumptions are necessary to realize a self-stabilizing gathering algorithm.

First we consider the CORDA model as a weaker synchronous model. Remind that cycles of robots are executed asynchronously in the CORDA model. Hence, it is possible that, after robot r observes the configuration and decides to move, some robots repeatedly observe and move before r actually moves.

Theorem 1. *There exists no probabilistic self-stabilizing gathering algorithm with the global-strong multiplicity detection in the CORDA model.*

Proof. Assume that there exists a probabilistic self-stabilizing gathering algorithm A that achieves gathering with probability at least $p(k,n)$ for some function p. Consider a n-node ring and $k = n$ robots $r_0, r_1, \ldots, r_{k-1}$ such that each node is occupied by one robot in the initial configuration. Note that each robot has the same view in the initial configuration. In this view, each robot has to move probabilistically, otherwise the configuration is never changed when they are activated synchronously (Note that, since the view of each robot is symmetric, all the robots move to the same direction by the scheduler if they move).

Consider the above configuration. For an arbitrary positive integer X, we define the procedure of the scheduler $Proc(X)$ as follows:

1. First the scheduler tries to make r_0 decide to move. To be concrete, the scheduler activates the look and compute phases of r_0. If r_0 decides to stay, the scheduler activates the move phase (Here r_0 does not move). Then, the scheduler activates the look and compute phases of r_0 again. This activation is repeated at most X times for r_0. If r_0 decides to move or r_0 is activated X times, the scheduler goes to the next step. Note that, after r_0 decides to move, the move phase is not activated here. This is possible because we consider the CORDA model.
2. Next, the scheduler similarly tries to make r_i $(i = 1, 2, \ldots, k-1)$ decide to move.
3. Then, the scheduler activates the move phase of r_i for each i.

The scheduler can make all robots move to the same direction, if they decide to move, since the view of any robot is symmetric. Consequently, if all robots decide to move, the configuration is not changed after $Proc(X)$. This implies that at least one robot must stay after $Proc(X)$ to achieve gathering. Let $P(X)$ be the probability that at least one robot stays after $Proc(X)$. It is clear that, for any positive number p', there exists a positive integer X' such that $P(X') < p'$.

Let p be a small constant satisfying $p < p(k,n)$. Let X_j $(j = 1, 2, \ldots)$ be a positive integer satisfying $P(X_j) < p/2^j$. We consider the scheduler such that it executes procedures $Proc(X_1), Proc(X_2), \ldots$ in this order. Note that this scheduler is fair because each robot is activated infinitely often. Then, letting P^* be the probability that A achieves gathering under this scheduler, we have $P^* < P(X_1) + P(X_2) + P(X_3) + \cdots < p$. This is a contradiction. $\qquad\square$

Next we consider the local-strong and global-weak multiplicity detection as the weaker multiplicity detection. For this case, we have a similar result.

Theorem 2. *There exists no probabilistic self-stabilizing gathering algorithm with the local-strong and global-weak multiplicity detection in the ATOM model.*

4   An Algorithm for the Gathering Problem

In the rest of the paper, we propose probabilistic self-stabilizing algorithms for the gathering problem, the orientation problem, and the set formation problem. All the algorithms assume the ATOM model and the global-strong multiplicity detection. Remind that we consider n-node and k-robot rings in the following.

In this section, we consider the gathering problem. The goal of the gathering problem is to form the configuration such that there exists exactly one tower node and all robots are on this tower. We denote a set of such configurations by C_g. For any configuration C, we define $M(C)$ as the maximum number of robots that occupy one node.

The behavior of each robot at configuration C ($C \notin C_g$) is given as follows.

- **Case 1:** Case where there exists exactly one $M(C)$-robot node. Let v_t be the $M(C)$-robot node. Let $N_C(v_i)$ be the number of robots on node v_i at configuration C.
  - For each x ($0 < x \leq \lceil n/2 \rceil$), every robot on node v_{t+x} such that $\sum_{i=1}^{x} N_C(v_{t+i}) < M(C)$ moves to v_{t+x-1}.
  - For each x ($0 < x < n - \lceil n/2 \rceil$), every robot on node v_{t-x} such that $\sum_{i=1}^{x} N_C(v_{t-i}) < M(C)$ moves to v_{t-x+1}.
- **Case 2:** Case where there exists more than one $M(C)$-robot node. For each $M(C)$-robot node v, we define h_v be the distance from v to its closer neighboring robot node. Let $h_{min} = \min\{h_v | v$ is a $M(C)$-robot node$\}$. Let V_1 be the set of robot nodes such that the distance to a $M(C)$-robot node is h_{min}. Let R_1 be the set of robots that occupy nodes in V_1. Note that R_1 is a set of robots that are closest to some other $M(C)$-robot node.
  - (Case 2-1) If $|R_1| = 1$, the robot in R_1 moves toward its closest $M(C)$-robot node.
  - (Case 2-2) If $|R_1| > 1$, each robot in R_1 moves toward its closest $M(C)$-robot node with probability $1/(2|R_1|)$.

First, we briefly explain the behavior to reach a configuration in C_g. In Case 1, there exists exactly one $M(C)$-robot node and other robots move to the $M(C)$-robot node. Consequently, the system reaches a configuration in C_g. In Case 2, there exists more than one $M(C)$-robot node. In Case 2-1, the robot in R_1 moves toward a $M(C)$-robot node and joins it. Then, the configuration becomes one in Case 1. In Case 2-2, exactly one robot moves toward a $M(C)$-robot node with constant probability. Then, the configuration becomes one in Case 1 (when the robot moves to a $M(C)$-robot node) or Case 2-1 (when the robot moves to a free node). Therefore, the system reaches a configuration in C_g eventually.

In the following, we prove the complexity of the algorithm. The important behavior of the algorithm is that, when d robots can make probabilistic moves, each robot decides to move with probability $1/(2d)$. Since the worst behavior of the algorithm is to make more than one robot move simultaneously, the adversarial scheduler may activate these d robots simultaneously. The following lemma says exactly one robot moves with probability $1/4$ even in this case. If the scheduler activates them separately, the probability becomes higher.

Lemma 1. *Consider the configuration in which there are d robots that move with probability $1/(2d)$ and other robots cannot move. Then, the probability that the configuration changes in one round and exactly one robot moves in the configuration change is at least $1/4$.*

From Lemma 1, we can show that the system reaches a configuration in C_g in $O(n \log k)$ rounds and $O(kn)$ moves with constant probability from any initial configuration. Even if the system does not reach a configuration in C_g, the system can reach the configuration by repeating the algorithm constant expected times. This implies the following theorem.

Theorem 3. *The proposed algorithm solves the gathering problem in $O(n \log k)$ expected rounds and $O(kn)$ expected moves from any initial configuration.*

5   An Algorithm for the Orientation Problem

The goal of the orientation problem in this paper is to make a configuration such that 1) it includes exactly one tower node and one 1-robot block with size ℓ (ℓ is a given input value) and 2) the tower node and the 1-robot block are neighboring (See Fig. 1). Our algorithm requires that $k \geq \ell + 2$, that is, there should exist enough number of robots to create one tower node and one 1-robot block with size ℓ.

Our orientation algorithm achieves such configuration from the gathering configuration. That is, we first execute the gathering algorithm and then execute the orientation algorithm. Note that, as we describe later, some configurations for the orientation algorithm are the same as those for the gathering algorithm. Since robots are oblivious, it seems to be impossible for robots to recognize which algorithm is executed in the configurations. However, by executing the orientation algorithm preferentially, robots can execute the orientation algorithm after the gathering algorithm. This means that the gathering algorithm is switched to the orientation algorithm as soon as the configuration becomes one included in the orientation algorithm.

In the following, we describe the overview of the orientation algorithm. For simplicity we assume $\ell \leq n-3$ (This assumption will be removed later). The orientation algorithm is divided into three phases. In the first phase, the algorithm achieves the target configuration for $\ell = 1$, i.e., it extracts one robot from the tower node. Note that the orientation is made in this phase because the configuration after the first phase is not symmetric. This orientation is conserved during

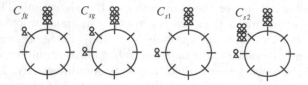

Fig. 2. The first and second phases of the orientation algorithm

the execution. The second phase achieves the target configuration for $\ell = 2$, and the third phase achieves the target configuration for any ℓ.

5.1   The First Phase

The goal of this phase is to reach configurations $\mathcal{C}_{fg}$ such that there exist one tower node and one 1-robot node neighboring to the tower node (See Fig. 2). If $\ell = 1$, the orientation algorithm finishes in the first phase.

In this phase we do not execute the orientation algorithm after the gathering algorithm, but execute the orientation algorithm and the gathering algorithm in parallel. More concretely, the first phase is as follows:

- If the configuration is in $\mathcal{C}_{fg}$, each robot does not move.
- If the configuration is in $\mathcal{C}_g$, each robot moves to its neighboring node with probability $1/(2k)$.
- Otherwise, each robot executes the gathering algorithm.

From Lemma 1, exactly one robot moves in a configuration in $\mathcal{C}_g$ with probability at least $1/4$, and then the system reaches a configuration in $\mathcal{C}_{fg}$. If multiple robots move, the system reaches a configuration in $\mathcal{C}_g$ again in $O(n \log k)$ expected rounds and $O(kn)$ expected moves from Theorem 3. Therefore, we have the following lemma.

Lemma 2. *From any initial configuration, the system reaches a configuration in $\mathcal{C}_{fg}$ in $O(n \log k)$ expected rounds and $O(kn)$ expected moves.*

5.2   The Second Phase

The goal of the second phase is to construct a configuration such that there exist one tower node and one 1-robot block with size 2 neighboring to the tower node. We denote such configurations by $\mathcal{C}_{sg}$ (See Fig. 2). If $\ell = 2$, the orientation algorithm finishes in the second phase.

We provide the behavior of robots from a configuration in $\mathcal{C}_{fg}$. First, a robot on the 1-robot node moves to its neighboring free node. After the move, the configuration becomes configurations $\mathcal{C}_{s1}$ such that there exists one free node between the tower node and the 1-robot node. Then, each robot on the tower node moves toward the 1-robot node with probability $1/(2(k-1))$. After the

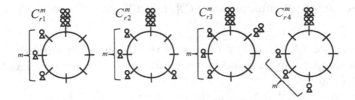

Fig. 3. The third phase of the orientation algorithm

move, the configuration becomes one in $\mathcal{C}_{sg}$ with probability at least $1/4$ from Lemma 1. Otherwise, if all robots move, the configuration becomes one in $\mathcal{C}_{fg}$ again. If multiple (not all) robots move, the configuration becomes one such that there exist two tower nodes. We denote such configurations by $\mathcal{C}_{s2}$. In $\mathcal{C}_{s2}$, each robot on the tower node neighboring to the 1-robot node moves to the other tower node. If all the robots move, the configuration becomes one in $\mathcal{C}_{s1}$. Due to the scheduler of the ATOM model, it is possible that not all robots move at the same time. If one robot remains, the configuration becomes one in $\mathcal{C}_{sg}$. Note that, since we assume $\ell \leq n - 3$, each configuration in the second phase is not symmetric.

In summary, the second phase of the orientation algorithm is as follows (Note that the algorithm includes the first phase and thus the algorithm works from any initial configuration):

- If the configuration is in $\mathcal{C}_{sg}$, each robot does not move.
- If the configuration is in $\mathcal{C}_{fg}$, a robot on the 1-robot node moves to its neighboring free node.
- If the configuration is in $\mathcal{C}_{s1}$, each robot on the tower node moves toward the 1-robot node with probability $1/(2(k-1))$.
- If the configuration is in $\mathcal{C}_{s2}$, each robot on the tower node neighboring to the 1-robot node moves to the other tower node.
- Otherwise, each robot executes the first phase of the orientation algorithm.

From the algorithm and Lemma 2, we can clearly have the following lemma.

Lemma 3. *From any initial configuration, the system reaches a configuration in $\mathcal{C}_{sg}$ in $O(n \log k)$ expected rounds and $O(kn)$ expected moves.*

5.3 The Third Phase

The goal of the third phase is the same as that of the orientation problem, that is, to construct a configuration such that 1) it includes only one tower node and one 1-robot block with size ℓ, and 2) the tower node and the 1-robot block are neighboring. Since the orientation algorithm finishes before the third phase in the case of $\ell < 3$, we assume $\ell \geq 3$ in the following.

First, we list all the possible configurations in this phase. We denote these configurations by regular configurations. Before we define regular configurations, we define some sets of configurations $\mathcal{C}_{r1}^m$, $\mathcal{C}_{r2}^m$, $\mathcal{C}_{r3}^m$, and $\mathcal{C}_{r4}^m$ for each $m \geq 2$ (see Fig. 3).

- Configuration C is in $\mathcal{C}_{r1}^m$ iff C satisfies the following conditions:
  - There exist one 1-robot block with size m, one tower node, and no other robot nodes,
  - and the 1-robot block and the tower node are neighbors.
- Configuration C is in $\mathcal{C}_{r2}^m$ iff C satisfies the following conditions:
  - There exist one 1-robot block with size m, one tower node, one isolated 1-robot node, and no other robot nodes,
  - and the 1-robot block and the tower node are neighbors.
- Configuration C is in $\mathcal{C}_{r3}^m$ iff C satisfies the following conditions:
  - There exist one 1-robot block with size m, two tower nodes, and no other robot nodes,
  - the 1-robot block and a tower node are neighbors,
  - and the two tower nodes are neighbors.
- Configuration C is in $\mathcal{C}_{r4}^m$ iff C satisfies the following conditions:
  - There exist one 1-robot block with size m, one tower node, and no other robot nodes,
  - and there exists exactly one free node between the 1-robot block and the tower node.

We define $\mathcal{C}_r^m = \mathcal{C}_{r1}^m \cup \mathcal{C}_{r2}^m \cup \mathcal{C}_{r3}^m \cup \mathcal{C}_{r4}^m$ and a set of regular configurations $\mathcal{C}_r = \bigcup_{2 \leq m \leq \ell-1} \mathcal{C}_r^m$. By definitions, the goal of the extracting phase is to reach a configuration C in $\mathcal{C}_e = \mathcal{C}_{r1}^\ell$. Note that, since we assume $\ell \leq n-3$, each regular configuration is not symmetric.

The behavior of each robot for the third phase is given as follows.

- **Case 1:** If $C \in \mathcal{C}_{r1}^m$, each robot on the tower node moves to its neighboring free node with probability $1/(2d)$, where $d = k - m$ is the number of robots on the tower node.
- **Case 2:** If $C \in \mathcal{C}_{r2}^m$, a robot on an isolated 1-robot node moves toward the 1-robot block.
- **Case 3:** If $C \in \mathcal{C}_{r3}^m$, each robot in the tower node that is not a neighbor of the 1-robot block moves to the other tower node.
- **Case 4:** If $C \in \mathcal{C}_{r4}^m$, each robot in the tower node moves to the free node between the 1-robot block and the tower node.
- **Goal:** If $C \in \mathcal{C}_e$, each robot does not move.
- **Other case:** If $C \notin \mathcal{C}_r \cup \mathcal{C}_e$, each robot executes the second phase of the orientation algorithm.

Clearly, after some robots move at regular configurations, the configuration is still regular or becomes one in $\mathcal{C}_e$. In the following, we prove the correctness of the algorithm.

Lemma 4. *From any configuration C such that $C \in \mathcal{C}_r^m$ and $2 \leq m \leq \ell - 1$, the system reaches a configuration in $\mathcal{C}_{r1}^{m+1}$ in $O(n)$ expected rounds and $O(n)$ expected moves.*

proposed algorithms. As an example application of our scheme, we provided a self-stabilizing algorithm for the set formation problem. This means any static set formation can be realized in a self-stabilizing manner in our model.

An interesting path for future research is to clarify the problems that could be solved in a self-stabilizing setting with weaker hypotheses (*e.g.* non-atomic CORDA model, no global-strong multiplicity detection, etc.). Another interesting path is to consider a weak scheduler. In this paper, we assume the strong scheduler that adapts to decisions of robots. It is interesting to consider the solvability under the scheduler that is oblivious to decisions of robots.

Acknowledgments. This work is supported in part by Grant-in-Aid for Scientific Research ((B)22300009, (B)23700056, (C)24500039) of JSPS.

References

1. Clement, J., Défago, X., Gradinariu, M., Izumi, T., Messika, S.: The cost of probabilistic agreement in oblivious robot networks. Information Processing Letters 110(11), 431–438 (2010)
2. Dieudonné, Y., Petit, F.: Self-stabilizing Deterministic Gathering. In: Dolev, S. (ed.) ALGOSENSORS 2009. LNCS, vol. 5804, pp. 230–241. Springer, Heidelberg (2009)
3. Elor, Y., Bruckstein, A.M.: Uniform multi-agent deployment on a ring. Theoretical Computer Science 412, 783–795 (2011)
4. Flocchini, P., Ilcinkas, D., Pelc, A., Santoro, N.: Computing Without Communicating: Ring Exploration by Asynchronous Oblivious Robots. In: Tovar, E., Tsigas, P., Fouchal, H. (eds.) OPODIS 2007. LNCS, vol. 4878, pp. 105–118. Springer, Heidelberg (2007)
5. Flocchini, P., Prencipe, G., Santoro, N., Widmayer, P.: Gathering of asynchronous robots with limited visibility. Theoretical Computer Science 337, 147–168 (2005)
6. Izumi, T., Izumi, T., Kamei, S., Ooshita, F.: Randomized Gathering of Mobile Robots with Local-Multiplicity Detection. In: Guerraoui, R., Petit, F. (eds.) SSS 2009. LNCS, vol. 5873, pp. 384–398. Springer, Heidelberg (2009)
7. Izumi, T., Izumi, T., Kamei, S., Ooshita, F.: Mobile Robots Gathering Algorithm with Local Weak Multiplicity in Rings. In: Patt-Shamir, B., Ekim, T. (eds.) SIROCCO 2010. LNCS, vol. 6058, pp. 101–113. Springer, Heidelberg (2010)
8. Kamei, S., Lamani, A., Ooshita, F., Tixeuil, S.: Asynchronous Mobile Robot Gathering from Symmetric Configurations without Global Multiplicity Detection. In: Kosowski, A., Yamashita, M. (eds.) SIROCCO 2011. LNCS, vol. 6796, pp. 150–161. Springer, Heidelberg (2011)
9. Klasing, R., Kosowski, A., Navarra, A.: Taking advantage of symmetries: Gathering of many asynchronous oblivious robots on a ring. Theoretical Computer Science 511, 3235–3246 (2010)
10. Klasing, R., Markou, E., Pelc, A.: Gathering asynchronous oblivious mobile robots in a ring. Theoretical Computer Science 390, 27–39 (2008)
11. Lamani, A., Potop-Butucaru, M.G., Tixeuil, S.: Optimal Deterministic Ring Exploration with Oblivious Asynchronous Robots. In: Patt-Shamir, B., Ekim, T. (eds.) SIROCCO 2010. LNCS, vol. 6058, pp. 183–196. Springer, Heidelberg (2010)
12. Suzuki, I., Yamashita, M.: Distributed anonymous mobile robots: Formation of geometric patterns. SIAM Journal of Computing 28(4), 1347–1363 (1999)

Optimal Grid Exploration by Asynchronous Oblivious Robots*

Stéphane Devismes[1], Anissa Lamani[2], Franck Petit[3],
Pascal Raymond[1], and Sébastien Tixeuil[3]

[1] VERIMAG UMR 5104, Université Joseph Fourier, Grenoble, France
firstname.lastname@imag.fr
[2] MIS, Université de Picardie Jules Verne, Amiens, France
anissa.lamani@u-picardie.fr
[3] LIP6 UMR 7606, UPMC Sorbonne Universités, Paris, France
firstname.lastname@lip6.fr

Abstract. We consider *deterministic terminating exploration* of a grid by a team of asynchronous oblivious robots. We first consider the semi-synchronous atomic model ATOM. In this model, we exhibit the minimal number of robots to solve the problem *w.r.t.* the size of the grid. We then consider the asynchronous non-atomic model CORDA. ATOM being strictly stronger than CORDA, the previous bounds also hold in CORDA, and we propose deterministic algorithms in CORDA that matches these bounds. The above results show that except in two particular cases, 3 robots are necessary and sufficient to deterministically explore a grid of at least three nodes. The optimal number of robots for the two remaining cases is: 4 for the $(2, 2)$-Grid and 5 for the $(3, 3)$-Grid, respectively.

1 Introduction

We consider autonomous robots that are endowed with motion actuators and visibility sensors, but that are otherwise unable to communicate. Those robots must collaborate to solve a collective task, here the *deterministic terminating grid exploration* (*exploration* for short), despite being limited with respect to input from the environment, asymmetry, memory, etc. So far, two universes have been studied: the *continuous two-dimensional Euclidean space* and the *discrete universe*. In the former, robots freely move on a plane using visual sensors with perfect accuracy that permit to locate all other robots with infinite precision (*e.g.*, [1,2,3]). In the latter, the space is partitioned into a finite number of locations, conventionally represented by a graph, where the nodes represent the possible locations that a robot can take and the edges the possibility for a robot to move from one location to another (*e.g.*, [4,5,6,7,8,9,10]).

In this paper, we pursue research in the discrete universe and focus on the *exploration problem* when the network is an anonymous unoriented grid, using a team of autonomous mobile robots. Exploration requires that robots explore the grid and stop when the task completion. In other words, every node of the grid must be visited by at least one robot and the protocol eventually terminates.

---

* This work has been supported in part by the ANR projet R-Discover (08-ANR-CONTINT).

A.W. Richa and C. Scheideler (Eds.): SSS 2012, LNCS 7596, pp. 64–76, 2012.
© Springer-Verlag Berlin Heidelberg 2012

The robots we consider are anonymous, uniform, and unable to communicate, however they can sense their environment and take decisions according to their own view. In addition, they are oblivious, *i.e.*, they do not remember their past actions.

The fact that robots have to stop after exploring all locations requires them to somehow remember at any time of the process which part of the graph has been visited yet. Nevertheless, under this weak scenario, robots have no memory and thus are unable to remember the various steps taken before. In addition, they are unable to communicate explicitly. Therefore the positions of the other robots are the only way to distinguish the different stages of the exploration process. The main complexity measure is then the minimal number of required robots. Since numerous symmetric configurations induce a large number of required robots, minimizing the number of robots turns out to be a difficult problem. As a matter of fact, in [8], it is shown that, in general, $\Omega(n)$ robots are necessary to explore a tree network of n nodes deterministically.

Related Work. In [7], authors proved that no deterministic exploration is possible on a ring when the number of robots k divides the number of nodes n. In the same paper, the authors proposed a deterministic algorithm that solves the problem using at least 17 robots provided that n and k are co-prime. In [10], Lamani *et al.* proved that there exists no deterministic protocol that can explore an even sized ring with $k \leq 4$ robots, even in the atomic model ATOM [3]. Impossibility results in ATOM naturally extend in the asynchronous non-atomic model CORDA [11]. Lamani *et al.* also provide in [10] a protocol in CORDA that allows 5 robots to deterministically explore any ring whose size is co-prime with 5. By contrast, four robots are necessary and sufficient to *probabilistically* explore of any ring of size at least 4 in ATOM [6,5].

To our knowledge, grid shaped networks were only considered in the context of anonymous and oblivious robot exploration [4] for a variant of the exploration problem where robots perpetually explore all nodes in the grid. Also, contrary to this paper, the protocols presented in [4] make use of a common sense of direction for all robots (common north, south, east, and west directions) and assume an essentially synchronous scheduling.

Contribution. In this paper, we propose optimal (*w.r.t.* the number of robots) solutions for the deterministic terminating exploration of a grid-shaped network by a team of k asynchronous oblivious robots in the CORDA model.

In more details, we first consider the ATOM model, which is a strictly stronger model than CORDA. We show that it is impossible to explore a grid of at least three nodes with less than three robots. Next, we show that it is impossible to explore a $(2,2)$-Grid with less than 4 robots, and a $(3,3)$-Grid with less than 5 robots, respectively. The two first results hold for both deterministic and probabilistic explorations, while the latter holds only in the deterministic case. Note also that these impossibility results naturally extend to CORDA.

Then, we propose several deterministic algorithms in CORDA to exhibit the optimal number of robots allowing to explore of a given grid. Our results show that except in two particular cases, 3 robots are necessary and sufficient to deterministically explore a grid of at least three nodes. The optimal number of robots for the two remaining cases is: 4 for the $(2,2)$-Grid and 5 for the $(3,3)$-Grid, respectively.

The above results show that, perhaps surprisingly, exploring a grid is easier than exploring a ring. In the ring, deterministic solutions essentially require five robots [10] while probabilities enable solutions with only four robots [6,5]. In the grid, three robots are necessary and sufficient in all but two cases even for deterministic protocols, the two latter cases do require four or five robots. Also, deterministically exploring a grid requires no primality condition while deterministically exploring a ring expects the number k of robots to be co-prime with n, the number of nodes.

Roadmap. Section 2 presents the system model and the problem to be solved. Lower bounds are shown in Section 3. The deterministic general solution using three robots is given in Section 4. (Note that exploring a $(2, 2)$-Grid using 4 robots is trivially possible, henceforth not considered in this paper.) Section 5 gives some concluding remarks. Due to the lack of space, the special case with five robots is omitted, see the technical report [12] for details.

2   Preliminaries

Distributed Systems. We consider systems of autonomous mobile entities called *agents* or *robots* evolving in a *simple unoriented connected graph* $G = (V, E)$, where V is a finite set of nodes and E a finite set of edges. In G, nodes represent locations that can be sensed by robots and edges represent the possibility for a robot to move from one location to another. We assume that G is an (i, j)-*Grid* (or a Grid, for short) where i, j are two positive integers, *i.e.*, G satisfies the following two conditions: (i) $|V| = i \times j$ and (ii) there exists an order on the nodes of V, $v_1, \ldots, v_{i \cdot j}$, such that $\forall x \in [1..i \times j]$, $(x \bmod i) \neq 0 \Rightarrow \{v_x, v_{x+1}\} \in E$, and $\forall y \in [1..i \times (j-1)]$, $\{v_y, v_{y+i}\} \in E$.

We denote by $n = i \times j$ the number of nodes in G. We denote by $\delta(v)$ the degree of node v in G. Nodes of the grid are anonymous. (We may use indices, but for notation purposes only.) Moreover, given two neighboring nodes u and v, there is no explicit or implicit labelling allowing the robots to determine whether u is either on the left, on the right, above, or below v. Remark that an (i, j)-*Grid* and a (j, i)-*Grid* are isomorphic. Hence, as the nodes are anonymous, we cannot distinguish an (i, j)-*Grid* from a (j, i)-*Grid*. So, without loss of generality, we always consider (i, j)-*Grids*, where $i \leq j$. Note also that any $(1, j)$-*Grid* is isomorphic to a chain. In any (i, j)-*Grid*, if $i = 1$, then either the grid consists of one single node, or two nodes are of degree 1 and all other nodes are of degree 2; otherwise, when $i > 1$, four nodes are of degree 2 and all other nodes are of degree either 3 or 4. In any grid, the nodes of smallest degree are called *corners*. In any $(1, j)$-*Grid* with $j > 1$, the unique chain linking the two corners is called the *borderline*. In any (i, j)-*Grid* such that $i > 1$, there exist four chains $v_1, \ldots, v_m$ of length at least 2 such that $\delta(v_1) = \delta(v_m) = 2$, and $\forall x, 1 < x < m, \delta(v_x) = 3$, these chains are also called the *borderlines*.

Robots and Computation. Operating on G are $k \leq n$ robots. The robots do not communicate in an explicit way; however they see the position of the other robots and can acquire knowledge based on this information. We assume that the robots cannot remember any previous observation nor computation performed in any previous step. Such robots are said to be *oblivious* (or *memoryless*).

Each robot operates according to its (local) *program*. We call *protocol* a collection of *k programs*, each one operating on one single robot. Here we assume that robots are *uniform* and *anonymous*, *i.e.*, they all have the same program using no local parameter (such as an identity) that could permit to differentiate them. The program of a robot consists in executing *Look-Compute-Move* (*LCM*) *cycles* infinitely many times. That is, the robot first observes its environment (Look phase). Then, based on its observation and according its program, the robot then decides to move or stay idle (Compute phase). When the robot decides to move, it moves from its current node to a neighboring node during the Move phase.

We consider two models: the semi-synchronous and atomic model called ATOM [3], and the asynchronous non-atomic model called CORDA [11]. In both models, time is represented by an infinite sequence of instants $0, 1, 2, \ldots$ No robot has access to this global time. Moreover, every robot executes cycles infinitely many times. Each robot performs its own cycles in sequence. However, the time between two cycles of the same robot and the interleavings between cycles of different robots are decided by an *adversary*. We are interested in algorithms that correctly operate despite the choices of the adversary. In particular, our algorithms should also work even if the adversary forces the execution to be fully sequential or fully synchronous. In ATOM, each LCM cycle execution is assumed to be *atomic*: every robot that is activated (by the adversary) at instant t instantaneously executes a full cycle between t and $t + 1$. In CORDA, LCM cycles are performed asynchronously by each robot: the time between Look, Compute, and Move operations is finite yet unbounded, and is decided by the adversary. The only constraint is that both Move and Look are instantaneous.

Note that in both models, any robot performing a Look operation sees all other robots on nodes and not on edges. However, in CORDA, a robot $\mathcal{R}$ may perform a Look operation at some time t, perceiving robots at some nodes, then Compute a target neighbor at some time $t' > t$, and Move to this neighbor at some later time $t'' > t'$ in which some robots are at different nodes from those previously perceived by $\mathcal{R}$ because in the meantime they moved. Hence, in CORDA robots may move based on significantly outdated perceptions. Of course, ATOM is stronger than CORDA. So, to be as general as possible, in this paper, our impossibility results are written assuming ATOM, while our algorithms assume CORDA.

Multiplicity. We assume that during the Look phase, every robot can perceive whether several robots are located on the same node or not. This ability is called *Multiplicity Detection*. We shall indicate by $d_i(t)$ the multiplicity of robots present in node u_i at instant t. We consider two kinds of multiplicity detection: the *strong* and *weak* multiplicity detections. Under the *weak* multiplicity detection, for every node u_i, d_i is a function $\mathbb{N} \mapsto \{\circ, \bot, \top\}$ defined as follows: $d_i(t)$ is equal to either $\circ$, $\bot$, or $\top$ according to u_i contains none, one or several robots at time instant t. If $d_i(t) = \circ$, then we say that u_i is *free* at instant t, otherwise u_i is said *occupied* at instant t. If $d_i(t) = \top$, then we say that u_i contains a *tower* at instant t. Under the *strong* multiplicity detection, for every node u_i, d_i is a function $\mathbb{N} \mapsto \mathbb{N}$ where $d_i(t) = j$ indicates that there are j robots in node u_i at instant t. If $d_i(t) = 0$, then we say that u_i is *free* at instant t, otherwise u_i is said *occupied* at instant t. If $d_i(t) > 1$, then we say that u_i contains a *tower (of $d_i(t)$ robots)* at instant t.

As previously, to be as general as possible, our impossibility results are written assuming the strong multiplicity detection, while our algorithms assume the weak multiplicity detection.

Configurations, Views and Execution. To define the notion of *configuration*, we need to use an arbitrary order $\prec$ on nodes. The system being anonymous, robots do not know this order. Let $v_1, \ldots, v_n$ be the list of the nodes in G ordered by $\prec$. The configuration at time t is $d_1(t), \ldots, d_n(t)$. We denote by *initial configurations* the configurations from which the system can start at time 0. Every configuration where all robots stay idle forever is said to be *terminal*. Two configurations $d_1, \ldots, d_n$ and $d'_1, \ldots, d'_n$ are *indistinguishable* (*distinguishable* otherwise) if and only if there exists an automorphism f on G satisfying the additional condition: $\forall v_i \in V$, we have $d_i = d'_j$ where $v_j = f(v_i)$.

The *view* of robot $\mathcal{R}$ at time t is a labelled graph isomorphic to G, where every node u_i is labelled by $d_i(t)$, except the node where $\mathcal{R}$ is currently located, this latter node u_j is labelled by $d_j(t), *$. (Indeed, any robot knows the multiplicity of the node where it is located.) Hence, from its view, a robot can compute the view of each other robot, and decide whether some other robots have the same view as its own.

Every decision to move is based on the view obtained during the last Look action. However, it may happen that some edges incident to a node v currently occupied by the deciding robot look identical in its view, *i.e.*, v lies on a symmetric axis of the configuration. In this case, if the robot decides to take one of these edges, it may take any of them. We assume the worst-case decision in such cases, *i.e.* the actual edge among the identically looking ones is chosen by the adversary.

We model the executions of our protocol in G by the list of configurations through which the system goes. So, an *execution* is a maximal list of configurations $\gamma_0, \ldots, \gamma_i$ such that $\forall j > 0$, we have: (i) $\gamma_{j-1} \neq \gamma_j$, ($ii$) γ_j is obtained from γ_{j-1} after some robots move from their locations in γ_{j-1} to a neighboring node, and (iii) For every robot $\mathcal{R}$ that moves between γ_{j-1} and γ_j, there exists $0 \leq j' \leq j$, such that $\mathcal{R}$ takes its decision to move according to its program and its view in $\gamma_{j'}$. An execution $\gamma_0, \ldots, \gamma_i$ is said to be *sequential* if and only if $\forall j > 0$, exactly one robot moves between γ_{j-1} and γ_j.

Exploration. We consider the *exploration* problem, where k robots, initially placed at different nodes, collectively explore an (i, j)-grid before stopping moving forever. By "collectively" explore we mean that every node is eventually visited by at least one robot. More formally, a protocol $\mathcal{P}$ *deterministically* (resp. *probabilistically*) solves the exploration problem if and only if every execution e of $\mathcal{P}$ starting from a *towerless configuration*[1] satisfies: (1) e terminates *in finite time* (resp. *with probability 1*), and (2) every node is visited by at least one robot during e.

Observe that the exploration problem is not defined for $k > n$ and is straightforward for $k = n$. (In this latter case the exploration is already accomplished in the initial towerless configuration.)

---

[1] The initial configuration must be towerless to make the exploration solvable in our model.

3 Bounds

In this section, we first show that, except for trivial case where $k = n$, if (i) robots are *oblivious*, (ii) the model is *ATOM*, and (iii) the multiplicity is *strong* (*i.e.*, the strongest possible assumptions), at least three robots are necessary to solve the (probabilistic or deterministic) exploration of any grid (Theorem 2). Moreover, in a $(2,2)$-Grid, four robots are necessary (Theorem 3). Finally, at least five robots are necessary to solve the deterministic exploration of a $(3,3)$-Grid (Theorem 4). In the two next sections, we show that all these bounds are also sufficient to solve the deterministic exploration in the asynchronous and non-atomic CORDA model.

Given that robots are oblivious, if there are more nodes than robots, then any terminal configuration should be distinguishable from any possible initial (towerless) configuration. So, we have:

Remark 1. *Any terminal configuration of any (probabilistic or deterministic) exploration protocol for a grid of n nodes using $k < n$ oblivious robots contains at least one tower.*

Theorem 2. *There exists no (probabilistic or deterministic) exploration protocol in ATOM using $k < 2$ oblivious robots for any (i, j)-Grid made of at least 3 nodes.*

Proof. By Remark 1, there is no protocol allowing one robot to explore any (i, j)-Grid made of at least 2 nodes. Indeed, any configuration is towerless in this case. Assume by contradiction, that there exists a protocol $\mathcal{P}$ in ATOM to explore with 2 oblivious robots an (i, j)-Grid made of at least 3 nodes. Consider a sequential execution e of $\mathcal{P}$ that terminates. (By definition, if we consider a deterministic exploration, then all executions should terminate; while if we consider a probabilistic exploration, at least one of the sequential execution should terminate.) Then, e starts from a towerless configuration (by definition) and eventually reaches a terminal configuration containing a tower (by Remark 1). As e is sequential, the two last configurations of e consist of a towerless configuration followed by a configuration containing one tower. These two configurations form a possible sequential execution that terminates while only two nodes are visited, thus a contradiction.   □

Any $(2,2)$-Grid is isomorphic to a 4-size ring. It is shown in [6] that no (probabilistic or deterministic) exploration using less than four oblivious robots is possible for any ring of size at least four in ATOM. So:

Theorem 3 ([6]). *There exists no (probabilistic or deterministic) exploration protocol using $k \leq 3$ oblivious robots in ATOM for a $(2,2)$-Grid.*

Theorem 4. *There exists no deterministic exploration protocol in ATOM using $k \leq 4$ oblivious robots for a $(3,3)$-Grid.*

Proof Outline. From Theorem 2, k must be greater or equal to 3. Consider first the case of $k = 3$ robots and, assume for the sake of contradiction, that there exists a deterministic protocol $\mathcal{P}$ in ATOM that uses 3 robots to explore a $(3,3)$-Grid. Then, we can show the following claims:

1. There exist sequential executions of $\mathcal{P}$, $e = \gamma_0, \ldots, \gamma_w$, in which: (a) for every x, y with $0 \le x < y$, γ_x and γ_y are distinguishable, and (b) only the first configuration γ_0 is towerless.
2. If there exists an execution of $\mathcal{P}$, $e = \gamma_0 \ldots \gamma_x \ldots$, where γ_x contains a tower of 3 robots, then there exists an execution e' starting with the prefix $e = \gamma_0 \ldots \gamma_x$ such that at most one new node can be visited after γ_x.
3. In any suffix $\gamma_w, \ldots, \gamma_z$ of any sequential execution of $\mathcal{P}$ where (a) for every x, y with $0 \le x < y$, γ_x and γ_y are distinguishable, and (b) γ_w contains a tower of 2 robots, then at most 4 new nodes can be visited from γ_w before a robot of the tower moves.

Using these three claims, we can show that there exist some executions of $\mathcal{P}$ that terminate while at least one node has not been visited, a contradiction.

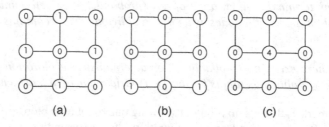

Fig. 1. Three possible configurations in a $(3, 3)$-Grid with 4 robots. Numbers inside the circles represent the multiplicity of the node.

Consider now the case of four robots. The proof consists in showing that, starting from particular configurations, the adversary can always maintain symmetries. To see this, refer to Figure 1 that depicts three possible configurations for a $(3, 3)$-Grid with 4 robots — numbers inside the circles represent the multiplicity of the node. Note that both Configuration (a) and (b) can be initial configurations. By activating the four robots synchronously and starting from Configuration (a), the adversary may lead the system in either Configuration (b) or Configuration (c). Then, in both cases, the adversary may prevent the termination of the exploration, no matter the protocol is.   □

4   Deterministic Solution Using Three Robots

In this section, we focus on the deterministic exploration of a grid by three robots, in CORDA, and assuming weak multiplicity detection. Recall that there exists no deterministic solution for the exploration using three robots in a $(2, 2)$- or $(3, 3)$-grid assuming that model (Section 3). Moreover, exploring a $(1, 3)$-grid using three robots is straightforward. So, we consider all remaining cases. We split our study in two cases. An overview of the deterministic solution for any (i, j)-grid such that $j > 3$ is given in Subsection 4.1. The particular case of the $(2, 3)$-grid is solved in Subsection 4.2.

4.1 Main Algorithm

Overview. Our algorithm works according to the following three phases:

- Set-Up. The aim of this phase is to reach a configuration, called Set-Up configuration, where there is a single line of robots starting at a corner and along one of the longest borderlines of the grid—refer to Figure 2. The phase is initiated from any towerless configuration that is not a Set-Up configuration. Note that no tower is created during this phase. Details about this phase are given in the next subsection.
- Orientation. This phase follows the Set-Up phase and consists of a single move where the robot which is at the corner move to its adjacent occupied node. Once it has moved, a tower is created. The resulting configuration is called an Oriented configuration in which, the robots can agree on a common coordinate system as show in Figure 3. The node with coordinates $(0,0)$ is the unique corner that is the closest to the tower. The x-axis is given by the vector linking the node $(0,0)$ to the node where the tower is located. The y-axis is given by the vector linking the node $(0,0)$ to its neighboring node that does not contain the tower.
- Exploration. This phase starts from an Oriented configuration. Note that in nodes of coordinates $(0,0)$, $(0,1)$, and $(0,2)$ have been visited. So, the goal is to visit all the other nodes. To ensure that the exploration phase remains distinct from the previous phases and keep the coordinate system, we only authorize the robot that does not belong to the tower to move. This robot is called the *explorer*.

  To explore all remaining nodes, the explorer should order all coordinates in such a way that (a) $(0,0)$ and $(0,1)$ are before its initial position (that is $(0,2)$) and all other coordinates are after; and (b) for all non-maximum coordinates (x,y), if (x',y') are successor of (x,y) in the order, then the nodes of coordinates (x,y) and (x',y') are neighbors. An example of such an order is $\preceq$, defined as follows: $(x,y) \preceq (x',y')$ if and only if $y < y' \vee [y = y' \wedge (x = x' \vee y \bmod 2 = 0 \wedge x < x' \vee y \bmod 2 = 1 \wedge x > x')]$.

  Using $\preceq$, the explorer moves as follows: While the explorer is not located at the node having the maximum coordinates according to $\preceq$, the explorer moves to the neighboring node whose coordinates are successors of the coordinates of its current position, as described in Figure 4.

The Set-Up Phase. In the following, we denote by $Dist(\mathcal{R}, \mathcal{R}')$ the *distance* (*i.e.*, the length of the shortest path) between the two nodes of the grid where $\mathcal{R}$ and $\mathcal{R}'$ are respectively located.

We now present the behavior of the three robots, respectively referred to as $\mathcal{R}1$, $\mathcal{R}2$, and $\mathcal{R}3$,[2] according to three main kinds of configurations: Leader, Choice, and Undefined. These classes will be split into several sub-classes.

I) The configuration is of type Leader: Any towerless configuration where there is exactly one robot that is at a corner of the grid. Let $\mathcal{R}1$ be this robot.

   Let consider the following subcases:

---

[2] Recall that robots are anonymous, so these notations are only used to ease the explanations.

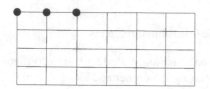

Fig. 2. `Set-Up` Configuration

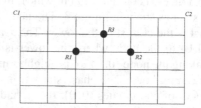

Fig. 3. Coordinate system built by the `Orientation` phase

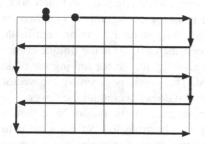

Fig. 4. Exploration phase

Fig. 5. Sample of a configuration of type `Undefined4-4`

A) The configuration is of type `Strict-Leader`: In such a configuration, there is no other robot on any borderline having the corner where $\mathcal{R}1$ is located as extremity. In this case, the robots that are the closest to $\mathcal{R}1$ are the ones allowed to move. Their destination is their adjacent free node on a shortest path towards the closest free node that is on a longest borderline having the corner where $\mathcal{R}1$ is located as extremity. (If there is several shortest paths, the adversary makes the choice.)

B) The configuration is of type `Half-Leader`: In such a configuration, among $\mathcal{R}2$ and $\mathcal{R}3$, only one robot, say $\mathcal{R}2$, is on a borderline having the corner where $\mathcal{R}1$ is located as extremity. Two subcases are possible:

- The configuration is of type `Half-Leader1`: $\mathcal{R}2$ is on a longest borderline. In this case, the third robot $\mathcal{R}3$ is the one allowed to move. Its destination is an adjacent free node towards a closest free node on the borderline that contains both $\mathcal{R}1$ and $\mathcal{R}2$. (If there is several shortest paths, the adversary makes the choice.)

- The configuration is of type `Half-Leader2`: $\mathcal{R}2$ is not on the longest borderline. In this case, $\mathcal{R}2$ is the one allowed to move, its destination is the adjacent free node outside the borderline, if any. In the case where there is no such a free node, $\mathcal{R}2$ moves to a free node on its own borderline. (In case of symmetry, the adversary makes the choice.)

C) The configuration is of type `All-Leader`: All the robots are on a borderline having the corner where $\mathcal{R}1$ is located as extremity. In this case, $\mathcal{R}2$ and $\mathcal{R}3$ are not necessarily on the same borderline. So, we have two subcases:

– The configuration is of type `Fully-Leader`: In such a configuration, all the robots are on the same borderline, $D1$. The two following subcases are then possible:

(1) The configuration is of type `Fully-Leader1`: In this case, $D1$ is a longest borderline. If the robots form a line, then the `Set-Up` configuration is reached and the phase is done. Otherwise, let $\mathcal{R}2$ be the closest robot from $\mathcal{R}1$. If $\mathcal{R}1$ and $\mathcal{R}2$ are not neighbors, then $\mathcal{R}2$ is the only one allowed to move and its destination is the adjacent free node towards $\mathcal{R}1$. In the other case, $\mathcal{R}3$ is the only robot allowed to move and its destination is the adjacent free node towards $\mathcal{R}2$.

(2) The configuration is of type `Fully-Leader2`: In this case, $D1$ is not a longest borderline. Then, the robot among $\mathcal{R}2$ and $\mathcal{R}3$ that is the closest to $\mathcal{R}1$ leaves the borderline by moving to its neighboring free node outside the borderline.

– The configuration is of type `Semi-Leader`: $\mathcal{R}2$ and $\mathcal{R}3$ are not on the same borderline. Two subcases are possible:

(1) The configuration is of type `Semi-Leader1`: In this case, $i \neq j$. The unique robot among $\mathcal{R}2$ and $\mathcal{R}3$ which is located on a smallest borderline moves to the adjacent free node outside its borderline.

(2) The configuration is of type `Semi-Leader2`: In this case, $i = j$. Let denote by $Dist(\mathcal{R}, \mathcal{R}')$ the *distance* (that is, the length of the shortest path) in the grid between the two nodes where $\mathcal{R}$ and $\mathcal{R}'$ are respectively located. If $Dist(\mathcal{R}1, \mathcal{R}2) \neq Dist(\mathcal{R}1, \mathcal{R}3)$, then the robot among $\mathcal{R}2$ and $\mathcal{R}3$ that is the closest to $\mathcal{R}1$ is the only one allowed to move, its destination is the adjacent free node outside the borderline. Otherwise $(Dist(\mathcal{R}1, \mathcal{R}2) = Dist(\mathcal{R}1, \mathcal{R}3))$, either (a) there is a free node between $\mathcal{R}1$ and $\mathcal{R}2$, or (b) $\mathcal{R}1$ is both neighbor of $\mathcal{R}2$ and $\mathcal{R}3$. In case (a), $\mathcal{R}1$ is the only robot allowed to move and its destination is an adjacent free node towards one of its two borderlines. (The adversary makes the choice.) In case (b), $\mathcal{R}2$ and $\mathcal{R}3$ move and their destination is their adjacent free node on their borderline.

II) The configuration is of type `Choice`: Any towerless configuration, where at least two robots are located at a corner.

We consider two cases:

A) The configuration is of type `Choice1`: In this configuration, there are exactly two robots that are located at a corner of the grid. Let $\mathcal{R}1$ and $\mathcal{R}2$ be these robots.

– In the case where $\mathcal{R}3$ is on the same borderline as either $\mathcal{R}1$ or $\mathcal{R}2$ but not both — suppose $\mathcal{R}1$ — then $\mathcal{R}2$ is the one allowed to move, its destination is the adjacent free node towards the closest free node of the borderline that contains both $\mathcal{R}1$ and $\mathcal{R}3$.

– In the case where the three robots are on the same borderline. Then:

(1) If $Dist(\mathcal{R}1, \mathcal{R}3) \neq Dist(\mathcal{R}2, \mathcal{R}3)$, then the robot among $\mathcal{R}1$ and $\mathcal{R}2$ that is farthest to $\mathcal{R}3$ moves to the adjacent free node on the borderline towards $\mathcal{R}3$.

(2) Otherwise $(Dist(\mathcal{R}1, \mathcal{R}3) = Dist(\mathcal{R}2, \mathcal{R}3))$, and $\mathcal{R}3$ has either or not an adjacent free node on the borderline. In the former case, $\mathcal{R}3$ moves to an adjacent free node on the borderline towards either $\mathcal{R}1$ or $\mathcal{R}2$. (The adversary makes the choice.) In the latter case, $\mathcal{R}3$ moves to its adjacent free node outside the borderline.

- If $\mathcal{R}3$ is not on any borderline, it moves to an adjacent free node on a shortest path towards the closest free node that is on a longest borderline that contains either $\mathcal{R}1$ or $\mathcal{R}2$. (In case of symmetry, the adversary makes the choice.)

B) The configuration is of type Choice2: In this configuration, all the robots are located at a corner. The robot allowed to move is the one that is located at a node that is common to the two borderlines of the other robots. Let $\mathcal{R}1$ be this robot. The destination of $\mathcal{R}1$ is the adjacent free node on a longest borderline. (In case of symmetry, the adversary makes the choice.)

III) The configuration is of type Undefined: Any towerless configuration where there is no robot that is located at any corner.

The cases below are then possible:

A) The configuration is of type Undefined1: In this case, $i = j$ and there is one borderline that contains two robots $\mathcal{R}1$ and $\mathcal{R}2$ such that $\mathcal{R}1$ is closer from a corner than $\mathcal{R}2$ and $\mathcal{R}3$. Let $D1$ be this borderline. $\mathcal{R}3$ is the only one allowed to move and its destination is an adjacent free node on a shortest path towards the closest free node of $D1$. (If there are several shortest paths, the adversary makes the choice.)

B) The configuration is of type Undefined2: It is any configuration different from Undefined1, where there is exactly one robot that is the closest to a corner. In this case, this robot is the only one allowed to move, its destination is an adjacent free node on a shortest path to a closest corner. (If there are several possibilities, the adversary makes the choice.)

C) The configuration is of type Undefined3: There are exactly two robots that are closest to a corner. Let $\mathcal{R}1$ and $\mathcal{R}2$ be these two robots.

- If $Dist(\mathcal{R}1, \mathcal{R}3) = Dist(\mathcal{R}2, \mathcal{R}3)$, then $\mathcal{R}3$ is the only one allowed to move, and either $Dist(\mathcal{R}1, \mathcal{R}3) = 1$ or $Dist(\mathcal{R}1, \mathcal{R}3) > 1$. In the former case, $\mathcal{R}3$ moves to an adjacent free node. (If there are two possibilities, the adversary makes the choice.) In the latter case, $\mathcal{R}3$ moves to an adjacent free node from which its distance to $\mathcal{R}1$ will be different from its distance to $\mathcal{R}2$. (There will be two possibilities and the adversary will make a choice.)
- If $Dist(\mathcal{R}1, \mathcal{R}3) \neq Dist(\mathcal{R}2, \mathcal{R}3)$, then the robot among $\mathcal{R}1$ and $\mathcal{R}2$ that is closest to $\mathcal{R}3$ is the only one allowed to move. Its destination is the adjacent free node that is on a shortest path to a closest corner. (If there are several possibilities, the adversary makes the choice.)

D) The configuration is of type Undefined4: There are three robots that are closest to a corner. Again, four cases are possible:

- The configuration is of type Undefined4-1: There is exactly one robot that is on a borderline. In this case, this robot is the only one allowed to move. Its destination is an adjacent free node that is on a shortest path to a closest corner. (In case of two shortest paths, the adversary breaks the symmetry in the first step.)
- The configuration is of type Undefined4-2: In such a configuration, there are exactly two robots on a borderline. Let $\mathcal{R}1$ and $\mathcal{R}2$ be these two robots. The robot allowed to move is $\mathcal{R}3$. Its destination is the adjacent free node towards a closest corner. (The adversary may have to break the symmetry.)
- The configuration is of type Undefined4-3: The three robots are on borderlines of the grid.

(1) There are more than one robot on the same borderline: In this case, there are exactly two robots on the same borderline, and let $\mathcal{R}1$ and $\mathcal{R}2$ be these robots. Then $\mathcal{R}3$ is the only one allowed to move and its destination is an adjacent free node towards a closest corner. (The adversary may have to break the symmetry.)

(2) There is at most one robot on each borderline: Exactly one borderline is perpendicular to the two others. Only the robot on that borderline moves and its destination is the adjacent node towards a closest corner. (The adversary may have to break the symmetry.)

- The configuration is of type Undefined4-4: In this case, there is no robot on any borderline.

(1) In the case where there are two robots, $\mathcal{R}1$ and $\mathcal{R}2$, that are closest to the same corner, and this corner is not a closest corner to $\mathcal{R}3$, then $\mathcal{R}3$ is the only robot allowed to move and its destination is an adjacent free node on a shortest path towards a closest corner. (If there are several possibilities, the adversary makes the choice.)

(2) In the case where there are two robots, $\mathcal{R}1$ and $\mathcal{R}2$, that are closest to corners $C1$ and $C2$, respectively, where $C1 \neq C2$, and $\mathcal{R}3$ is closest to both $C1$ and $C2$, then $\mathcal{R}3$ is the only one allowed to move (see Figure 5), and it moves toward $C1$ or $C2$ according to a choice of the adversary.

(3) In the case where all the robots are closest to different corners, there is one robot $\mathcal{R}1$ whom corner is between the two corners targeted by $\mathcal{R}2$ and $\mathcal{R}3$. The robot allowed to move is $\mathcal{R}1$, its destination is an adjacent free node on a shortest path towards its closest corner. (If there are several shortest paths, the adversary makes the choice.)

The next theorem can be proven using the state diagram of the algorithm:

Theorem 5. *The three phases* Set-Up, Orientation, *and* Exploration *deterministically solve the exploration problem with 3 oblivious robots in CORDA for any* (i,j)-*Grid such that* $j > 3$.

4.2 Exploring a (2,3)-Grid

The idea for the $(2, 3)$-Grid is rather simple. Consider the two longest borderlines of the grid. Since there are initially three isolated robots on the grid, there exists one of the two longest borderlines, say D, that contains either all the robots or exactly two robots. In the second case, the robot that is not part of D moves to the adjacent free node on the shortest path towards the free node of D. Thus, the three robots are eventually located on D. Next, the robot not located at any corner moves to one of its two neighboring occupied nodes. (The destination is chosen by the adversary.) Thus, a tower is created. Once the tower is created, the grid is oriented. Then, the single robot moves to the adjacent free node in the longest borderline that does not contain any tower. Next, it explores the nodes of this line by moving towards the tower. When it becomes neighbor of the tower, all the nodes of the $(2, 3)$-Grid have been explored.

Theorem 6. *The deterministic exploration of a* $(2, 3)$-*Grid can be solved in CORDA using 3 oblivious robots.*

5 Conclusion

We presented necessary and sufficient conditions to explore a grid with a team of k asynchronous oblivious robots. Our results show that, perhaps surprisingly, exploring a grid is easier than exploring a ring. In the ring, deterministic (respectively, probabilistic) solutions essentially require five (resp., four) robots. In the grid, three robots are necessary (even in the probabilistic case) and sufficient (even in the deterministic case) in the all but two cases, while the two remaining instances do require four and five robots, respectively. Note that the general algorithm given in that paper requires exactly three robots. It is worth investigating whether exploration of a grid of n nodes can be achieved using any number k ($3 > k \geq n - 1$) of robots, in particular when k is even.

References

1. Das, S., Flocchini, P., Santoro, N., Yamashita, M.: On the computational power of oblivious robots: forming a series of geometric patterns. In: Proceedings of the ACM Symposium on Principles of Distributed Computing (PODC 2010), pp. 267–276 (2010)
2. Dieudonné, Y., Labbani-Igbida, O., Petit, F.: Circle formation of weak robots. ACM Transactions on Adaptive and Autonomous Systems (TAAS) 3(4), 16:1–16:20 (2008)
3. Suzuki, I., Yamashita, M.: Distributed anonymous mobile robots: Formation of geometric patterns. SIAM J. Comput. 28(4), 1347–1363 (1999)
4. Baldoni, R., Bonnet, F., Milani, A., Raynal, M.: On the Solvability of Anonymous Partial Grids Exploration by Mobile Robots. In: Baker, T.P., Bui, A., Tixeuil, S. (eds.) OPODIS 2008. LNCS, vol. 5401, pp. 428–445. Springer, Heidelberg (2008)
5. Devismes, S.: Optimal exploration of small rings. In: Proceedings of the Third International Workshop on Reliability, Availability, and Security, WRAS 2010, pp. 9:1–9:6. ACM, New York (2010)
6. Devismes, S., Petit, F., Tixeuil, S.: Optimal Probabilistic Ring Exploration by Semi-synchronous Oblivious Robots. In: Kutten, S., Žerovnik, J. (eds.) SIROCCO 2009. LNCS, vol. 5869, pp. 195–208. Springer, Heidelberg (2010)
7. Flocchini, P., Ilcinkas, D., Pelc, A., Santoro, N.: Computing Without Communicating: Ring Exploration by Asynchronous Oblivious Robots. In: Tovar, E., Tsigas, P., Fouchal, H. (eds.) OPODIS 2007. LNCS, vol. 4878, pp. 105–118. Springer, Heidelberg (2007)
8. Flocchini, P., Ilcinkas, D., Pelc, A., Santoro, N.: Remembering without Memory: Tree Exploration by Asynchronous Oblivious Robots. In: Shvartsman, A.A., Felber, P. (eds.) SIROCCO 2008. LNCS, vol. 5058, pp. 33–47. Springer, Heidelberg (2008)
9. Klasing, R., Markou, E., Pelc, A.: Gathering asynchronous oblivious mobile robots in a ring. Theor. Comput. Sci. 390(1), 27–39 (2008)
10. Lamani, A., Potop-Butucaru, M.G., Tixeuil, S.: Optimal Deterministic Ring Exploration with Oblivious Asynchronous Robots. In: Patt-Shamir, B., Ekim, T. (eds.) SIROCCO 2010. LNCS, vol. 6058, pp. 183–196. Springer, Heidelberg (2010)
11. Prencipe, G.: *Instantaneous Actions* vs. *Full Asynchronicity*: Controlling and Coordinating a Set of Autonomous Mobile Robots. In: Restivo, A., Ronchi Della Rocca, S., Roversi, L. (eds.) ICTCS 2001. LNCS, vol. 2202, pp. 154–171. Springer, Heidelberg (2001)
12. Devismes, S., Lamani, A., Petit, F., Raymond, P., Tixeuil, S.: Optimal grid exploration by asynchronous oblivious robots. Technical report, UPMC (2011),
http://arxiv.org/abs/1105.2461

Terminating Population Protocols via Some Minimal Global Knowledge Assumptions[*]

Othon Michail[1,2], Ioannis Chatzigiannakis[1,2], and Paul G. Spirakis[1,2]

[1] Computer Technology Institute & Press "Diophantus" (CTI), Patras, Greece
[2] Computer Engineering and Informatics Department (CEID), University of Patras
{michailo,ichatz,spirakis}@cti.gr

Abstract. We extend the population protocol model with a *cover-time service* that informs a walking state every time it covers the whole network. This is simply a known upper bound on the cover time of a random walk. This allows us to introduce *termination* into population protocols, a capability that is crucial for any distributed system. By reduction to an oracle-model we arrive at a very satisfactory lower bound on the computational power of the model: we prove that it is *at least as strong as a Turing Machine of space* $\log n$ *with input commutativity*, where n is the number of nodes in the network. We also give a $\log n$-space, but nondeterministic this time, upper bound. Finally, we prove interesting similarities of this model to linear bounded automata.

1 Introduction

Networks of tiny artifacts will play a fundamental role in the computational environments and applications of tomorrow. As a result, over the last decade, there has been a strong focus on theoretical models of pervasive systems, consisting of great numbers of computationally restricted, communicating entities. One such model, called the *Population Protocol* (*PP*) model, has been recently introduced by Angluin *et al.* [AAD+06]. Their aim was to model sensor networks consisting of tiny computational devices (called *agents*) with sensing capabilities that follow some unpredictable and uncontrollable mobility pattern. Due to the minimalistic nature of their model, the class of computable predicates was proven [AAER07] to be fairly small: it is the class of *semilinear predicates* [GS66], which does not support e.g. multiplications, exponentiations, and many other important operations on input variables. Additionally, population protocols do not halt. No

[*] This work has in part been supported by the EU (European Social Fund - ESF) and Greek national funds through (i) the Operational Programme "Education and Lifelong Learning" (EdLL), under the title "Foundations of Dynamic Distributed Computing Systems" (FOCUS), and (ii) the National Strategic Reference Framework (NSRF) (Regional Operational Programme - Western Greece) under the title "Advanced Systems and Services over Wireless and Mobile Networks" (number 312179).

A.W. Richa and C. Scheideler (Eds.): SSS 2012, LNCS 7596, pp. 77–89, 2012.
© Springer-Verlag Berlin Heidelberg 2012

agent of the population running the protocol can know whether the computation is completed. The agents forever interact in pairs while their outputs (but not necessarily their states) stabilize to a certain value.

An interesting question that quickly emerged was whether complex computations could be performed by using simple protocols and combining their functionality. Given the protocols stabilizing behavior, their sequential execution was impossible. To circumvent this problem, Angluin *et al.* introduced the *stabilizing inputs PPs* [AAC+05] and they showed that multiple protocols can run in parallel and once one stabilized the others could run correctly (by taking appropriate actions to restore correct execution) using the stabilized output of the former as their input. This approach is, however, fairly slow in terms of the number of interactions (provided some probabilistic assumption on the interaction pattern) since it requires to implement phase clocks based on epidemic protocols (see [AAE08]).

In this work, we follow an alternative approach. We augment the original model of computation with a *cover-time service* (we abbreviate the new model as *CTS*) that informs a walking state every time it covers the whole network. This is simply a known upper bound on the cover time of a random walk. This allows us to introduce *termination* into population protocols, a capability that is crucial for any distributed system. Then we reduce this model to population protocols augmented with an *absence detector*. An absence detector is an oracle that gives hints about *which states are not present in the population*. Each process can interact with this special agent (the absence detector) that monitors other agents in the system, and maintains flags for each state of the protocol. The rest of the model is the same as the PP model. All agents, apart from the absence detector, are modeled as *finite-state machines* that run the *same protocol*. Agents interact in pairs according to some *interaction graph* which specifies the permissible interacting pairs, and update their states in the process. *No agent can predict or control its interactions*. Within this framework, we explore the computational capabilities of this new extension, that we call *Population Protocols with Absence Detector* (*AD*), and study its properties on a purely theoretical ground. As we shall see the AD model is computationally stronger than PPs but this is not what sets it apart. A major new feature of this model is its capability to perform *halting computations*, which allows sequential execution of protocols. Note that although we are currently unaware of how to construct such detectors, in the future, our detector may be implemented via a Bulletin Board regarding the existing states (e.g. each device marks its current state in the board, and all devices can read this board). Such Boards can be implemented easily and have been used in the past [Edi86].

2   Other Previous Work

In the population protocol model [AAD+06], n computational agents are passively mobile, interact in ordered pairs, and the temporal connectivity assumption is a *strong global fairness condition* according to which all configurations that may always occur, occur infinitely often. These assumptions give rise to some sort of structureless interacting automata model. The usually assumed *anonymity* and *uniformity* (i.e. n is not known) of protocols only allow for commutative computations that eventualy stabilize to a desired configuration. Most computability issues in this area have now been established. Constant-state nodes on a complete interaction network (and several variations) compute the *semilinear predicates* [AAER07]. Semilinearity persists up to $o(\log \log n)$ local space but not more than this [CMN+11]. If constant-state nodes can additionally leave and update fixed-length pairwise marks then the computational power dramatically increases to the commutative subclass of **NSPACE**(n^2) [MCS11a]. For a very recent introductory text see [MCS11b]. Finally, our CTS model is different than the cover-times considered in [BBCK10] in that we allow protocols know the cover times and as their cover-times refer to the time for an agent to meet all other agents.

3   Our Results - Roadmap

In Sections 4 and 5, the newly proposed models are formally defined. Subsection 5.1 in particular, defines halting and output stabilizing computations, as well as the classes of predicates that the AD model can compute in both cases. In Section 6, we illustrate the new model with a simple leader election protocol and give some properties of the AD concerning halting computations. Section 7 first establishes the computational equivalence of the CTS and AD models and then deals with the computational power of the latter. In particular, Section 7.1 shows that all semilinear predicates (whose class is denoted by **SEM**) are stably computable by halting ADs. In Section 7.2, several improved computational lower bounds and an upper bound are presented. In particular, it is first shown that the class **HAD**, of all predicates computable by some AD with a unique leader, includes all multiplication predicates of the form $(bN_1^{d_1} N_2^{d_2} \cdots N_k^{d_k} < c)$, where b, c, d_i, k are constants, $b, c \in \mathbb{Z}$ and $d_i, k \in \mathbb{Z}^+$. We do so by constructing an AD (Protocol 2) that performs *iterative computation*. Then in Subsection 7.2 it is shown that halting ADs can compute any predicate whose support (corresponding language on the input alphabet) is decidable by a Turing Machine (TM) of $O(\log n)$ space. This is shown by *simulating a One Way k-Counter Machine* (*k*-CM) [FMR68, Min61] with halting ADs. Moreover, it is shown that all predicates in **HAD** are stably computable by a TM of $O(\log^2 n)$ space. Finally, some similarities of the AD model with *Multilset Linear Bounded Automata with Detection* (*MLBADs*) are pointed out and it is established (however, the proof being left for the full paper) that ADs can simulate such automata. In Section 8, we conclude and present potential future research directions.

4   A Cover-Time Service

We equip pairwise-interacting agents with the following natural capability: *swapping states can know when they have covered the whole population*. Note that we

refer to states and not to nodes. A node may possibly not be ever able to interact with all other nodes, however if nodes constantly swap their states then the
resulting random walk must be capable of covering the whole population (e.g.
in a complete graph the cover time of a random walk is $n \log n$).

We assume a unique leader in the population which jumps from node to node.
What we require is that the leader state *knows* when it has passed from all nodes
and we require this to hold iteratively, that is after it knows that it has covered
the whole population it can know the same for the next walk, and so on. So
we just assume a *cover-time service* which is a black-box for the protocol. We
call this extension of PPs with leader and a cover-time service the *Cover-Time
Service (CTS)* model.

Formally, we are given a population of n agents s.t. initially a node u is in state
$(l, D, 0)$ while all other nodes are in state $\perp$. What we require is that $D \in \mathbb{N}$
satisfies the following. If in every interaction (v, w), s.t. the state of v is (l, D, i)
and the state of w is $\perp$, v updates to $\perp$ and w to $(l, D, i + 1)$ (swapping their
states and increasing i by one) if $D > i + 1$ and to $(l, D, 0)$ otherwise, then in
every D consecutive steps $s_1, \ldots, s_D$ (where we can w.l.o.g. assume that a single
interaction occurs in each step) it holds that $\{z \in V : z$ has obtained l at least
once in the interval $[s_1, s_D]\} = V$. That is D is an upper bound on the time
needed for a swapping state (here l) to visit all nodes (called the *cover-time*).
The leader state, no matter which node it lies on, can detect the coverage of V
when the step/interaction counter i becomes equal to D. We assume that both
D and i are only used for coverage detection and not as additional storage for
internal computation (nodes keep operating as finite-state machines). Another
way to appreciate this is by imagining that all nodes have access to a global
clock that ticks every D rounds.

We explore the computability of the CTS model. In particular, we arrive at
an exact characterization of its computational power. We do so by reducing the
CTS model to an artificial but convenient variant of population protocols that
is equipped with a powerful oracle-node capable of detecting the presence or
absence of any state from the population. Our oracle model is of particular theoretical interest as it seems that most PP variants equipped with some capability
to detect termination, and not only our particular CTS example, may as well
reduce to it.

5   Absence Detectors

A *Population Protocol with Absence Detector (AD)* is a 7-tuple $(X, Y, Q, I, \omega, \delta, \gamma)$
where X, Y and Q are finite sets and X is the *input alphabet*, Y is the *output
alphabet*, Q is a set of *states*, $I : X \to Q$ is the *input function*, $\omega : Q \to Y$ is
the output function, δ is the transition function $\delta : Q \times Q \to Q \times Q$ and γ is
the *detection transition function* $\gamma : Q \times \{0, 1\}^{|Q|} \to Q$. If $\delta(a, b) = (c, d)$, where
$a, b, c, d \in Q$, we call $(a, b) \to (c, d)$ a *transition* and we define $\delta_1(a, b) = c$ and
$\delta_2(a, b) = d$. We also call transition any $(q, a) \to c$, where $q, c \in Q$, $a \in \{0, 1\}^{|Q|}$
so that $\gamma(q, a) = c$.

An AD runs on the nodes of an interaction graph $G = (V, E)$ where G is a directed graph without self-loops and multiple edges, V is a *population* of n *agents* plus a single *absence detector* ($n + 1$ entities in total), and E is the set of permissible, ordered interactions between two agents or an agent and the absence detector. An absence detector is a special node whose state is a vector $a \in \{0, 1\}^{|Q|}$, called *absence vector*, always representing the absence or not of each state from the population; that is, $q \in Q$ is absent from the population in the current configuration iff $a[q] = 1$. From now on we will denote the absence detector by a unless stated otherwise. Throughout the section we consider only complete interaction graphs, that is all agents may interact with each other and with the absence detector.

Initially, each agent except the absence detector senses its environment (as a response to a global start signal) and receives an input symbol from X. We call an *input assignment* to the population, any string $x = \sigma_1 \sigma_2 \ldots \sigma_n \in X^*$, where by n we denote the population size. Then all agents that received an input symbol apply the input function on their symbols and obtain their initial states. Given an input assignment x the absence detector is initialized by setting $a[q] = 0$ for all $q \in Q$ so that $\exists \sigma_k \in x : I(\sigma_k) = q$ and $a[q] = 1$ for all other $q \in Q$.

A *population configuration*, or more briefly a *configuration* is a mapping $C : V \to Q \cup \{0, 1\}^{|Q|}$ specifying a state $q \in Q$ for each agent of the population and a vector $a \in \{0, 1\}^{|Q|}$ for the absence detector. We call an *initial configuration*, a configuration that specifies the initial state of each agent of the population and the initial absence vector of the absence detector w.r.t. a given input assignment x (as previously described). Let C, C' be two configurations and $u \in V - \{a\}$, $a \in \{0, 1\}^{|Q|}$ be an agent and the absence vector of the detector, respectively. We denote by $C(u)$ the state of agent $u \in V$ under configuration C. We say that C *yields* C' *via encounter* $(u, a) \in E$ and denote by $C \xrightarrow{(u,a)} C'$, if $C'(u) = \gamma(C(u), a)$, $C'(w) = C(w)$, $\forall w \in (V - \{u, a\})$ and $C'(a) = a'$ so that $a'[q] = 0$, $\forall q \in Q$ where $\exists w \in V : C'(w) = q$ and $a'[q] = 1$ otherwise. The previous transition can be similarly defined for the reverse interaction (a, u). In addition, given two distinct agents $u, v \in V$, where $u, v \neq a$, we say that C *yields* C' *via encounter* $e = (u, v) \in E$ and denoted by $C \xrightarrow{e} C'$, if $C'(u) = \delta_1(C(u), C(v))$, $C'(v) = \delta_2(C(u), C(v))$, $C'(w) = C(w)$, for all $w \in (V - \{u, v, a\})$ and $C'(a) = a'$ updated as previously. We say that C can go to C' in one step, denoted $C \to C'$, if $C \xrightarrow{t} C'$ for some $t \in E$. We write $C \xrightarrow{*} C'$ if there is a sequence of configurations $C = C_0, C_1, \ldots, C_k = C'$, such that $C_i \to C_{i+1}$ for all $i, 0 \le i < k$, in which case we say that C' is *reachable* from C.

We call an *execution* any finite or infinite sequence of configurations $C_0, C_1, C_2, \ldots$, where C_0 is an initial configuration and $C_i \to C_{i+1}$, for all $i \ge 0$. The interacting pairs are chosen by an adversary. A strong global *fairness condition* is imposed on the adversary to ensure the protocol makes progress. An infinite execution is *fair* if for every pair of configurations C and C' such that $C \to C'$, if C occurs infinitely often in the execution then so does C'. An adversary scheduler is fair if it always leads to fair executions. A *computation* is an infinite fair execution. An interaction between two agents is called *effective* if at least one of the initiator's or the responder's states is modified (that is, if C, C' are the configurations before and after the interaction, respectively, then $C' \neq C$).

Note that since X, Y, and Q are finite, the description of an AD is independent from the population size n. Moreover, agents cannot have unique identifiers (uids) since their are unable to store them in their memory. As a result, the AD model preserves both *uniformity* and *anonymity* properties that the basic Population Protocols have.

5.1   Stable Computation

We call a *predicate over X^** any function $p : X^* \to \{0, 1\}$. p is called *symmetric* if for every $x \in X^*$ and any x' which is a permutation of x's symbols, it holds that $p(x) = p(x')$ (in words, permuting the input symbols does not affect the predicate's outcome). In this work we are interested in the computation of symmetric predicates.

A configuration C is called *output stable* if for every configuration C' that is reachable from C it holds that $\omega(C'(u)) = \omega(C(u))$ for all $u \in V$, where $\omega(C(u))$ is the output of agent u under configuration C. In simple words, no agent changes its output in any subsequent step and no matter how the computation proceeds. We assume that a is the only agent that does not have an output. So the output of the population concerns only the rest of the agents.

A predicate p over X^* is said to be *stably computable* by the AD model, if there exists a AD $\mathcal{A}$ such that for any input assignment $x \in X^*$, any computation of $\mathcal{A}$ on a complete interaction graph of $|x| + 1$ nodes beginning from the initial configuration corresponding to x reaches an output stable configuration in which all agents except a output $p(x)$.

The existence of an absence detector allows for halting computations. An AD $\mathcal{A} = (X_\mathcal{A}, Y_\mathcal{A}, Q_\mathcal{A}, I_\mathcal{A}, \omega_\mathcal{A}, \delta_\mathcal{A}, \gamma_\mathcal{A})$, is *halting* if there are two special subsets $Q_{h\_accept}, Q_{h\_reject} \subseteq Q_\mathcal{A}$, in which any agent stops participating in effective interactions (halts), giving output $1, 0$ respectively. We say that a predicate p over X^* is *computable by a halting AD $\mathcal{A}$* if for any input assignment $x \in X^*$, any computation of $\mathcal{A}$ on a complete interaction graph of $|x| + 1$ nodes beginning from the initial configuration corresponding to x reaches an output stable configuration in which, *after a finite number of interactions*, all agents, except for a, are in states of Q_{h_accept} if $p(x) = 1$ and of Q_{h_reject} otherwise.

Let **SPACE**$(f(n))$ (**NSPACE**$(f(n))$) be the class of languages decidable by some (non) deterministic TM in $O(f(n))$ space. For any class **L** denote by **SL** its commutative subclass. In addition, we denote by **SEM**, the class of the semilinear predicates, consisting of all predicates definable by first-order logical formulas of Presburger arithmetic (see, e.g., [GS66]).

6   Examples and Properties

We begin with a leader-election AD. $X = \{1\}$, $Q = \{l, f, q_{halt}\}$, $I(1) = f$, δ is defined as $(l, f) \to (l, q_{halt})$, and γ as $(f, a) \to l$, if $a[l] = 1$ and $(l, a) \to q_{halt}$, if

$a[f] = 1$. Note that both the output alphabet and the output function are not specified since the output is meaningless in this setting. The interactions that are not specified in δ and γ are ineffective.

Proposition 1. *The above protocol is a leader election AD.*

Proof. It is easy to see that a leader is initially generated that halts the non-leaders computation. The leader halts once it is informed by the absence detector that all non-leaders have halted. $\qquad\square$

The following are some interesting properties of the AD model.

Proposition 2. *Any AD with stabilizing states has an equivalent halting AD.*

Proof. $\{0,1\}^{|Q|}$ can be partitioned into a state stable subset and a state unstable subset. $a \in \{0,1\}^{|Q|}$ is state stable iff for all $q_1, q_2 \in Q$ (not necessarily distinct) such that $a[q_1] = a[q_2] = 0$, $\delta(q_1, q_2) = (q_1, q_2)$ and $\gamma(q_1, a) = q_1$. If we let all agents know in advance the above partitioning (note that this is constant information, so storing it is feasible) then we have the required termination criterion; that is, an agent halts iff it encounters a detector with a state stable absence vector. $\qquad\square$

From now on, we only consider ADs that halt.

A very interesting feature of ADs is that they can be sequentially composed. This means that given two ADs $\mathcal{A}$ and $\mathcal{B}$ we can construct a AD $\mathcal{C}$ which has the input of $\mathcal{A}$ and the output of $\mathcal{B}$ given $\mathcal{A}$'s output as input. First, $\mathcal{C}$ runs as $\mathcal{A}$ on its inputs and once the absence detector detects $\mathcal{A}$'s halt, $\mathcal{C}$ starts $\mathcal{B}$'s execution on using the output of $\mathcal{A}$ as input. The next theorem exploits the sequential composition of ADs to show that any AD can assume the existence of a unique leader.

Proposition 3. *Any AD $\mathcal{A}$ has an equivalent AD $\mathcal{B}$ that assumes a unique leader which does not obtain any input.*

Proof. For the one direction, $\mathcal{B}$ may trivially simulate $\mathcal{A}$ by ignoring the leader. Then for all computations of $\mathcal{A}$ on n agents there is an equivalent computation of $\mathcal{B}$ on $n + 1$ agents. For the other direction, $\mathcal{A}$ first elects a unique leader and then simulates $\mathcal{B}$ by considering the input of the agent that has been elected as a leader as a "virtual" agent. The leader creates a bit which moves between the non-leaders. Whenever the leader encounters the bit it interacts with the virtual agent that it carries in its own state. The role of the leader in the "virtual" interaction, that is, whether it is the initiator or the responder can be determined by its role in the real interaction in which it encountered the bit. Note that $\mathcal{B}$'s computations on $n + 1 \geq 3$ agents are simulated by $\mathcal{A}$ on n agents. $\qquad\square$

Based on this fact, we only consider ADs that assume the existence of such a unique leader in the initial configuration that is responsible for all effective interactions (non-leader interactions do not cause state modifications). We denote by **HAD** *the class of all predicates computable by some AD with a unique leader.*

6.1   The Power of 2 Protocol

We now construct an AD that computes the non-semilinear predicate $(N_1 = 2^d)$, which is true if the number of 1s in the input is a power of 2 (Protocol 1). This protocol illustrates the ability of ADs to perform iterative computations (which was impossible in PP model).

Protocol 1. *Power of 2*

1: $X = \{1\}, Q = (\{l\} \times \{q_0, q_1, q_2, q_3, q_4\}) \cup (\{n\} \times \{1, \bar{1}, 1'\}) \cup \{q_{accept}, q_{reject}\}$,
2: $I(1) = (n, 1)$ only for the non-leaders,
3: the leader is initialized to (l, q_0),
4: δ:

$$(l, q_0), (n, 1) \rightarrow (l, q_1), (n, \bar{1})$$
$$(l, q_1), (n, 1) \rightarrow (l, q_2), (n, \bar{1})$$
$$(l, q_2), (n, 1) \rightarrow (l, q_3), (n, 1')$$
$$(l, q_3), (n, 1) \rightarrow (l, q_2), (n, \bar{1})$$
$$(l, q_4), (n, 1') \rightarrow (l, q_4), (n, 1)$$

5: γ:

$$(l, q_2), a \rightarrow q_{accept}, \text{ if } a[n, 1] = a[n, 1'] = 1$$
$$\rightarrow (l, q_4), \text{ if if } a[n, 1] = 1 \text{ and } a[n, 1'] = 0$$
$$(l, q_3), a \rightarrow q_{reject}, \text{ if } a[n, 1] = 1 \text{ and } a[n, 1'] = 0$$
$$(l, q_4), a \rightarrow (l, q_1), \text{ if } a[n, 1'] = 1$$

---

7   Computational Power

We now explore the computational power of the CTS model via the AD model. In particular, we provide several lower bounds and an upper bound for the class **HAD**. By Theorem 1, that we just present, these results carry over to the class of languages computable by CTS protocols.

Theorem 1. *The CTS model is computationally equivalent to the leader-AD model.*

Proof. The CTS-leader may form an absence vector by walking around and keeping track of present states until it covers the whole population. The AD-leader detects the completion of a covering by marking all nodes that it meets and asking the absence detector whether all nodes have been marked.   □

7.1 PPs vs. ADs

In [AAER07], they defined the k-truncate of a configuration $c \in \mathbb{N}^Q$ as $\tau_k(c)[q] := \min(k, c[q])$ for all $q \in Q$.

Lemma 1. *For all finite k and any initial configuration $c \in \mathbb{N}^Q$, there is an AD that aggregates in one agent $\tau_k(c)$.*

Proof. The unique leader is aware of the finite bound k and initiates a $|Q|$-vector full of zeros except for a 1 in the position of its own state (note that since the leader election protocol is halting we are allowed to first elect a leader and then execute a second procedure based on the assumption of a leader). When a leader interacts with a non-leader, then the non-leader halts and if the leader's counter corresponding to the non-leader's state was less than k, then the leader increments it by one. The leader halts when the absence detector informs it that non-leaders are absent.   □

Theorem 2. SEM ⊆ HAD.

Proof. It was proved in [AAER07] that, for any PP with stabilizing outputs, there exists a finite k such that a configuration is output stable iff its k-truncate is output stable (and the output values are preserved). We let the AD know the k corresponding to the simulated PP. The AD-leader performs a constant number of simulation steps, e.g. k, and then does the following. It marks all non-leaders one after the other, while gathering the k-truncate of their current configuration c. When the detector informs the leader that no unmarked non-leaders have remained, the leader checks whether $\tau_k(c)$ is output-stable (since k is finite and independent of the population size, we may as in Proposition 2 assume that the leader knows in advance the subset of output stable k-truncates). If it is, then c must also be output stable and the protocol halts. If not, then neither is c and the leader drops this truncate, restores one after the other all non-leaders and when no marked non-leader has remained it continues the PP's simulation for another constant number of steps, and so on.   □

Taking into account Theorem 2 and the non-semilinear power of 2 predicate (Protocol 1) we have that **SEM ⊊ HAD**.

7.2 Better Lower Bounds and an Upper Bound

We construct now an AD that computes the predicate $(bN_1^{d_1} N_2^{d_2} \cdots N_k^{d_k} < c)$, where b and c are integer constants and d_i and k are nonnegative constants. We again make w.l.o.g. the assumption of a unique leader, and for further simplification we forget about the leader's input.

To simplify the description we first present an AD (Protocol 2) that computes $(bN_1^d < c)$. Define $[c] := \{0, 1, \ldots, |c|\}$ if $c < 0$ and $[c] := \{-c, -c+1, \ldots, 0\}$ if $c \geq 0$. Define u_{-i} to be the subvector of a vector u consisting of all components of u except from component i. We write a vector u as (j, u_{-i}) when we want to

---

Protocol 2. *VarPower*

1: $X = \{s_1\}, Q = (\{l_1, l_2, \ldots, l_d, l_1^e, l_2^e, \ldots, l_d^e\} \times [c]) \cup \{0,1\}^d \cup \{q_{accept}, q_{reject}\}$,
2: $I(s_1) = 0^d$,
3: the initial state of the leader is $(l_1, -c)$,
4: δ:

$$(l_i, w), (0, u_{-i}) \to (l_{i+1}, w), (1, u_{-i}), \text{ if } i < d$$
$$\to q_{accept}, \text{ if } i = d \text{ and } c \geq 0, w + b \leq -c \text{ or } c < 0, w + b < 0$$
$$\to q_{reject}, \text{ if } i = d \text{ and } c \geq 0, w + b \geq 0 \text{ or } c < 0, w + b \geq -c$$
$$\to (l_i, w + b), (1, u_{-i}), \text{ if } i = d \text{ and } c \geq 0, -c \leq w + b < 0 \text{ or }$$
$$c < 0, 0 \leq w + b < |c|$$
$$(l_i^e, w), (1, u_{-i}) \to (l_i^e, w), (0, u_{-i})$$

5: γ:

$$(l_i, w), a \to (l_i^e, w), \text{ if } a[0, u_{-i}] = 1 \text{ and } i > 1$$
$$\to q_{accept}, \text{ if } a[0, u_{-i}] = 1, i = 1 \text{ and } w < 0$$
$$\to q_{reject}, \text{ if } a[0, u_{-i}] = 1, i = 1 \text{ and } w \geq 0$$
$$(l_i^e, w), a \to (l_{i-1}, w), \text{ if } a[1, u_{-i}] = 1$$

---

emphasize that component i of u has the value j. Given an absence vector a, $a[j, u_{-i}] = 1$ is true iff (j, u_{-i}) is absent from the population for all u_{-i}.

We now extend the above construction to devise an AD for the predicate $(bN_1^{d_1} N_2^{d_2} \cdots N_k^{d_k} < c)$, where b and c are integer constants and k is a nonnegative constant. The idea is simple. The leader now holds a k-vector of vectors, l, where l_i is a d_i-vector of states, similar to those of Protocol 2, in order to execute k copies of Protocol 2. The leader still holds a unique counter initialized to $-c$. Similarly, each agent has k components, one for each subprotocol. The AD, in fact, produces all possible assignments of states to l_{ij}. Initially, one step of each subprotocol is executed, then all steps of subprotocol k is executed, then k is reinitialized, $k - 1$ is proceeded for one step and again all possible steps of k are executed, when all possible combinations of $k - 1$ and k have been exhausted, $k - 2$ proceeds for one step, and all possible combinations of $k - 1$ and k are reproduced, and so on. After each step, except for the first $k - 1$ steps, the terminating conditions of Protocol 2 are checked and if no one is satisfied b is added to the leader's counter.

Finally, by exploiting the above constructions we devise an AD that computes the predicate $\sum_{d_1, d_2, \ldots, d_k = 0}^{l} a_{d_1, d_2, \ldots, d_k} N_1^{d_1} N_2^{d_2} \cdots N_k^{d_k} < c$, where $a_{d_1, d_2, \ldots, d_k}$ and c are integer constants and l and k are nonnegative constants. Here, a difference to the previous protocol is that we have many copies of it running in parallel, their number being equal to the number of nonzero coefficients, and each one of them adds to the counter its own coefficient $a_{d_1, d_2, \ldots, d_k}$.

A key difference is that the counter bounds are now set to $-s, s$, where $s :=$ $\max(\max_{d_1, d_2, \ldots, d_k = 0, \ldots, l} |a_{d_1, d_2, \ldots, d_k}|, |c|)$, and that when we say "in parallel" we can implement this in a round-robin fashion, and let the protocol terminate when no subprotocol can proceed without exceeding the bounds. Then the halting decision simply depends on whether the leader's counter is negative or not. We conclude with the following lower bound on **HAD**.

Theorem 3. *Any predicate of the form $\sum_{d_1, d_2, \ldots, d_k = 0}^{l} a_{d_1, d_2, \ldots, d_k} N_1^{d_1} N_2^{d_2} \cdots N_k^{d_k} < c$, where $a_{d_1, d_2, \ldots, d_k}$ and c are integer constants and l and k are nonnegative constants, is in* **HAD**.

Simulating a Counter Machine. In this Section, we prove that ADs and *one-way (online) counter machines* (CMs) [FMR68, Min61] can simulate each other.

The *space* required by a CM in processing its input is the maximum value that any of its counters obtains in the course of the computation. A language $L \subseteq \Sigma^*$ is said to be *CM-decidable in $O(f(n))$ space* if some CM which operates in space $O(f(n))$ accepts any $w \in L$ and rejects any $w' \in \Sigma^* \backslash L$. Let **CMSPACE**$(f(n))$ (**NCMSPACE**$(f(n))$ for nondeterministic CMs) be the class of all languages that are CM-decidable in $O(f(n))$ space. Recall that by **SCMSPACE**$(f(n))$ (**SNCMSPACE**$(f(n))$) we denote its symmetric subclass. The following well-known theorem states that any CM of space $O(f(n))$ can be simulated by a TM of space $O(\log f(n))$ and conversely.

Theorem 4 ([FMR68]). **CMSPACE**$(f(n))$ $=$ **SPACE**$(\log f(n))$ *and* **NCMSPACE**$(f(n))$ = **NSPACE**$(\log f(n))$.

The above result can also be found as Lemma 3, page 94, in [Iba04].

Corollary 1. **SCMSPACE**$(f(n))$ $=$ **SSPACE**$(\log f(n))$ *and* **SNCMSPACE**$(f(n))$ = **SNSPACE**$(\log f(n))$.

We are now ready to establish our final bounds on **HAD**.

Theorem 5. **SSPACE**$(\log n)$ $=$ **SCMSPACE**(n) $\subseteq$ **HAD** $\subseteq$ **SNSPACE**$(\log n)$ $\subseteq$ **SSPACE**$(\log^2 n)$.

Proof. For the lower bound, we show that ADs can simulate CMs (**SSPACE**$(\log n)$ = **SCMSPACE**(n) is from [FMR68]). The CM consists of a control unit, an input terminal, and a constant number of counters. The AD simulates the control unit by its unique leader, which is responsible for carrying out the simulation. The input terminal is formed by the actual input slots of the agents. The k counters are stored by creating a k-vector of bits in the memory of each agent. In this manner, each counter is distributed across the agents. The value of the ith counter at any time is determined by the number of 1s appearing in the ith components of the agents. Since the number of agents is equal to the number of input symbols the space of each counter is linear to the input size (in fact, we can easily make this $O(n)$ by allowing c bits in each component instead of just one). To take a step, the CM reads or not the next symbol from the input and the sign (0 or positive) of each tape and then, if it read the input, moves to the next input symbol and updates the contents of the counters. The leader of the AD waits or not to encounter an agent whose input is not erased (unread), in the former case erases that input symbol, and waits to encounter the absence detector to learn the set of zero counters. When the latter happens, the leader obtains a vector of -1s, 0, and 1, representing the value to be added to each counter. From that point on, the leader adds these values wherever possible until all of them have been added. Then the leader continues the simulation as above. The proof for the upper bound is similar to the one of Theorem 15 in [AAD+06]. We construct a TM that, starting from any initial configuration, nondeterministically guesses all reachable configurations and always stores at most one. We also invoke Savitch's theorem [Sav70].   □

In the full paper, we also prove that ADs can simulate *Multiset Linear Bounded Automata with Detection (MLBAD)* [CVMVM01, Vas08]. This implies that ADs can compute any language produced by random context grammars. Finally, we establish that nondeterministic ADs are computationally equivalent to the deterministic ones.

8   Conclusions

In this work, we proposed the CTS model a new extension of the PP model of Angulin *et al.* that additionally assumes the existence of a cover-time service. By reduction to the absence detector oracle model we were able to investigate and almost completely characterize the computational power of the new model. The introduced global knowledge enables CTSs to perform halting computations, a feature that was missing from the PP model. We explored the properties and the computability of the new model and focused more on halting computations. We showed that all predicates in **SSPACE**$(\log n)$ are also in **HAD** and that the latter is a subset of **SSPACE**$(\log^2 n)$.

Many interesting questions remain open. The bounds given in this work for halting ADs are not tight. An exact characterization of **HAD** is still elusive. In addition, what happens in the case where the detector does not correctly detect the existing states in the population? Do the protocols presented here work correctly in the case of an adversarial detector? In addition, how is the computability of graph properties of the interaction graph affected by the absence detectors presence? Finally, can one simplify the proof of the upper bound of PPs [AAER07] by simulating them by a one-way 1-CM or by a nondeterministic pushdown automaton?

Acknowledgements. We would like to particularly thank James Aspnes for bringing to our attention some similarities of our model to the eventual leader detector Ω of [FJ06] and also thank Stavros Nikolaou for his useful comments throughout the preparation of this work.

References

[AAC+05]   Angluin, D., Aspnes, J., Chan, M., Fischer, M.J., Jiang, H., Peralta, R.: Stably Computable Properties of Network Graphs. In: Prasanna, V.K., Iyengar, S.S., Spirakis, P.G., Welsh, M. (eds.) DCOSS 2005. LNCS, vol. 3560, pp. 63–74. Springer, Heidelberg (2005)

[AAD+06]   Angluin, D., Aspnes, J., Diamadi, Z., Fischer, M.J., Peralta, R.: Computation in networks of passively mobile finite-state sensors. Distributed Computing, 235–253 (2006)

[AAE08]   Angluin, D., Aspnes, J., Eisenstat, D.: Fast computation by population protocols with a leader. Distributed Computing 21(3), 183–199 (2008)

[AAER07]   Angluin, D., Aspnes, J., Eisenstat, D., Ruppert, E.: The computational power of population protocols. Distributed Computing 20(4), 279–304 (2007)

[BBCK10]   Beauquier, J., Burman, J., Clement, J., Kutten, S.: On utilizing speed in networks of mobile agents. In: Proceedings of the 29th ACM SIGACT-SIGOPS Symposium on Principles of Distributed Computing, PODC 2010, pp. 305–314. ACM, New York (2010)

[CMN+11]   Chatzigiannakis, I., Michail, O., Nikolaou, S., Pavlogiannis, A., Spirakis, P.G.: Passively mobile communicating machines that use restricted space. Theor. Comput. Sci. 412(46), 6469–6483 (2011)

[CVMVM01] Csuhaj-Varjú, E., Martín-Vide, C., Mitrana, V.: Multiset Automata. In: Calude, C.S., Pun, G., Rozenberg, G., Salomaa, A. (eds.) Multiset Processing. LNCS, vol. 2235, pp. 69–84. Springer, Heidelberg (2001)

[Edi86]   Edighoffer, J.L.: Distributed, replicated computer bulletin board service. PhD thesis, Stanford, CA, USA, UMI order no. GAX86-19742 (1986)

[FJ06]   Fischer, M., Jiang, H.: Self-stabilizing Leader Election in Networks of Finite-State Anonymous Agents. In: Shvartsman, M.M.A.A. (ed.) OPODIS 2006. LNCS, vol. 4305, pp. 395–409. Springer, Heidelberg (2006), http://dx.doi.org/10.1007/11945529_28

[FMR68]   Fischer, P.C., Meyer, A.R., Rosenberg, A.L.: Counter machines and counter languages. Mathematical Systems Theory 2(3), 265–283 (1968)

[GS66]   Ginsburg, S., Spanier, E.H.: Semigroups, presburger formulas, and languages. Pacific Journal of Mathematics 16, 285–296 (1966)

[Iba04]   Ibarra, O.H.: On the computational complexity of membrane systems. Theor. Comput. Sci. 320, 89–109 (2004)

[MCS11a]   Michail, O., Chatzigiannakis, I., Spirakis, P.G.: Mediated population protocols. Theor. Comput. Sci. 412, 2434–2450 (2011)

[MCS11b]   Michail, O., Chatzigiannakis, I., Spirakis, P.G.: New Models for Population Protocols. In: Lynch, N.A. (ed.) Synthesis Lectures on Distributed Computing Theory. Morgan & Claypool (2011)

[Min61]   Minsky, M.L.: Recursive unsolvability of post's problem of "tag" and other topics in theory of turing machines. The Annals of Mathematics 74(3), 437–455 (1961)

[Sav70]   Savitch, W.J.: Relationships between nondeterministic and deterministic tape complexities. J. Comput. System Sci. 4(2), 177–192 (1970)

[Vas08]   Vaszil, G.: Multiset grammars, multiset automata, and membrane systems. In: Colloquium on the Occasion of the 50th Birthday of Victor Mitrana, pp. 1–10. Springer (2008)

Brief Announcement: The Degrading Effect of Forgetting on a Synchronizer*

Matthias Függer[1], Alexander Kößler[1], Thomas Nowak[2], and Martin Zeiner[1]

[1] ECS Group, TU Wien, Vienna, Austria
{fuegger,koe,mzeiner}@ecs.tuwien.ac.at
[2] Laboratoire d'Informatique, École polytechnique, Palaiseau, France
nowak@lix.polytechnique.fr

Abstract. A strategy to increase an algorithm's robustness against internal memory corruption is to let processes actively discard part of their accumulated knowledge during execution. We study how different strategies of forgetting affect the performance of a synchronizer in an environment with probabilistic message loss.

Introduction. Network synchronizers allow to tolerate asynchrony, as well as certain types of failures, while using programs devised for lock-step synchronous execution. We study a retransmission-based variant of the α-synchronizer introduced by Awerbuch [1] as the first in a series of synchronizer algorithms for asynchronous message-passing systems. Its main idea is that each process continuously broadcasts its current round number together with the corresponding application data. A process starts the next round when it has received the messages of its current round from all other processes.

In distributed systems such as low-power wireless sensor networks, one can observe two types of failures: (i) Messages can be dropped or corrupted, and (ii) the processes' internal memory can be corrupted. Failures of type (i) are already dealt with by the synchronizer itself: Since each process continuously retransmits its current round message until it starts its next round, dropping messages may only result in larger times between round switches, but not in incorrect behavior. The occurrence of corrupted messages can be made negligible by using error detection codes, often directly supported by transceiver chips. In this paper we thus assume that a message is either correctly received or dropped. Failures of type (ii) may occur for instance by ionized particle hits in memory cells. The longer the time between the write of a memory cell and its successive read, the higher is the likelihood that the read returns corrupted data. By actively resetting (part of) the nodes' internal memory, one reduces the likelihood of reading corrupted memory content. More "forgetful" strategies correspond to maintaining less internal state, which should increase robustness against failures but decrease performance.

* M. Függer, A. Kößler, and M. Zeiner were supported in part by the Austrian Science Fund (FWF): P21694-N23, S11405-N23.

A.W. Richa and C. Scheideler (Eds.): SSS 2012, LNCS 7596, pp. 90–91, 2012.

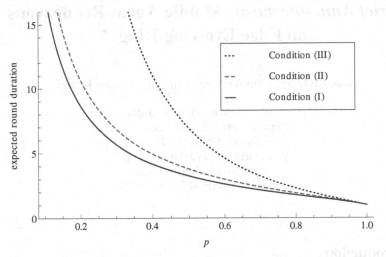

Fig. 1. Expected round durations in systems with three processes

System model and algorithm. Processes $1, \ldots, N$ take steps simultaneously at all integral times, but each message transmission succeeds only with constant independent probability p. Messages that do arrive have a transmission delay of 1. A step consists in (a) receiving messages from other processes, (b) performing local computations, and (c) broadcasting a message to the other processes (i.e., performing $N - 1$ point-to-point message transmissions). Processes continuously broadcast their local round number and maintain a *knowledge vector* which contains the information on other processes' local round numbers accumulated via received messages. After updating its local round number, a process may *forget*, i.e., reset its knowledge vector. We consider three different conditions on when processes forget: (I) Never. (II) When starting a new local round. (III) Always, in every step.

Results. We state an explicit formula for the expected asymptotic round duration for condition (III) and give efficiently computable bounds for the other two conditions. These bounds are shown to approximate the exact value well if the probability p of successful message transmission is high. We show that for all three conditions, the expected round durations collapse when $p \to 1$: All three expected round durations, as well as their first derivatives as a function of p, coincide in $p = 1$. We prove that for $p \to 0$, the expected round durations for conditions (I) and (II) follow the same order of growth, namely $\Theta(p^{-1})$, whereas condition (III) gives rise to $\Theta(p^{-(N-1)})$. Fig. 1 shows the behavior of the expected round duration in three-processor systems as a parameter of the probability parameter p. Monte Carlo simulations support our analytic results.

Reference

1. Awerbuch, B.: Complexity of Network Synchronization. J. ACM 32, 804–823 (1985)

Brief Announcement: Mobile Agent Rendezvous on Edge Evolving Rings*

Tomoko Izumi[1], Yukiko Yamauchi[2], and Sayaka Kamei[3]

[1] Ritsumeikan University, Japan
izumi-t@fc.ritsumei.ac.jp
[2] Kyushu University, Japan
yamauchi@inf.kyushu-u.ac.jp
[3] Hiroshima University, Japan
s-kamei@se.hiroshima-u.ac.jp

1 Introduction

The *rendezvous problem* of *mobile agents* is to make agents, which are initially distributed in a network, meet at a non-predefined location. The challenging issue is to design rendezvous algorithms which work in anonymous systems. Previous works such as [2,4,5] characterized its solvability with the symmetricity and periodicity of network topology and initial locations of agents. However, most existing works (except [3]) assume "static" networks, where its topology does not change during the execution.

As dynamic computer networks, where the network topology and/or the participants continuously change (e.g., the Internet, P2P networks, MANETs), become widely used, distributed systems over such networks are expected to autonomously adapt to dynamic changes. Our question is "is it possible to rendezvous in dynamic networks?". In a "static" network, all agents recognize the same network, i.e., the sequence of local connectivity (such as the adjacent links) at each node represents the global network. However, in a "dynamic" network, each agent only recognizes temporal connectivity at each node, and all agents do not always recognize the same global network.

This paper newly introduces the rendezvous problem in dynamic networks modeled with *edge evolving graphs* [1]. Given a graph G, an evolving graph of G is a sequence of subgraphs of G. As original graph G, we focus on anonymous undirected oriented rings, which are one of the simplest topologies with periodicity and symmetricity. Our interest is to reveal the solvability of the rendezvous problem on the edge evolving rings[1]. We try to characterize the solvability on evolving rings by a given evolving graph and initial locations of agents. We first show an impossibility result: If the initial allocation of agents and every subgraph of evolving rings have the same periodicity, the rendezvous problem cannot be solved. We then present some deterministic rendezvous algorithms, and show their memory complexities and the graph classes where the algorithms realize the rendezvous and terminate.

---

* This work is supported in part by KAKENHI no.22700017, no.22700074 and no.2370019.
[1] If a given edge evolving ring is in the impossible case, then we allow agents to continue their execution forever.

A.W. Richa and C. Scheideler (Eds.): SSS 2012, LNCS 7596, pp. 92–94, 2012.
© Springer-Verlag Berlin Heidelberg 2012

2 Preliminaries

Given a graph $G = (V, E)$, an *edge evolving graph* of G is an infinite sequence $S_G = G_0, G_1, \ldots$ where for each $G_i = (V_i, E_i)$ $(0 \leq i)$, $V_i = V$ and $E_i \subseteq E$. We assume that for each edge e in E, graphs which have e appear in sequence S_G infinitely often. Every edge is locally labeled in a globally consistent way, and the label is fixed during an execution. Each node is provided with a *whiteboard*, which is local storage where agents on the node can write and read some data. We assume that each agent knows the number k of agents (otherwise, the rendezvous is not solvable [2]), and that the system is *asynchronous*.

About the relationship between the timing of graph transition and the behavior of agents, we make following assumptions:1) An agent is not destroyed by deletion of edges, and 2) the time interval of the transition of graphs is long enough for the agents to visit all the nodes on a segment (i.e., a connected component). As for the detection of graph transitions, we introduce three models: Any agent can detect a transition 1) any-time in *global detection* model, 2) when the edges incident to the nodes in the segment where the agent resides change in *semi-local detection* model, and 3) when the edges incident to the node where it stays change in *local detection* model.

If ring G is represented by a periodic sequence of segment lengths, then G is called periodic. The *periodic number* is defined by the number of copies in the sequence of G, and its set is denoted by $P(G)$. For an initial allocation of agents, the periodicity and periodic number are also defined similarly. Let α be a periodic allocation of agents and $P(\alpha)$ be the set of periodic numbers of α. The maximum and minimum periodic number of α are denoted by $p_{max}(\alpha)$ and $p_{min}(\alpha)$, respectively.

3 Overview of the Results

For the rendezvous problem on static graphs, several impossibilities are caused by the periodicity of graphs and agents allocation [2]. For dynamic networks, we have a similar negative result.

Theorem 1. *Assume that an initial allocation α of agents is periodic. Then, even in the global detection model, the rendezvous is unsolvable if every G_i in S_G is periodic with $p_{min}(\alpha) \in P(G_i)$ or a ring.*

We also show some positive results. In all our algorithms, every agent collects the initial allocation α of agents. So, if α is not periodic, the rendezvous can be solved. In the followings, we discuss the other solvable cases. First, consider a simple case: We assume the semi-local detection model and the *edge occurrence restriction*, where evolving ring S_G satisfies that for any i, if $\{u, v\} (\in E) \notin E_i$ then $\{u, v\} \in E_{i+1}$. Graph G is said to have *p-periodic segments* if the sequence of segment lengths of G contains the equally-spaced p segments of the same length.

Theorem 2. *Let G_i do not have cp-periodic segments for any $p \in P(\alpha)$, where c is a positive integer. In the semi-local detection model, there is a deterministic rendezvous algorithm with $O(n \cdot \log n)$ bits memory per agent if S_G satisfies the edge occurrence restriction and contains graph G_i.*

The outline of our algorithm is as follows: To agree on a rendezvous node, each agent collects the allocation of home nodes (i.e., initial nodes of agents) and the lengths of segments where it stays (by using $O(n \cdot \log n)$ bits memory). Then, the agent shares the collected information with the others by writing and reading on the home nodes. By comparing the sequence of segment lengths which each agent collects, the agent can decide which it is a winner or loser. If there is a non-periodicity in the allocation of home nodes of winner agents, they recognize and agree on a rendezvous node.

For the subclass of instances defined in Theorem 2, we can reduce the memory complexity to $O(n)$ bits: Instead of segment lengths, each agent keeps the locations of clockwise end nodes on each segment (by using $O(n)$ bits memory). By comparing the sequences of the recorded locations, the agents select the winners among them, and decide the rendezvous node if the locations of winners' home nodes have a non-periodicity.

Theorem 3. *Let G_i have a segment whose length l satisfies $(n/p_{min}(\alpha)) + 1 \le l \le n - 1$. In the semi-local detection model, there is a deterministic rendezvous algorithm with $O(n)$ bits memory per agent if S_G satisfies the edge occurrence restriction and contains graph G_i.*

Next, we consider the case without the edge occurrence restriction. In this case, unfortunately, we cannot take the same approach above because there may be some agents who do not notice a transition of graphs in which some segments do not change their topologies. The outline of the algorithm is as follows: Each agent moves in the clockwise direction, and on each transition of graphs, if it moves at least one edge on a graph then it records the location of the end node. For each lap, every track of agents are shared and merged on each agent. Let the merged track denote by S. The agents decide the rendezvous node by S, a conjunctive and disjunctive sequence of S and α.

Theorem 4. *In the semi-local detection model, the algorithm solves the rendezvous on edge evolving rings if there is a lap in which S is non-periodic or in which the number of recorded nodes in S is coprime to $p_{max}(\alpha)$.*

The edge evolving rings satisfying the above conditions can be characterized by simulating the agent behavior, which is omitted due to the space restriction.

In the local detection model, we can get the same positive results by modifying the above algorithms: When a transition of ring G_i to non-ring G_{i+1} occurs, the agents decide the non-periodicity of the evolving graph based on their home nodes and end nodes of segments where they stay.

Theorem 5. *For the local detection model, Theorem 2, 3, and 4 also hold.*

References

1. Ferreira, A.: Building a reference combinatorial model for dynamic networks: Initial results in evolving graphs, INRIA, RR-5041 (2003)
2. Flocchini, P., Kranakis, E., Krizanc, D., Santoro, N., Sawchuk, C.: Multiple Mobile Agent Rendezvous in a Ring. In: Farach-Colton, M. (ed.) LATIN 2004. LNCS, vol. 2976, pp. 599–608. Springer, Heidelberg (2004)
3. Flocchini, P., Mans, B., Santoro, N.: Exploration of Periodically Varying Graphs. In: Dong, Y., Du, D.-Z., Ibarra, O. (eds.) ISAAC 2009. LNCS, vol. 5878, pp. 534–543. Springer, Heidelberg (2009)
4. Fraigniaud, P., Pelc, A.: Deterministic Rendezvous in Trees with Little Memory. In: Taubenfeld, G. (ed.) DISC 2008. LNCS, vol. 5218, pp. 242–256. Springer, Heidelberg (2008)
5. Kranakis, E., Krizanc, D., Santoro, N., Sawchuk, C.: Mobile agent rendezvous in a ring. In: Proc of ICDCS, pp. 592–599 (2003)

High-Level Executable Specifications
of Distributed Algorithms

Yanhong A. Liu, Scott D. Stoller, and Bo Lin

Computer Science Department, State University of New York at Stony Brook
{liu,stoller,bolin}@cs.stonybrook.edu

Abstract. This paper describes a method for specifying complex distributed algorithms at a very high yet executable level, focusing in particular on general principles for making properties and invariants explicit while keeping the control flow clear. This is critical for understanding the algorithms and proving their correctness. It is also critical for generating efficient implementations using invariant-preserving transformations, ensuring the correctness of the optimizations.

We have studied and experimented with a variety of important distributed algorithms, including well-known difficult variants of Paxos, by specifying them in a very high-level language with an operational semantics. In the specifications that resulted from following our method, critical properties and invariants are explicit, making the algorithms easier to understand and verify. Indeed, this helped us discover improvements to some of the algorithms, for correctness and for optimizations.

1   Introduction

Distributed algorithms are at the core of distributed systems, which are increasingly indispensable in our daily lives. Yet, understanding and proving the correctness of distributed algorithms remain challenging, recurring tasks. Study of distributed algorithms has relied on either pseudo code with English, which is high-level but imprecise, or formal specification languages, which are precise but harder to understand or not executable.

For example, the well-known Paxos algorithm for distributed consensus, from when Lamport first described it in 1990 [16], through all the variations, investigations, and practical deployments (including Google's Chubby distributed locking and storage service [6]) over the years, e.g., [8, 17, 5], remains as actively studied as ever in specification and verification, e.g., [20, 33]. The description by van Renesse [33] finally provides precise pseudo code for full Paxos—multi-Paxos—with comprehensive detailed explanations.

This paper describes a method to help make it easier to understand and verify complex distributed algorithms by specifying them at a very high yet executable level. The method focuses in particular on general principles for making properties and invariants explicit while keeping the control flow clear. It exploits message history sequences and queries over sets and sequences to abstract the

A.W. Richa and C. Scheideler (Eds.): SSS 2012, LNCS 7596, pp. 95–110, 2012.
© Springer-Verlag Berlin Heidelberg 2012

handling of received messages, and to abstract synchronization, when to send what messages to whom, and sending of messages collectively.

Making properties and invariants explicit is critical also for generating efficient implementations using invariant-preserving transformations, ensuring the correctness of the optimizations. In fact, it was during the study of these optimizations in the last several years, while trying to better understand and teach distributed algorithms, that we developed the abstractions and the specification method.

We have studied and experimented with a variety of important distributed algorithms, including well-known difficult variants of Paxos, by specifying them in a very high-level language with an operational semantics. In the specifications that resulted from following our method, critical properties and invariants are explicit, making the algorithms easier to understand and verify. Indeed, this helped us discover improvements to some of the algorithms, both for correctness and for optimizations, and also exposed some remaining correctness concerns.

2   Language and Case Studies

We use a very high level, executable language, called DistAlgo, that has an operational semantics [23]. We use parts of two case studies as examples in describing our method.

Language. To support distributed programming at a high level, we add four main concepts to commonly used object-oriented programming languages, such as Java and Python: (1) processes as objects, and sending of messages, (2) yield points and waits for control flows, and handling of received messages, (3) computations using high-level queries and message history sequences, and (4) configuration of processes and communication mechanisms. The following paragraphs describe the constructs that support these concepts in DistAlgo. For other constructs, we mostly use Python syntax (indentation for scoping, ':' for separation, '#' for comments, etc.), for succinctness, except with a few conventions from Java. The skip statement does nothing. We adopt the convention that any method named setup implicitly assigns each of its parameters to a field with the same name as the parameter before executing the rest of its body.

Processes and Sending of Messages. Process definition is done by defining classes that extend a special class Process. This is analogous to thread definition in Java and Python, which is done by defining classes that extend a special class Thread. The class must define a run method. The start method inherited from Process starts the execution of the process, which executes its run method. Processes can be created using constructors of process classes. Those constructors have an optional additional parameter that specifies the site (machine) on which the new process should be created. Processes can also be created by calling newprocesses(n,P,s), which creates and returns a set of n processes of class P on site s.

A send-statement `send m to p` sends a message m to a process p. If p is a set of processes, m is sent to each process in the set. A message can be a tuple, where the first component is a string specifying the kind of the message.

Control Flows and Handling of Received Messages. The key idea is to use labels to specify program points where control flow can yield to handling of messages and resume afterwards. A yield point is a statement of the form `-- l`, where l is a label that names this point in the program. Messages are handled only at yield points, so code segments not containing yield points are atomic. Handling of received messages is expressed using receive-definitions, which are members of class definitions for processes and are of the form:

```
receive m₁ from p₁,...,mₖ from pₖ at l₁,...,lⱼ: stmt
```

where each m_i is a variable or tuple pattern. This allows messages that match any one of m_1 from p_1, ..., m_k from p_k to be handled at yield points labeled any one of $l_1,...,l_j$, by executing the statement stmt at those points. A tuple pattern is a tuple in which each component is a constant, a variable possibly prefixed with "=", or a wildcard. A variable prefixed with "=" means that the corresponding part of the tuple being matched must equal the value of the variable for pattern matching to succeed. A variable that is not prefixed with "=" matches any value and gets bound to the corresponding part of the tuple being matched. A wildcard, written as "_", matches any value. The at-clause is optional, and the default means all yield points. The from-clause is also optional. As syntactic sugar, a receive-definition used at only one yield point can be written at that point.

Synchronization uses the await-statement, whose general form is

```
await bexp₁: stmt₁ or ... or bexpₖ: stmtₖ timeout t: stmt
```

This statement waits for one of the Boolean expressions $bexp_i$ to become true or until t seconds have passed and then executes the corresponding statement. The statements $stmt_i$ and the timeout-clause are optional. An await-statement must be preceded by a yield point; if a yield point is not specified explicitly, the default is that all message handlers can be executed at this point.

High-Level Queries. Synchronization conditions can be expressed using high-level queries—quantifications, comprehensions, and aggregates—over sets of processes and sequences of messages. We define operations on sets; operations on sequences are the same except that elements are processed in order, and square brackets are used in place of curly braces.

— Quantifications are of the following two forms. Each variable v_i enumerates elements of the set value of expression exp_i; the return value is whether, for each or some, respectively, combination of values of $v_1,...,v_k$, the value of Boolean expression bexp is true.

```
each v₁ in exp₁, ..., vₖ in expₖ | bexp
some v₁ in exp₁, ..., vₖ in expₖ | bexp
```

- Comprehensions are of the following form. Each variable v_i enumerates elements of the set value of expression exp_i; for each combination of values of $v_1, \ldots v_k$, if the value of Boolean expression bexp is true, the value of expression exp forms an element of the resulting set.

  {exp: v_1 in exp_1, ..., v_k in exp_k | bexp}

  We abbreviate {v: v in exp | bexp} as {v in exp | bexp}.
- Aggregates are of the form agg(exp), where agg is an operation, such as count or min, specifying the kind of aggregation over the set value of exp.
- In the query forms above, each v_i can also be a tuple pattern, in which case each enumerated element of the set value of exp_i is matched against the pattern before bexp is evaluated. We omit |bexp when bexp is true.

We use {} for empty set; s.add(x) and s.del(x) for element addition and deletion, respectively; and x in s and x not in s for membership test and its negation, respectively. We overload or to work for sets; s_1 or s_2 returns s_1 if s_1 is nonempty, otherwise it returns s_2.

DistAlgo has two built-in sequences, received and sent, containing all messages received and sent, respectively, by a process.

- Sequence received is updated only at yield points. An arrived message m for which the program contains a matching receive-definition is added to received when the program reaches a yield point where m is handled, and all matching message handlers associated with that yield point are executed for m. An arrived message for which the program contains no matching receive-definitions is added to received at the next yield point. The sequence sent is updated at each send-statement.
- received(m from p) is a shorthand for m from p in received; from p is optional, but when it is used, each message in received is automatically associated with the corresponding sender. sent(m to p) is a shorthand for m to p in sent; to p is optional, but when it is used, p is the process or set of processes in the corresponding send-statement.

Configuration. Configuration statements can specify various aspects of configuration. For example, use fifo_channel and use reliable_channel specify that channels are required to be FIFO and reliable, respectively; by default, channels are not required to be FIFO or reliable. The configuration statement use Lamport_clock specifies that Lamport logical clock [15, 9, 25] is used; this configures sending and receiving of messages to update the clock, and defines a function Lamport_clock() that returns the value of the clock.

Case Studies. We use parts of two important algorithms as case studies: (1) van Renesse's pseudo code for multi-Paxos for distributed consensus [33], which has been worked on for a long time, with the pseudo code remaining the same for a year or more, and is in the process of being made a technical report, and (2) Lamport's description of distributed mutual exclusion algorithm [15], which Lamport developed to illustrate the logical clock he invented. We use them because they are the clearest descriptions we found for these problems.

van Renesse's pseudo code for multi-Paxos is for a set of leaders, commanders, scouts, and acceptors to reach consensus among a set of replicas in serving a sequence of requests from clients. A replica receives client requests and proposes to leaders, and receives decisions from leaders and replies back to clients; a leader spawns off commander and scouts to do the two phases of the consensus algorithm; commander and scouts communicates with acceptors to try to have proposed values accepted.

Lamport's distributed mutual exclusion is for a set of processes accessing a shared resource that can only be used by one process at a time. A process maintains a queue of pending requests sorted by their logical timestamps, adds self to the request queue and sends a message to all others to request the resource, waits for all others to reply and for self to be first on the queue to get access, and sends release messages to all and dequeues itself afterwards; it enqueues any request upon receiving the request message, and dequeues it upon receiving the release message.

3   High-Level Specifications of Distributed Algorithms

Our method aims to specify distributed algorithms at a high level while keeping them fully executable as they are designed for. The key idea is to preserve the sending and receive of messages while abstracting away details of local computations.

Abstractions for Specifying Distributed Algorithms. Our method exploits two basic abstractions—message history sequences and queries over sets and sequences—and has four main components:

1. abstracting waiting on received messages using high-level synchronization with explicit wait,
2. abstracting when to send messages using high-level assertions over sets and sequences,
3. abstracting what to send in messages to whom using high-level set and aggregate computations, and
4. abstracting what messages to send collectively using loops and high-level queries.

These abstractions help make invariants maintained in distributed algorithms explicit, and thus help make the algorithms easier to understand and to verify. Note that our method does not yet make all invariants explicit, if that is possible.

The method emphasizes sending of messages and synchronization, because a process has no control over when it receives what messages from whom, but only when and how to handle them once they arrive, and handling of received messages is driven by the need to send messages, besides waiting and yielding. Therefore, handling is implied by the four components above, especially as they all heavily use queries over received messages.

Message Sequences. For a distributed process to make decisions, the key input is the history of messages it has sent and received. Therefore, at a high level, these decisions should be expressed in terms of the sequences of messages sent and received, not lower-level local updates after each message is sent or received.

High-Level Queries. Because distributed computations involve sets of processes and sequences of message, decision making mainly involves assertions and other computations over sets and sequences. To specify these assertions and computations at a high level, our method uses queries extensively, including logic quantifications, set comprehensions, and aggregate computations.

Overall Method. The four components of our method are orthogonal and can be applied independently. We describe these components in more detail in four subsections and show precisely how they help specify distributed algorithms at a higher level.

Incremental Computations. Although abstractions with high-level queries help make algorithms easier to understand and to verify, computations using these abstractions can be extremely inefficient, because they involve iteration over sets and sequences, and they are performed repeatedly as the sets and sequences are updated. This can take asymptotically much more time than necessary, and furthermore the space usage may be unbounded if the history of messages sent and received is used in actual implementations.

Optimization by incrementalization, e.g., [28, 12, 22, 21], transforms such expensive computations into efficient incremental maintenance of appropriate auxiliary values as the sets and sequences are updated. For distributed algorithms, the resulting incremental computations become efficient message handlers [23]. In fact, it was during the study of such optimizations in the last several years that we developed the abstractions, which we believe was instrumental in leading us to discover improvements to some of the algorithms.

3.1   Explicit High-Level Synchronization

Synchronization is at the core of distributed systems. It requires waiting for certain conditions to become true before taking the corresponding actions. Because message passing is generally asynchronous in distributed systems, synchronization must be achieved by explicitly tracking synchronization conditions, maintaining their truth values as messages are received, until the conditions become true, and then taking the corresponding actions.

Expressing such synchronization at a low level requires, in general, sophisticated updates driven by the events of different kinds of messages being received, making it difficult to understand and verify the conditions that the process is waiting for.

We use three principles in specifying such synchronization at a high level: (1) specify the waiting on the conditions and corresponding actions explicitly using await-statements, (2) express the conditions using high-level queries over sequences of messages sent and received, and (3) minimize local updates in the actions.

Example. In multi-Paxos [33], a commander process is spawned by a leader for each adopted triple of ballot number, slot number, and proposal, to try to have it accepted by acceptors and notify replicas of the decisions, and in case of being preempted by a different ballot number, to notify the leader.

```
process Commander(λ, acceptors, replicas, ⟨b, s, p⟩)
  var waitfor := acceptors;

  ∀α ∈ acceptors : send(α, ⟨p2a, self(), ⟨b, s, p⟩⟩);
  for ever
    switch receive()
      case ⟨p2b, α, b'⟩ :
        if b' = b then
          waitfor := waitfor − {α};
          if |waitfor| < |acceptors|/2 then
            ∀ρ ∈ replicas :
              send(ρ, ⟨decision, s, p⟩);
            exit();
          end if;
        else
          send(λ, ⟨preempted, b'⟩);
          exit();
        end if;
      end case
    end switch
  end for
end process
```

Fig. 1. Pseudo code for a commander in multi-Paxos [33]

Fig. 1 shows the pseudo code for a commander in multi-Paxos. A commander maintains `waitfor`— the set of acceptors from which it waits for p2b messages. It sends a p2a message to all acceptors and then handles each p2b message it receives from an acceptor, maintaining `waitfor` in one of two cases. When |waitfor|<|acceptors|/2 in the first case, it sends a decision message to all replicas and exits; it sends a preempted message in the second case.

We specify a commander at a high level as follows. First, we specify the synchronization explicitly using an await-statement. Then, we note that `waitfor` can be queried from the set of p2b messages received and the given set of acceptors, so we do not maintain `waitfor` explicitly; instead of starting from all acceptors and removing certain acceptors until a minority remain, we directly check whether those certain acceptors are a majority. Finally, the corresponding actions are simply single send-actions, yielding the specification in Fig. 2.

The result is that the flow that leads to each send-action is made clearer, and the conditions for the actions can easily be read off. Similar improvements can be made to the specification of a scout.

3.2 Direct High-Level Assertions

Determining the state of a distributed system is key to synchronization and to making decisions in general. Because there is no shared memory, a process must assert the state to the best of its knowledge through sending and receiving messages. The truth values of assertions about the state must be updated as messages are sent and received.

We express assertions using high-level queries over sequences of messages sent and received, as for synchronization conditions. The queries may be in the forms

```
class Commander extends Process:
  def setup(leader, acceptors, replicas, b, s, p): skip

  def run():
    send ('p2a', b, s, p) to acceptors
    await count({a: received(('p2b', =b) from a)}) > count(acceptors)/2:
      send ('decision', s, p) to replicas
    or received('p2b', b2) and b2!=b:
      send ('preempted', b2) to leader
```

Fig. 2. Higher-level specification for a commander in multi-Paxos

of quantifications, comprehensions, and aggregates. However, a same assertion may be expressed using different forms of queries. Because quantifications are usually not supported in executable languages, loops and low-level updates are most often used. Even in many high-level specifications, comprehensions and aggregates are often used in place of quantifications; this can be error-prone or lead to poor performance.

For example, an existential quantification may be specified indirectly as a set comprehension followed by an emptiness test, but this may incur unnecessary space for maintaining the intermediate set. For another example, a universal quantification asserting that a number is greater than all elements in a set may be specified indirectly as the number being greater than the maximum element in the set, but this causes an error when the set is empty; a special boundary value may be used in case the set is empty, but this is error-prone and may be sensitive to the maximum or minimum number that can be represented, which may be determined by the memory word size.

Our core principle in specifying assertions at a high level is to express existentially and universally quantified properties directly using logic quantifications, not indirectly using aggregates or comprehensions. Quantifications are easier and clearer for correctly stating the requirements, and can be systematically converted to aggregates and comprehensions that allow the best optimizations [23].

Example. In Lamport's distributed mutual exclusion [15], a process that requests a resource at time c needs to wait for the following two key conditions to hold before it is granted the resource:

(i) the request time (c,self) in its request queue is ordered before every other request in the queue, and (ii) it has received an acknowledgment message from every other process timestamped later than c.

We express the assertion directly using three quantifications, including a nested quantification in the second condition. The result is that the conditions can be directly read off the assertion.

```
each ('request',c2,p2) in q | (c2,p2)!=(c,self) implies (c,self) < (c2,p2)
and each p2 in s | some ('ack', c2, =p2) in received | c2 > c
```

3.3   Straightforward High-Level Computations

A distributed algorithm is designed for a set of processes to achieve a goal via sending and receiving messages. Computations needed for achieving the goal generally involve various collections of processes and messages. This means that the algorithm specification must capture the effects of sending and receiving messages on the needed computations.

Expressing these computations at a low level requires explicitly storing the results of these computations and updating their values appropriately as relevant messages are sent and received. Maintaining these low-level values correctly through updates can be challenging and error-prone; some of them require combinations of sophisticated data structures, while others are tedious.

We use three principles in specifying such computations at a high level: (1) specify computations of aggregate values using aggregate queries over message sequences, (2) specify computations of set values using comprehensions over message sequences, and (3) specify repeated computations straightforwardly where the results are used.

Example. In multi-Paxos [33], an acceptor process responds to p1a messages from scouts with p1b messages in the first phase, and responds to p2a messages from commanders with p2b messages in the second phase.

Fig. 3 shows the pseudo code for an acceptor in multi-Paxos. An acceptor maintains ballot_num—a ballot number, and accepted a set of accepted triples of ballot number, slot number, and proposal. It handles a p1a message by updating ballot_num and replying with a p1b message containing ballot_num and accepted, and handles a p2a message by updating ballot_num and accepted and replying with a p2a message containing ballot_num.

We specify an acceptor at a high level as follows. First, we note that ballot_num is updated to be the maximum from p1a and p2a messages, so we compute it using an aggregate. Then, we compute it straightforwardly where it is used in message handlers, yielding the specification in Fig. 4.

```
process Acceptor()
  var ballot_num := ⊥, accepted := ∅;

  for ever
    switch receive()
      case ⟨p1a, λ, b⟩ :
        if b > ballot_num then
          ballot_num := b;
        end if;
        send(λ, ⟨p1b, self(), ballot_num, accepted⟩);
      end case
      case ⟨p2a, λ, ⟨b, s, p⟩⟩ :
        if b ≥ ballot_num then
          ballot_num := b;
          accepted := accepted ∪ {⟨b, s, p⟩};
        end if
        send(λ, ⟨p2b, self(), ballot_num⟩);
      end case
    end switch
  end for
end process
```

Fig. 3. Pseudo code for an acceptor in multi-Paxos [33]

The result is that the invariants relating the sent messages to the received messages are made clearer. In particular, it allowed us to make explicit the property that (b,s,p) is added to accepted only if b equals ballot_num.

```
class Acceptor extends Process:
  def setup(): self.accepted = {}

  def run(): await false

  receive m:
    self.ballot_num = max({b: received('p1a',b)}+{b: received('p2a',b,_,_)} or {(-1,-1)})

  receive ('p1a', _) from scout:
    send ('p1b', ballot_num, accepted) to scout

  receive ('p2a', b, s, p) from commander:
    if b == ballot_num: accepted.add((b,s,p))
    send ('p2b', ballot_num) to commander
```

Fig. 4. Higher-level specification for an acceptor in multi-Paxos

3.4   Collective Send-Actions

Distributed algorithms generally involve sending and receiving collections of related messages. Precise specifications of distributed algorithms are commonly centered around handling of individual received messages. This lower-level model makes it harder than necessary to understand the overall working of the algorithms.

In contrast, a distributed algorithm can be viewed as driven by send-actions, because send-actions are observable externally, which then incur the needed computations. Thus, distributed algorithms may be expressed at a higher level by specifying send-actions collectively.

Our method aims to specify send-actions collectively in three steps: (1) identify the kinds of sent messages, (2) for each kind of sent messages, collect all situations in which messages of this kind are sent, and (3) express the collective situations using loops, choosing for-loops over while-loops if possible.

Example. In multi-Paxos [33], a replica process holds the state of the application; it handles requests of operations from clients and proposes them with minimum slot numbers to leaders, and it handles decisions of operations from leaders, applies the operations following the order of slot numbers, and sends the results to clients.

Fig. 5 shows the pseudo code for a replica in multi-Paxos. A replica maintains state—the state of the application, slot_num—a slot number for the next operation to be applied, proposals—the set of proposals it sent to leaders, and decisions—the set of decisions it received from leaders. It handles a request message by calling function propose. It handles a decision message by repeatedly checking decisions, re-proposing a proposal if overridden by a decision, and calling function perform. Function propose(p) checks that requested operation p is not in decisions, finds a minimum unused slot number for it, updates proposals, and sends a propose message. Function perform checks whether the operation in the argument is in `decisions`; if so, it only increments `slot_num`; otherwise, it applies the operation to `state`, atomically updates `state` and increments `slot_num`, and sends the result to the client.

```
process Replica(leaders, initial_state)
  var state := initial_state, slot_num := 1;
  var proposals := ∅, decisions := ∅;

  function propose(p)
    if ∄s : ⟨s, p⟩ ∈ decisions then
      s' := min{s | s ∈ ℕ⁺ ∧
        ∄p' : ⟨s, p'⟩ ∈ proposals ∪ decisions};
      proposals := proposals ∪ {⟨s', p⟩};
      ∀λ ∈ leaders : send(λ, ⟨propose, s', p⟩);
    end if
  end function

  function perform(⟨κ, cid, op⟩)
    if ∃s : s < slot_num ∧
        ⟨s, ⟨κ, cid, op⟩⟩ ∈ decisions then
      slot_num := slot_num + 1;
    else
      ⟨next, result⟩ := op(state);
      atomic
        state := next;
        slot_num := slot_num + 1;
      end atomic
      send(κ, ⟨response, cid, result⟩);
    end if
  end function

  for ever
    switch receive()
      case ⟨request, p⟩ :
        propose(p);
      case ⟨decision, s, p⟩ :
        decisions := decisions ∪ {⟨s, p⟩};
        while ∃p' : ⟨slot_num, p'⟩ ∈ decisions do
          if ∃p'' : ⟨slot_num, p''⟩ ∈ proposals ∧
              p'' ≠ p' then
            propose(p'');
          end if
          perform(p');
        end while;
    end switch
  end for
end process
```

Fig. 5. Pseudo code for a replica in multi-Paxos [33]

We specify a replica process at a high level as follows. First, we identify the two send-actions as the driving goals of the process. Then, we collect all situations in which **propose** messages are sent: they are for all **request** messages received, including those already proposed but whose proposed slots are overridden by decisions. Here, we add details to replace the set of positive natural numbers $\mathbb{N}^+$ with the range of integers from 1 to the maximum of the slot numbers used plus 1. Finally, we collect all situations in which **response** messages are sent: they are for all **decision** messages received, applied in increasing order of slot numbers. Here we increment `slot_num` in both branches together, not worrying about breaking the atomic block, because the local updates are atomic by default without any yield point in between. We obtain the specification in Fig. 6.

4 Experiments

We experimented with specifying a variety of important distributed algorithms in DistAlgo, including the same algorithms specified at both high levels and low levels, and discovered improvements to some of the algorithms. We also implemented DistAlgo, as described in [23], by automatically generating Python code from DistAlgo specifications following the operational semantics, and we tested the invariants and performance by running the generated implementations on many inputs.

Algorithm specifications. Table 1 lists five algorithms with which we had the most interesting experiences. The last two columns show the sizes of DistAlgo

```
class Replica extends Process:
  def setup(leaders, initial_state):
    self.state = initial_state
    self.slot_num = 1

  def run():
    while true:
      -- propose
      for ('request',p) in received:
        if each ('propose',s,=p) in sent | some received('decision',=s,p2) | p2!=p:
          s = min({s in 1.. max({s: sent('propose',s,_)}+{s: received('decision',s,_)})+1
                   | not (sent('propose',s,_) or received('decision',s,_))})
          send ('propose', s, p) to leaders
      -- perform
      while some ('decision', =slot_num, p) in received:
        if not some ('decision', s, =p) in received | s < slot_num:
          client, cmd_id, op = p
          state, result = op(state)
          send ('respond', cmd_id, result) to client
        slot_num += 1
```

Fig. 6. Higher-level specification for a replica in multi-Paxos

specifications at a high level and sizes of DistAlgo specifications containing low-level incremental updates; for multi-Paxos in the last row, the second size is for a specification corresponding to the pseudo code in [33]. Each specification includes specification of a driver for configuring and running the algorithm.

These sizes are clearly smaller than specifications in other languages. For example, our high-level specification for La Paxos is 44 lines, compared with 83 lines of PlusCal [26], 145 lines of I/O automata [13], 230 lines of Overlog [27], and 157 lines of Bloom [29]. For multi-Paxos, our high-level specification is 86 lines, compared with 130 lines of pseudo code in [33], and about 3000 lines of Python in an implementation of that pseudo code [32].

Table 1. Distributed algorithms and sizes of DistAlgo specifications (number of lines)

Algorithm	Description	Spec size	Incr size
La mutex	Lamport's distributed mutual exclusion [15]	31	43
2P commit	Two-phase commit [11]	32	55
La Paxos	Lamport's Paxos for distributed consensus [16, 17]	44	59
CL Paxos	Castro-Liskov's Byzantine Paxos [5]	72	81
vR Paxos	van Renesse's pseudo code for multi-Paxos [33]	86	132

Improvements. We discovered improvements to some of the algorithms, as well as correctness and performance issues, explained below.

La mutex. Our method specifies the key synchronization conditions using quantifications directly, as discussed in Section 3.2. Transforming them into best forms of set and aggregate queries led to two discoveries: (1) Lamport's original algorithm can be simplified to not enqueue and dequeue a process's own request, and (2) a standard heap-like data structure for maintaining the minimum of all pending requests in $O(\log n)$ time per update can be removed, and the number of pending earlier requests can be maintained instead in $O(1)$ time per update.

2P commit. Our method leads to a succinct specification of a coordinator process consisting mainly of 4 queries: 2 await-conditions, an if-condition, and a set comprehension. Even though the core algorithm does not specify timeout for the waits, the succinct specification makes it easy to see that allowing timeout of the first await-statement is safe, but allowing timeout of the second await-statement is not safe.

La Paxos and CL Paxos. Our method eventually led to specifications that use quantifications directly and cleanly, almost exactly as stated in the original informal algorithm descriptions. Our earlier versions used aggregates, and we discovered later that some of them were incorrect, while others needed to use special boundary values.

vR Paxos. Our method led to a specification easier to understand, as discussed in Sections 3.1, 3.3, and 3.4. The clearer specification led to two discoveries: (1) for a commander and scout, if the division operator /, which returns an integer in common programming languages, is used directly, the original checking of minority would be incorrect, and (2) for a replica, re-proposals, due to earlier proposals being overridden, are delayed unnecessarily.

Code Generation. The table below shows the sizes (number of lines) of Python implementations generated from DistAlgo specifications, and the compilation time (ms) for generating the implementations. Our generated implementation of multi-Paxos corresponding to the pseudo code in [33] is 1099 lines of Python, much smaller than a manually written implementation of 3000 lines of Python [32]. Smaller higher-level specifications may take longer to compile than larger lower-level specifications, because transforming queries that use received and sent takes extra time, and may produce longer, more generic code.

We also measured time and space performance of generated implementations from both high-level and low-level DistAlgo specifications for these algorithms. The measurements confirmed the analyzed time and space complexities. The graph below shows the running times of generated implementations of 2P commit and 2P commit incr, for the commit case and abort case.

Algorithm	Spec size	Gen'd size	Compil time
La mutex	31	951	4.451
La mutex incr	43	960	4.988
2P commit	32	978	5.910
2P commit incr	55	1001	6.816
La Paxos	44	1003	9.121
La Paxos incr	59	999	7.613
CL Paxos	72	1044	13.055
CL Paxos incr	81	1024	12.348
vR Paxos	86	1116	19.064
vR Paxos incr	132	1099	21.602

"incr" indicates specifications containing low-level incremental updates.

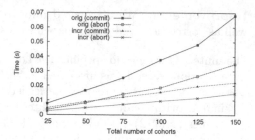

Running times are averaged over 50 rounds and 15 independent runs, measured on an Intel Core-i7 2600K CPU with 16GB of main memory, running Linux 3.0.0 kernel and Python 3.2.2.

5   Related Work

There has been much study on distributed algorithms, e.g., [30, 24, 10, 31], including especially much work on Paxos, from original [16], Byzantine [5, 20], made simple [17], made live in Google's Chubby service [6], and many more, to most recently precise pseudo code for full Paxos [33]. Distributed algorithms have been heavily and increasingly studied both because of their importance in increasingly more distributed applications, e.g., Google's computing infrastructure, and because of challenges in precisely specifying, implementing, and improving them to satisfy the needs of applications.

Distributed algorithms have been expressed in a wide range of languages and notations, from informal pseudo code to formal state machine based specifications, with many variations in between. Formal specification languages, such as I/O automata [24, 14], TLA+ [18], and PlusCal [19], are instrumental in precise verification. While study of languages is important, making specifications higher level is orthogonal, because the most essential language features are already present in many existing languages.

Besides state-machine based approaches, e.g., I/O automata [24, 14], established specification methods include notably the actor model [1] and general event-driven models where events include receipts of messages. These models focus on specifying actions and state transitions driven by the receipts of individual messages. Our specification method aims to make it easier to understand the algorithms at a high level, by abstracting away low-level state updates. It focuses on relating send-actions, which are externally observable, with the history of messages sent and received at a high level, by using high-level queries to express the assertions and computations.

More declarative languages for expressing distributed algorithms have also been studied, e.g., Datalog-based languages Overlog [2] and Bloom [3], and a logic-based language EventML [4, 7]. More declarative languages generally abstract away some or all control flow information and may be more succinct, but they are also harder to understand when used for specifications of algorithms, in which control flow is essential. Our method uses declarative queries over sets and sequences to express assertions and computations, and keeps the control flow of sending and receiving messages clear.

Our method can make the resulting executable specifications extremely inefficient if executed straightforwardly, because of repeated expensive high-level queries. Optimization by incrementalization [28, 12, 22, 21, 23] transforms such expensive queries into efficient incremental maintenance of appropriate auxiliary values. Invariants made explicit following our specification method not only help prove the correctness of the algorithms, but also help apply the optimizations. How to make more or all invariants explicit to make verification of distributed algorithms even easier is open for future study; so is the verification.

References

[1] Agha, G.: Actors: a model of concurrent computation in distributed systems. MIT Press (1986)

[2] Alvaro, P., Condie, T., Conway, N., Hellerstein, J., Sears, R.: I do declare: Consensus in a logic language. ACM SIGOPS Operating Systems Review 43(4), 25–30 (2010)

[3] Berkeley Orders of Magnitude. Bloom Programming Language, http://www.bloom-lang.net/

[4] Bickford, M.: Component Specification Using Event Classes. In: Lewis, G.A., Poernomo, I., Hofmeister, C. (eds.) CBSE 2009. LNCS, vol. 5582, pp. 140–155. Springer, Heidelberg (2009)

[5] Castro, M., Liskov, B.: Practical Byzantine fault tolerance and proactive recovery. ACM Transactions on Computer Systems 20, 398–461 (2002)

[6] Chandra, T.D., Griesemer, R., Redstone, J.: Paxos made live—An engineering perspective. In: Proceedings of the 26th Annual ACM Symposium on Principles of Distributed Computing (PODC), pp. 398–407 (2007)

[7] CRASH Project. EventML, http://www.nuprl.org/software/#WhatisEventML (last dated February 13, 2012)

[8] De Prisco, R., Lampson, B., Lynch, N.: Revisiting the Paxos algorithm. Theoretical Computer Science 243, 35–91 (2000)

[9] Fidge, C.J.: Timestamps in message-passing systems that preserve the partial ordering. In: Proceedings of the 11th Australian Computer Science Conference, pp. 56–66 (1988)

[10] Garg, V.K.: Elements of Distributed Computing. Wiley (2002)

[11] Gray, J.: Notes on Data Base Operating Systems. In: Flynn, M.J., Jones, A.K., Opderbeck, H., Randell, B., Wiehle, H.R., Gray, J.N., Lagally, K., Popek, G.J., Saltzer, J.H. (eds.) Operating Systems. LNCS, vol. 60, pp. 393–481. Springer, Heidelberg (1978)

[12] Gupta, A., Mumick, I.S., Subrahmanian, V.S.: Maintaining views incrementally. In: Proceedings of the 1993 ACM SIGMOD International Conference on Management of Data, pp. 157–166 (1993)

[13] http://groups.csail.mit.edu/tds/ioa/distributions/IOA_Toolkit-tools.tar.gz, The Paxos code is under Examples/Paxos

[14] Kaynar, D., Lynch, N., Segala, R., Vaandrager, F.: The Theory of Timed I/O Automata, 2nd edn. Morgan Claypool Publishers (2010)

[15] Lamport, L.: Time, clocks, and the ordering of events in a distributed system. Communications of the ACM 21, 558–565 (1978)

[16] Lamport, L.: The part-time parliament. ACM Transactions on Computer Systems 16(2), 133–169 (1998)

[17] Lamport, L.: Paxos made simple. SIGACT News (Distributed Computing Column) 32(4), 51–58 (2001)

[18] Lamport, L.: Specifying Systems: The TLA+ Language and Tools for Hardware and Software Engineers. Addison-Wesley (2002)

[19] Lamport, L.: The PlusCal Algorithm Language. In: Leucker, M., Morgan, C. (eds.) ICTAC 2009. LNCS, vol. 5684, pp. 36–60. Springer, Heidelberg (2009)

[20] Lamport, L.: Byzantizing Paxos by Refinement. In: Peleg, D. (ed.) DISC 2011. LNCS, vol. 6950, pp. 211–224. Springer, Heidelberg (2011)

[21] Liu, Y.A., Gorbovitski, M., Stoller, S.D.: A language and framework for invariant-driven transformations. In: Proceedings of the 8th International Conference on Generative Programming and Component Engineering, pp. 55–64 (2009)

[22] Liu, Y.A., Stoller, S.D., Gorbovitski, M., Rothamel, T., Liu, Y.E.: Incrementalization across object abstraction. In: Proceedings of the 20th ACM Conference on Object-Oriented Programming, Systems, Languages, and Applications, pp. 473–486 (2005)

[23] Liu, Y.A., Stoller, S.D., Lin, B., Gorbovitski, M.: From clarity to efficiency for distributed algorithms. In: Proceedings of the 27th ACM SIGPLAN Conference on Object-Oriented Programming, Systems, Languages and Applications (2012)

[24] Lynch, N.A.: Distributed Algorithms. Morgan Kaufman (1996)

[25] Mattern, F.: Virtual time and global states of distributed systems. In: Proc. International Workshop on Parallel and Distributed Algorithms, pp. 120–131 (1989)

[26] Mechanically checked safety proof of a Byzantine Paxos algorithm
http://research.microsoft.com/en-us/
um/people/lamport/tla/byzpaxos.html
(last modified September 1, 2011)

[27] https://svn.declarativity.net/overlog-paxos/src/olg/core/

[28] Paige, R., Koenig, S.: Finite differencing of computable expressions. ACM Transactions on Programming Languages and Systems 4(3), 402–454 (1982)

[29] https://github.com/bloom-lang/bud-sandbox/tree/master/paxos

[30] Raynal, M.: Distributed Algorithms and Protocols. Wiley (1988)

[31] Raynal, M.: Communication and Agreement Abstractions for Fault-Tolerant Asynchronous Distributed Systems. Morgan & Claypool (2010)

[32] Sirer, E.G.: Email, August 12 (2011)

[33] van Renesse, R.: Paxos made moderately complex, October 11 (2011), An online version is at http://www.cs.cornell.edu/courses/CS7412/2011sp/paxos.pdf

Formal Verification of Security Preservation for Migrating Virtual Machines in the Cloud

Yosr Jarraya[1], Arash Eghtesadi[1], Mourad Debbabi[1], Ying Zhang[2], and Makan Pourzandi[3]

[1] Computer Security Laboratory,
CIISE, Concordia University, Montreal, Quebec, Canada
{y_jarray,a_eghte,debbabi}@encs.concordia.ca
[2] Ericsson Research Sillicon Valley Lab, San Jose, CA, USA
ying.zhang@ericsson.com
[3] Ericsson Research Canada, Montreal, Quebec, Canada
makan.pourzandi@ericsson.com

Abstract. Firewalls are a prerequisite for securing any communication network. In cloud computing environments, virtual machines are dynamically and frequently migrated across data centers. This frequent modification in the topology requires frequent reconfiguration of security appliances, particularly firewalls. In this paper, we address the issue of security policy preservation in a distributed firewall configuration within a highly dynamic context. Thus, we propose a systematic procedure to verify security compliance of firewall policies after VM migration. First, the distributed firewall configurations in the involved data centers are defined according to the network topology expressed using Cloud Calculus. Then, these configurations are expressed as propositional constraints and used to build a verification model based on the constraint satisfaction problem framework, which allows reasoning on security policy preservation. Finally, we present a case study inspired from Amazon EC2 to show the applicability and usefulness of our approach.

1 Introduction

Virtualization enables a dynamic computing infrastructure supporting the elastic nature of service provisioning and de-provisioning as requested by users while maintaining high levels of reliability and security [1]. In this setting, Virtual Machines (VMs) are software implementations created within a virtualization layer and their capacity to be easily moved, copied, and reassigned between host servers is a key-enabler technology that enhances load balancing, scheduled maintenance, as well as power management. However, VM migration creates new security challenges in the data centers.

VMs are protected using various security mechanisms including firewalls, intrusion detection/prevention, etc. Specifically, firewalls are used to allow only authorized traffic to reach the protected VMs. While VMs lively migrate around, not only the memory and the states on the hypervisor need to be migrated, but

A.W. Richa and C. Scheideler (Eds.): SSS 2012, LNCS 7596, pp. 111–125, 2012.

also the network states including firewall rules. Failing to do this may expose the running services on the migrated VM to security problems. An illustrative example of this case is firewall access control lists (ACLs). Assume that a VM migrates to a new location under a different firewall configuration. On the one hand, if the ACLs at the new location are more permissive than those at the original location, some packets that should be blocked may be allowed. This may open up several security vulnerabilities to the VM. On the other hand, if they are less permissive, some packets that should be allowed may be blocked. Furthermore, some virtual machine's running services might require specific filtering rules. As virtual machines are dynamically and frequently moved between sites, managing manually complex firewall rules can be time-consuming and error-prone. Furthermore, scale and complexity of data centers are continually increasing, which makes it difficult to rely on the administrators to update and validate the security mechanisms.

In our previous work [2], we proposed an algebraic framework named cloud calculus that can be used to specify cloud networks topology and the migration of virtual machines along with their security policies. We also defined based on the concept of testing equivalence the formal foundation for the verification of security policy consistency. However, the need for test cases generation, which might be tedious and incomplete, hinders the practical use of such an approach. In this paper, we propose an alternative formal and systematic approach for the verification of security policy preservation after VM migration that has the advantage of being more automatable and complete. Furthermore, we consider multiple paths in data centers with distributed firewall configurations. More specifically, we address the issue of security policy preservation in dynamic cloud computing environments focusing on distributed firewalls as the principal security mechanism. Binary Decision Diagram (BDD), propositional satisfiability problem, and model-checking are the three principal approaches that are proposed in the state-of-the-art for verifying firewalls configuration conformance to security policy. The bottleneck of using BDD is the amount of memory required to store and manipulate BDDs [3], which can grow exponentially. Furthermore, the most performance degradation points in the BDD is the building and initialization time, which make it impractical for the analysis of dynamic environments [4]. Additionally, model-checking based approaches do not scale well. Also, it was shown that propositional satisfiability problems can be solved with modern SAT solvers without suffering from space explosion problem [3].

Thus, we propose to model security policy consistency preservation as a constraint satisfaction problem (CSP) and use Sugar [5], a SAT-based constraint solver, to asses security of VMs in the cloud after VMs migration. The main contributions of this paper are threefold. (1) Extend Cloud Calculus to handle distributed asymmetric firewall configurations (2) Define the concept of security policy preservation in dynamic cloud computing environment. (3) Define a systematic procedure to validate security policy preservation using a constraint satisfaction problem solver. The remaining of the paper is organized as follows. Section 2 provides an overview on related work in the context of firewall security policy verification. Section 3 presents the extended Cloud Calculus framework. Section 4 introduces a language for specifying distributed firewall composition. Section 5 is dedicated for presenting the paradigm of constraint satisfaction problems and encoding of distributed firewall configurations into CSP. Section 6 defines the concept of security policy preservation and presents our approach to verify security preservation in cloud data centers after VM migration. Section 7 is dedicated for a case study showing the applicability of our approach and illustrating scenarios where the migration is performed with errors and how our approach can be used to detect such a problem.

2   Related Work

In this section, we review the state-of-the-art in the verification and validation of firewall policy with respect to security requirements. Yuan et al. [6] propose FIREMAN, a static analysis toolkit implemented using BDDs and their related operations such as intersection and union. It performs symbolic model-checking of a set of networked firewalls configurations and analyze them in order to detect misconfigurations such as policy violations, inconsistencies, and inefficiencies at intra-firewall, inter-firewall, and cross-path levels. Jeffrey and Samak [4] propose bounded model-checking based on a SAT solver for the analysis of a network of IPtables firewall policy configurations. Reachability of a given rule and cyclicity in the firewall configuration are investigated. Ben Youssef et al. [7] propose an automated approach for the verification of the conformance of a distributed firewalls configuration to a predefined security policy based on Satisfiability Modulo Theories (SMT) technique. Their approach detects conflicts within the security policy and returns key elements for the correction of flawed firewall configurations. Gawanmeh et al. [8] propose an approach based on domain restriction for modeling and verifying firewall configuration. The approach is implemented in Event-B. They use invariant checking to verify the consistency of firewall configurations in Event-B theorem proving framework. Al-Shaer et al. [9] propose symbolic model-checking based on BDDs in order to verify network reachability and security requirements. The network model specified as a state machine captures the end-to-end behavior of access control configurations of a network including routers, IPSec, and firewalls. The model can be very large as it captures all possible types of packet headers. The verified properties are expressed in the Computation Tree Logic (CTL). Acharya and Gouda [10] study the equivalence of firewall verification and firewall redundancy checking problems for stateles firewalls. They demonstrate that any algorithm that can be used to solve either problem can be also used to solve the other problem with the same time and space complexity. Kotenko et al. [11] propose a model-checking approach intended for detection and resolution of filtering anomalies in the specification of security policy using SPIN model-checker. Anomalies detection is based on the verification of a set of LTL properties. Gouda et at. [12] propose a method to verify the correctness of firewall networks configuration with tree topologies based on Firewall Decision Diagram (FDD). The method consists of two algorithms that can be used to decide whether a given firewall tree satisfies a given, accept or discard, property of that tree. Yin et al. [13] propose to map the verification of consistency between security policy and firewall policy into CSP. The problem is then solved using the Sugar CSP solver. This latter work is the closest to our work. However, we consider distributed firewalls with multiple ACL rules and we do not verify the consistency of a firewall policy with respect to a given security policy but we derived an approach that ensures that the modification of a distributed firewall configurations does not introduce security breaches, which is useful in network where policy and firewall configuration modifications are frequently performed.

3   Cloud Calculus

Cloud Calculus (CC) [2] is a process algebra used to specify cloud network topology and virtual machines migrations. In this section, we briefly present CC and focus on its use to express distributed firewalls topology and firewall rules migration. Cloud calculus is built upon a subset of the Mobile Ambients (MA) [14] and the Non-interfering Boxed Ambients [15]. However, it extends them to handle specific security related features, including security appliances and cloud-related concepts, including dynamic firewall re-configuration.

According to Cardelli and Gordon [14], an ambient is a bounded place, where the boundary determines its inside and its outside. Ambients can be nested and moved as a whole. Each ambient has a name and a collection of local processes that represent computations running directly within the ambient and, in a sense, control it. Ambients allow representing any type of resources including firewalls, switches, routers, gateways, physical hosts, and VMs. Initially, MA calculus is based on the concepts of hierarchy and grouping. However, we extend it with a construct that allows referring to an already defined ambient n. This enables expressing topologies with multiple paths leading to a given same ambient. The syntax of cloud calculus is presented in Figure 1. In the following, we only detail a subset of the processes and the firewall constructs. The explanation of the other constructs can be found in [2].

A process P can be defined as the inactive process 0, the parallel composition of two processes $P \mid Q$, the restriction of a new name n within the scope P, denoted by $(\nu n)P$, an ambient named n containing a running process P, denoted by $n[P]$, a security ambient named n containing a running process P and protected by a security policy defined in F, denoted by $F :: n[P]$, a reference to an ambient named n, the unbounded replication of the process P, denoted by $!P$, and finally the process that executes a capability M, and then continues as P, denoted by $M.P$. The syntax of a firewall configuration language in BNF is presented in Figure 2. The proposed syntax, an improved version of the language presented in [2], allows expressing a wide packet filtering firewall systems where both single, and multiple linked ACLs can be specified. Multiple ACL, in the IPtables style, are useful to express different access control lists for different attributes of the packets' headers, which has a performance advantage over filtering using single list. The bit-length of the allocated network prefix is denoted

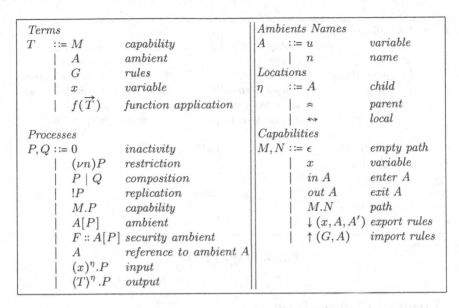

Terms		
T ::= M	capability
| A	ambient
| G	rules
| x	variable
| $f(\overrightarrow{T})$	function application
Processes		
P, Q ::= 0	inactivity
| $(\nu n)P$	restriction
| $P \mid Q$	composition
| $!P$	replication
| $M.P$	capability
| $A[P]$	ambient
| $F :: A[P]$	security ambient
| A	reference to ambient A
| $(x)^{\eta}.P$	input
| $\langle T \rangle^{\eta}.P$	output

Ambients Names		
A ::= u	variable
| n	name
Locations		
η ::= A	child
| $\approx$	parent
| $\leftrightsquigarrow$	local
Capabilities		
M, N ::= ϵ	empty path
| x	variable
| $in\ A$	enter A
| $out\ A$	exit A
| $M.N$	path
| $\downarrow (x, A, A')$	export rules
| $\uparrow (G, A)$	import rules

Fig. 1. Cloud Calculus Syntax

by *num* and the name of a given interface of the firewall is denoted by *iface*. The symbol *, depending on its position, denotes the range of possible values in terms of IP, port, or protocol. A firewall configuration F can be composed of a number of ACLs L. For a given category of firewalls, the configuration language, rules' organization, and the interaction between multiple ACLs are the main variation factors between firewalls from different vendors. An ACL, denoted by L, is associated with a name m. The latter allows naming ACLs in order to link an ACL to another using the construct *Jump m*. The firewall rules in a given ACL are organized in sequential order. Let f_i be a single firewall rule, denoted by $p_i \mapsto d_i$ where p_i is a predicate representing the filtering condition of the rule and d_i is the corresponding decision. The predicate p_i is the conjunction of the set of predicates on the proceeded packet's attributes. The commonly used attributes in the packet header are the protocol, the source IP address, the destination IP address, the source port number, and the destination port number. For instance, the topology of the data center $DC1$ depicted in Figure 4 can be expressed using cloud calculus as follows:

$D_1 = F1 :: G1[\ F2 :: S1[\ S3[\ PS1[P_{WEB1}]\ ]\ ]\ ]\ |\ P]$

where $P = F3 :: S2[\ S3\ |\ S4[\ PS2[P_{API}]\ ]\ ]$ and $P_{WEB1} = VM_5\ |\ VM_6\ |\ VM_7$

The topology of the data center $DC2$ can be expressed as follows:

$D_2 = F4 :: G2[\ F5 :: S5[\ S6[\ PS3[P_{DB1}]\ ]\ |\ PS4[VM_1\ |\ VM_2\ |\ VM_3\ |\ VM_4]]\ ]]$

The CC operational semantics is defined in terms of reduction rules and structural congruence. Firewall rules migration can be described using the CC reduction rules. Because of lack of space, we refer the reader to [2] for full description of the operational semantics of cloud calculus.

Firewall Configuration			Rule Predicate		
F	$::= \{m : L, \cdots, m : L\}$	multiple ACL	p	$::= sip \bowtie add$	source addr
L	$::= nop$	empty		$\mid ps \bowtie port$	source port
	$\mid (p \mapsto d).L$	sequence		$\mid dip \bowtie add$	destination addr
d	$::= allow$	allow decision		$\mid pd \bowtie port$	destination port
	$\mid deny$	deny decision		$\mid pr = prot$	protocol
	$\mid Jump\ m$	link to ACL m		$\mid p \wedge p$	conjunction
ip	$::= val.val.val.val$		$add ::= *$		
$subnet$	$::= ip/num$			$\mid subnet$	
val	$\in [0, 255]$			$\mid ip$	
$pval$	$\in [0, 65535]$		$port ::= *$		
$prot$	$::= tcp \mid udp \mid *$			$\mid pval$	
$\bowtie$	$\in \{=, \subset\}$			$\mid pval .. pval$	

Fig. 2. Firewall Syntax

4   Firewall Composition

In the case of a well-engineered network with distributed firewalls, multiple paths may exist to reach a given destination and dynamic routing is used in order to improve performance and reliability. Packets crossing different paths may be processed by different firewalls rules. Consequently, a packet could traverse different ACL at different times. In this section, we define a language to express distributed firewalls composition, denoted by T. Two firewalls may be either composed in serial or in parallel. The syntax of T is provided in BNF as follows:

$$T ::= F \mid T \odot T \mid T \oplus T$$

where F is a single firewall configuration, $T_1 \odot T_2$ denotes serial composition of T_1 and T_2, and $T_1 \oplus T_2$ is the parallel composition of two firewall configurations T_1 and T_2. In serial composition, $T_1 \odot T_2$ means that a packet that survives filtering of rules of T_1 is then necessarily filtered by T_2. The operator $\odot$ is associative and distributive over $\oplus$. With respect to parallel composition[1], $T_1 \oplus T_2$ means that a packet is either filtered by T_1 or by T_2. The operator $\oplus$ is commutative and associative.

Given a cloud calculus term expressing the topology of a cloud data center, one can parse it in order to infer the resulting firewalls composition expressed in the above syntax. Thus, we define a function $\mathscr{P}$ that takes as input a cloud calculus term and an ambient name A and returns the firewall composition expression. For instance, for the data center expressed in Section 3 using CC as D_1, $\mathscr{P}(D_1, PS1) = (FW1 \odot FW2) \oplus (FW1 \odot FW3)$. In contrast, $\mathscr{P}(D_1, PS2) = FW1 \odot FW3$. For the data center expressed as D_2, $\mathscr{P}(D_2, PS4) = (FW4 \odot FW5)$.

---

[1] The parallel firewalling operation is useful for better high availability. In this case if one of the links goes down, the second is used to carry the traffic to the destination.

5   Encoding Firewall Configuration in CSP

Constraint satisfaction is the process of finding a solution to a propositional reasoning problem that is specified using a vector of variables that must satisfy a set of constraints. A solution is therefore a vector of values that satisfies all constraints. Many problems including those of scheduling, test generation, and verification can be encoded in CSP. Constraint satisfaction problems are typically identified with problems based on constraints on a finite domain. More formally, a CSP is defined by a set of variables $\{x_i\}_{1 \leq i \leq n}$ and a set of constraints $\{C_j\}_{1 \leq j \leq m}$. Each variable x_i is defined within a domain D_i of possible values. Each constraint C_j involves all or a subset of the variables and specifies the allowable combinations of values for that variables. A state of the problem is defined by an assignment of values to some or all of the variables. A consistent or legal assignment is one that does not violate any constraint. A complete assignment is one in which all variables are assigned values. A solution to a CSP is a complete assignment that satisfies all the constraints. There exist programs that solves CSP problems and are called constraints solver. We use Sugar CSP solver, a SAT-based constraint solver based on a new SAT-encoding method named "order encoding" [5]. Sugar accepts Lisp-like expressions. For instance, the constraint $C_1 \wedge C_2$ is equivalent to the expression *(and C_1 C_2)* in Sugar syntax. The complete language accepted by Sugar can be found in [16]. After submitting a problem to Sugar, two possible conclusion are output: either *satisfiable* (denoted hereafter as SAT), if all constraints are satisfied or *unsatisfiable* (denoted hereafter as UNSAT), otherwise. For instance, for a conjunction of constraints $c_1 \wedge \cdots \wedge c_n$, a SAT conclusion allows to infer that $\{c_i\}_{1 \leq i \leq n}$ are not disjoint whereas UNSAT conclusion asserts that they are indeed disjoint.

In the following, we present how we encode a single firewall and then a distributed firewall configuration in Sugar. The CSP variables are the set of integer variables V needed to encode the condition filters of a given firewall rule. In order to represent an IP address, 4 integer variables within the range $[0, 255]$ are used. A source (resp. destination) IP address is represented by $\{sip_i\}_{1 \leq i \leq 4}$ (resp. $\{dip_i\}_{1 \leq i \leq 4}$). The integer variable $pr \in [0, 255]$ represents the protocol number. We also define two integer variables to encode the source and destination port numbers, respectively ps and pd within the range of values $[0, 65535]$. Thus, the set of integer variables is $V = \{pr, sip1, sip2, sip3, sip4, ps, dip1, dip2, dip3, dip4, pd\}$. Declaring an integer variable in Sugar syntax, for instance pr, within the range $[0, 255]$ is denoted by *(int pr 0 255)*. Each single firewall rule predicate p is encoded as a CSP constraint. It is a conjunctive logical formula over the variables in V. The corresponding CSP constraint is written as follows:

$$pr = v_1 \ \wedge \ sip1 = v_2 \ \wedge \ sip2 = v_3 \ \cdots \ \wedge \ dip4 = v_{10} \ \wedge pd = v_{11}$$

where v_i is to be replaced by the actual value in the corresponding firewall rule. The firewall ACL is encoded as a constraint $\mathcal{C}$ built as a disjunctive logical formula over all firewall rules formulas. Thus, the ordered sequence of firewall rules $(p_n \to d_n).(p_{n-1} \to d_{n-1}). \ \cdots \ .nop$ are encoded as the logical formula $p_1 \vee p_2 \vee \cdots \vee p_n$. In Sugar syntax, this is denoted by *(or p_1 ... p_n)*. Since we consider that all rules have "allow" decisions, this constraint represents the set of packets accepted by the firewall configuration. Sugar parses $\mathcal{C}$ and returns *satisfiable* with a complete assignment solution of the problem, which is a packet that matches one of the firewall rules predicate. A $!\mathcal{C}$ represents the set of packets denied by the firewall configuration. With respect to distributed firewalls, we consider each possible path to the migrating VM in source and destination data centers. Given the cloud calculus term, one can infer the firewall composition of the data center topology expressed in the syntax defined in Section 4. Therein, paths are composed using the $\oplus$ operator, i.e. $P_1 \oplus \cdots \oplus P_n$, where P_i consists of the serial composition of k firewalls, denoted by $F_1 \odot \cdots \odot F_k$.

6   Preservation of Security Consistency as CSP

In this section, we present our approach to verify security policy preservation in dynamic cloud computing environment. First, we present security policy preservation concept and summarize our assumptions. Then, we formally define security policy preservation in source and destination data centers as well as for a migrating VM. Afterward, we elaborate on the CSP constrains, which satisfiabilities allow verifying the defined security policy preservation. Finally, we describe the proposed verification procedure and explain the interpretation the outcome of Sugar solver.

In dynamic cloud computing environment, a virtual machine may leave a data center D_1, called source data center, to be relocated in another data center D_2, called destination data center. During migration, the security enforcement rules located initially in D_1 should follow the VM. Thus, they have to be removed from the source data center and then reinforced at the destination data center. Thus, it is very important to ensure each time that the migrating VM security requirements have not been compromised. Furthermore, as this involves modification of security rules in both source and destination data centers, we also have to ensure that security requirements of the non-migrating virtual machines located therein have not been compromised. We suppose that all firewalls are anomalies-free and that all rules decisions are of type "allow" and the default one is a "deny" rule. Although, in case of existence of both deny and allow rules, one can use the algorithm defined in [17], which computes the effective representation of the firewall rules consisting of the equivalent allow rules. Furthermore, we assume the initial configurations in both data centers are compliant with the pre-defined security policy.

In the following, we formally define security preservation in dynamic cloud computing environment. Let A_{src}^b, A_{src}^a, A_v be the accepted traffic in the source data center before migration, the accepted traffic in the source data center after migration, and the accepted traffic destined to the migrating VM v, respectively. Intuitively, security is preserved in the source data center if the only difference between traffic accepted before and after migration is the one destined to the migrating VM v. This is defined formally as follows:

Definition 1. *Security Preservation in Source Data Center*
Security is preserved in source data center if and only if for any path, we have
$A_{src}^{a} = A_{src}^{b} \smallsetminus A_v$ *and* $A_v \neq \varnothing$. □

Note here that we require $A_v \neq \varnothing$ otherwise, this will be a trivial case where no rule is migrated. In the destination data center, security preservation is defined as follows:

Definition 2. *Security Preservation in Destination Data Center*
Security is preserved in destination data center if and only if for any path, we have $A_{dst}^{b} = A_{dst}^{a} \smallsetminus A_v$ *and* $A_v \neq \varnothing$. □

Since we are assuming that security requirements of the migrating VM are met in the source data center, its security is preserved if the traffic accepted to that VM in the destination data center after migration and the source data center before migration are equal.

Definition 3. *Security Preservation for the Migrating VM*
Security is preserved for the migrated VM if and only if for any path in the destination data center $A_{dst}^{a} \smallsetminus A_{dst}^{b} = A_{src}^{b} \smallsetminus A_{src}^{a}$. □

In order to verify security preservation in both data centers and for the migrating VM, we encode all firewall rules in both data centers as explained in Section 5 and use the aforementioned definitions in order to infer the corresponding equivalent constraint satisfiability problem.

Let $\mathcal{C}_{src}^{b}(P_i)$ (resp. $\mathcal{C}_{dst}^{b}(P_j)$) be the constraint that encodes the filtering conditions of the firewall at the source (resp. destination) data center before migration on path P_i (resp. P_j). The constraints $\mathcal{C}_{src}^{b}(P_i)$ and $\mathcal{C}_{dst}^{b}(P_j)$ represent the encoding in CSP of A_{src}^{b} and A_{dst}^{b}, respectively. Let $\mathcal{C}_{src}^{a}(P_i)$ (resp. $\mathcal{C}_{dst}^{a}(P_j)$) be the constraint that encodes the filtering conditions of the firewall at the source (resp. destination) data center after migration. The constraints $\mathcal{C}_{src}^{a}(P_i)$ and $\mathcal{C}_{dst}^{a}(P_j)$ represent the encoding in CSP of A_{src}^{a} and A_{dst}^{a}, respectively. Let $\mathcal{C}_v$ be the constraint that specifies the packets that are destined to the migrating VM v. According to the set theory, two sets A and B are equal, denoted $A = B$, if and only if $A \subseteq B$ and $B \subseteq A$. We use this concept in order to prove security preservation as defined in Definition 1, Definition 2, and Definition 3 using CSP framework. From Definition 1, $A_{src}^{a} = A_{src}^{b} \smallsetminus A_v$ if and only if $A_{src}^{a} \subseteq A_{src}^{b} \smallsetminus A_v$ and $A_{src}^{b} \smallsetminus A_v \subseteq A_{src}^{a}$. This condition holds if the following CSP problems are unsatisfiable for all paths:

$$\mathcal{C}_{src}^{a}(P_i) \wedge !(\mathcal{C}_{src}^{b}(P_i) \wedge !\mathcal{C}_v) \tag{1}$$

$$\mathcal{C}_{src}^{b}(P_i) \wedge !\mathcal{C}_v \wedge !\mathcal{C}_{src}^{a}(P_i) \tag{2}$$

Equation (1) is equivalent to $(\mathcal{C}_{src}^{a}(P_i) \wedge !\mathcal{C}_{src}^{b}(P_i)) \vee (\mathcal{C}_{src}^{a}(P_i) \wedge \mathcal{C}_v)$.

The condition $A_v \neq \varnothing$ is verified if $\mathcal{C}_{src}^{b}(P_i) \wedge !\mathcal{C}_{src}^{a}(P_i)$ is satisfiable. Therefore, proving security preservation in source data center is equivalent to prove for all paths that:

- $\mathcal{C}_1 = \mathcal{C}_{src}^b(P_i) \wedge !\mathcal{C}_{src}^a(P_i)$ is satisfiable
- $\mathcal{C}_2 = \mathcal{C}_{src}^a(P_i) \wedge !\mathcal{C}_{src}^b(P_i)$ is unsatisfiable
- $\mathcal{C}_3 = \mathcal{C}_{src}^a(P_i) \wedge \mathcal{C}_v$ is unsatisfiable
- $\mathcal{C}_4 = \mathcal{C}_{src}^b(P_i) \wedge !\mathcal{C}_v \wedge !\mathcal{C}_{src}^a(P_i)$ is unsatisfiable

From Definition 2, $A_{dst}^b = A_{dst}^a \smallsetminus A_v$ if and only if $A_{dst}^b \subseteq A_{dst}^a \smallsetminus A_v$ and $A_{dst}^a \smallsetminus A_v \subseteq A_{dst}^b$. This condition holds if the following CSP problems are unsatisfiable for all paths:

$$\mathcal{C}_{dst}^b(P_j) \wedge !(\mathcal{C}_{dst}^a(P_j) \wedge !\mathcal{C}_v) \tag{3}$$

$$\mathcal{C}_{dst}^a(P_j) \wedge !\mathcal{C}_v \wedge !\mathcal{C}_{dst}^b(P_j) \tag{4}$$

Equation (3) is equivalent to $\mathcal{C}_{dst}^b(P_j) \wedge !\mathcal{C}_{dst}^a(P_j) \vee \mathcal{C}_{dst}^b(P_j) \wedge \mathcal{C}_v$. The unsatisfiability of formula $\mathcal{C}_{dst}^b(P_j) \wedge \mathcal{C}_v$ states that before migration none of the rules concern v. This trivially holds thus, we do not consider it in the verification process. The condition $A_v \neq \varnothing$ is verified if $\mathcal{C}_{dst}^a(P_i) \wedge !\mathcal{C}_{dst}^b(P_i)$ is satisfiable. Thus, proving security preservation in the destination data center is equivalent to prove for all paths that:

- $\mathcal{C}_5 = \mathcal{C}_{dst}^a(P_j) \wedge !\mathcal{C}_{dst}^b(P_j)$ is satisfiable.
- $\mathcal{C}_6 = \mathcal{C}_{dst}^b(P_j) \wedge !\mathcal{C}_{dst}^a(P_j)$ is unsatisfiable.
- $\mathcal{C}_7 = \mathcal{C}_{dst}^a(P_j) \wedge !\mathcal{C}_v \wedge !\mathcal{C}_{dst}^b(P_j)$ is unsatisfiable.

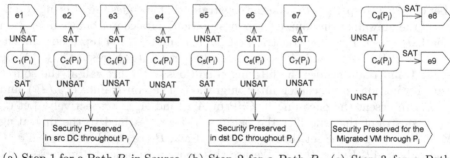

(a) Step 1 for a Path P_i in Source Data Center

(b) Step 2 for a Path P_j in Destination Data Center

(c) Step 3 for a Path P_j in Destination Data Center

Fig. 3. Security Verification Approach

For Definition 3, $A_{dst}^a \smallsetminus A_{dst}^b = A_{src}^b \smallsetminus A_{src}^a$ hold if and only if $A_{dst}^a \smallsetminus A_{dst}^b \subseteq A_{src}^b \smallsetminus A_{src}^a$ and $A_{src}^b \smallsetminus A_{src}^a \subseteq A_{dst}^a \smallsetminus A_{dst}^b$. This condition holds if the following CSP problems are unsatisfiable for all paths P_j, with a reference path in the source data center P_{ref}:

$$\mathcal{C}_8 = \mathcal{C}_{src}^b(P_{ref}) \wedge !\mathcal{C}_{src}^a(P_{ref}) \wedge !(\mathcal{C}_{dst}^a(P_j) \wedge !\mathcal{C}_{dst}^b(P_j)) \tag{5}$$

$$\mathcal{C}_9 = \mathcal{C}_{dst}^a(P_j) \wedge !\mathcal{C}_{dst}^b(P_j) \wedge !(\mathcal{C}_{src}^b(P_{ref}) \wedge !\mathcal{C}_{src}^a(P_{ref})) \tag{6}$$

Table 1. Interpretations of the Unexpected Constraints' Satisfaction Values

e1	$A_{src}^b \subseteq A_{src}^a$
e2	$A_{src}^b \subset A_{src}^a$
e3	$\exists p \mid p \in A_v$ and $p \in A_{src}^a$
e4	$\exists p \mid p \in A_{src}^b$ and $p \notin A_v$ and $p \notin A_{src}^a$
e5	$A_{dst}^a \subseteq A_{dst}^b$
e6	$A_{dst}^a \subset A_{dst}^b$
e7	$\exists p \mid p \in A_{dst}^a$ and $p \notin A_v$ and $p \notin A_{dst}^b$
e8	$A_{v,dst} \subset A_{v,src}$, some rules from source data center did not migrate
e9	$A_{v,src} \subset A_{v,dst}$, more rules than migrated in destination data center

Thus, proving security preservation for the migrating VM is equivalent to prove for all paths in destination data center that both C_8 and C_9 are unsatisfiable. The satisfiability of any one of them implies that there is discrepancy between the migrated rules from source data center and the rules migrated into the destination data center for path P_j. Figure 3 illustrates the verification approach, which consists of three steps: security preservation in source data center, security preservation in destination data center and then security preservation of the migrated VM. Note that the horizontal bar in this figure means that all conditions have to hold before concluding on the security preservation. For instance, in Figure 3a, C_1 has to be satisfiable and C_2, C_3, and C_4 have to be unsatisfiable in order to conclude on the security preservation in source data center. The evaluation of these constraints is interpreted relatively to a given path in source or destination data center. In the case of a constraint satisfiability, the CSP solver provides a solution that can be used to identify the problematic rule(s). The interpretation of the undesired outputs as identified in Figure 3 are summarized in Table 1.

7   Case Study

To better illustrate our approach, we present a case study consisting of two data centers $DC1$ and $DC2$ with distributed firewall settings as depicted in Figure 4, inspired from Amazon Elastic Compute Cloud (Amazon EC2) [18]. The service is built using a three-tier architecture: web, application, and database. Table 2 summarizes the firewall rules in both data centers before migration. We suppose that for the sake of load balancing, $VM1$ has to be migrated from the physical server $PS4$ in data center $DC2$ to $PS1$ in data center $DC1$. The need for virtual machine mobility across data centers, has been expressed by many providers as it serves several reasons including data center infrastructure maintenance, disaster avoidance, or data center expansion to address power, cooling, and space constraints. Even though the technology is not widespread at the moment, but we believe it is coming in the near future. The traffic destined to application group should traverse $FW1$ and $FW3$, whereas traffic destined to web group 1

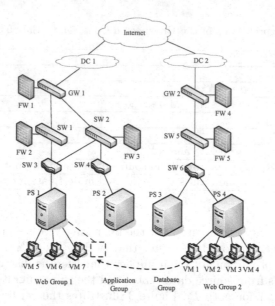

Fig. 4. Cloud Network Model Case Study

can either traverse $FW1$ followed by $FW2$, or $FW1$ followed by $FW3$. Thus, all firewall configurations along the paths to the destination physical server $PS1$ in data center $DC1$ have to be updated. In order to demonstrate the applicability of our verification approach, we consider three scenarios:

Scenario 1 - Migration Error 1. The administrator correctly updated $FW2$ but omitted to add the rules to $FW3$. In such a scenario, $FW3$ rules after migration will be the same as before ($FW3$ in Table 2).

Scenario 2 - Migration Error 2. The administrator correctly migrated the firewall rules to $FW2$ but missed some rules in $FW3$.

Scenario 3 - Correct Migration. The firewall rules are correctly migrated on every path of the network and are provided in Table 3. Note that $FW1$ and $FW4$ do not need to be modified after migration.

In order to verify security preservation, we translate the distributed firewall configuration for each scenario into CSP syntax and use Sugar SAT-solver. The verification results for the three scenarios are summarized in Table 4. Therein, we show only the results for the path that has a firewall configuration error (i.e. $FW1 \odot FW3$). Values in bold show the constraints, which satisfactions are not as expected. When the solver returns satisfiable for a constraint expected to be unsatisfiable, a solution is provided that pinpoints one of the rules that makes security requirements fails. This indicates a possible error that should be investigated in order to correct the firewall configuration. In order to have an assessment of the performance overhead, we performed a set of experiments on an Intel Core i7 2.67 GHz processor with 12Gbytes of RAM. The verification performance depends on the total number of firewall rules. Table 5 summarizes

Table 2. Firewall Rules in Data Centers $DC1$ and $DC2$- Before Migration

FW1					
1. TCP	*.*.*.*	ANY	*.*.*.*	80	Allow
2. TCP	*.*.*.*	ANY	*.*.*.*	443	Allow
3. TCP	*.*.*.*	ANY	*.*.*.*	22	Allow
4. TCP	*.*.*.*	ANY	*.*.*.*	8000	Allow
FW2					
1. TCP	*.*.*.*	ANY	VM5,VM6,VM7	80	Allow
2. TCP	*.*.*.*	ANY	VM5,VM6,VM7	443	Allow
3. TCP	CorpIP	ANY	VM5,VM6,VM7	22	Allow
FW3					
1. TCP	*.*.*.*	ANY	VM5,VM6,VM7	80	Allow
2. TCP	*.*.*.*	ANY	VM5,VM6,VM7	443	Allow
3. TCP	CorpIP	ANY	VM5,VM6,VM7	22	Allow
4. TCP	VM1,VM2,VM3,VM4,VM5,VM6,VM7	ANY	AP1	8000	Allow
5. TCP	CorpIP	ANY	AP1	22	Allow
FW4					
1. TCP	*.*.*.*	ANY	*.*.*.*,	80	Allow
2. TCP	*.*.*.*	ANY	*.*.*.*,	443	Allow
3. TCP	*.*.*.*	ANY	*.*.*.*,	22	Allow
4. TCP	*.*.*.*	ANY	*.*.*.*	3306	Allow
FW5					
1. TCP	*.*.*.*	ANY	VM1,VM2,VM3,VM4	80	Allow
2. TCP	*.*.*.*	ANY	VM1,VM2,VM3,VM4	443	Allow
3. TCP	CorpIP	ANY	VM1,VM2,VM3,VM4	22	Allow
4. TCP	AP1	ANY	DB1	3306	Allow
5. TCP	CorpIP	ANY	DB1	22	Allow

Table 3. Updated Firewall Rules in Data Centers $DC1$ and $DC2$- After Migration

FW2					
1. TCP	*.*.*.*	ANY	VM5,VM6,VM7,VM1	80	Allow
2. TCP	*.*.*.*	ANY	VM5,VM6,VM7,VM1	443	Allow
3. TCP	CorpIP	ANY	VM5,VM6,VM7,VM1	22	Allow
FW3					
1. TCP	*.*.*.*	ANY	VM5, VM6,VM7, VM1	80	Allow
2. TCP	*.*.*.*	ANY	VM5, VM6,VM7, VM1	443	Allow
3. TCP	CorpIP	ANY	VM5, VM6,VM7, VM1	22	Allow
4. TCP	VM1,VM2,VM3,VM4,VM5,VM6,VM7	ANY	AP1	8000	Allow
5. TCP	CorpIP	ANY	AP1	22	Allow
FW5					
1. TCP	*.*.*.*	ANY	VM2,VM3,VM4	80	Allow
2. TCP	*.*.*.*	ANY	VM2,VM3,VM4	443	Allow
3. TCP	CorpIP	ANY	VM2,VM3,VM4	22	Allow
4. TCP	AP1	ANY	DB1	3306	Allow
5. TCP	CorpIP	ANY	DB1	22	Allow

Table 4. Sugar CSP Solver Results for the Three Scenarios

	C_1	C_2	C_3	C_4	C_5	C_6	C_7	C_8	C_9
Scen. 1	SAT	UNSAT	UNSAT	UNSAT	**UNSAT**	UNSAT	UNSAT	**SAT**	UNSAT
Scen. 2	SAT	UNSAT	UNSAT	UNSAT	SAT	UNSAT	UNSAT	**SAT**	UNSAT
Scen. 3	SAT	UNSAT	UNSAT	UNSAT	SAT	UNSAT	UNSAT	UNSAT	UNSAT

Table 5. Performance Evaluation

Number of Rules	Number of VMs	CPU Time (seconds)
22	5	0.278
202	50	0.324
2002	500	0.340
20002	5000	0.762
40002	10000	2.150

the result in terms of CPU time for an increased number of rules which is mostly due to increasing the number of VMs. The result shows that the CPU time consumption increases approximately linearly, also confirmed by [19].

8   Conclusion

In this paper, we addressed the issue of security policy preservation in elastic cloud computing environment with distributed firewalls as the principal security mechanism. We proposed a novel verification and validation approach based on the notion of security policy preservation and the constraint satisfaction problems framework. First, the formal definition of security preservation in source and destination data center as well as for the migrating VM was provided. Then, we elaborated a framework that describes these security preservation problems in terms of constraint satisfaction problems based on Sugar, a SAT-based constraint solver. In order to automate the encoding, we proposed to model cloud network topology using cloud calculus and to use an intermediate syntax in order to express serial and parallel composition of firewalls. The presented automated approach is helpful for practitioners to tackle the uprising issues of network security in highly dynamic cloud computing. For future work, we are going to continue on the verification and validation of security policies in the cloud considering not only packet filtering firewalls, but also stateful firewalls, intrusion detection and prevention, and secure tunneling.

References

1. Malcolm,   D.:   The   Five   Pillars   of   Cloud   Computing   (2009),
   http://soa.sys-con.com/node/904780; SOA & WOA magazine, Cloud Expo
   article (last visited, April 2012)
2. Jarraya, Y., Eghtesadi, A., Debbabi, M., Zhang, Y., Pourzandi, M.: Cloud calculus:
   Security verification in elastic cloud computing platform. In: The Proceeding of the
   2012 International Conference on Collaboration Technologies and Systems (CTS),
   pp. 447–454. IEEE (2012)
3. Biere, A., Cimatti, A., Clarke, E.M., Strichman, O., Zhu, Y.: Bounded Model
   Checking. Advances in Computers, vol. 58, pp. 117–148. Elsevier (2003)
4. Jeffrey, A., Samak, T.: Model Checking Firewall Policy Configurations. In: IEEE
   International Symposium on Policies for Distributed Systems and Networks, POL-
   ICY 2009, pp. 60–67 (July 2009)

5. Tamura, N., Banbara, M.: Sugar: A CSP to SAT Translator Based on Order Encoding. In: The Proceedings of the Second International CSP Solver Competition, pp. 65–69 (2008)
6. Yuan, L., Chen, H., Mai, J., Chuah, C.-N., Su, Z., Mohapatra, P.: Fireman: a toolkit for firewall modeling and analysis. In: IEEE Symposium on Security and Privacy, pp. 199–213 (May 2006)
7. Ben Youssef, N., Bouhoula, A.: Automatic Conformance Verification of Distributed Firewalls to Security Requirements. In: 2010 IEEE Second International Conference on Social Computing (SocialCom), pp. 834–841 (August 2010)
8. Gawanmeh, A., Tahar, S.: Modeling and Verification of Firewall Configurations Using Domain Restriction Method. In: 6th International Conference on Internet Technology and Secured Transactions (December 2011)
9. Al-Shaer, E., Marrero, W., El-Atawy, A., ElBadawi, K.: Network Configuration in a Box: Towards End-to-End Verification of Network Reachability and Security. In: 17th IEEE International Conference on Network Protocols, ICNP 2009, pp. 123–132 (October 2009)
10. Acharya, H., Gouda, M.: Firewall Verification and Redundancy Checking are Equivalent. In: 2011 Proceedings IEEE INFOCOM, pp. 2123–2128 (April 2011)
11. Kotenko, I., Polubelova, O.: Verification of Security Policy Filtering Rules by Model Checking. In: The Proceedings of the IEEE 6th International Conference on Intelligent Data Acquisition and Advanced Computing Systems (IDAACS), vol. 2, pp. 706–710 (September 2011)
12. Gouda, M., Liu, A., Jafry, M.: Verification of Distributed Firewalls. In: Global Telecommunications Conference, IEEE GLOBECOM 2008, pp. 1–5. IEEE (December 2008)
13. Yin, Y., Xu, J., Takahashi, N.: Verifying Consistency between Security Policy and Firewall Policy by Using a Constraint Satisfaction Problem Server. In: Zhang, Y. (ed.) Future Wireless Networks and Information Systems. LNEE, vol. 144, pp. 135–146. Springer, Heidelberg (2012)
14. Cardelli, L., Gordon, A.D.: Mobile Ambients. Theoretical Computer Science 240(1), 177–213 (2000)
15. Bugliesi, M., Crafa, S., Merro, M., Sassone, V.: Communication and Mobility Control in Boxed Ambients. Inf. Comput. 202(1), 39–86 (2005)
16. Syntax of sugar csp description (2010), http://bach.istc.kobe-u.ac.jp/sugar/sugar-v1-14-7/docs/syntax.html (last modified: Tuesday June 29, 13:09:26, 2010 JST)
17. Lu, L., Safavi-Naini, R., Horton, J., Susilo, W.: Comparing and debugging firewall rule tables. IET Information Security 1(4), 143–151 (2007)
18. Amazon.com, Amazon web services: Overview of security processes (May 2011), http://awsmedia.s3.amazonaws.com/pdf/AWS_Security_Whitepaper.pdf
19. van Harmelen, F., Lifschitz, V., Porter, B.: Handbook of Knowledge Representation. Elsevier Science (2008)

Evaluating Practical Tolerance Properties of Stabilizing Programs through Simulation: The Case of Propagation of Information with Feedback

Jordan Adamek[1], Mikhail Nesterenko[1], and Sébastien Tixeuil[2,*]

[1] Kent State University
[2] UPMC Sorbonne Universités & IUF

Abstract. We simulate a stabilizing propagation of information with feedback (PIF) program to evaluate its response to perturbations. Under several classic execution models, we vary the extent of the fault as well as the system scale. We study the program's speed of stabilization and overhead incurred by the fault. Our simulation provides insight into practical program behavior that is sometimes lacking in theoretical correctness proofs. This indicates that such simulation is a useful research tool in studies of fault tolerance.

1 Introduction

System stabilization [2, 12, 8, 1] of various flavors is an attractive approach to optimistic failure recovery. A system is stabilizing if, regardless of the initial state, it eventually arrives at a legitimate state. This allows the program to recover from any fault, regardless of its nature, after the influence of the fault stops. This property allows researchers in this area to effectively ignore the nature of the fault. Classic papers on stabilization usually contain the algorithm description, proof of its correctness, and performance bound estimates.

Extensive performance evaluations are relatively rare in the field [4–7, 13]. If stabilization simulation is carried out, the researchers tend to focus on time of algorithm recovery from randomly chosen initial global states. We believe that such studies give an incomplete picture of robust algorithm behavior. A random initial state is expected to represent a systemic fault. However, uniformly random states tend to present a rather mild challenge to the algorithm as individual process states end up being evenly distributed across the state space. Moreover, such initial states may not adequately represent the states that occur after faults influence legitimate states of the algorithm. In effect, random initial states tend to hide the complexity of faulty behavior and resultant algorithm recovery. Another simplification is the focus on recovery time, a staple of stabilization research. We believe that other characteristics, such as the expense of

---

* This work was supported in part by ANR project SHAMAN.

A.W. Richa and C. Scheideler (Eds.): SSS 2012, LNCS 7596, pp. 126–132, 2012.
© Springer-Verlag Berlin Heidelberg 2012

recovery in terms of fault-induced extra steps, is also an important characteristic of a stabilizing algorithm.

In this paper, we describe the performance evaluation of a stabilizing propagation of information with feedback [11] algorithm. Variants of such algorithm have been extensively studied in stabilization literature. Taking this algorithm as an example, we studied its recovery from faults of increasing scale under classic execution semantics. We measured the algorithm's stabilization time as well as its stabilization overhead. The result is a detailed chart of the algorithm's behavior across fault scales and system sizes.

2   Algorithm Description

The algorithm implements propagation of information with feedback (PIF) for rooted trees. Each process has access to the read-only variables *parent* and *Ch* that respectively contain the identifier of the parent, and the set of identifiers of the children for this process. Each process can be in one of the three states: idle, requesting and replying. This state is encoded in the variable *st* as **i**, **rq**, and **rp** respectively. The root can only be requesting or idle while a leaf can be either idle or replying. Each process can read the state of its neighbors and update its own in a single atomic step. The actions of the algorithm are shown in Figure 1. Let us consider any chain of processes from the root to a leaf and possible legitimate states in this chain. In case the request has not reached the leaf, the chain starts with a possibly empty sequence of requesting processes, followed by at least one idle process and concluding by a possibly empty sequence of replying processes that belong to the previous request. Once the request has reached the leaf, the chain starts with a non-empty sequence of requesting processes followed by a non-empty chain of replying processes. This algorithm is proven self- and ideally-stabilizing [8, 9]. That is, regardless of the initial state, the algorithm achieves one of the above legitimate states in a specified sequence and remains in a legitimate state afterwards. A variant of this algorithm is proven snap-stabilizing [1]. That is, the algorithm transitions to a legitimate state within a single wave cycle.

$$
\begin{aligned}
&request: & st.root = \mathbf{i} \quad\wedge\ (\forall q \in Ch.root : st.q = \mathbf{i}) &\longrightarrow st.root := \mathbf{rq}\\
&clear: & st.root = \mathbf{rq} \wedge\ (\forall q \in Ch.root : st.q = \mathbf{rp}) &\longrightarrow st.root := \mathbf{i}\\
&forward: st.parent = \mathbf{rq} \wedge st.p = \mathbf{i} \quad\wedge\ (\forall q \in Ch.p : st.q = \mathbf{i}) &\longrightarrow st.p := \mathbf{rq}\\
&back: \quad st.parent = \mathbf{rq} \wedge st.p = \mathbf{rq} \quad\wedge\ (\forall q \in Ch.p : st.q = \mathbf{rp}) &\longrightarrow st.p := \mathbf{rp}\\
&stop: \quad st.parent = \mathbf{i} \quad\wedge st.p \neq \mathbf{i} &\longrightarrow st.p := \mathbf{i}\\
&reflect: \quad st.parent = \mathbf{rq} \wedge st.leaf = \mathbf{i} &\longrightarrow st.leaf := \mathbf{rp}\\
&reset: \quad st.parent = \mathbf{i} \quad\wedge st.leaf = \mathbf{rp} &\longrightarrow st.leaf := \mathbf{i}
\end{aligned}
$$

Fig. 1. PIF algorithm actions. Actions *request* and *clear* belong to the root process; actions *forward*, *back*, and *stop* – to an intermediate processes; actions *reflect* and *reset* – to a leaf.

3 Experiment Description and Results

Tree Generation. The PIF algorithm evaluation requires rooted tree selection. Unbiased tree selection is a non-trivial task. We use Prüfer sequences [10]. A labeled sequence of size $n - 2$ uniquely defines one of all possible trees of n nodes. Hence, selecting a uniformly random labeled sequence of length $n - 2$ gives each tree an equal probability of being chosen. An example tree is shown in Figure 2. For the generated tree, we select the root uniformly at random.

Initial State Selection. For the initial state of the algorithm computation, we select a legitimate state and then perturb it by a fault. The initial state selection for PIF also requires care: in the execution of the algorithm, certain states may appear more often than others. For example, in a tree of large size, in most of the states, the root is requesting. Indeed, once the root receives the feedback from one wave, it immediately starts the next one. Hence, the global states where the root process is idle are rare. Due to uneven occurrence of global state in a computation, the states are not evenly exposed to faults. In other words, faults are more likely to occur in states of the algorithm that happen more often. To generate an initial legitimate state, we randomly select the number of execution steps between zero and the number that is ten times the system size. We then start the algorithm from the legitimate initial state where all processes are idle and run the algorithm for the selected number of steps. Thus obtained state is used as the initial state for our experiment.

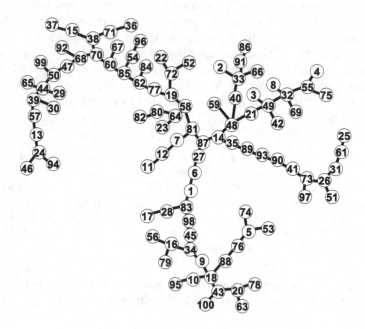

Fig. 2. Example random tree

Execution Semantics. To produce the computations of our algorithm we implement three classic algorithm execution semantics (also known as schedulers or daemons [3]): interleaving (centralized), powerset (distributed) and (maximally) synchronous. To produce the next state of the computation, for each execution semantics we evaluate each process to determine which actions are enabled. The execution semantics differ by the selection of enabled actions for execution. For *interleaving semantics*, we randomly select one of the enabled actions to execute. For the other two semantics the selection procedure is more complicated. The algorithm is proven correct in interleaving semantics only. Thus, the actions of two neighbor processes cannot be executed in a single step without compromising the correctness of the algorithm. The enabled action selection is as follows. We randomly choose one of the enabled actions. After that, we eliminate the neighbor process actions from consideration and repeat the selection. For *powerset semantics* the number of selected enabled actions is chosen at random between 1 and the total number of enabled actions. For *synchronous semantics* we continue the selection until no more actions remain.

Selection of Fault Model. To measure the robustness of our algorithm, we introduce faults in the initial state of the system. In a faulty process, the state is randomly selected from the range of possible states. Note that the fault may perturb the process back into the legitimate state. In other words, a fault may have no observable effect. This method sounds counterintuitive. However, it precludes the correct state of the process from influencing the faulty state. If every process is faulty, the resultant state is completely random.

Stabilization Time and Overhead. We focus on two stabilization metrics: stabilization time and processing overhead. The *stabilization time* is the number of execution steps it takes the algorithm to achieve the legitimate state. The

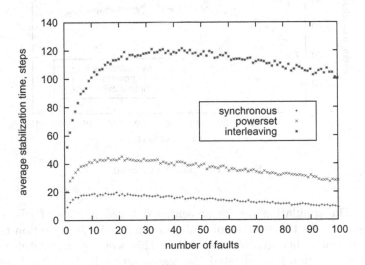

Fig. 3. Stabilization time

overhead is the number of extra action executions that the fault induces the algorithm to perform. To describe out definition of overhead, let us revisit a chain of processes from the root to a leaf. Even in an illegitimate state there is an non-empty sequence of processes that starts with the root and conforms to the definition of PIF legitimacy. Let us consider the longest such sequence. An action is counted as overhead if it is executed outside this sequence and not counted as overhead otherwise. In other words, the overhead actions are those that the algorithm executes before it achieves the legitimate state excluding the actions involved in the root request propagation. In the literature on snap-stabilization [1], for the interleaving execution semantics this metric is called wait time.

Experiments. We ran two sets of experiments. We used the system of 100 processes and varied the number of faults from one to 100. For each number of faults, we run $1,000$ experiments. In each experiment we selected a random tree and a random initial state for it. The generated trees had the average height of 21.6 ± 4.9 and the average number of children was 37.5 ± 3.1. As we varied the faults, we calculated the stabilization time and overhead for the three execution semantics. The results are shown in Figures 3 and 4. In the second set of experiments, we fixed the particular fault rate and varied the scale of the system. The results are shown in Figure 5.

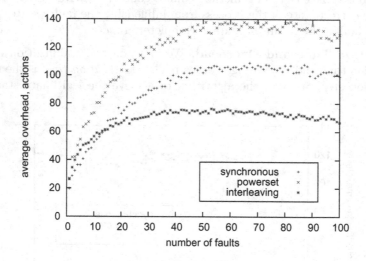

Fig. 4. Processing overhead

Analysis. The simulation results present a detailed picture of PIF fault recovery behavior. As the number of faults increases, the stabilization time and overhead rises and then gradually subsides. This seems counterintuitive. However, further investigation indicated the reason for such algorithm behavior. If a state is legitimate, a single fault may initiate a spurious wave that runs in the opposite direction to the legitimate wave. This happens, for example, if the reply propagates towards the root and the fault changes the state of one of the replying processes to idle. This may also happen if the wave propagates towards the leaves and the fault switches the state of one of the requesting processes to replying. Stabilization from such faults takes time proportional to the system size. Further faults tend to break up these long spurious waves and decrease stabilization time.

The overhead and stabilization time of parallel and power-set execution semantics is lower than that of the interleaving semantics. The execution semantics that allow greater concurrency lead to faster stabilization and thus lower overhead. As the scale set of experiments indicates, as the size of the system grows, the stabilization time grows linearly. Similarly to the first experiment set, the growth for the completely random initial state (100% fault rate) is lower than for the smaller number of faults. For 1% rate, the stabilization time is about twice the system size, while for 100% fault rate, it is about one and a half.

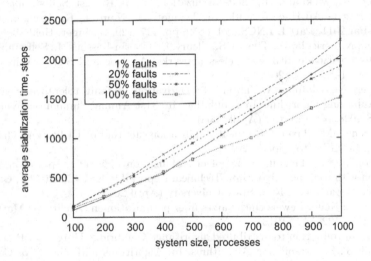

Fig. 5. Stabilization time dependence on system size. Interleaving semantics.

4 Conclusion

The performance of PIF is by no means exhaustive. For example, depending on its location, a fault affects stabilization of the algorithm differently. A fault closer to the root may be a lot more detrimental since it has greater potential to spread state corruption throughout the tree. Similarly, estimating the reliability of our simulation with confidence intervals would be useful. More extensive investigation of PIF performance could be the subject of further research.

However, performance evaluation of the stabilizing PIF algorithm in this paper makes a case for more extensive simulation studies of stabilizing algorithms.

We believe this greater engagement with applied algorithm study would benefit stabilizing algorithm design itself. Once the researchers observe the algorithm behavior in the case of practical faults, they will construct stabilizing algorithms that are specifically designed to counteract such realistic conditions. This will lead to greater applicability of stabilizing research overall.

References

1. Bui, A., Datta, A.K., Petit, F., Villain, V.: Snap-stabilization and PIF in tree networks. Distributed Computing 20(1), 3–19 (2007)
2. Dolev, S.: Self-Stabilization. MIT Press (2000)
3. Dubois, S., Tixeuil, S.: A taxonomy of daemons in self-stabilization. Technical Report 1110.0334, ArXiv eprint (October 2011)
4. Flatebo, M., Datta, A.K.: Simulation of self-stabilizing algorithms in distributed systems. In: Proceedings of the 25th Annual Simulation Symposium, pp. 32–41 (1992)
5. Johnen, C., Mekhaldi, F.: Self-stabilization versus Robust Self-stabilization for Clustering in Ad-Hoc Network. In: Jeannot, E., Namyst, R., Roman, J. (eds.) Euro-Par 2011, Part I. LNCS, vol. 6852, pp. 117–129. Springer, Heidelberg (2011)
6. Mitton, N., Séricola, B., Tixeuil, S., Fleury, E., Guérin-Lassous, I.: Self-stabilization in self-organized multihop wireless networks. Ad Hoc and Sensor Wireless Networks 11(1-2), 1–34 (2011)
7. Mullner, N., Dhama, A., Theel, O.: Derivation of fault tolerance measures of self-stabilizing algorithms by simulation. In: 41st Annual Simulation Symposium, ANSS 2008, pp. 183–192 (April 2008)
8. Nesterenko, M., Tixeuil, S.: Ideal stabilization. Journal of Utility and Grid Computing (JUGC) (to appear, 2012)
9. Nesterenko, M., Tixeuil, S.: Proof of stabilization of ideal propagation of information with feedback algorithm. Technical Report TR-KSU-CS-2012-1, Computer Science Department, Kent State University (April 2012)
10. Prüfer, A.: Neuer beweis eines Satzes über permutationen. Archiv für Mathematik Physik 27, 122–142 (1918)
11. Tel, G.: Introduction to distributed algorithms. Cambridge University Press (1994)
12. Tixeuil, S.: Self-stabilizing Algorithms. In: Algorithms and Theory of Computation Handbook, 2nd edn., pp. 26.1–26.45. CRC Press, Taylor & Francis Group (November 2009)
13. Wahba, S.K., Hallstrom, J.O., Srimani, P.K., Sridhar, N.: SFS [3]: a simulation framework for self-stabilizing systems. In: McGraw, R.M., Imsand, E.S., Chinni, M.J. (eds.) Proceedings of the 2010 Spring Simulation Multiconference, SpringSim 2010, Orlando, Florida, USA, April 11-15, pp. 172–181. SCS/ACM (2010)

Self-stabilizing End-to-End Communication in (Bounded Capacity, Omitting, Duplicating and non-FIFO) Dynamic Networks[*]
(Extended Abstract)

Shlomi Dolev[1], Ariel Hanemann[1],
Elad Michael Schiller[2], and Shantanu Sharma[1]

[1] Department of Computer Science, Ben-Gurion University of the Negev, Israel
{dolev,hanemann,sharmas}@cs.bgu.ac.il[**]
[2] Department of Computer Science and Engineering, Chalmers University of
Technology, Sweden
elad@chalmers.se[* * *]

Abstract. End-to-end communication over the network layer (or data link in overlay networks) is one of the most important communication tasks in every communication network, including legacy communication networks as well as mobile ad hoc networks, peer-to-peer networks and mash networks. We study end-to-end algorithms that exchange packets to deliver (high level) messages in FIFO order without omissions or duplications. We present a self-stabilizing end-to-end algorithm that can be applied to networks of bounded capacity that omit, duplicate and reorder packets. The algorithm is network topology independent, and hence suitable for always changing dynamic networks with any churn rate.

1 Introduction

End-to-end communication is a basic primitive in communication networks. A *sender* must transmit messages to a *receiver* in an exactly once fashion, where no omissions, duplications and reordering are allowed. Errors occur in transmitting packets among the network entities – one significant source of error is noise in the transmission media. Thus, error detection and error correcting techniques are employed as an integral part of the transmission in the communication network. These error detection and correction codes function with high probability. Still,

---

[*] Also appears as a technical report in [10].
[**] Partially supported by Deutsche Telekom, Rita Altura Trust Chair in Computer Sciences, Lynne and William Frankel Center for Computer Sciences, Israel Science Foundation (grant number 428/11), Cabarnit Cyber Security MAGNET Consortium, Grant from the Institute for Future Defense Technologies Research named for the Medvedi of the Technion, Israeli Internet Association, and Israeli Defense Secretary (MAFAT).
[* * *] Work was partially supported by the EC, through project FP7-STREP-288195, KARYON (Kernel-based ARchitecture for safetY-critical cONtrol).

A.W. Richa and C. Scheideler (Eds.): SSS 2012, LNCS 7596, pp. 133–147, 2012.
© Springer-Verlag Berlin Heidelberg 2012

when there is a large volume of communication sessions, the probability that an error will not be detected becomes high, leading to a possible malfunction of the communication algorithm. In fact, it can lead the algorithm to an arbitrary state from which the algorithm may never recover unless it is *self-stabilizing* [8]. By using packets with enough distinct labels infinitely often, we present a self-stabilizing end-to-end communication algorithm that can be applied to dynamic networks of bounded capacity that omit, duplicate and reorder packets.

Contemporary communication and network technologies enhance the need for automatic recovery and interoperability of heterogeneous devices and the means of wired and wireless communications, as well as the churn associated with the totally dynamic communication networks. Having a self-stabilizing, predictable and robust basic end-to-end communication primitive for these dynamic networks facilitates the construction of high-level applications. Such applications are becoming extremely important nowadays where countries' main infrastructures, such as the electrical smart-grid, water supply networks and intelligent transportation, are based on cyber-systems. Defining the communication network as a bounded capacity network that allows omissions, duplications and reordering of packets and building (efficient) exactly once message transmission using packets, allows us to abstract away the exact network topology, dynamicity and churn.

The dynamic and difficult-to-predict nature of electrical smart-grid and intelligent transportation systems give rise to many fault-tolerance issues and require efficient solutions. Such networks are subject to transient faults due to hardware/software temporal malfunctions or short-lived violations of the assumed settings for the location and state of their nodes. Fault-tolerant systems that are *self-stabilizing* [8,7] can recover after the occurrence of transient faults, which can drive the system to an arbitrary system state. The system designers consider *all* configurations as possible configurations from which the system is started. The self-stabilization design criteria liberate the system designer from dealing with specific fault scenarios, the risk of neglecting some scenarios, and having to address each fault scenario separately.

Related Work and Our Contribution. End-to-end communication and data-link algorithms are fundamental for any network protocol [25]. End-to-end algorithms provide the means for message exchange between senders and receivers over unreliable communication links. Not all end-to-end communication and data-link algorithms assume initial synchronization between senders and receivers. For example, Afek and Brown [1] presented a self-stabilizing alternating bit protocol (ABP) for FIFO packet channels without the need for initial synchronization. Self-stabilizing token passing was used as the bases for self-stabilizing ABP over unbounded capacity and FIFO preserving channels in [17,11]. Spinelli [24] introduced two self-stabilizing sliding window ARQ protocols for unbounded FIFO channels. Dolev and Welch [15] considered tolerating network errors in dynamic networks with FIFO non-duplicating communication links, and use source routing over paths to cope with crashes. In contrast, we do not consider known network topology nor base our algorithms on a specific routing policy. We merely assume bounded network capacity.

In [2], an algorithm for self-stabilizing unit capacity data link over a FIFO physical link is assumed. Flauzac and Villai [16] described a snapshot algorithm that uses bidirectional and FIFO communication channels. Cournier et al. [5] considered a snap-stabilizing algorithm [3] for message forwarding over message switched network. They ensure one time delivery of the emitted message to the destination within a finite time using destination based buffer graph and assuming underline FIFO packet delivery.

In the context of dynamic networks and mobile ad hoc networks, Dolev, Schiller and Welch [14,12,13] presented self-stabilizing algorithms for token circulation, group multicast, group membership, resource allocation and estimation of network size. Following [14,12,13], similar approaches to cope with constantly changing networks have been investigated [22] in addition to other fundamental problems such as clock synchronization [21], dissemination [18,20], leader election [19,6,4], and consensus [23] to name a few. In this paper, we investigate the basic networking tasks of end-to-end communication over the network layer (or overlay networks), that are required for the design of fundamental problems, such as the aforementioned problems considered in [21,22,18,20,19,6,4,23].

Recently, Dolev et al. [9] presented a self-stabilizing data link algorithm for reliable FIFO message delivery over bounded non-FIFO and non-duplicating channel. This paper presents the first, to the best of our knowledge, self-stabilizing end-to-end algorithms for reliable FIFO message delivery over bounded non-FIFO and *duplicating* channel.

Due to space limit, some of the proofs are omitted from this extended abstract and can be found in [10].

2   System Settings

We consider a distributed system that includes *nodes* (or processors), $p_1, p_2, \ldots, p_N$. We represent a distributed system by a *communication graph* that may change over time, where each processor is represented as a node. Two *neighboring* processors, p_i and p_j, that can exchange packets directly are connected by a link in the communication graph. Packet exchange between neighbors is carried via (directed) communication links, where packets are sent from p_i to p_j through the directed link (p_i, p_j) and packets are sent from p_j to p_i through (p_j, p_i), the opposite directed link. End-to-end communication among non-neighbor nodes, p_s and p_r, is facilitated by packet relaying from one processor to neighbors. Thus, establishing a (virtual) communication link between p_s and p_r in which p_s is the sender and p_r is the receiver. We assume the communication graph is dynamic, and is constantly changed, while respecting N as the upper bound on the number of nodes in the system. Packets are exchanged by the sender and the receiver in order to deliver (high level) messages in a reliable fashion. We assume that the entire number of packets in the system at any given time, does not exceed a known bound. We allow any churn rate, assuming that joining processors reset their own memory, and by that assist in respecting the assumed bounded packet capacity of the entire network.

The communication links are bidirectional. Namely, between every two nodes, p_i and p_j, that can exchange packets, there is a unidirectional *channel (set)* that transfers packets from p_i to p_j and another unidirectional channel that transfer packets from p_j to p_i. We model the *(communication) channel*, from node p_i to node p_j as a (non-FIFO order preserving) packet set that p_i has sent to p_j and p_j is about to receive. When p_i sends a packet m to p_j, the operation *send* inserts a copy of m to the channel from p_i to p_j as long as the upper bound of packets in the channel is respected. Once m arrives, p_j triggers the *receive* event and m is deleted from the set. The communication channel is non-FIFO and has no reliability guarantees. Thus, at any time the sent packets may be omitted, reordered, and duplicated, as long as the link capacity bound is not violated. We note that transient faults can bring the system to consist of arbitrary, and yet capacity bounded, channel sets from which convergence should start. We assume that when node p_i sends a packet, *pckt*, infinitely often through the communication link from p_i to p_j, p_j receives *pckt* infinitely often. We intentionally do not specify (the possible unreliable) routing scheme that is used to forward a packet from the sender to the receiver, e.g., flooding, shortest path routing. We assume that the overall network capacity allows a channel from p_i to p_j to contain at most *capacity* packets at any time, where *capacity* is a known constant. However, it should be noted that although the channel has a maximal capacity, packets in the channel may be duplicated infinitely many times because even if the channel is full, packets in the channel may be either lost or received. This leaves places for other packets to be (infinitely often) duplicated and received by p_j.

Self-stabilizing algorithms do not terminate (see [8]). The non-termination property can be easily identified in the code of a self-stabilizing algorithm: the code is usually a do forever loop that contains communication operations with the neighbors. An *iteration* is said to be complete if it starts in the loop's first line and ends at the last (regardless of whether it enters branches).

Every node, p_i, executes a program that is a sequence of *(atomic) steps*. Where a step starts with local computations and ends with a single communication operation, which is either *send* or *receive* of a packet. For ease of description, we assume the interleaving model, where steps are executed atomically, a single step at any given time. An input event can either be the receipt of a packet or a periodic timer going off triggering p_i to send. Note that the system is totally asynchronous and the non-fixed spontaneous send of nodes and node processing rates are irrelevant to the correctness proof.

The *state*, s_i, of a node p_i consists of the value of all the variables of the node including the set of all incoming communication channels. The execution of an algorithm step can change the node state. The term *(system) configuration* is used for a tuple of the form $(s_1, s_2, \cdots, s_N)$, where each s_i is the state of node p_i (including packets in transit for p_i). We define an *execution (or run)*

$R = c[0], a[0], c[1], a[1], \ldots$ as an alternating sequence of system configurations $c[x]$ and steps $a[x]$, such that each configuration $c[x + 1]$ (except the initial configuration $c[0]$) is obtained from the preceding configuration $c[x]$ by the execution of the step $a[x]$. We often associate the notation of a step with its executing node p_i using a subscript, e.g., a_i. An execution R is *fair* if every node, p_i, executes infinitely many steps in R. We represent the omissions, duplications and reordering using environment steps that are interleaved with the steps of the processors in the run R. In every fair run, the environment steps do not prevent communication, namely, infinite *send* operations of p_i of a packet, *pckt*, to p_j implies infinite *receive* operations of *pckt* by p_j.

The system is asynchronous and the notion of time, for example, when considering system convergence to legal behavior, is measured by the number of *asynchronous rounds*, where the first asynchronous round is the minimal prefix of the execution in which every node sends at least one packet to every neighbor and one of these packets is received by each neighbor. Thus, we nullify the infinite power of omissions, duplications and reordering when measuring the algorithm performance. Moreover, we ensure that packets sent are eventually received; otherwise the channel is, in fact, disconnected. The second asynchronous round is the first asynchronous round in the suffix of the run that follows the first asynchronous round, and so on. We measure the communication costs by the number of packets sent in synchronous execution in which each packet sent by p_s arrives to its destination, p_r, in one time unit, and before p_s sends any additional packet to p_r.

We define the system's task by a set of executions called *legal executions* (LE) in which the task's requirements hold. A configuration c is a *safe configuration* for an algorithm and the task of LE provided that any execution that starts in c is a legal execution (belongs to LE). An algorithm is *self-stabilizing* with relation to the task LE when every (unbounded) execution of the algorithm reaches a safe configuration with relation to the algorithm and the task.

The *self-stabilizing end-to-end communication* (S^2E^2C) algorithm provides FIFO guarantee for bounded networks that omit duplicate and reorder packets. Moreover, the algorithm considers arbitrary starting configurations and ensures error-free message delivery. In detail, given a system's execution R, and a pair, p_s and p_r, of sending and receiving nodes, we associate the message sequences $s_R = m_0, m_1, m_2, \ldots$, of messages fetched by p_s, with the message sequence $r_R = m'_0, m'_1, m'_2, \ldots$ of messages delivered by p_r. Note that we list messages according to the order they are fetched (from the higher level application) by the sender, thus two or more (consecutive or non-consecutive) messages can be identical. The S^2E^2C task requires that for every legal execution $R \in LE$, there is an infinite suffix, R', in which infinitely many messages are delivered, and $s_{R'} = r_{R'}$. It should be noted that packets are not actually received by the receiver in their correct order but eventually it holds that messages are delivered by the receiver (to higher level application) in the right order.

3   The End-to-End Algorithm

Dynamic networks have to overcome a wide range of faults, such as message corruption and omission. It often happens that networking techniques, such as retransmissions and multi-path routing, which are used for increasing robustness, can cause undesirable behavior, such as message duplications and reordering. We present a self-stabilizing end-to-end communication algorithm that uses the network's bounded capacity, to cope with packet corruptions, omissions, duplications, and reordering. We abstract the entire network by two directed channels, one from the sender to the receiver and one from the receiver to the sender, where each abstract channel is of a bounded capacity. These two abstract channels can omit, reorder and duplicate packets. We regard two nodes, p_s, p_r, as sender and receiver, respectively. Sender p_s sends packets with distinct labels infinitely often until p_s receives a sufficient amount of corresponding distinct acknowledgment labels from the receiver p_r.

For the sake of readability, we start describing the algorithm using large overhead, before showing ways to dramatically reduce the overhead. The sender repeatedly sends each message m with a three state *alternating index*, which is either 0, 1 or 2. We choose to discuss, without the loss of generality, the case of a message with alternating index 0, where $\langle 0, m \rangle$ is repeatedly sent in $(2 \cdot capacity + 1)$ packet types. Each type uses a distinct label in the range 1 to twice the capacity plus 1. Namely, the types are: $\langle 0, 1, m \rangle$, $\langle 0, 2, m \rangle$, ..., $\langle 0, 2 \cdot capacity + 1, m \rangle$. The sender waits for an acknowledgment of the packet arrival for each of the $(2 \cdot capacity + 1)$ distinct labels, and an indication that the receiver delivered a message due to the arrival of $(capacity + 1)$ packets with alternating index 0. The receiver accumulates the arriving packets in an array of $(2 \cdot capacity + 1)$ entries, where each entry, j, stores the last arriving packet with distinct label j. Whenever the receiver finds that $(capacity + 1)$ recorded array entries share the same alternating index, for example 1, the receiver delivers the message m encapsulated in one in-coming packet recorded in the array – this packet has the alternating index of the majority of recorded packets; 1 in our example. Then, the receiver resets its array and starts accumulating packets again, until $(capacity + 1)$ recorded copies, with the same alternating index reappear. The receiver always remembers the last delivered alternating index, *ldai*, that caused the reset of its array, and does not deliver two successive messages with the same alternating index. Each packet $\langle ai, lbl, m \rangle$ that arrives to the receiver is acknowledged by $\langle lbl, ldai \rangle$. The sender accumulates the arriving packet in an array of $(2 \cdot capacity + 1)$ entries and waits to receive a packet for each entry, and to have a value of *ldai* that is equal to the alternating index the sender is currently using in the sent packets in at least $(capacity + 1)$ of the recorded packets. Once such a packet set arrives, the sender resets its array, fetches a new message, m', to be delivered, and increments the alternating index by 1 modulo 3 for the transmission process of the next message, m'.

The correctness considers the fact that the receiver always acknowledges incoming packets, and hence the sender will infinitely often fetch messages. Following the first fetch of the sender, the receiver follows the sender's alternating index, records it in $ldai$, and acknowledges this fact. We consider an execution in which the sender changes the alternating index in to x, $x+1$, $x+2$, x (all modulo 3). In this execution, the sender is acknowledged that the receiver changes $ldai$ to $x+1$ and then to $x+2$, while the sender does not send packets with alternating index x, thus, the last x delivery in the sequence must be due to fresh packets, packets sent after the packets with alternating index $x+2$ were sent, and cause a delivery.

In the preceding text a simplified algorithm with a large overhead was presented – a more efficient algorithm is described in the following. The basic idea is to enlarge the arrays to have more than $n > (2 \cdot capacity + 1)$ recorded packets. Roughly speaking, in such a case the minority of the distinct label packets accumulated in the arrays are erroneous, i.e., packet copies that were accumulated in the network prior to the current fetch (maximum $capacity$). The other $(n - capacity)$ distinct label accumulated packets are correct. Thus, as we know the maximal amount of unrelated packets, we can manipulate the data so that the $n - capacity$ correct packets, each of length pl will encode, by means of error correcting codes, pl messages each of length ml, a length slightly shorter than n. The sender fetches a window of pl messages each of length ml, where pl is the maximal packet length beyond the header. The sender then uses error correcting codes so that a message of length ml is coded by a word of length n, such that the encoded word can tolerate up to $capacity$ erroneous bits. The pl encoded messages of length n are then converted to n packets of length pl in a way that the ith message out of the ml fetched messages is encoded by the ith bits of all the n distinct packets that are about to be transmitted. So eventually, the first bit of all distinct labeled packets, ordered by their distinct labels, encode, with redundancy, the first message, and the second bit of all distinct labeled packets, encode, with redundancy, the second message, etc. Fig. 1 shows the formation of the n packets from the pl messages. When the receiver accumulates n distinct label packets, the $capacity$ of the packets may be erroneous. However, since the ith packet, out of the n distinct packets, encodes the ith bits of all the pl encoded messages, if the ith packet is erroneous, then the receiver can still decode the data of the original pl messages each of length $ml < n$. The ith bit in each encoded message may be wrong, in fact, capacity of packets maybe erroneous yielding capacity of bits that may be wrong in each encoded message, however, due to the error correction, all the original pl messages of length ml can be recovered, so the receiver can deliver the correct pl messages in the correct order.

In this case, the sender repeatedly sends n distinct packets and the receiver keeps sending $(capacity + 1)$ packets each with a distinct label in the range 1 to $(capacity + 1)$. In addition, each of these packets contains the receiver's current value of $ldai$. The packets from the receiver are sent infinitely often, not necessarily as a response to its received packets. When the receiver accumulates n distinct label packets with the same alternating index, it recovers the original pl messages, delivers them, resets its received packets array and changes its $ldai$ to the alternating index of the packets that it just delivered. We note that these received packets must be different from its current $ldai$ because the receiver does not accumulate packets if their alternating index is equal to its current $ldai$. The sender may continue sending the n packets with alternating index $ldai$, until the sender accumulates $(capacity + 1)$ distinct label acknowledging packets with alternating index $ldai$. However, because now the packets' alternating index is equal to its current $ldai$, the receiver does not accumulate them, and hence does not deliver a duplicate. Once the sender accumulates $(capacity+1)$ packets with $ldai$ equal to its alternating index, it will fetch pl new messages, encode and convert them to n distinct label packets and increase its alternating index by 1 modulo 3.

The correctness arguments use the same facts mentioned above in the majority based algorithm. Eventually, we will reach an execution in which the sender fetches a new set of messages infinitely often and the receiver will deliver the messages fetched by the sender before the sender fetches the next set of messages.

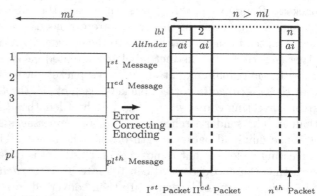

Fig. 1. Packet formation from messages

Eventually, every set of pl fetched messages is delivered exactly once because after delivery the receiver resets its packets record array and changes $ldai$ to be equal to the senders alternating index. The receiver stops accumulating packets from the sender until the sender fetches new messages and starts sending packets with a new alternating index. Between two delivery events of the receiver, the receiver will accumulate n distinct label packets of an identical alternating index, where $(n - capacity)$ of them must be fetched by the sender after the last delivery of messages by the receiver. The fact, which reflects such behavior at the receiver node, is that the sender only fetches new messages after it gets $(capacity + 1)$ distinct packets with $ldai$ equal to its current alternating index. When the receiver holds n distinct label packets with maximum capacity erroneous packets, it can convert the packets back to the original messages by applying the error correction code capabilities and deliver the original message correctly.

Algorithm Description. Algorithms 1 and 2 implement the proposed S^2E^2C sender-side and receiver-side algorithms, respectively. The two nodes, p_s and p_r, are the sender and the receiver nodes respectively. The Sender algorithm consists of a do forever loop statement (line 2 of the Sender algorithm), where the sender, p_s, assures that all the data structures comprises only valid contents. I.e., p_s checks that the ACK_set_s holds packets with alternating index equal to the senders current $AltIndex_s$ and the labels are between 1 and $(capacity + 1)$.

Algorithm 1. Self-Stabilizing End-to-End Algorithm (Sender)

Persistent variables:

$AltIndex$: an integer $\in [0,2]$ that states the current alternating index value

ACK_set: at most $(capacity + 1)$ acknowledgment set, where items contain labels and last delivered alternating indexes, $\langle lbl, ldai \rangle$

$packet\_set$: n packets, $\langle AltIndex, lbl, dat \rangle$, to be sent, where $lbl \in [1,n]$ and dat is data of size pl bits

Interface:

$Fetch(NumOfMessages)$ Fetches $NumOfMessages$ messages from the application and returns them in an array of size $NumOfMessages$ according to their original order

$Encode(Messages[])$ receives an array of messages of length ml each, M, and returns a message array of identical size M', where message $M'[i]$ is the encoded original $M[i]$, the final length of the returned $M'[i]$ is n and the code can tolerate $capacity$ errors

1 **Do forever begin**
2   **if** $(ACK\_set \nsubseteq \{AltIndex\} \times [1, capacity + 1])$ **then**
      $(ACK\_set, messages) \leftarrow (\emptyset, Encode(Fetch(pl)))$
3   **foreach** $pckt \in packet\_set()$ **do send** $pckt$

4 **Upon receiving** $ACK = \langle lbl, ldai \rangle$ **begin**
5   **if** $lbl \in [1, capacity + 1] \wedge ldai = AltIndex$ **then**
6       $ACK\_set \leftarrow ACK\_set \cup \{ACK\}$
7   **if** $capacity <| ACK\_set |$ **then begin**
8         $AltIndex \leftarrow (AltIndex + 1) \bmod 3$
9         $(ACK\_set, messages) \leftarrow (\emptyset, Encode(Fetch(pl)))$

10 **Function** $packet\_set()$ **begin**
11   **foreach** $(i,j) \in [1,n] \times [1,pl]$ **do let** $data[i].bit[j] = messages[j].bit[i]$
12   **return** $\{\langle AltIndex, i, data[i] \rangle\}_{i \in [1,n]}$

In case any of these conditions is unfulfilled, the sender resets its data structures (line 2 of the Sender algorithm). Subsequently, p_s triggers the *Fetch* and the *Encode* interfaces (line 2 of the Sender algorithm). Before sending the packets, p_s executes the *packet_set()* function (line 3 of the Sender algorithm).

The Sender algorithm, also, handles the reception of acknowledgments $ACK_s = \langle lbl, ldai \rangle$ (line 4 of the Sender algorithm). Each ACK_s has distinct labels, corresponding to already transmitted packets. On the reception of the $(capacity + 1)$ distinct label ACK_s, p_s keeps ACK_s in ACK_set_s (line 6 of the Sender algorithm), if ACK_s have the value of $ldai$ (last delivered alternating index) equals to $AltInex$ (line 5 of the Sender algorithm). When p_s gets an ACK_s packet $(capacity + 1)$ times (line 7 of the Sender algorithm), p_s changes $AltIndex_s$ (line 8 of the Sender algorithm). Afterwards, p_s does reset ACK_set_s and calls $Fetch()$ and $Encode()$ interfaces (line 9 of the Sender algorithm).

142   S. Dolev et al.

Algorithm 2. Self-Stabilizing End-to-End Algorithm (Receiver)

Persistent variables:
packet_set: packets, $\langle AltIndex, lbl, dat \rangle$, received, where $label \in [1, n]$ and dat is data of size pl bits
LastDeliveredIndex: an integer $\in [0, 2]$ that states the alternating index value of the last delivered packets

Interface:
$Decode(Messages[])$ receives an array of encoded messages, M', of length n each, and returns an array of decoded messages of length ml, M, where $M[i]$ is the decoded $M'[i]$. The code is the same error correction coded by the sender and can correct up to *capacity* mistakes
$Deliver(messages[])$ receives an array of messages and delivers them to the application by the order in the array

Macros:
$P(ind) = \{\langle ind, *, * \rangle \in packet\_set\}$

1 **Do forever begin**
2   **if** $\{\langle ai, lbl \rangle : \langle ai, lbl, * \rangle \in packet\_set\} \nsubseteq$
       $\{[0, 2] \setminus \{LastDeliveredIndex\}\} \times [1, n] \times \{*\} \vee$
       $(\exists \langle ai, lbl, dat \rangle \in packet\_set : \langle ai, lbl, * \rangle \in packet\_set \setminus \{\langle ai, lbl, dat \rangle\}) \vee$
       $(\exists pckt = \langle *, *, data \rangle \in packet\_set :| pckt.data | \neq pl) \vee$
       $1 <| \{AltIndex : n \leq| \{\langle AltIndex, *, * \rangle \in packet\_set\} |\} |$ **then**
       $packet\_set \leftarrow \emptyset$
3   **foreach** $i \in [1, capacity + 1]$ **do send** $\langle lbl, LastDeliveredIndex \rangle$

4 **Upon receiving** $pckt = \langle ai, lbl, dat \rangle$ **begin**
5   **if** $\langle ai, lbl, * \rangle \notin packet\_set \wedge$
       $\langle ai, lbl \rangle \in (\{[0, 2] \setminus \{LastDeliveredIndex\}\} \times [1, n]) \wedge | dat |= pl$ **then**
6       $packet\_set \leftarrow packet\_set \cup \{pckt\}$
7   **if** $\exists \, ! \, ind : ind \neq LastDeliveredIndex \wedge n \leq| P(ind) |: P(ind) =$
          $\{\langle ind, *, * \rangle \in packet\_set\}$ **then**
8   **foreach** $(i, j) \in [1, pl] \times [1, n]$ **do**
9   **let** $messages[i].bit[j] = data.bit[i] : \langle ind, j, data \rangle \in P(ind)$
10         $(packet\_set, LastDeliveredIndex) \leftarrow (\emptyset, ind)$
11         $Deliver(Decode(messages))$

The Receiver algorithm executes at the receiver side, p_r. The receiver p_r assures its data structure, namely, $packet\_set_r$, in do forever loop (line 2 of the Receiver algorithm). The receiver p_r audits: (*i*) the $packet\_set_r$ holds packets with alternating index, $ai \in [0, 2]$, except $LastDeliveredIndex_r$, labels (*lbl*) between 1 and n and data of size pl; (*ii*) the $packet\_set_r$ holds exactly one group of ai that has at least n elements. When any of the aforementioned conditions are falsified, p_r assigns the empty set to $packet\_set_r$. In addition, p_r acknowledges p_s by $(capacity + 1)$ packets (line 3 of the Receiver algorithm).

Node p_r receives a packet $pckt_r = \langle ai, lbl, dat \rangle$, see line 4 of the Receiver algorithm. If $pckt_r$ has data (dat) in the size of pl bits and $pckt_r$ has alternating index (ai) in the range from 0 to 2, excluding the $LastDeliveredIndex$ and $pckt_r$ has a label (lbl) in the range of 1 to n (line 5 of the Receiver algorithm), p_r puts $pckt_r$ in $packet\_set_r$ (line 6 of the Receiver algorithm). When p_r gets n distinct label packets of identical ai (line 7 of the Receiver algorithm), p_r forms the message from the packets (line 9 of the Receiver algorithm). Subsequent steps include the reset of the $packet\_set_r$ data structure and change of $LastDeliveredIndex_r$ to ai (line 10 of the Receiver algorithm). Next, p_r decodes and delivers the message (line 11 of the Receiver algorithm).

Correction proof. The correct packet exchange between the sender and the receiver requires coordination. The sender should wait after fetching a new message batch, i.e., executing lines 8 to 9 of the Sender algorithm, until the receiver delivers a message batch, i.e., executing line 11 of the Receiver algorithm. We describe the set of legal executions for correct packet exchange before demonstrating that the Sender and the Receiver algorithms satisfy these requirements in Theorem 1, which says that the studied algorithms implement self-stabilizing end-to-end communication (S^2E^2C) task.

Let a_{s_α} be the αth time that the sender is fetching a new message batch, i.e., executing lines 8 to 9 of the Sender algorithm. Let a_{r_β} be the βth time that the receiver is delivering a message batch, i.e., executing line 11 of the Receiver algorithm. With respect to the self-stabilizing end-to-end communication (S^2E^2C) task and the algorithms of the Sender and the Receiver, the legal execution set includes executions, R, that interleave the a_{s_α} and the a_{r_β} steps in a manner that matches the alternating index labels. Namely, after the occurrence of $a_{s_\alpha} \in R$ in which the sender fetches a new message batch, the step $a_{s_{\alpha+1}}$ should not occur before $a_{r_\beta} \in R$ in which the receiver delivers *that* message batch (Lemma 3). Similarly, after the occurrence of $a_{r_\beta} \in R$ in which the receiver delivers a message batch, the step $a_{r_{\beta+1}}$ should not occur before $a_{s_\alpha} \in R$ in which the sender fetches the next message batch (Lemma 4).

In addition, the a_{s_α} and the a_{r_β} steps should have matching alternating indices. The proof shows that the sender, p_s, increments its $AltIndex_s = s\_index_\alpha$ value on every a_{s_α} in a modulo 3 fashion, and the receiver, p_r, adopts s_index_α and deliver its message batch in step a_{r_β} after receiving at least $(n - capacity)$ packets that are tagged by s_index_α. Similarly, p_r acknowledges the received packets using the tag $LastDeliveredIndex_r = r\_index_\beta$, and then p_s proceeds to fetch a next message batch in $a_{s_{\alpha+1}}$ after receiving at least more than $capacity$ acknowledgments.

We note that the proof implies that within a constant number of asynchronous rounds, the receiver, p_r, receives an entire batch of n packets from its incoming abstract channel out of which $(n - capacity)$ packets are from the sender, p_s. This is true because: (1) we assume that when the sender sends a packet infinitely often through the abstract channel, the receiver receives the packet infinitely often, and (2) the proof shows that the sender does not stop sending its current batch of messages, before guaranteeing that the current message batch had arrived to the receiver, p_r, and p_r had delivered it. Moreover, analogous arguments to arguments (1) and (2) above imply the number of asynchronous rounds, in which the sender, p_s, receives an entire batch of $(capacity + 1)$ acknowledgments that at least one of them is from the receiver.

Lemmas 1 and 2 are needed for the proof of lemmas 3 and 4. Throughout we refer to R as an execution of the Sender and the Receiver algorithms, where p_s executes the Sender algorithm and p_r executes the Receiver algorithm.

Lemma 1. *Let $c_{s_\alpha}(x)$ be the xth configuration between a_{s_α} and $a_{s_{\alpha+1}}$ and $ACK_\alpha = \{ack_\alpha(\ell)\}_{\ell \in [1, capacity+1]}$ be a set of acknowledgment packets, where $ack_\alpha(\ell) = \langle \ell, s\_index_\alpha \rangle$. For any given $\alpha > 0$, there is a single index value, $s\_index_\alpha \in [0, 2]$, such that for any $x > 0$, it holds that $AltIndex_s = s\_index_\alpha$ in $c_{s_\alpha}(x)$. Moreover, between a_{s_α} and $a_{s_{\alpha+1}}$ there is at least one configuration c_{r_β}, in which $LastDeliveredIndex_r = s\_index_\alpha$. Furthermore, between a_{s_α} and $a_{s_{\alpha+1}}$, the sender, p_s, receives from the channel from p_r to p_s, the entire set, ACK_α, of acknowledgment packets (each packet at least once), and between (the first) c_{r_β} and $a_{s_{\alpha+1}}$ the receiver must send at least one $ack_\alpha(\ell) \in ACK_\alpha$ packet, which p_s receives.*

Proof. We start by showing that s_index_α exists before showing that c_{r_β} exists and that p_s receives ack_α from p_r between a_{s_α} and $a_{s_{\alpha+1}}$.

The value of $AltIndex_s = s\_index_\alpha$ is only changed in line 8 of the Sender algorithm. By the definition of a_{s_α}, line 8 is not executed by any step between a_{s_α} and $a_{s_{\alpha+1}}$. Therefore, for any given α, there is a single index value, $s\_index_\alpha \in [0, 2]$, such that for any $x > 0$, it holds that $AltIndex_s = s\_index_\alpha$ in $c_{s_\alpha}(x)$.

We show that c_{r_β} exists by showing that, between a_{s_α} and $a_{s_{\alpha+1}}$, there is at least one acknowledge packet, $\langle lbl, ldai \rangle$, that p_r sends and p_s receives, where $ldai = s\_index_\alpha$. This proves the claim because p_r's acknowledgments are always sent with $ldai = LastDeliveredIndex_r$, see line 3.

We show that, between a_{s_α} and $a_{s_{\alpha+1}}$, the receiver p_r sends at least one of the $ack_\alpha(\ell) \in ACK_\alpha$ packets that p_s receives. We do that by showing that p_s receives, from the channel from p_r to p_s , more than $capacity$ packets, i.e., the set ACK_α. Since $capacity$ bounds the number of packets that, at any time, can be in the channel from p_r to p_s , at least one of the ACK_α packets, say $ack_\alpha(\ell')$, must be sent by p_r and received by p_s between a_{s_α} and $a_{s_{\alpha+1}}$. This in fact proves that p_r sends $ack_\alpha(\ell')$ after c_{r_β}.

In order to demonstrate that p_s receives the set ACK_α, we note that $ACK\_set = \emptyset$ in configuration $c_{s_\alpha}(1)$, which immediately follows a_{s_α}, see line 9 of the Sender algorithm. The sender tests the arriving acknowledgment packet, ack_α, in line 5 of the Sender algorithm. It tests ack_α's label to be in the range of $[1, capacity + 1]$, and that they are of ack_α's form. Moreover, it counts that $(capacity + 1)$ different packets are added to ACK_set by adding them to ACK_set, and not executing lines 8 to 9 of the Sender algorithm before at least $(capacity + 1)$ distinct packets are in ACK_set.

Lemma 2 (proof appears in [10]). *Let $c_{r_\beta}(y)$ be the yth configuration between a_{r_β} and $a_{r_{\beta+1}}$, and $PACKET_\beta(r\_index'_\beta) = \{packet_\beta(\ell, r\_index'_\beta)\}_{\ell \in [1,n]}$ be* *a packet set, where $packet_{\beta, r\_index'_{\beta}}(\ell) = \langle r\_index'_{\beta}, \ell, * \rangle$. For any given $\beta >$ 0, there is a single index value, $r\_index_{\beta} \in [0, 2]$, such that for any $y >$ 0, it holds that $LastDeliveredIndex_r = r\_index_{\beta}$ in configuration $c_{r_{\beta}}(y)$. Moreover, between $a_{r_{\beta}}$ and $a_{r_{\beta+1}}$ there is at least one configuration, $c_{s_{\alpha}}$, such that $AltIndex_s \neq r\_index_{\beta}$. Furthermore, there exists a single $r\_index'_{\beta} \in [0, 2] \setminus \{r\_index_{\beta}\}$, such that the receiver, p_r, receives all the packets in $PACKET_{\beta}(r\_index'_{\beta})$ at least once between $c_{s_{\alpha}}$ and $a_{r_{\beta+1}}$, where at least $n - capacity > 0$ of them are sent by the sender p_s between $a_{r_{\beta}}$ and $a_{r_{\beta+1}}$.*

Lemmas 3 and 4 borrow their notations from lemmas 1 and 2. Lemma 4 shows that between $a_{s_{\alpha}}$ and $a_{s_{\alpha+1}}$, there is exactly one $a_{r_{\beta}}$ step.

Lemma 3. *Between $a_{s_{\alpha}}$ and $a_{s_{\alpha+1}}$, the receiver takes exactly one $a_{r_{\beta}}$ step, and that between $a_{r_{\beta}}$, and $a_{r_{\beta+1}}$, the sender takes exactly one $a_{s_{\alpha+1}}$ step.*

Proof. We start by showing that between $a_{s_{\alpha}}$ and $a_{s_{\alpha+1}}$, there is at least one $a_{r_{\beta}}$ step before showing that there is exactly one such $a_{r_{\beta}}$ step when $\alpha > 2$. Then, we consider a proof for showing that between $a_{r_{\beta}}$ and $a_{r_{\beta+1}}$, there is at least one $a_{s_{\alpha}}$ step before showing that between $a_{r_{\beta}}$ and $a_{r_{\beta+1}}$, there is exactly one $a_{s_{\alpha}}$ step when $\beta > 2$.

By Lemma 1 and line 8 of the Sender algorithm, in any configuration, $c_{s_1}(x)$, that is between a_{s_1} and a_{s_2}, the sender is using a single alternating index, s_index_1, and in any configuration, $c_{s_2}(x)$, that is between a_{s_2} and a_{s_3}, the sender is using a single alternating index, s_index_2, such that $s\_index_2 = s\_index_1 + 1 \bmod 3$. In a similar manner, we consider configuration, $c_{s_{\alpha}}(x)$, that is between $a_{s_{\alpha}}$ and $a_{s_{\alpha+1}}$.

Lemma 1 also shows that for $\alpha \in (1, 2, \ldots)$, there are configurations, $c_{r_{\alpha}}$, in which $LastDeliveredIndex_r = s\_index_{\alpha}$. This implies that between $a_{s_{\alpha}}$ and $a_{s_{\alpha+1}}$, the receiver changes the value of $LastDeliveredIndex_r$ at least once, where $\alpha \in (1, 2, \ldots)$. Thus, by $a_{r_{\beta}}$'s definition and line 10 of the Receiver algorithm, there is at least one $a_{r_{\beta}}$ step between $a_{s_{\alpha}}$ and $a_{s_{\alpha+1}}$.

To see that when $\alpha > 2$ there is exactly one such $a_{r_{\beta}}$ step between $a_{s_{\alpha}}$ and $a_{s_{\alpha+1}}$, we consider the case in which between $a_{s_{\alpha}}$ and $a_{s_{\alpha+1}}$, there are several $a_{r_{\beta}}$ steps, i.e., $a_{r_{\beta_{first}}}, \ldots, a_{r_{\beta_{last}}}$. In particular we consider the $a_{s_{\alpha-1}}, a_{r_{\beta-1_{last}}}, a_{s_{\alpha}}$, $a_{r_{\beta_{first}}}, a_{r_{\beta_{last}}}, a_{s_{\alpha+1}}$ steps and show that $a_{r_{\beta+1_{first}}} = a_{r_{\beta+1_{last}}}$. Let us assume, in the way of a proof by contradictions that $a_{r_{\beta+1_{first}}} \neq a_{r_{\beta+1_{last}}}$. We show that there is an $a_{s_{\alpha'}}$ step between $a_{r_{\beta+1_{first}}}$ and $a_{r_{\beta+1_{last}}}$.

By Lemma 2, between $a_{r_{\beta_{first}}}$ and $a_{r_{\beta_{last}}}$, there is at least one configuration, $c_{s_{\alpha'}}(x)$, for which $AltIndex_s \neq r\_index_{\beta-1_{last}}$, and at least one configuration, $c_{s_{\alpha''}}(x)$, for which $AltIndex_s \neq r\_index_{\beta+1_{first}}$.

Suppose that $\alpha' = \alpha''$. By $a_{s_{\alpha}}$'s definition, line 3 of the Sender algorithm and the function $packet\_set()$, the sender changes $AltIndex_s$'s value in step $a_{s_{\alpha'}}$ that occurs between $a_{r_{\beta+1_{first}}}$ and $a_{r_{\beta+1_{last}}}$. For the case of $\alpha' \neq \alpha''$, we use similar arguments and consider the sequence of all $c_{s_{\alpha'}}(x), c_{s_{\alpha''}}(x), \ldots$ configurations between $a_{r_{\beta_{first}}}$ and $a_{r_{\beta_{last}}}$ and their corresponding $AltIndex_s$'s values. By similar arguments to the case of $\alpha' = \alpha''$, any consecutive pair of

AltIndex$_s$ implies the existence of an a_{s_α} between $a_{r_{\beta_{first}}}$ and $a_{r_{\beta_{last}}}$. Thus, a contradiction.

Lemma 4 shows that between a_{r_β} and $a_{r_{\beta+1}}$, there is exactly one a_{s_α} step, and its proof follows similar arguments as the ones in Lemma 3.

Lemma 4 (proof appears in [10]). *Between a_{r_β} and $a_{r_{\beta+1}}$, the sender takes exactly one $a_{s_{\alpha+1}}$ step.*

Lemmas 3 and 4 facilitates the proof of Theorem 1.

Theorem 1 (S^2E^2C). *Within a constant number of asynchronous rounds, the system reaches a safe configuration (from which a legal execution starts). Moreover, following a safe configuration, Algorithm 2 delivers every new sent message batch within a constant number of asynchronous rounds.*

4   Conclusions

Self-stabilizing end-to-end data communication algorithms for bounded capacity dynamic networks have been presented in this extended abstract. The proposed algorithms inculcate error correction techniques for the delivery of messages to their destination without omissions, duplications or reordering. We consider two nodes, one as the sender and the other as the receiver. In many cases, however, two communicating nodes may act both as senders and receivers simultaneously. In such situations, acknowledgment piggybacking may reduce the overhead needed to cope with the capacity irrelevant packets that exist in each direction, from the sender to the receiver *and* from the receiver to the sender. Using piggybacking, the overhead is similar in both directions. The obtained overhead is proportional to the ratio between the number of bits in the original message, and the number of bits in the coded message, which is a code that withstands *capacity* corruptions. Thus, for a specific *capacity*, assuming the usage of efficient encoding, the overhead becomes smaller as the message length grows.

References

1. Afek, Y., Brown, G.M.: Self-stabilization over unreliable communication media. Distributed Computing 7(1), 27–34 (1993)
2. Awerbuch, B., Patt-Shamir, B., Varghese, G.: Self-stabilization by local checking and correction. In: FOCS, pp. 268–277. IEEE Computer Society (1991)
3. Bui, A., Datta, A.K., Petit, F., Villain, V.: State-optimal snap-stabilizing pif in tree networks. In: Workshop on Self-stabilizing Systems (ICDCS 1999), pp. 78–85. IEEE Computer Society (1999)
4. Chung, H.C., Robinson, P., Welch, J.L.: Brief Announcement: Regional Consecutive Leader Election in Mobile Ad-Hoc Networks. In: Scheideler, C. (ed.) ALGOSENSORS 2010. LNCS, vol. 6451, pp. 89–91. Springer, Heidelberg (2010)

5. Cournier, A., Dubois, S., Villain, V.: A snap-stabilizing point-to-point communication protocol in message-switched networks. In: 23rd IEEE International Symposium on Parallel and Distributed (IPDPS 2009), pp. 1–11 (2009)
6. Datta, A.K., Larmore, L.L., Piniganti, H.: Self-stabilizing Leader Election in Dynamic Networks. In: Dolev, S., Cobb, J., Fischer, M., Yung, M. (eds.) SSS 2010. LNCS, vol. 6366, pp. 35–49. Springer, Heidelberg (2010)
7. Dijkstra, E.W.: Self-stabilizing systems in spite of distributed control. Commun. ACM 17(11), 643–644 (1974)
8. Dolev, S.: Self-Stabilization. MIT Press (2000)
9. Dolev, S., Dubois, S., Potop-Butucaru, M., Tixeuil, S.: Stabilizing data-link over non-fifo channels with optimal fault-resilience. Inf. Process. Lett. 111(18), 912–920 (2011)
10. Dolev, S., Hanemann, A., Schiller, E.M., Sharma, S.: Self-stabilizing data link over non-fifo channels without duplication. Technical Report 2012:01, Chalmers University of Technology (2012) ISSN 1652-926X
11. Dolev, S., Israeli, A., Moran, S.: Resource bounds for self-stabilizing message-driven protocols. SIAM J. Comput. 26(1), 273–290 (1997)
12. Dolev, S., Schiller, E., Welch, J.L.: Random walk for self-stabilitzing group communication in ad hoc networks. In: PODC, p. 259 (2002)
13. Dolev, S., Schiller, E., Welch, J.L.: Random walk for self-stabilizing group communication in ad-hoc networks. In: 21st Symposium on Reliable Distributed Systems (SRDS 2002), pp. 70–79 (2002)
14. Dolev, S., Schiller, E., Welch, J.L.: Random walk for self-stabilizing group communication in ad hoc networks. IEEE Trans. Mob. Comput. 5(7), 893–905 (2006)
15. Dolev, S., Welch, J.L.: Crash resilient communication in dynamic networks. IEEE Trans. Computers 46(1), 14–26 (1997)
16. Flauzac, O., Villain, V.: An implementable dynamic automatic self-stabilizing protocol. In: ISPAN, pp. 91–97. IEEE Computer Society (1997)
17. Gouda, M.G., Multari, N.J.: Stabilizing communication protocols. IEEE Trans. Computers 40(4), 448–458 (1991)
18. Haeupler, B., Karger, D.R.: Faster information dissemination in dynamic networks via network coding. In: 30th Annual ACM Symposium on Principles of Distributed Computing (PODC 2011), pp. 381–390 (2011)
19. Ingram, R., Shields, P., Walter, J.E., Welch, J.L.: An asynchronous leader election algorithm for dynamic networks. In: 23rd IEEE International Symposium on Parallel and Distributed Processing (IPDPS 2009), pp. 1–12 (2009)
20. Jelasity, M., Montresor, A., Babaoglu, Ö.: Gossip-based aggregation in large dynamic networks. ACM Trans. Comput. Syst. 23(3), 219–252 (2005)
21. Kuhn, F., Locher, T., Oshman, R.: Gradient clock synchronization in dynamic networks. Theory Comput. Syst. 49(4), 781–816 (2011)
22. Kuhn, F., Lynch, N.A., Oshman, R.: Distributed computation in dynamic networks. In: ACM Symposium on Theory of Computing (STOC 2010), pp. 513–522 (2010)
23. Kuhn, F., Oshman, R., Moses, Y.: Coordinated consensus in dynamic networks. In: 30th ACM Symposium on Principles of Distributed Computing (PODC 2011), pp. 1–10 (2011)
24. Spinelli, J.: Self-stabilizing sliding window arq protocols. IEEE/ACM Trans. Netw. 5(2), 245–254 (1997)
25. Tanenbaum, A.S.: Computer networks, 4th edn. Prentice-Hall (2002)

Self-stabilizing Distributed Data Fusion

Bertrand Ducourthial*, Véronique Cherfaoui, and Thierry Denoeux

Lab. Heudiasyc UMR CNRS-UTC 7253
Université de Technologie de Compiègne France
Bertrand.Ducourthial@utc.fr

Abstract. The Theory of Belief Functions is a formal framework for reasoning with uncertainty that is well suited for representing unreliable information and weak states of knowledge. In information fusion applications, it is mainly used in a centralized way, by gathering the data on a single node before computation.

In this paper, a distributed algorithm is proposed to compute the neighborhood confidence of each node, by combining all the data of its neighbors using an adaptation of the well known Dempster's rule. Moreover, a distributed algorithm is proposed to compute the distributed confidence of each node, by combining all the data of the network using an adaptation of the cautious operator. Then, it is shown that when adding a discounting to the cautious operator, it becomes an r-operator and the distributed algorithm becomes self-stabilizing. This means that it converges in finite time despite transient faults.

Using this approach, uncertain and imprecise distributed data can be processed over a network without gathering them on a central node, even on a network subject to failures, saving important computing and networking resources. Moreover, our algorithms converge in finite time whatever is the initialization of the system and for any unknown topology.

This contribution leads to new interesting distributed applications dealing with uncertain and imprecise data. This is illustrated in the paper: an application for sensors networks is detailed all along the paper to ease the understanding of the formal approach and to show its interest.

1 Introduction

Algorithms for gathering data spread out over a network of communicating process units are well known [17,25,7]. However, in the real world, information is almost always tainted with various kinds of imperfection, such as imprecision, uncertainty, ambiguity, etc. Following [10], if a variable X takes its values in Ω (domain or *frame of discernment*), an item of information about X could be represented as a pair (*value, confidence*). The *value* component corresponds to a subset of Ω while the *confidence* component is an indication on the reliability of the item of information. Imprecision is related to the *value*, uncertainty is related to the *confidence*. For instance, when using the output of any disposal (sensor, algorithm, model, expert...), it would be preferable to distinguish between the following pieces of information: "the value is between 15 and 25", "the

---

* Corresponding author.

A.W. Richa and C. Scheideler (Eds.): SSS 2012, LNCS 7596, pp. 148–162, 2012.

value is probably 20", "the value is probably between 15 and 25". The first one is imprecise but certain, the second is precise but uncertain while the last is both imprecise and uncertain. The Set-Membership approach can represent the imprecision but lacks robustness while the Probability theory models aleatory uncertainty but does not express any notion of imprecision. The Theory of Belief Functions has been introduced by Dempster (1968) [5] and Shafer (1976) [18], and has been further developed by Smets (Transferable Belief Model) in the 1990's [23]. It is also known as Dempster-Shafer theory or Evidence. It is a formal framework for representing and reasoning from partial (uncertain, imprecise) information, by generalizing both the Set-Membership approach and the Probability Theory. Many applications in the field of data fusion are developed through belief functions framework [21]. However, even if the sources of data are distributed in space or in time, the proposed approaches are variant of centralized fusion methods [16].

As more and more sensors are present in our life (in smart-phones, vehicles, clothes, body, etc.), and as more and more networking connections appear between all these devices, a distributed approach for computing belief functions appear useful and is promising to many applications. In fact, such an approach would not be limited to information produced by sensors but could be applied to *any* imprecise and uncertain information, even on the distributed system itself. Recent works have been done in [3,2] where each node discounts information according to the distance and the age of the received message before to combine it with a local knowledge. The notion a data contamination due to the vehicular network context was taken into account for the choice of the combination rules. This work has been extended in [26]. In [15], a spanning tree is used for dealing with the loops of the network. In all these works, the network is supposed to be reliable.

Instead of gathering the information and then processing it in a central node, it would be very advantageous in terms of networking and computing resources to compute locally the belief functions. Generally, every node produces locally an information and then a local belief function (called in the following *direct confidence*). It would be very interesting to enrich such a confidence with information from other nodes. However in many cases, the result will depend on the position of the node and it is expected that node u should have a different result as compared to that of node v. In this (very common) case, computing the belief function locally using a distributed algorithm appears to be the best approach.

Nevertheless, distributed algorithms are subject to faults, especially when the devices are cheap and the underlying network opportunistic. We present in this paper algorithms able to compute a belief function on every node of a network subject to crash and transient faults. Our first algorithm computes on every node its *neighborhood confidence* relying on the direct confidences of neighbors. The second algorithm builds on every node its *distributed confidence*, taken into account all the direct confidences produced in the network, while favoring the closest ones. Our algorithms are self-stabilizing, so that they recover correct behavior after finite time starting from an arbitrary global state caused by a transient fault [8,9]. All these results are given for a simplified communication model relying on a simple `push` action, periodically called by the nodes. This can be implemented in an idealized WiFi network or in the classical shared-register model. The correctness of the algorithms is shown thanks to previous works on *r-operators* [12]. By modeling local algorithms with operators, global properties (termination, self-stabilization in different communication model) can be inferred by checking the algebraic properties of the operators [14,13,4]. However, for applying such a general scheme (and reusing generic proofs), the problem to be solved has to be modeled as an algebraic operator.

The contributions of our paper are threefold. First we explain how the processing of uncertain and imprecise data in a distributed system can be modeled by algebraic operators over a specific finite set, namely *vectors of discretized weights*. Second we propose two distributed algorithms for computing data fusion over distributed data in a network of unknown topology, the first one combining close information, the second one combining also remote information. Finally, we show that this second algorithm can be modeled as an r-operator (namely *discounted cautious* over the vectors of discretized weights), that satisfies the requirements for ensuring the self-stabilization of the distributed system.

Such contributions allows to process uncertain and imprecise distributed data without gathering them on a central node, even on a network subject to failures, saving important computing and networking resources. Moreover, our algorithms converge in finite time whatever is the initialization of the system and for any unknown topology. We believe that many applications can take benefit of this approach; we detail an application for sensors networks all along the paper to ease the understanding of the formal approach and to show its interest.

In Section 2, we present the distributed system we consider. Then, in Section 3, we explain how to model the processing of uncertain and imprecise data using local computations based on an adaptation of the Dempster'rule over a specific set (the vectors of discretized weights), and we present an algorithm for neighborhood confidence computation. In Section 4, we extend these results by presenting a distributed algorithm able to process all the uncertain and imprecise data of the distributed system. We show that such algorithm can be modeled as an r-operator (discounted cautious) and is self-stabilizing.

2   Self-stabilizing Distributed Systems

System. We consider a distributed system $\mathcal{S}$ composed of communicating computing nodes. Each node owns a local memory and a sequential computing unit so that it is able to run a local algorithm. Nodes are not synchronized. The local memory of node v is composed by its *private memory* $\mathtt{PRIV}_v$, an *incoming memory* $\mathtt{IN}_v$ and an *output memory* $\mathtt{OUT}_v$. The private memory of v contains its direct confidence and is regularly updated thanks to an external local disposal (eg. a sensor). The output memory will store the result of the local computation on v, namely its *neighborhood confidence* (Algorithm 1, Section 3) or its *distributed confidence* (Algorithm 2, Section 4). Communications are done through a simple atomic action called **push**: when a *sender* node u executes **push(m)**, the value m stored in its output memory is copied into the input memories of some *receiver* nodes $v_1, v_2, \ldots, v_k$.

We assume transient faults sometimes occur at the memories. To circumvent this problem, we will introduce *self-stabilization*.

Moving Topology. The receivers of a **push** action on v are not known from the sender v and do not know v. They are determined by the current topology of $\mathcal{S}$ and could be different from those of a previous **push** on the same node v. There is a *link* (u, v) between u and v if a data m pushed by u is received by v. Such a link disappears when a data m' pushed by u is not received by v. A link (u, v) may exist while the link (v, u) does not exist. The channel capacity is a single message.

In order our algorithms stabilizes, it is required that the topology remains stable for a period longer than the stabilization phase. We say that the topology of $\mathcal{S}$ *stabilizes* if it remains the same for further **push** actions (same links, that is, same receivers for a given sender). Such a topology is modeled by a directed graph $G(V, E)$ where V is the set of nodes and E is the set of current links. We denote by Γ_v^{01} the set of ancestors of v included v itself: $\Gamma_v^{01} = \{v\} \cup \{u \in V, (u, v) \in E\}$ and by Γ_v the set of all ancestors of v included v itself: $\Gamma_v = \{v\} \cup \{u \in V, \exists u_1, \ldots, u_k \in V \; s.t. \; (u, u_1), (u_1, u_2), \ldots, (u_k, v) \in E\}$.

Example. This communication scheme can be implemented on a wireless network with a link capacity of a single message: a push is implemented using a local broadcast followed by an idle period longer than the maximal communication duration (which is bounded in wireless protocols such as IEEE 802.11). Nodes moves and collisions add/delete links according to the communication range.

When the topology remains stable, this communication model can also be implemented through shared registers: a **push** by a writer u is simply a write into the register it shares with some readers $v_1, \ldots, v_n$. Then transformers can be used to extend this model to other communication models [1,11].

In the rest of this paper, we develop an example in the context of wireless sensor networks, where each node regularly push its result to potential neighbors. Nodes only own a local clock and may push their results at different frequencies.

Self-stabilization. A *configuration* of a distributed system $\mathcal{S}$ is an instance of the states of its processors and links. The set of configurations of $\mathcal{S}$ is denoted as $\mathcal{C}$. A distributed algorithm is a collection of local algorithms running on every node of $\mathcal{S}$. Processors actions change the global system configuration. An *execution* e is a sequence of configurations $c_1, c_2, \ldots$. Configuration c_1 is the *initial configuration* of execution e.

A *specification* is a predicate on executions that are admissible for a distributed system. A system *matches its specification* if all its possible executions match the specification. This paper considers problems whose solutions consist in computing a global result (static task); the specification can then be given in terms of a set of configurations. The set of configurations that matches the specification of static problems is called the set of *legitimate* configurations (denoted as $\mathcal{L}$).

Self-stabilization is defined through the concept of closed attractor.

Definition 1 (Closed Attractor). *Let $\mathcal{C}_a$ and $\mathcal{C}_b$ be subsets of $\mathcal{C}$. $\mathcal{C}_b$ is an attractor for $\mathcal{C}_a$ if and only if for any initial configuration $c_1 \in \mathcal{C}_a$, for any execution $e = c_1, c_2, \ldots,$ there exists $i \geq 1$ such that $c_i \in \mathcal{C}_b$. It is closed if for any $j \geq i$, $c_j \in \mathcal{C}_b$.*

In the usual (non-stabilizing) distributed systems, possible executions can be restricted by allowing the system to start only from some well-defined initial configurations. In stabilizing systems, problems cannot be solved using this convenience, since all possible configurations are admissible initial configurations.

Definition 2 (Self-stabilization). *A system $\mathcal{S}$ is called self-stabilizing if and only if there exists a non-empty subset $\mathcal{L} \subset \mathcal{C}$ of legitimate configurations such that $\mathcal{L}$ is a closed attractor for $\mathcal{C}$.*

3   Neighborhood Confidence Algorithm

In this section, we consider a network where each node owns a private data and we propose a distributed algorithm for computing a neighborhood confidence. After summarizing our approach, we explain how to build the domain of our variables (*vectors of discretized weights*). Next we introduce an adaptation of the Dempster operator for data combination. We then present our algorithm and its properties. We terminate by explaining how to exploit its outputs.

3.1   Neighborhood Confidence Principle

We consider a network where each node owns a private data. Such an information is regularly updated using a local external disposal (sensor, other algorithm...). As the data are uncertain and imprecise, instead of collecting on each node the data of its neighbors, the purpose of our algorithm is to evaluate a *neighborhood confidence* using the *direct confidences*, these lasts being computed by each node starting from their private data and their local external disposal.

Our scheme is general enough for covering many applications but to fix ideas, we illustrate it all along the paper using an example (marked with a vertical rule): a very simple weather forecast application. We assume that each node is able to measure the local atmospheric pressure and to determine whether it is decreasing, stable or increasing, allowing us to deduce a weather forecast. As the accuracy of the measurement is not perfect, we consider intervals instead of reals: each pressure measurement is an interval $I \subset \mathbb{R}^+$ and the pressure gradient ΔI computed with the two last measures I_k and I_{k-1} is then an interval of $\mathbb{R}$. Moreover, the sensor is not totally trusted because it could be damaged. Hence, we consider a confidence in the information, by affecting so-called *masses* to the sets ΔI and $\mathbb{R}$ in such a way that the sums of the masses is 1. The mass on $\mathbb{R}$ corresponds to the proportion of time when the sensor is not working correctly; the more the sensor is reliable, the lower is the mass on $\mathbb{R}$. Hence, thanks to its disposal, each node v obtains a result which can be interpreted as follows: "I have a confidence of 80% that the atmospheric pressure is increasing or stable, announcing a good weather". This is the *direct confidence* of node v.

The direct confidences are the local inputs of our algorithms. Starting from them, our first algorithm builds on each node v its *Neighborhood Confidence* by combining the direct confidence of v with those it receives from its direct ancestors. For this purpose, the confidences are stored as *vectors of discretized weights*; they are combined using an adaptation of the Dempster'rule.

3.2 Domain $\mathbb{K}$: Vectors of Discretized Weights

In this section, the domain on which operate our algorithms is introduced.

The state of belief of a node is expressed on a *frame of discernment* Θ using a *basic belief assignment* (BBA for short). Such a BBA can be represented by several means, the most common one being with a *mass function*. A mass function m^Θ is a mapping from the set of subsets of Θ, denoted $\mathcal{P}(\Theta)$, to the set of *masses* $[0,1] \subset \mathbb{R}$ such that $\sum_{X \subset \Theta} m^\Theta(X) = 1$. A set $X \subset \Theta$ such that $m(X) > 0$ is called *focal set*. If every focal set X satisfies $|X| = 1$, m is said to be Bayesian and it corresponds to a probability mass function. However, the main interest of the Theory of Belief Functions is to consider every subset X of Θ. The more a node is confident in X, the higher is $m^\Theta(X)$. If the empty set $\emptyset$ is not a focal set, the mass is *normal*. A mass on $\emptyset$ is used to model conflict between pieces of evidence on which m is based. If Θ is not a focal set, the mass is *dogmatic*. A mass on Θ is used to model lack of knowledge. The higher $m^\Theta(\Theta)$ is, the less the mass function m^Θ is informative. If $m^\Theta(\Theta) = 1$, the mass function is *vacuous*. Finally, a mass function is *simple* if it admits at most two focal sets including Θ.

In our example, the pressure gradient interval ΔI belongs to $\Theta = \mathbb{R}$. Each node then determines a simple mass function m^Θ such that $m^\Theta(\Delta I) = 1 - \alpha$ and $m^\Theta(\Theta) = \alpha$. The size of pressure measure interval (and then the size of ΔI) is related to the accuracy of the measure, while α is related to the reliability of the measure disposal (sensor).

Starting from a mass function m^Θ on the frame of discernment Θ, it is convenient to build another mass function on a coarser, finite frame of discernment Ω. Such a *coarsening* allows us to work on a finite set with simple interpretation. It will also limit the amount of data exchanged between nodes.

For our simple weather forecast example, we consider $\Omega = \{wet, cloud, sun\}$. Each node determines a simple mass function m^Ω depending on the position of $\Delta I \in \mathbb{R}$ regarding 0. If $\Delta I << 0$ (case **a** in Fig. 1), then $m^\Omega(\{wet\}) = 1 - \alpha$ while if $\Delta I >> 0$ (case **d**), then $m^\Omega(\{sun\}) = 1 - \alpha$. When ΔI is close to 0, there are some uncertainties: if $0 \in \Delta I$ (case **e** in Fig. 1), then $m^\Omega(\Omega) = 1$ because a node cannot determine whether the pressure increase or not; if

$0 < \Delta I$ (case c) then $m^{\Omega}(\{\text{cloud}, \text{sun}\}) = 1 - \alpha$, while if $\Delta I < 0$ (case b), then $m^{\Omega}(\{\text{wet}, \text{cloud}\}) = 1 - \alpha$.

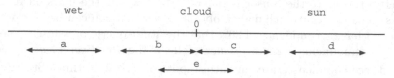

Fig. 1. Determining m^{Ω} from the comparison of ΔI with 0

Besides classical mass functions, a basic belief assignment can be represented by other functions, such as commonality and weights functions. Our algorithms work with weights, which are obtained from masses using commonalities [20] [6], as summarized in the following table.

mass function	commonality function	weight function
$m : \mathcal{P}(\Omega) \to [0,1]$	$q : \mathcal{P}(\Omega) \to [0,1]$	$\mu : \mathcal{P}(\Omega) \setminus \Omega \to \mathbb{R}^+$
$A \quad \mapsto m(A)$	$A \quad \mapsto q(A)$	$A \quad \mapsto w(A)$
$\sum_{A \subset \Omega} m(A) = 1$	$q(A) = \sum_{B \subset \Omega, A \subseteq B} m(B)$	$\mu(A) = \Pi_{B \subset \Omega, A \subseteq B} q(B)^{(-1)^{|B|-|A|+1}}$

In our example, we considered simple mass functions m^{Ω} defined by $m^{\Omega}(X) = 1 - \alpha$ for a single subset $X \subset \Omega$ and $m^{\Omega}(\Omega) = \alpha$. We then obtain $q^{\Omega}(\emptyset) = q^{\Omega}(X) = 1$ and $q^{\Omega}(Y) = \alpha$ for any other subset Y of Ω not included in X. Regarding the weight functions, we obtain $\mu^{\Omega}(X) = \alpha$ and $\mu^{\Omega}(Y) = 1$ for any other $Y \subsetneq \Omega$ (our approach works also with more complex mass functions).

Whenever the mass functions are not dogmatic ($m(\Omega) > 0$), the weights are strictly positive. Moreover, any separable mass function ensures that the weights are smaller than or equal to 1 and reciprocally. A mass function m is *separable* ([18] Chapter 4) if it admits a canonical decomposition in simple mass functions m_i so that the conjunctive combination of these simple mass functions is equal to the mass function itself: $m = \bigcirc m_i$. We introduce the conjunctive operator $\bigcirc$ hereafter. Hence, by restricting the considered mass functions to the set of separable non dogmatic normalized mass functions, we can represent them as weight functions from $\mathcal{P}(\Omega) \setminus \{\Omega, \emptyset\}$ to the interval $(0,1] \subset \mathbb{R}$. The data set we consider is then a set of values in $(0,1]$, one per subset of Ω except $\emptyset$ and Ω.

However, to ensure convergence in finite time, finite memory consumption and finite message size, we consider a discretization of $(0,1]$, denoted by $\mathbb{W}$: $\mathbb{W} \subset (0,1]$ with $|\mathbb{W}| \in \mathbb{N}$ and $1 \in \mathbb{W}$. We denote by $\epsilon \in \mathbb{W}$ the smallest element of $\mathbb{W}$.

As a conclusion, the data set of our algorithms is $\mathbb{W}^{2^{|\Omega|}-2}$, that is vectors of $2^{|\Omega|} - 2$ values taken into $\mathbb{W}$, which is a discretization of the weights that represent a BBA expressing a state of knowledge over a frame of discernment Ω. We call this set *vectors of discretized weights* and we denote it $\mathbb{K}$. Any vector of weights $\mathbf{w}$ in $\mathbb{K}$ can be coded with $(2^{|\Omega|} - 2) \ln(|\mathbb{W}|)$ bits. We denote by $\mathbf{w}_{\perp}$ (resp. $\mathbf{w}_{\top}$) the element of $\mathbb{K}$ composed only with weights ϵ (resp. 1).

In our example, supposing we discretize $(0, 1]$ up to the thousandth, as $|\Omega| = 3$, the vectors of weights require a size of 60 bits.

3.3 Operations on $\mathbb{K}$: Discretized Dempster Operator

The BBAs can be combined using some operators in the aim of forging a better knowledge from several sources of information. Given two mass functions m_1 and m_2 over the same discernment set Ω, the *conjunctive operator* $\odot$ builds a new mass function denoted $m_{1 \odot 2}$ by emphasizing the agreement between the sources that induced the BBAs, providing they are reliable [19]. The sources should be independent, that is, they provide distinct, non overlapping pieces of evidence [18]. The conflict between two BBAs m_1 and m_2 is given by $m_{1 \odot 2}(\emptyset)$. It can be spread over other sets when the conflict is ignored. The resulting operator is called *Dempster*'s rule, denoted by $\oplus$. Operators $\odot$ and $\oplus$ are commutative and associative and admit the vacuous mass function as neutral element.

Conjunctive operator	Dempster operator
$m_{1 \odot 2}(A) = \sum_{B \cap C = A} m_1(B) \cdot m_2(B)$	$m_{1 \oplus 2}(A) = m_{1 \odot 2}(A) / \left(1 - m_{1 \odot 2}(\emptyset)\right) \quad A \neq \emptyset$ $\qquad\qquad\qquad 0 \qquad\qquad\qquad\qquad A = \emptyset$

In our example, supposes that node u determines its direct confidence as a mass function m_{du} such that $m_{du}(\{\text{cloud}, \text{sun}\}) = 0.8$ and $m_{du}(\Omega) = 0.2$ (hence its disposal is reliable at 80% but the pressure gradient ΔI was close above 0). Supposes that a neighbor v of u determines its direct confidence as a mass function m_{dv} such that $m_{dv}(\{\text{sun}\}) = 0.7$ and $m_{dv}(\Omega) = 0.3$ (v trusts its disposal at 70% only but the pressure gradient is clearly above 0). Then, by combining these two BBAs, we find: $m_{du \oplus dv}(\{\text{sun}\}) = 0.7$. Now, if another neighbor w determines its direct confidence as a mass function m_{dw} such that $m_{dw}(\{\text{wet}, \text{cloud}\}) = 0.9$ and $m_{dw}(\Omega) = 0.1$, the belief in "sun" decreases to 0.538, but is not null because w does not fully trust its disposal.

When the BBAs are expressed with weight functions, the Dempster operator becomes a product: if μ_1 and μ_2 are two weight functions expressing BBAs on the same discernment frame Ω, then $\mu_{1 \oplus 2} = \mu_1 \oplus \mu_2$ is defined by: $\mu_{1 \oplus 2}(A) = \mu_1(A) \times \mu_2(A)$. Nevertheless, as the weights we manipulate belong to the finite set $\mathbb{W}$, we need to introduce a product operation on $\mathbb{W}$, that we denote by $*$. We then obtain a discretized Dempster-like operator denoted $\boxplus$ on $\mathbb{K}$ as follows. For any vector $\mathbf{w}_1$ and $\mathbf{w}_2$ belonging to $\mathbb{K}$, $\mathbf{w}_{1 \boxplus 2} = \mathbf{w}_1 \boxplus \mathbf{w}_2$ is defined by: $\mathbf{w}_{1 \boxplus 2}(A) = \mathbf{w}_1(A) * \mathbf{w}_2(A)$ for any subset A of Ω except Ω and $\emptyset$. By lack of place, the "discrete multiplication" $*$ is not defined here.

As a conclusion, in our first algorithm, the direct confidence expressed as vectors of $\mathbb{K}$ will be combined using the operator $\boxplus$, an adaptation of the Dempster operator using the operator $*$ for multiplying the weights of $\mathbb{W}$.

3.4 Algorithm 1: Neighborhood Confidence Computation

Now that we have defined the data set and the operator used to combine the data, the algorithm is simply described as follows. The direct confidence of each node is regularly updated by an external mean, as explained previously, and stored in the private memory $\mathtt{PRIV}_v$. It is coded (as all other variables) by a vector of discretized weights belonging to the finite set $\mathbb{K}$. The incoming memory $\mathtt{IN}_v$ on node v stores all data pushed by some ancestors since the last timer expiration. The output memory $\mathtt{OUT}_v$ contains the neighborhood confidence computed by v.

Nodes are not synchronized. Timers are given by local clocks and may have an unbounded drift. Upon timer expiration, each node computes its neighborhood confidence by combining its own direct confidence with those it has received since the last timer expiration, using operator $\boxplus$. It also pushes its direct confidence.

Algorithm 1: **Neighborhood Confidence, node** v

```
1    Upon timer expiration:
2       PRIVᵥ ← current direct confidence
3       OUTᵥ ← PRIVᵥ              ▷ Initializing the iterative computation
4       for each entry u in INᵥ do  ▷ Iterative computation of the output
5          OUTᵥ ← OUTᵥ ⊞ INᵥ[u]
6       end for
7       push( PRIVᵥ )             ▷ Sending the direct confidence to neighbors
8       Reset INᵥ
9       Restart the timer
```

The legitimate configurations of Algorithm 1 can only be defined when the topology is stable as well as the direct confidences stabilized. Indeed, in case the direct ancestors or their direct confidences vary, no stabilization of the outputs can be obtained. Assuming these conditions are fulfilled, the set of legitimate configurations $\mathcal{L}_1$ of Algorithm 1 is defined by:

$$\forall c \in \mathcal{L}_1, \quad \forall v \in \mathcal{S}, \qquad \mathtt{OUT}_v(c) = \bigcirc_{u \in \Gamma_v^{01}} \mathtt{PRIV}_u(c)$$

Proposition 1. *Algorithm 1 is self-stabilizing: it converges in finite time to a legitimate configuration of $\mathcal{L}_1$ after the last occurrence of a transient fault and the last modification of either the topology or the direct confidences (inputs).*

Proof. Let e be an execution of Algorithm 1 on the distributed system $\mathcal{S}$. Let $c \in e$ be the first configuration from which the topology and the inputs are stable and such that there is no transient fault from c in e. Note that there is no more crash faults from c as they affect the topology. As there is no more transient faults from c, the private memories do contain the direct confidences. Let $c' \in e$ a configuration reachable from c such that, for any node v, its timer has expired between c and c'. Then all the incoming memories have been purged (line 8). Let $c'' \in e$ a configuration reachable from c' such that, for any node v, its timer has expired between c' and c''. Since the topology is stable and there is no more transient fault, the direct confidence of each node u has been copied into the incoming memory of any node v such that u is a direct ancestor of v. Then any node v will compute $\bigcirc_{u \in \Gamma_v^{01}} \mathtt{PRIV}_u(c)$ that will be stored in $\mathtt{OUT}_v$. Hence, any configuration of e from c'' belongs to $\mathcal{L}_1$. $\square$

3.5 Exploiting the Output: From Discretized Weights to Decision

By considering focal sets of cardinality larger than one (e.g., $\{wet, cloud\}$), the Theory of Belief Functions generalizes the Bayesian Probability Theory and is well adapted for representing weak states of knowledge. Nevertheless, when a decision has to be taken, one need to go back to focal sets of cardinality one. For this purpose the result BBA (expressed as a vector of weights) is converted in a mass function m and is then mapped to a *pignistic probability* function P [22], defined by: $P(A) = \sum_{\emptyset \neq B \subset \Omega} (B) \frac{|A \cap B|}{|B|}$.

Applying to our example, the decision would be: Is the umbrella necessary? By computing the pignistic probability on our previous numerical example, we find for instance that $P(\{sun\}) = 0.84$ when considering only the direct confidences of u and v while it is equal to 0.645 when considering the direct confidence of w, which did not agree with u and v.

4 Distributed Confidence Algorithm

Starting from Algorithm 1, we present an algorithm that computes on every node its *distributed confidence*, by combining the direct confidence of *all* the nodes, not only those of its neighbors.

4.1 Distributed Confidence Principle

The algorithm presented in the previous section is able to compute the so-called neighborhood confidence of every node by combining the direct confidence of its direct ancestors. The algorithm relies on local exchanges of belief functions represented as vector of masses belonging to $\mathbb{K}$. However, the information produced by a node will never impact nodes at more than one hop in the network. Yet in many cases it would be interesting to take into account remote information.

For instance, in our weather forecast example, the neighborhood confidence is preferable to the direct confidence because it relies on several measures. However it cannot determine the weather by advance. To the contrary, if remote measures are taken into account in the computation, a node could be warn about a depression before it arrives on it (supposing the distributed algorithm converges more rapidly than the wind!).

In order to preserve the networking and computing resources over the network, it is preferable that each node computes its distributed confidence using the one computed by its neighbors instead of using the direct confidence of remote nodes. By the way, the modification to be done in Algorithm 1 is at line 7: each node v will push its output OUT_v, containing the result of its local computation, instead of its input IN_v containing its direct confidence.

7   **push**(OUT_v)

This has some consequences on the distributed algorithm, and the operator has to be changed at line 5. We first introduce Algorithm 2a in Section 4.2, that uses the *cautious* operator. Then we show it cannot support transient failures and we introduce Algorithm 2b in Section 4.3, based on the cautious operator and a *discounting* function. This last one is self-stabilizing.

4.2   Cautious Operator: Algorithm 2a

While it makes sense to use the Dempster operator to combine all the direct confidences, this is no more suitable with our algorithm modified at line 7 to push the output of each node. Indeed, whenever the network admits two distinct paths between nodes u and v, the direct confidence of u will be taken into account several times in the result built by node v. This problem is known as *data incest*. By the way, Algorithm 1 with the above mentioned modification at line 7 is only suitable for stable networks having a topology corresponding to a tree.

Besides the data incest, the algorithm would converge to the vector $\mathbf{w}_\perp \in \mathbb{K}$ (composed only with ϵ values) whenever there is a loop in the network because the multiplications by operator $*$ will converge to ϵ. As explained in [12], an idempotent operator is required for ensuring the convergence in a network with circuits.

In [6], an idempotent operator has been introduced for combining non dogmatic BBAs: the *cautious* operator denoted by $\oslash$. It is based on the *Least Commitment Principle*, which states that: "when several belief functions are compatible with a set of constraints, the least informative should be selected". When the BBAs are represented by weight functions, it is computed by taking the minimum of each component: $\mu_{1 \oslash 2} = \mu_1 \oslash \mu_2$ is defined by $\mu_{1 \oslash 2}(A) = \mu_1(A) \wedge \mu_2(A)$ for any $A \subsetneq \Omega$, where $\wedge$ denotes the minimum operator on $\mathbb{R}$.

Translated in $\mathbb{K}$, the discretization is here straightforward. We have, for any subset A of Ω with $A \neq \Omega$ and $A \neq \emptyset$, $\mathbf{w}_1 \oslash \mathbf{w}_2[A] = \mathbf{w}_1[A] \wedge \mathbf{w}_2[A]$, where $\mathbf{w}[A]$ denotes the component of the vector $\mathbf{w}$ corresponding to the subset of A, and $\wedge$ the minimum operator on $\mathbb{W}$. This operator is associative, commutative and idempotent on $\mathbb{K}$. It admits $\mathbf{w}_\top$ as neutral element (vector composed only with some 1). It solves the data incest problem.

In fact, besides solving the data incest problem, operator $\oslash$ also ensures the termination of the distributed computation. Let Algorithm 2a be the algorithm obtained from Algorithm 1 with line 7 replaced by push(OUT$_v$) and line 5 modified to use operator $\oslash$ instead of $\boxplus$. Let c_0 be the initial configuration defined by: for all nodes v in $\mathcal{S}$, IN$_v$ is empty and OUT$_v = \mathbf{w}_\top$. Assuming the topology is stable and the direct confidences stabilized, the set of legitimate configurations $\mathcal{L}_2$ of Algorithm 2 is defined by:

$$\forall c \in \mathcal{L}_{2a}, \quad \forall v \in \mathcal{S}, \quad \text{OUT}_v(c) = \oslash_{u \in \Gamma_v} \text{PRIV}_u(c)$$

As the cautious operator is a law of an idempotent semi-group, the following proposition holds (Proposition 4 in [14]).

Proposition 2. *Algorithm 2a stabilizes in a fixed topology starting from configuration c_0, assuming the direct confidences (inputs) stabilizes.*

4.3   Cautious and Discounting: Algorithm 2b

In contrast with Algorithm 1, Algorithm 2 stabilizes to a legitimate configuration only when it starts from the initial configuration c_0 (cf. Propositions 1 and 2). Indeed, an associative, commutative and idempotent operator leads to a self-stabilizing distributed algorithm only on networks corresponding to trees. For instance, consider a distributed system S in form of a loop composed of two nodes u and v and suppose that, due to a transient fault, the vector of weights $\mathbf{w}_\perp$ appears in the incoming memory of u. The next output of u will be $\mathbf{w}_\perp$, which will be sent to v. Both nodes will then converge to $\mathbf{w}_\perp$ whatever are their direct confidences (Proposition 7 in [14]).

On another hand, one may object that the legitimate configurations of Algorithm 2a are not always satisfactory. Indeed, it gives a single result per connected components of the network. When the information admits a local meaning (such as the weather forecast in our example), the result on a node u should differ from the result of a far node v except if all the nodes agree on their direct confidence. Hence, while it is useful to take into account remote information, all the nodes should not always converge to the same belief function.

We then introduce a discounting function $\mathbf{r}$, which is applied to each incoming data before the computation with the cautious operator (line 5). We call Algorithm 2b the algorithm obtained by modifications of the line 7 (for pushing $\mathtt{OUT}_v$) and of the line 5 as follows:

5      $\mathtt{OUT}_v \leftarrow \mathtt{OUT}_v \oslash \mathbf{r}(\mathtt{IN}_v[u])$

The function $\mathbf{r}$ is called a *discounting*; it is used to decrease the information in a given basic belief function. The choice of the discounting is application-dependent. Nevertheless, we impose two conditions on r. As $\oslash$ is associative, commutative and idempotent, it defines an order relation denoted $\prec_\oslash$ by: $\mathbf{w}_1 \prec_\oslash \mathbf{w}_2$ if and only if $\mathbf{w}_1 \neq \mathbf{w}_2$ and $\mathbf{w}_1 \oslash \mathbf{w}_2 = \mathbf{w}_1$.

Condition 1. *The discounting function $\mathbf{r}$ is an endomorphism of $(\mathbb{K}, \oslash)$: for any $\mathbf{w}_1$ and $\mathbf{w}_2$ in $\mathbb{K}$, $\mathbf{r}(\mathbf{w}_1)$ and $\mathbf{r}(\mathbf{w}_2)$ belong to $\mathbb{K}$ and $\mathbf{r}(\mathbf{w}_1 \oslash \mathbf{w}_2) = \mathbf{r}(\mathbf{w}_1) \oslash \mathbf{r}(\mathbf{w}_2)$.*

Condition 2. *The function $\mathbf{r}$ is expansive on $\mathbb{K}$: $\forall \mathbf{w} \in \mathbb{K} \setminus \{\mathbf{w}_\top\}$, $\mathbf{w} \prec_\oslash \mathbf{r}(\mathbf{w})$ and $\mathbf{r}(\mathbf{w}_\top) = \mathbf{w}_\top$.*

Condition 1 is justified as follows. Consider a path $u_1, u_2, \ldots, u_k$ in a stable network and suppose that the algorithm has converged (all the outputs of the nodes do not change any more). Then we have: $\mathtt{OUT}_{u_k} = \mathtt{PRIV}_{u_k} \oslash r(\mathtt{OUT}_{u_{k-1}}) \oslash \cdots$. Recursively, $\mathtt{OUT}_{u_{k-1}} = \mathtt{PRIV}_{u_{k-1}} \oslash r(\mathtt{OUT}_{u_{k-2}}) \oslash \cdots$. Since r is an homomorphism, we have $\mathtt{OUT}_{u_k} = \mathtt{PRIV}_{u_k} \oslash r(\mathtt{PRIV}_{u_{k-1}}) \oslash r^2(\mathtt{PRIV}_{u_{k-2}}) \cdots$. Hence, thanks to Condition 1, the output of a node takes into account every received direct confidence a single time but discounted accordingly to the distance from the sender. The second condition is required for discounting the received BBA compared to the local direct confidence. It is also required for the convergence (else every node v in a loop would converge to $\mathbf{w}_\top$).

In our example, the weights being discretized up to the thousandth, the application $\mathbf{r} : \mathbf{w} \to \mathbf{r}(\mathbf{w})$ defined by $\mathbf{r}(\mathbf{w})[A] = \min(1, \mathbf{w}[A] + 0.1)$ for any $A \subset \Omega$ ($A \neq \Omega$ and $A \neq \emptyset$) is convenient.

4.4   Self-stabilizing Property of Algorithm 2b

It is a remarkable result that the cautious operator along with a discounting is a strictly idempotent r-operator. Under certain conditions, the r-operators lead to self-stabilization of the global computation [12,14,13,4]. This is a convenient way to design new self-stabilizing silent tasks: by only checking algebraic properties of the operator modeling the local computation, global properties over the whole networks are ensured.

An *r-operator* is the law of an r-semi-group [12], which generalizes the idempotent Abelian semi-group. Let $(\mathbb{S}, \diamond)$ be a set endowed by an operator $\diamond$ (*magma*). It admits a right-identity element $e_\diamond$ if $\forall x \in \mathbb{S}$, $x = x \diamond e_\diamond$. It is *weak left cancellative* iff $\forall y, z \in \mathbb{S}$, $(\forall x \in \mathbb{S}, x \diamond y = x \diamond z) \Leftrightarrow (y = z)$. Let $r : \mathbb{S} \to \mathbb{S}$ be a mapping. Then $(\mathbb{S}, \diamond)$ is *r-associative* iff $\forall x, y, z \in \mathbb{S}$, $x \diamond (y \diamond z) = x \diamond y \diamond r(z)$. It is *r-commutative* iff $\forall x, y \in \mathbb{S}$, $r(x) \diamond y = r(y) \diamond x$. It is *r-idempotent* iff $\forall x \in \mathbb{S}$, $r(x) \diamond x = r(x)$.

Definition 3 (r-semi-group). *Let $(\mathbb{S}, \lhd)$ be a weak left cancellative magma admitting the right identity element $e_\lhd$, and let $r : \mathbb{S} \to \mathbb{S}$ be an endomorphism. Then $(\mathbb{S}, \lhd)$ is an r-semi-group if it is r-associative, r-commutative, r-idempotent with the application r.*

Proposition 3. *Let $r : \mathbb{K} \to \mathbb{K}$ a mapping satisfying Conditions 1 and 2. Let $\lhd$ the operator defined on $\mathbb{K}$ by $\mathbf{w}_1 \lhd \mathbf{w}_2 = \mathbf{w}_1 \oslash r(\mathbf{w}_2)$. Then $(\mathbb{K}, \lhd)$ is a strictly idempotent r-semi-group.*

Assuming the topology is stable and the direct confidences stabilized, the set of legitimate configurations $\mathcal{L}_{2b}$ of Algorithm 2b is defined by (we states $\mathrm{dist}(v, v) = 0$):

$$\forall c \in \mathcal{L}_{2b}, \quad \forall v \in \mathcal{S}, \quad \mathtt{OUT}_v(c) = \oslash_{u \in \Gamma_v} \mathtt{PRIV}_u(c) = \oslash_{u \in \Gamma_v} \mathbf{r}^{\mathrm{dist}(u,v)}(\mathtt{PRIV}_u(c))$$

Proposition 4. *Algorithm 2b is self-stabilizing: it converges in finite time to a legitimate configuration of $\mathcal{L}_{2b}$ after the last occurrence of a transient fault and the last modification of either the topology or the direct confidences (inputs).*

Proof. As $\oslash$ induces a partial order relation on $\mathbb{K}$ ($\prec_\oslash$ based on $\wedge$ component per component of vectors), we apply results of [13], proved for the shared register model. As soon as the topology stabilizes, the distributed system $\mathcal{S}$ is assimilated to a shared-registers system, with the difference that links are unforeseen (not known at the beginning, not known by the senders and the receivers when the system is stabilized). Moreover, as the topology was moving, any value could have been copied in the incoming memories. This means that, during the stabilizing phase, Algorithm 2b runs on an unknown directed topology starting from *any* configuration. Thanks to Proposition 4 and Condition 2, Theorem 9 of [13] applies and Algorithm 2b is self-stabilizing. □

Let k be the integer defined by $r^k(\mathbf{w}_\perp) = \mathbf{w}_\top$ and D the diameter of the stabilized topology. Supposing a synchronous system, the stabilization time is $O(k + D)$. In a system without transient fault, when starting from the good initial configuration c_0 (§ 4.2), the convergence time is $O(D)$.

In our weather forecast example, our discounting function $\mathbf{r}$ satisfies $k = 10$.

5   Conclusion

In this paper, two algorithms have been presented for dealing with distributed imprecise an uncertain data in a network. The first one builds the neighborhood confidence of each node based on the inputs of its neighbors. The second one extends this computation to the whole network: each input is taken into account while favoring close information. These algorithms are self-stabilizing, meaning that, they converge in finite time in a legitimate configuration after the topology and the inputs become stable.

These results rely on the r-operators introduced for stabilizing distributed computations and on the cautious operator introduced for dealing with data incest in the Theory of Belief Functions, completed with a discounting for ensuring the self-stabilization and discretized for ensuring the convergence in finite time.

We believe that a large set of applications, either fundamental or practical, could take benefit of this approach. In particular, our simple weather forecast application is more efficient than other schemes based on data gathering while allowing to process uncertain and imprecise data given by cheap sensors. It supports crash faults of sensors, network reconfigurations and transient faults affecting memories. It can be implemented on wireless sensors networks.

Future work will concern extension of this approach as well as the study of its applications.

References

1. Attiya, H., Bar-Noy, A., Dolev, D.: Sharing memory robustly in message-passing systems. Journal of the ACM 1(42), 124–142 (1995)
2. Cherfaoui, V., Denoeux, T., Cherfi, Z.-L.: Confidence management in Vehicular Network. In: Vehicular Networks: Techniques, Standards, and Applications, pp. 357–378, CRC Press (2009) ISBN: 9781420085716
3. Cherfaoui, V., Denoeux, T., Cherfi, Z.L.: Distributed data fusion: application to confidence management in vehicular networks. In: Proceedings of the 11th International Conference on Information Fusion (FUSION 2008), Germany (2008)
4. Delaët, S., Ducourthial, B., Tixeuil, S.: Self-stabilization with r-operators revisited. Journal of Aerospace Computing, Information, and Com. (2006)
5. Dempster, A.P.: A generalization of bayesian inference. Journal of the Royal Statistical Society 30, 205–247 (1968)

6. Denœux, T.: Conjunctive and disjunctive combination of belief functions induced by non distinct bodies of evidence. Artificial Intelligence 172, 234–264 (2008)
7. Dieudonné, Y., Ducourthial, B., Senouci, S.-M.: Design and experimentation of a self-stabilizing data collection protocol for vehicular ad-hoc networks. In: IEEE Intelligent Vehicle Symposium 2012, Madrid (June 2012)
8. Dijkstra, E.W.: Self-stabilizing systems in spite of distributed control. Commun. ACM 17(11), 643–644 (1974)
9. Dolev, S.: Self-Stabilization. MIT Press (2000)
10. Dubois, D., Prade, H.: Representation and combination of uncertainty with belief functions and possibility measures. Computer intelligence 4, 244–264 (1988)
11. Dubois, S.: Tolerating Transient, Permanent, and Intermittent Failures. PhD thesis, Université Pierre et Marie Curie, Paris, France (2011)
12. Ducourthial, B.: r-Semi-Groups: A Generic Approach for Designing Stabilizing Silent Tasks. In: Masuzawa, T., Tixeuil, S. (eds.) SSS 2007. LNCS, vol. 4838, pp. 281–295. Springer, Heidelberg (2007)
13. Ducourthial, B., Tixeuil, S.: Self-stabilization with path algebra. Theor. Comput. Sci. 293(1), 219–236 (2003)
14. Ducourthial, B., Tixeuil, S.: Self-stabilization with r-operators. Distributed Computing 14(3), 147–162 (2001)
15. Gasparri, A., Fiorini, F., Di Rocco, M., Panzieri, S.: A networked transferable belief model approach for distributed data aggregation. IEEE Transactions on Systems, Man, and Cybernetics, Part B (99) (2011)
16. Hall, D.L., Llinas, J.: Handbook of Multisensor Data Fusion. CRC Press (2001)
17. Segall, A.: Distributed network protocols. IEEE Trans. Inf. Theory 29(1), 23–34 (1983)
18. Shafer, G.: A mathematical theory of evidence. Princeton, N.J. (1976)
19. Smets, P.: The combination of evidence in the Ttransferable Belief Model. IEEE Transactions on Pattern Analysis and Machine Intelligence 12(5), 447–458 (1990)
20. Smets, P.: The canonical decomposition of a weighted belief. In: Int. Joint Conf. on Artificial Intelligence, pp. 1896–1901. Morgan Kaufmann, San Mateo (1995)
21. Smets, P.: Data fusion in the transferable belief model. In: Proceedings of. 3rd Intern. Conf. Information Fusion, Paris, France (2000)
22. Smets, P.: Decision making in the TBM: the necessity of the pignistic transformation. Int. Journal of Approximate Reasoning 38, 133–147 (2005)
23. Smets, P., Kennes, R.: The transferable belief model. Artificial Intelligence 66, 191–234 (1994)
24. Tel, G.: Topics in Distributed Algorithms. Cambridge International Series on Parallel Computation, vol. 1. Cambridge University Press (1991)
25. Tel, G.: Introduction to Distributed Algorithms. Cambridge University Press (1994)
26. El Zoghby, N., Cherfaoui, V., Ducourthial, B., Denœux, T.: Distributed Data Fusion for Detecting Sybil Attacks in VANETs. In: Denœux, T., Masson, M.-H. (eds.) Belief Functions: Theory & Appl. AISC, vol. 164, pp. 351–358. Springer, Heidelberg (2012)

From Self- to Self-stabilizing with Service Guarantee 1-hop Weight-Based Clustering*

Colette Johnen and Fouzi Mekhaldi

LaBRI, University of Bordeaux, CNRS. F-33405 Talence Cedex, France

Abstract. We propose a transformer building a silent self-stabilizing with service guarantee 1-hop clustering protocol $\mathcal{TP}$ of an input silent self-stabilizing 1-hop clustering protocol $\mathcal{P}$. From an arbitrary configuration, $\mathcal{TP}$ reaches a safe configuration in at most 3 rounds, where the following useful minimal service is provided: "each node belongs to a 1-hop cluster having an effective leader". During stabilization of $\mathcal{TP}$, the minimal service is preserved, so the clustering structure is available throughout the entire network. The minimal service is also maintained despite the occurrences of some external disruptions, called *highly tolerated disruptions*, denoted $\mathcal{HTD}$. $\mathcal{TP}$ reaches a terminal (also legitimate) configuration in at most $4 * S_{\mathcal{P}}$ rounds where $S_{\mathcal{P}}$ is the stabilization time of $\mathcal{P}$ protocol. Moreover, $\mathcal{TP}$ requires only 2 bits per node more than $\mathcal{P}$.

1 Introduction

Self-stabilization has a major limitation: during stabilization periods, a self-stabilizing protocol does not guarantee any property (except the eventual convergence) even if perturbations could be handled in a safe manner. Thus, self-stabilization is suited for distributed systems with intermittent disruptions, where the delay between successive disruptions is so large that the system can recover to a legitimate configuration providing its optimum service for some time. However, in large scale dynamic networks, the network topology changes very often, and the paradigm of self-stabilization is no more satisfying. Indeed, the system may be continuously disrupted, causing a total loss of service. As consequence, the availability and reliability of self-stabilizing systems are compromised when disruptions are frequent. To overcome these drawbacks, the paradigm *self-stabilization with service guarantee* has been recently introduced in [17,21,18].

A protocol $\mathcal{P}$ is self-stabilizing with service guarantee if: (1) $\mathcal{P}$ is self-stabilizing; (2) from an arbitrary configuration, $\mathcal{P}$ quickly reaches a safe configuration, where a safety property is satisfied, so a minimal service is provided; (3) the safety property (minimal service) holds during progress of $\mathcal{P}$ towards the optimum service (i.e., during stabilization despite actions of $\mathcal{P}$) and, (4) the safety property (minimal service) is also maintained despite the occurrences of some specific external disruptions, called *highly tolerated disruptions*, denoted $\mathcal{HTD}$.

---

* This work was partially supported by the ANR projects ALADDIN and Displexity.

A.W. Richa and C. Scheideler (Eds.): SSS 2012, LNCS 7596, pp. 163–178, 2012.

Whatever the occurrences of $\mathcal{HTD}$ disruptions, the useful minimal service is still provided. Whereas, other disruptions are handled by self-stabilization, i.e., after their occurrences, the system may behave arbitrarily, but it will quickly reach a safe configuration. Therefore, the service guarantee property is provided through both: fast recovering to the minimal service, and preservation of the minimal service despite the occurrences of $\mathcal{HTD}$ disruptions.

Clustering. This work addresses the transformation of a silent self-stabilizing 1-hop weight-based clustering protocol to a self-stabilizing with service guarantee one. The clustering of networks consists of partitioning network nodes into non-overlapping groups called clusters. Each cluster has a single head, called leader, that acts as local coordinator of the cluster, and eventually a set of standard nodes. In 1-hop clusters, the standard nodes are neighbor (at distance 1) of their leader. Clustering is found very attractive in infrastructure-less networks, like ad-hoc networks, since it limits the responsibility of network management only to leaders, and it allows the use of hierarchical routing. This is why numerous clustering protocols were proposed in the literature [1,2,6,11,15,17,20,21,22,24].

When the clustering is weight-based, each node of the network has a weight value that can change during time. The weight value represents the capability of nodes to be leaders. Hence, in weight-based clustering protocols, leaders are chosen according to their weight value in order to be the most suitable nodes in their clusters. Protocols proposed in [1,6,16,17,20,21] are weight-based.

Related Works. Self-stabilization with service guarantee is related to snap-stabilization [4], safe convergence [22] and super-stabilization [13]. The common goal of these approaches is to provide a desired safety property during the convergence phase, after the occurrence of one or several well defined events.

A protocol is *snap-stabilizing* if it always behaves according to its specification whatever its initial configuration. The safety property in snap-stabilization is *user-centric* [10] (not *system-centric* as in safe convergence, super-stabilization and self-stabilization with service guarantee approaches). It ensures that the answer to a properly initiated request by the protocol is correct. This approach is thus suited for service-oriented protocols, but not to silent protocols like clustering protocols. The *safe convergence* ensures that (1) the system quickly converges to a safe configuration, and (2) the safety property stays satisfied during the stabilization under protocol actions. However, external disruptions are not handled in safe convergence. Let us study the self-stabilizing with service guarantee protocol [18] building the knowledge of 1-hop neighbor clusters. The stabilization time of this protocol is 4 rounds as the time to reach a safe configuration. In this case, the safe convergence contributes nothing compared to the self-stabilization (they become equivalents). The main specifity of [18] is the maintain of safety property in spite of disruptions made by clustering protocol (i.e., reconstruction of clusters). A *super-stabilizing* protocol guarantees that (1) starting from a legitimate configuration, a safety property is preserved after only one specific topology change (of a set $\mathcal{HTD}$), and (2) the safety property is maintained during recovering to a legitimate configuration assuming that no more topology change occurs during stabilization phase. Self-stabilization with service guarantee provides and maintains the safety property even before stabilization, unlike super-stabilization. For example, the super-stabilizing coloring algorithm [13] stabilizes in $O(N)$ rounds (N is the number of nodes), but from an illegitimate configuration it does not quickly converge to a safe configuration. Furthermore, a self-stabilizing with service guarantee protocol preserves the safety property in spite of several $\mathcal{HTD}$ disruptions that are simultaneous or not. Whereas, a super-stabilizing protocol handles only one disruption: if disruptions occur in bursts, super-stabilizing protocol handles them as a self-stabilizing protocol.

Some transformers related to previous approaches were proposed. In [23], the proposed protocol transforms almost all non self-stabilizing protocols to self-stabilizing one. The method proposed in [8] transforms a self-stabilizing wave protocol with a unique initiator to a snap-stabilizing one. In [7], authors propose a snap-stabilizing version of four fundamental protocols: reset, snapshot, leader election, termination detection, based on a snap-stabilizing PIF (Propagation of Information with Feedback) algorithm. Thereafter, they propose a method to provide a snap-stabilizing version of any protocol. In [3], the proposed method transforms a self-stabilizing protocol constructing spanning tree and optimizing any arbitrary tree metric to a loop-free super-stabilizing protocol.

Motivation and Contributions. The stabilization time of weight-based clustering protocols is proportional to the network diameter [21]. Nevertheless, a crucial challenge of ad-hoc networks is the fast establishment and maintenance of clustering structure in spite of topological changes like node/link failures.

In this paper, we propose a generic scheme to transform a silent self-stabilizing 1-hop weight-based clustering protocol $\mathcal{P}$, to a silent self-stabilizing with service guarantee protocol, called transformed protocol $\mathcal{TP}$. $\mathcal{TP}$ quickly reaches, in at most 3 rounds, a safe configuration from any initial one, and thereafter it reaches a terminal configuration in at most $4 * S_\mathcal{P}$ rounds where $S_\mathcal{P}$ is stabilization time of $\mathcal{P}$ protocol. In a safe configuration, each standard node belongs to a cluster, and each cluster has an effectual leader; so the clustering structure is available throughout the entire network. This safety property holds during stabilization phases even despite the occurrence of $\mathcal{HTD}$ disruptions (Definition 5). Moreover, compared to $\mathcal{P}$ protocol, $\mathcal{TP}$ requires only 2 extra bits per node.

Paper Outline. The rest of the paper is organised as follows. In section 2, communication and computation models are defined, and the general form of original protocol $\mathcal{P}$ is described. Transformed protocol $\mathcal{TP}$ is presented in section 3. In sections 4 , 5 and 6, we give the sketch proof of service guarantee, correctness and termination of $\mathcal{TP}$ protocol. Finally, in section 7, the memory space and time complexity of $\mathcal{TP}$ protocol as well as the futur works are discussed.

2   Model and Concepts

A distributed system S is an undirected graph $G = (V, E)$ where vertex set V is the set of (mobile) nodes and edge set E is the set of communication links.

A link $(u, v) \in E$ if and only if u and v can directly communicate (links are bidirectional); so, u and v are neighbors. We note by N_v the set of v's neighbors: $N_v = \{u \in V \mid (u, v) \in E\}$. Furthermore, every node v in the network is assigned a unique identifier, and a weight value w_v (a real number). The weight value of a node can increase or decrease during time reflecting changes in the node's state. For the sake of simplicity, we assume that nodes weight are different (the tie in node's weight could be broken using nodes identifier id).

We use the *local shared memory model* introduced in [12]. Each node v maintains a set of local variables such that v can read its own variables and those of its neighbors, but it can modify only its variables. The *state* of a node is defined by the values of its local variables. The union of states of all nodes determines the *configuration* of the system. The *program* of each node is a set of *rules*. Each rule has the form: $Rule_i :< Guard_i > \longrightarrow < Action_i >$. The *guard* of a v's rule is a Boolean expression involving the state of the node v, and those of its neighbors. The *action* of a v's rule updates v's state. A rule can be executed only if it is *enabled*, i.e., its guard evaluates to true. A node is said to be enabled if at least one of its rules is enabled. In a *terminal configuration*, no node is enabled.

Nodes are not synchronized; nevertheless several nodes may perform their actions at the same time. During a *computation step* $c_i \to c_{i+1}$, one or several enabled nodes perform an enabled action and the system reaches the configuration c_{i+1} from c_i. A *computation* e is a sequence of configurations $e = c_0, c_1, ..., c_i, ...$, where c_{i+1} is reached from c_i by one computation step: $\forall i \geqslant 0, c_i \to c_{i+1}$. We say that a computation e is *maximal* if it is infinite, or if it reaches a terminal configuration. A computation is *weakly fair*, if for any node v that is always enabled along this computation, it eventually performs an action. In this paper, we study only weakly fair computations. We note by $\mathcal{C}$ the set of all possible configurations, and by $\mathcal{E}$ the set of all weakly fair computations. The set of weakly fair computations starting from a particular configuration $c \in \mathcal{C}$ is denoted $\mathcal{E}_c$. $\mathcal{E}_A$ denotes the set of weakly fair computations where the initial configuration belongs to the set of configurations $A \subset \mathcal{C}$.

We say that a node v is *neutralized* during a computation step cs $c_i \to c_{i+1}$, if v is enabled in c_i and disabled in c_{i+1}, but it did not execute any action during cs. The neutralization of a node v happens when one v's neighbor changes its state during cs, and after this change, the guard of all v's actions are not verified.

We use the *round* notion to measure the time complexity. The first round of a computation $e = c_1, ..., c_j, ...$ is the minimal prefix $e_1 = c_1, ..., c_j$, such that every enabled node v in c_1 either executes a rule or it is neutralized during a computation step of e_1. Let e_2 be the suffix of e such that $e = e_1 e_2$. The second round of e is the first round of e_2, and so on.

Definition 1 (Attractor). *Let B_1 and B_2 be subsets of $\mathcal{C}$. B_2 is an attractor from B_1, if and only if the following conditions hold:*

- **Convergence:** $\forall c \in B_1$, *If* $(\mathcal{E}_c = \emptyset)$ *then* $c \in B_2$
  $$\forall e \in \mathcal{E}_{B_1}(e = c_1, c_2, ...), \exists i \geqslant 1, c_i \in B_2$$
- **Closure:** $\forall e \in \mathcal{E}_{B_2}(e = c_1, ...), \forall i \geqslant 1 : c_i \in B_2.$

Definition 2 (Self-stabilization). *A distributed system S is self-stabilizing if and only if there exists a non-empty set $\mathcal{L} \subseteq \mathcal{C}$, called set of legitimate configurations, such that the following conditions hold:*

- *$\mathcal{L}$ is an attractor from $\mathcal{C}$.*
- *Configurations of $\mathcal{L}$ match the specification problem.*

A self-stabilizing protocol is *silent* if once the system is stabilized, no node modifies its state.

Stabilization time. The stabilization time is the number of disjoint rounds of a computation reaching a legitimate configuration from any initial one.

Definition 3 (Self-stabilization with service guarantee). *Let $\mathcal{SP}$ be the safety predicate that stipulates the minimal service (safety property), and $\mathcal{HTD}$ be the set of highly tolerated disruptions. A self-stabilizing system has service guarantee despite $\mathcal{HTD}$ if and only if the set of configurations satisfying $\mathcal{SP}$ is:*

- *An attractor from $\mathcal{C}$.*
- *Closed under any disruption of $\mathcal{HTD}$.*

2.1 The Original Protocol $\mathcal{P}$

We are placing in the context of clustering protocols where nodes proclaim themselves leaders like [1,2,6,11,15,17,20,21,24], and not in the context of protocols where leaders are nominated by other nodes like [5,9].

The general form of the original silent self-stabilizing weight-based 1-hop clustering protocol $\mathcal{P}$ is described in Protocol 1. Such protocol has four class of rules. The Election, Affiliation and Resignation rules for a node v update at least the head identity of v's cluster (i.e., Head(v)). Whereas the Complementary rules (named $Complement(v)$) update other variables if there exist.

Protocol 1. The original protocol $\mathcal{P}$ on node v

Output variables
- Head(v) $\in N_v \cup \{v\}$; Head(v) returns the head's identity of the v's cluster.
- NextHead(v) $\in N_v \cup \{v\}$; NextHead(v) returns the identity of head that will be chosen by the affiliation or resignation rule if it is enabled. It return v if the Election rule is enabled. Otherwise, it returns Head(v).

Rules
   Election(v) : GE(v) $\longrightarrow$ AE(v); The election rule
   Affiliation(v) : GA(v) $\longrightarrow$ AA(v); The affiliation rule
   Resignation(v) : GR(v) $\longrightarrow$ AR(v); The resignation rule
   Complement(v) : GC(v) $\longrightarrow$ AC(v); Complementary rules if there exist

---

The variable Head(v) indicates the identity of v's head and, whether v is a leader (i.e., Head(v) $= v$) or v is a standard node (i.e., Head(v) $\neq v$).

Note that rules of $\mathcal{P}$ protocol are not necessarily explicitly written in this form, but they can be distinguished according to how they update Head(v) variable. Any rule does not updating Head(v) is classified as Complementary rule.

Election rule is enabled only by standard nodes verifying the election guard GE (1st Precondition). Upon execution of Election rule, the standard node becomes leader. Conversely, Resignation rule is enabled only by leaders verifying the resignation guard GR (2nd Precondition), and after execution of Resignation rule, the leader chooses a new head and it becomes a standard node. Nodes having Affiliation rule enabled are standard nodes verifying the affiliation guard GA (3rd Precondition). By performing this rule, the standard node changes its cluster. Both actions AE, AR and AA are called *clustering actions* because they modify $\text{Head}(v)$ and they set it to $\text{NextHead}(v)$. When Election rule is enabled, then $\text{NextHead}(v) = v$ (1st Precondition). If Resignation or Affiliation rule is enabled, then $\text{NextHead}(v) \neq v$ (2nd and 3rd Preconditions), $\text{NextHead}(v) \neq \text{Head}(v)$ and $\text{NextHead}(v)$ is currently leader (4th Precondition).

$\mathcal{P}$ is weight-based clustering protocol. In weight-based clustering protocols, each node v has a dynamic input value, its weight named w_v, representing its suitability to be leader. Such protocols select nodes having a higher weight to be leader, and try as soon as possible to assign standard nodes to the best leader in their neighborhood. Thus, the value of NextHead in such protocols depends intrinsically on the weight of nodes (see 5th Precondition on $\mathcal{P}$).

The fact that $\mathcal{P}$ is self-stabilizing and weight-based, is summarized by the following Preconditions 1-5, whereas Preconditions 6-7 are consequences of silence property of $\mathcal{P}$. The formal description of these preconditions in follows facilitates the proof of service guarantee, correctness and termination of $\mathcal{TP}$ protocol.

1. $\text{GE}(v) \Rightarrow \text{Head}(v) \neq v \wedge \text{NextHead}(v) = v$

2. $\text{GR}(v) \Rightarrow \text{Head}(v) = v \wedge \text{NextHead}(v) \neq v$

3. $\text{GA}(v) \Rightarrow \text{Head}(v) \neq v \wedge \text{NextHead}(v) \neq v$

4. $\text{GA}(v) \vee \text{GR}(v) \Rightarrow$

$$\text{NextHead}(v) \neq \text{Head}(v) \wedge \text{Head}(\text{NextHead}(v)) = \text{NextHead}(v) \quad (1)$$

5. The function updating NextHead is based on node's weight,

$$(\text{NextHead}(v) \neq \text{Head}(v)) \Rightarrow (\text{NextHead}(v) = v) \vee (w_{\text{NextHead}(v)} > w_v) \quad (2)$$

6. Along a computation where a standard node v never changes of cluster (so, its $\text{Head}(v)$ value), v performs a finite number of time Complementary rules.

7. Along a computation where the cluster of a leader v does not change, v performs a finite number of time Complementary rules.

3   The Transformed Protocol $\mathcal{TP}$

During stabilization of $\mathcal{P}$ protocol, a node may not belong to a cluster. One goal of $\mathcal{TP}$ protocol is to avoid such situation: once a node is in a cluster, it will belong to a cluster having an effectual leader during all stabilization period despite the occurrence of $\mathcal{HTD}$ events. The main idea of transformation is to control the execution of $\mathcal{P}$ protocol by changing/adding some rules in order: (1) to form temporary clusters, (2) to delay actions by making cluster-heads resign only after their clusters become empty, and by avoiding standard nodes to affiliate with a currently resigning leader. Moreover, this transformation modifies the execution of $\mathcal{P}$ since it forces some nodes to become leaders although the Election rule is disabled in $\mathcal{P}$ protocol. This forced election does not impact the final clusters produced by $\mathcal{TP}$ protocol compared to final clusters of $\mathcal{P}$ (see Correction proofs, Sec 5). Transformed protocol $\mathcal{TP}$ is described in Protocols 2 and 3.

Protocol 2. Variables and predicates of the Transformed Protocol $\mathcal{TP}$

Output variables

- $\text{Status}_v \in \{CH, O, NO, NCH\}$; Hierarchical status of node v. It can be Cluster-head (CH), Ordinary (O), Nearly Ordinary (NO) and Nearly Cluster-head (NCH).

Input variables

- $\text{Ready}_v \in \{RO, RCH\}$; It indicates if v is ready to become cluster-head ($\text{Ready}_v = RCH$) or ordinary ($\text{Ready}_v = RO$).

Predicates

- $\text{Is\_Leader}(v) \in \{T, F\}$; It indicates if v is a leader or a standard node. If $\text{Head}(v) = v$ then v is leader ($\text{Is\_Leader}(v) = T$), otherwise v is a standard node ($\text{Is\_Leader}(v) = F$); i.e., $\text{Is\_Leader}(v) \equiv (\text{Head}(v) = v)$.

- $\text{ClusterEmpty}(v) \in \{T, F\}$; It indicates if the v's cluster is empty or not. $\text{ClusterEmpty}(v) \equiv \forall u \in N_v, \text{Head}(u) \neq v$.

- $\text{MustAffiliate}(v) \in \{T, F\}$; It indicates if node v must affiliate with the NextHead or not. $\text{MustAffiliate}(v) \equiv \text{GA}(v) \wedge \text{Status}_{\text{NextHead}(v)} = CH$.

- $\text{MustResign}(v) \in \{T, F\}$; It indicates if node v has to resign and join the cluster headed by NextHead or not. $\text{MustResign}(v) \equiv \text{GR}(v) \wedge \text{Status}_{\text{NextHead}(v)} = CH$.

- $\text{MustBecomeHead}(v) \in \{T, F\}$; It indicates if the node v has to become cluster-head: if $\text{GE}(v)$ is enabled or v cannot affiliate with NextHead and it cannot join an existing cluster. $\text{MustBecomeHead}(v) \equiv \text{GE}(v) \vee (\neg\text{MustAffiliate}(v) \wedge \text{Status}_{\text{Head}(v)} \neq CH)$.

Our transformation is applied to a class of original clustering protocols that can have a deep difference between them. The original protocol may build a dominating set, independent dominating set, k-fold dominating set, capacitated dominating set, connected or weakly connected dominating set etc. The transformed protocol builds the same kind of clusters as the original protocol. The computations of original protocol are however modified to ensure the service guarantee to $\mathcal{TP}$ protocol despite $\mathcal{HTD}$ disruptions. Protocols GDMAC [1], building a k-fold dominating set, and BSC [20] building a capacitated dominating set, are transformed respectively to R-GDMAC [21], and R-BSC [17] using

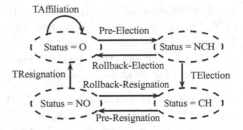

Fig. 1. Status transition in $\mathcal{TP}$ protocol

our transformer. To ensure the service guarantee, $\mathcal{TP}$ protocol maintains, in addition to variables of $\mathcal{P}$ protocol, a variable Status that indicates the hierarchical status of a node. The hierarchical status of a node v is : *cluster-head* (Status$_v = CH$), *ordinary node* (Status$_v = O$), *nearly ordinary* (Status$_v = NO$), or *nearly cluster-head* (Status$_v = NCH$). The status transition diagram of a node v is illustrated in Figure 1, where transitions are the rules executed by v (and defined in Protocol 3).

Protocol 3. Rules of the Transformed Protocol $\mathcal{TP}$

Correct1(v) : Is_Leader$(v) \wedge ($Status$_v = O \vee$ Status$_v = NCH) \longrightarrow$ Status$_v := CH$

Correct2(v) : $\neg$Is_Leader$(v) \wedge ($Status$_v = CH \vee$ Status$_v = NO) \longrightarrow$ Status$_v := O$

Pre-Election(v) : Status$_v = O \wedge \neg$Is_Leader$(v) \wedge$ MustBecomeHead(v)
$$\longrightarrow \text{Status}_v := NCH;$$

TElection(v) : Status$_v = NCH \wedge \neg$Is_Leader$(v) \wedge$ Ready$_v = RCH \wedge$
$$\text{MustBecomeHead}(v) \longrightarrow \text{Status}_v := CH; \text{ AE}(v);$$

Rollback-Election(v) : Status$_v = NCH \wedge \neg$Is_Leader$(v) \wedge \neg$MustBecomeHead$(v) \wedge$
$$\neg\text{MustAffiliate}(v) \longrightarrow \text{Status}_v := O;$$

Pre-Resignation(v) : Status$_v = CH \wedge$ Is_Leader$(v) \wedge$ MustResign(v)
$$\longrightarrow \text{Status}_v := NO;$$

TResignation(v) : Status$_v = NO \wedge$ Is_Leader$(v) \wedge$ ClusterEmpty$(v) \wedge$
$$\text{Ready}_v = RO \wedge \text{MustResign}(v) \longrightarrow \text{Status}_v := O; \text{ AR}(v);$$

Rollback-Resignation(v) : Status$_v = NO \wedge$ Is_Leader$(v) \wedge \neg$MustResign(v)
$$\longrightarrow \text{Status}_v := CH;$$

TAffiliation(v) : $\neg$Is_Leader$(v) \wedge$ MustAffiliate$(v) \longrightarrow$ Status$_v := O; \text{ AA}(v);$

TComplement(v) : GC$(v) \longrightarrow$ AC$(v);$ // Complementary rules are not changed.

The value of Ready variable is an input to $\mathcal{TP}$ protocol, and it is updated by an upper-layer hierarchical protocol, called $\mathcal{UHP}$. Ready does not have any impact on the transformation of $\mathcal{P}$ to $\mathcal{TP}$, i.e., $\mathcal{TP}$ is self-stabilizing with service guarantee without using Ready variable. Ready allows just the control of $\mathcal{TP}$ actions by $\mathcal{UHP}$ in order to ensure the service guarantee of $\mathcal{UHP}$ protocol. For example, $\mathcal{UHP}$ can be the knowledge of neighbor clusters protocol proposed in [18], where the minimal service is "the permanent availability of paths leading to the head of each neighbor cluster". Ready is thus an interface that enables the implantation of self-stabilizing with service guarantee protocols on the top of $\mathcal{TP}$ protocol, as hierarchical routing protocols. The value RO (resp. RCH) of Ready$_v$ indicates that v is ready to become ordinary (resp. cluster-head) without violating some properties on $\mathcal{UHP}$. For ordinary nodes the default value of Ready is RO, and for cluster-heads the default value is RCH.

Assumption 1. *Let v be a node. If* Status$_v = NCH$ *(resp.* Status$_v = NO)$ *and* Ready$_v = RO$ *(resp.* Ready$_v = RCH)$, *there exist successive enabled actions from the $\mathcal{UHP}$ protocol that set* Ready$_v$ *to RCH (resp. RO) in a finite time.*

Predicates and Rules. Correction rules Correct1(v) and Correct2(v) update initially the value of Status(v) according to the value of Is_Leader(v) predicate.

Only one of these rules is enabled at a time by a node v. After execution of one of these rules, both rules are disabled forever on v.

Affiliation process. In $\mathcal{P}$ protocol, a node v affiliates to NextHead's cluster if $GA(v)$ is satisfied. However, if v and $NextHead(v)$ perform respectively Affiliation and Resignation rules during the same computation step, v will be affiliated to a standard node (v is now orphan, because its head is not leader). To avoid generating orphan nodes, $\mathcal{TP}$ protocol authorises the affiliation of v to cluster of NextHead only if $GA(v) \wedge Status_{NextHead(v)} = CH$ (i.e., $MustAffiliate(v)$).

Resignation process. For the same reason above, it is not enough that a leader v satisfying $GR(v)$ resigns its leadership. Otherwise, v could be orphan, and it could generate orphan nodes after its resignation. This is why in $\mathcal{TP}$ protocol, a leader v must satisfy the predicate $MustResign(v)$, and its cluster should be empty before becoming a standard node. The resignation process is thus done in two steps. First, a cluster-head v satisfying $MustResign(v)$ has the Pre-Resignation rule enabled. By the execution of Pre-Resignation rule, v becomes nearly ordinary (it still behaves as leader). In this state (i.e., $Status_v = NO$), no node u having $NextHead_u = v$ can join the v's cluster because $\neg MustAffiliate(u)$ and $\neg MustResign(u)$ are satisfied. Furthermore, the members of v's cluster have to leave their cluster, because they satisfy $MustAffiliate \vee MustBecomeHead$, and so they eventually quit the v's cluster. In the other hand, while v is nearly ordinary, $\mathcal{UHP}$ protocol will update Ready to RO in a finite time (Assumption 1). Once the v's cluster is empty (i.e., $ClusterEmpty(v) = T$) and $Ready_v = RO$, the rule TResignation(v) is enabled. By performing TResignation(v) rule, v becomes ordinary, and the Resignation action $AR(v)$ is executed. If $MustResign(v)$ becomes unsatisfied when $Status_v = NO$, then Rollback-Resignation(v) rule is enabled. Execution of Rollback-Resignation stops the resignation process. These conditions guarantee that during the construction/maintenance of clusters, no cluster-head abandons its leadership and generates orphan nodes.

Election process. A standard node v has to become leader if $MustBecomeHead(v)$ is verified: either due to the satisfaction of $GE(v)$, or because v has to leave its cluster (the v's head is nearly ordinary) but v cannot affiliate with another cluster. The election process is done in two steps. First, an ordinary node satisfying $MustBecomeHead(v)$ has the Pre-Election rule enabled. After its execution, v takes the nearly cluster-head status (it still behaves as a standard node). While v is nearly cluster-head, the protocol $\mathcal{UHP}$ will update Ready to RCH in a finite time (Assumption 1). Once $Ready_v = RCH$ and $MustBecomeHead(v)$ is satisfied, the rule TElection is enabled for v. By executing TElection(v), v becomes cluster-head, and it performs the Election action $AE(v)$. If $MustBecomeHead(v)$ is no more satisfied when $Status_v = NCH$, then Rollback-Election(v) rule is enabled. Its execution leads v to ordinary status and stops the election process.

4 Service Guarantee of the Transformed Protocol $\mathcal{TP}$

In this section, we prove that $\mathcal{TP}$ protocol quickly reaches a safe configuration, in at most 3 rounds. Moreover, the safety property is preserved under any action of $\mathcal{TP}$ protocol and also despite the occurrence of $\mathcal{HTD}$ disruptions. Some proofs are omitted due to lack of space. They can be found in [19].

Lemma 1. $A_1 = \{c \in C \mid \forall v \in V : (\texttt{Is\_Leader}(v) \Rightarrow \texttt{Status}_v \in \{CH, NO\}) \wedge (\neg\texttt{Is\_Leader}(v) \Rightarrow \texttt{Status}_v \in \{NCH, O\})\}$ *is an attractor from C in one round.*

Observation 1. *In a configuration of A_1, the rules Correct1(v) and Correct2(v) are disabled for any node v.*

Definition 4 (Safety Predicate). *Let us define the safety predicate $\mathcal{SP}$ as follows:* $\mathcal{SP}_v \equiv \texttt{Head}(\texttt{Head}(v)) = \texttt{Head}(v)$
$$\mathcal{SP} \equiv \forall v \in V : \mathcal{SP}_v$$

Notation 1. *Let c be a configuration, and $\mathcal{X}$ be a variable or a predicate. We note by $\mathcal{X}[c]$ the value of $\mathcal{X}$ in the configuration c.*

Lemma 2. *Following the execution of TElection, TResignation or TAffiliation rule by a node v, $\mathcal{SP}_v$ is satisfied.*

Proof. Let c_1 be a configuration of A_1, and cs be a computation step of $\mathcal{TP}$ protocol $c_1 \xrightarrow{cs} c_2$. Let v be a node. During cs, if v performs the TElection rule, the predicate $\mathcal{SP}_v$ is verified in c_2 ($\texttt{Head}(v)[c_2] = v$).
Let us study the case where v performs TResignation or TAffiliation rule during cs. We note u the head selected by v during cs ($\texttt{NextHead}(v)[c_1] = u$). In c_1, we have $\texttt{Status}_u = CH$, otherwise predicates $\texttt{MustResign}(v)$ and $\texttt{MustAffiliate}(v)$ are not satisfied in c_1. $\mathcal{SP}_v[c_2]$ is satisfied because u cannot modify the value of $\texttt{Head}(u)$ by performing TResignation or TAffiliation rule during cs.   ∎

Lemma 3. *The set of configurations $A_2 = A_1 \cap \{c \in C \mid \mathcal{SP} \text{ is satisfied }\}$ is closed under any computation step of the $\mathcal{TP}$ protocol.*

Proof. Let c_1 be a configuration of A_2, and cs be a computation step of $\mathcal{TP}$ protocol $c_1 \xrightarrow{cs} c_2$. Let v be a node. During cs, there are two possibilities.
• v **did not change its head during** cs. Let u be the head of v in c_1, i.e., $u = \texttt{Head}(v)[c_1] = \texttt{Head}(v)[c_2]$, and $\texttt{Head}(u)[c_1] = u$. TElection(u) and TAffiliation(u) rules are disabled in c_1. So, TResignation(u) is the only rule that modifies the value of $\texttt{Head}(u)$. However, TResignation(u) is disabled in c_1 because $\texttt{ClusterEmpty}(u)[c_1]$ is not satisfied. Thus, $\mathcal{SP}_v$ stays satisfied in c_2.
• v **changes its head during** cs. Note that the Pre-Election, Rollback-Election, Pre-Resignation, Rollback-Resignation, TComplementary rules do not change the v's head identity. During cs, if v performs the other rules, $\mathcal{SP}_v$ becomes verified in c_2 (according to Lemma 2).

We conclude that A_2 is closed under any computation step of $\mathcal{TP}$ protocol.   ∎

Theorem 1. A_2 *is an attractor for $\mathcal{TP}$ protocol from A_1 in at most two rounds.*

Corollary 1. *A safe configuration is reached in at most 3 rounds.*

Proof. Each configuration of A_2 is safe. The remaining of the proof follows directly from Lemma 1 and Theorem 1.   ∎

Definition 5 (Highly Tolerated Disruptions). *The set of highly tolerated disruptions* HTD *handled by the protocol* $\mathcal{TP}$ *is:*

- *the change of node's weight,*
- *the crash of standard nodes,*
- *the failure of a link between (1) two leaders, or (2) two standard nodes,*
- *the joining of sub-networks verifying the predicate* $\mathcal{SP}$.

Theorem 2. $\mathcal{SP}$ *is closed under any disruption of* $\mathcal{HTD}$.

Proof. Let v be a standard node (v is ordinary or nearly cluster-head), and u its head (u is cluster-head or nearly ordinary). Let $c \in A_2$. Starting from c, $\mathcal{SP}_v$ will be not verified only if one of the following events occurs: u's removal from the network or crash, or failure of the communication link between u and v. Therefore, $\mathcal{SP}$ is preserved under any disruption of $\mathcal{HTD}$.   ∎

5   Correctness of the Transformed Protocol $\mathcal{TP}$

In this section, we prove that a terminal configuration of $\mathcal{TP}$ protocol is not due to a deadlock situation, but it corresponds to a terminal configuration of $\mathcal{P}$.

Theorem 3. *In a terminal configuration c of $\mathcal{TP}$ protocol, no action of $\mathcal{P}$ protocol is enabled.*

Proof. Let u, v, w be nodes, and let c_t be a terminal configuration of $\mathcal{TP}$ protocol. According to Theorem 1, c_t belongs to $A2$. In the configuration c_t, all rules of $\mathcal{TP}$ protocol are disabled.

Assume that in c_t, v satisfies $\neg$Is_Leader(v). In the configuration c_t we have:
- Status$_v = NCH \vee$ Status$_v = O$, since $c_t \in A_1$.
- $\neg$MustBecomeHead(v) is satisfied, otherwise the Pre-Election or TElection rule is eventually enabled according to Observation 1.
- Status$_v = O$, because otherwise the rule Rollback-Election is enabled.
- $\neg$MustAffiliate(v) is satisfied, otherwise the rule TAffiliation is enabled.
- $\neg$GE(v) $\wedge$ Status$_{\text{Head}(v)} = CH$, since $\neg$MustBecomeHead(v) is satisfied.

We conclude that in c_t, $\neg$Is_Leader(v) $\Rightarrow$

$$\text{Status}_v = O \wedge \neg\text{GE}(v) \wedge \neg\text{MustAffiliate}(v) \wedge \text{Status}_{\text{Head}(v)} = CH \qquad (3)$$

In addition, according to 2nd and 3rd Preconditions, we have

$$\text{Is\_Leader}(v) \Rightarrow \neg\text{GA}(v) \wedge \neg\text{GE}(v) \Rightarrow \neg\text{MustAffiliate}(v) \wedge \neg\text{GE}(v)$$

Therefore, in c_t, we have :

$$\forall v \in V : \neg\text{MustAffiliate}(v) \wedge \neg\text{GE}(v) \qquad (4)$$

Assume that in c_t the node w satisfies Is_Leader(w), and it is nearly ordinary (Status$_w = NO$). According to our assumptions, in c_t we have:
- MustResign(w) is satisfied, otherwise the rule Rollback-Resignation is enabled.

- ¬ClusterEmpty(w) is satisfied, otherwise TResignation(w) is eventually enabled (Observation 1). Thus, $\exists u \in N_w : \text{Head}(u) = w$ (i.e., ¬Is_Leader(u)). We have, Status$_{\text{Head}(u)} = NO$. According to Equation 3, node u does not exist.
- There is a contradiction, in c_t Is_Leader(w) implies Status$_w \neq NO$.

Assume now that in c_t w is cluster-head, thus in c_t we have:
- ¬MustResign(w) is satisfied, otherwise Pre-Resignation(w) is enabled.
We establish that in c_t,

$$\text{Is\_Leader}(w) \Rightarrow \text{Status}_w = CH \wedge \neg\text{MustResign}(w) \tag{5}$$

According to 1st Precondition, ¬Is_Leader(w) $\Rightarrow$ ¬GR(w) $\Rightarrow$ ¬MustResign(w). Therefore, in c_t, we have:

$$\forall v \in V : \neg\text{MustResign}(v) \tag{6}$$

According to Equation 1, in c_t we have: GA(v) $\Rightarrow$ Is_Leader(NextHead(v)). Thus, Status$_{\text{NextHead}(v)} = CH$ (Equation 5). We conclude that in c_t,

$$\neg\text{MustAffiliate}(v) \Rightarrow \neg\text{GA}(v) \tag{7}$$

Similarly, according to Equation 1, in c_t we have: GR(w) $\Rightarrow$ Is_Leader(NextHead(w)). Thus, Status$_{\text{NextHead}(w)} = CH$ (Equation 5). We conclude that in c_t,

$$\neg\text{MustResign}(w) \Rightarrow \neg\text{GR}(w) \tag{8}$$

In c_t, GC(v) guards are disabled because TComplementary(v) rules are disabled.

In terminal configuration c_t, the guards GE(v) (Equation 4), GA(v) (Equations 4 and 7), GR(v) (Equations 5 and 8) and GC(v) are disabled for any node v. This is a terminal configuration for $\mathcal{P}$.   ∎

6   Termination of the Transformed Protocol $\mathcal{TP}$

The proof of termination of $\mathcal{TP}$ protocol poses a technical challenge. Indeed, some times the rule TElection in $\mathcal{TP}$ protocol may be enabled whereas the Election rule in $\mathcal{P}$ protocol is disabled, i.e., GE is not verified but MustBecomeHead is verified. The execution of TElection rule when MustBecomeHead $\wedge$ ¬GE allows to empty a cluster headed by a Nearly-ordinary node, and so it ensures the convergence of $\mathcal{TP}$ protocol.

Requirement 1. *For the following, we assume that $A_p = A_2 \cap \{c \in C \mid \forall v \in V, P1(v) \wedge P2(v)\}$ is an attractor for $\mathcal{TP}$ protocol from A_2 where:*

$$P1(v) \equiv (\text{GA}(v) \vee \text{GE}(v)) \wedge (\text{Head}(\text{Head}(v)) = \text{Head}(v))$$
$$\Rightarrow w_{\text{NextHead}(v)} > w_{\text{Head}(v)}$$

$P2(v) \equiv (\forall u \in V, w_u < w_v$ *or u will never perform a clustering action) $\Rightarrow$*
The value of GR(v) does not change while v does not perform an action.

The predicate $P1$ is related to the fact that $\mathcal{P}$ is weight-based: a standard node of a well-formed cluster (its head is a leader) changes of cluster only to affiliate to a better leader. The predicate $P2$ is related to silent and weigh-based properties of $\mathcal{P}$: a leader v is neutralized only by an action of a stronger node (its weight is larger than v's weight).

Termination Scheme: Let e be a computation of $\mathcal{TP}$ protocol starting from a configuration of $A_2 \cap A_p$. Along e, the stabilization of nodes of V is done in steps. At the end of the ith step, a suffix e_i of e is reached where all nodes of S_i executes only Pre-Election and Rollback-Election rules. We define the set S_i, and the suffix e_i as follows:

- $S_0 = \emptyset$; $e_0 = e$; $i \geqslant 1$;
- $V_i = V - S_{i-1}$;
- Let vi be the node of V_i having the highest weight.
- Let e_i be a suffix of e_{i-1}, such that along e_i the following *stabilization properties* are always satisfied for the node vi:
  1. $\text{Status}_{vi} \in \{CH, NCH, O\}$, and vi will never change its head identity.
  2. If vi is cluster-head, then vi is disabled forever, and the vi's cluster is stable (i.e., no node joins or leaves the cluster headed by vi).
  3. If vi is ordinary or nearly cluster-head, then vi only executes Pre-Election and Rollback-Election rules.
- $S_i = S_{i-1} \cup \{vi\}$.

Lemma 4. *For all $i \geqslant 1$, the suffix e_i of e_{i-1} exists assuming that the suffix e_{i-1} of c_0 exists.*

Theorem 4. *All computations of $\mathcal{TP}$ protocol, starting from a configuration of $A_2 \cap A_p$, reach a terminal configuration.*

Proof. Let $j = |V|$ be an integer. The suffix e_j exists (where *stabilization properties* are satisfied for all nodes of V), and it is reached by any computation of $\mathcal{TP}$ protocol (Lemma 4). Along e_j, nodes may only execute Pre-Election and Rollback-Election rules. So, no node executes a clustering action (i.e., AA, AE, AR, and AC actions), and the value of guards $\text{GA}(v)$, $\text{GE}(v)$, $\text{GR}(v)$, and $\text{GC}(v)$ does not change for any node v. Furthermore, along e_j, $\forall v \in V, \text{Status}_v \neq NO$.
Assume that e_j is infinite. So, there exists a set of nodes, denoted $\text{Inf} \neq \emptyset$, that perform infinitely often Pre-Election and Rollback-Election rules. Let v be the node of Inf having the highest weight.
Along e_j, each time v satisfies $\text{MustBecomeHead}(v)$ (to perform Pre-Election rule) then the guard $\text{GE}(v)$ is satisfied, because $\text{Status}_{\text{Head}(v)} = CH$. Since no node performs a clustering action, the node v satisfying $\text{GE}(v)$ stays enabled along e_j unless it performs a clustering action. By fairness, v executes TElection rule after Pre-Election rule and it leaves its cluster. This is impossible along e_j. We conclude that $\text{GE}(v)$ is not verified along e_j. Moreover, along e_j we have $\text{Status}_{\text{Head}(v)} = CH$. Thus, MustBecomeHead(v) is never satisfied along e_j.
Therefore, along e_j, Pre-Election(v) is disabled forever, and after the execution of Rollback-Election(v) rule, v is disabled forever.

We conclude that v does not perform infinitely often the Pre-Election and Rollback-Election rules: $\text{Inf} = \emptyset$. So, e_j reaches a terminal configuration. ■

7   Complexity Measures and Concluding Remarks

Time Complexity. A comparison between the time complexity of $\mathcal{P}$ and $\mathcal{TP}$ protocols is illustrated in Table 1, where $\mathcal{UHP}$ rules are rules of $\mathcal{UHP}$ protocol updating the variable $Ready$, and U is the time required by $\mathcal{UHP}$ rules to achieve such update. We conclude that an upper bound of the stabilization time of $\mathcal{TP}$ protocol is $(4 + 2U) * S_{\mathcal{P}}$, where $S_{\mathcal{P}}$ is the stabilization time of $\mathcal{P}$ protocol.

Memory Space Complexity. Let $M_{\mathcal{P}}$ be the memory requirement of protocol $\mathcal{P}$ at each node. The protocol $\mathcal{TP}$ differs from $\mathcal{P}$ by the variable `Status` added at each node. This variable has 4 values, so it can be coded by 2 bits. Thus, the memory space complexity of $\mathcal{TP}$ protocol is $M_{\mathcal{P}} + 2$ bits per node.

Table 1. Comparison between time complexity of $\mathcal{P}$ and $\mathcal{TP}$ protocols

Protocol $\mathcal{P}$		Protocol $\mathcal{TP}$	
Rule	Number of rounds	Rule	Number of rounds
Complementary	1 round	TComplementary	1 round
Affiliation	1 round	TAffiliation	1 round
Election	1 round	Pre-Election + $\mathcal{UHP}$ rules + TElection	$2 + U$ rounds
Resignation	1 round	Pre-Resignation + (Pre-Election + $\mathcal{UHP}$ rules + TElection **or** TAffiliation) + $\mathcal{UHP}$ rules + TResignation	$4 + 2U$ rounds

The proposed scheme constructs a silent self-stabilizing with service guarantee 1-hop clustering protocol $\mathcal{TP}$ starting from a silent self-stabilizing one $\mathcal{P}$. In at most 3 rounds (Corollary 1), $\mathcal{TP}$ provides the following useful minimal service: "each node belongs to a cluster having an effectual leader". The service guarantee property of $\mathcal{TP}$ protocol ensures that this minimal service stays provided during the stabilization phase, even despite the occurrences of disruptions $\mathcal{HTD}$ (see Definition 5). Thus, the hierarchical organization of the network is quickly available and it is maintained over the time, which allows the continuity of operation of upper-layer hierarchical protocols.

Futur Works. The presented transformer is adapted only to self-stabilizing 1-hop weight-based protocols. A first generalization of this work is the design of a transformer dealing with k-hops weight-based protocols (i.e. the cluster-head being at distance at most k of its cluster's members). A second generalization is the design of a transformer adapted to any k-hops protocol; for instance [14] where the selection of cluster-heads is randomized and not weight-based.

References

1. Basagni, S.: Distributed and mobility-adaptive clustering for multimedia support in multi-hop wireless networks. In: International Vehicular Technology Conference (VTC 1999), pp. 889–893 (1999)

2. Bein, D., Datta, A.K., Jagganagari, C.R., Villain, V.: A self-stabilizing link-cluster algorithm in mobile ad hoc networks. In: International Symposium on Parallel Architectures, Algorithms and Networks (ISPAN 2005), pp. 436–441 (2005)
3. Blin, L., Potop-Butucaru, M.G., Rovedakis, S., Tixeuil, S.: Loop-Free Super-Stabilizing Spanning Tree Construction. In: Dolev, S., Cobb, J., Fischer, M., Yung, M. (eds.) SSS 2010. LNCS, vol. 6366, pp. 50–64. Springer, Heidelberg (2010)
4. Bui, A., Datta, A.K., Petit, F., Villain, V.: Snap-stabilization and PIF in tree networks. Distributed Computing 20, 3–19 (2007)
5. Caron, E., Datta, A.K., Depardon, B., Larmore, L.L.: self-stabilizing k-clustering algorithm for weighted graphs. Journal of Parallel and Distributed Computing 70, 1159–1173 (2010)
6. Chatterjee, M., Das, S.K., Turgut, D.: WCA: A weighted clustering algorithm for mobile ad hoc networks. Journal of Cluster Computing 5(2), 193–204 (2002)
7. Cournier, A., Datta, A.K., Petit, F., Villain, V.: Enabling snap-stabilization. In: Conference on Distributed Computing Systems (ICDCS 2003), pp. 12–19 (2003)
8. Cournier, A., Devismes, S., Villain, V.: From Self- to Snap- Stabilization. In: Datta, A.K., Gradinariu, M. (eds.) SSS 2006. LNCS, vol. 4280, pp. 199–213. Springer, Heidelberg (2006)
9. Datta, A.K., Larmore, L.L., Vemula, P.: A self-stabilizing o(k)-time k-clustering algorithm. The Computer Journal 53, 342–350 (2010)
10. Delaët, S., Devismes, S., Nesterenko, M., Tixeuil, S.: Snap-Stabilization in Message-Passing Systems. In: Garg, V., Wattenhofer, R., Kothapalli, K. (eds.) ICDCN 2009. LNCS, vol. 5408, pp. 281–286. Springer, Heidelberg (2008)
11. Demirbas, M., Arora, A., Mittal, V., Kulathumani, V.: A fault-local self-stabilizing clustering service for wireless ad hoc networks. IEEE Transactions on Parallel and Distributed Systems 17, 912–922 (2006)
12. Dijkstra, E.W.: Self-stabilizing systems in spite of distributed control. Communications of the ACM 17(11), 643–644 (1974)
13. Dolev, S., Herman, T.: Superstabilizing protocols for dynamic distributed systems. Chicago J. Theor. Comput. Sci. (1997)
14. Dolev, S., Tzachar, N.: Empire of colonies: Self-stabilizing and self-organizing distributed algorithm. Theoretical Computer Science 410, 514–532 (2009)
15. Drabkin, V., Friedman, R., Gradinariu, M.: Self-stabilizing Wireless Connected Overlays. In: Shvartsman, M.M.A.A. (ed.) OPODIS 2006. LNCS, vol. 4305, pp. 425–439. Springer, Heidelberg (2006)
16. Gerla, M., Tsai, J.T.: Multicluster, mobile, multimedia radio network. Journal of Wireless Networks 1(3), 255–265 (1995)
17. Johnen, C., Mekhaldi, F.: Robust Self-stabilizing Construction of Bounded Size Weight-Based Clusters. In: D'Ambra, P., Guarracino, M., Talia, D. (eds.) Euro-Par 2010, Part I. LNCS, vol. 6271, pp. 535–546. Springer, Heidelberg (2010)
18. Johnen, C., Mekhaldi, F.: Self-stabilizing computation and preservation of knowledge of neighbor clusters. In: IEEE International Conferences on Self-Adaptive and Self-Organizing Systems (SASO 2011), pp. 41–50 (2011)
19. Johnen, C., Mekhaldi, F.: From self- to self-stabilizing with service guarantee 1-hop weight-based clustering. Technical Report RR1462-12, LaBRI (2012), http://hal.archives-ouvertes.fr/
20. Johnen, C., Nguyen, L.H.: Self-stabilizing construction of bounded size clusters. In: International Symposium on Parallel and Distributed Processing with applications (ISPA 2008), pp. 43–50 (2008)
21. Johnen, C., Nguyen, L.H.: Robust self-stabilizing weight-based clustering algorithm. Theoretical Computer Science 410(6-7), 581–594 (2009)

22. Kamei, S., Kakugawa, H.: A Self-stabilizing Approximation for the Minimum Connected Dominating Set with Safe Convergence. In: Baker, T.P., Bui, A., Tixeuil, S. (eds.) OPODIS 2008. LNCS, vol. 5401, pp. 496–511. Springer, Heidelberg (2008)
23. Katz, S., Perry, K.J.: Self-stabilizing extensions for meassage-passing systems. Distributed Computing 7, 17–26 (1993)
24. Mitton, N., Fleury, E., Guérin-Lassous, I., Tixeuil, S.: Self-stabilization in self-organized multihop wireless networks. In: International Conference on Distributed Computing Systems Workshops (WWAN 2005), pp. 909–915 (2005)

Brief Announcement: Verification of Stabilizing Programs with SMT Solvers

Jingshu Chen and Sandeep Kulkarni

Michigan State University,
3115 Engineering Building, 48824 East Lansing, US

Abstract. We focus on the verification of stabilizing programs using SMT solvers. SMT solvers have the potential to convert the verification problem into a satisfiability problem of a Boolean formula and utilize efficient techniques to determine whether it is satisfiable. In this work, we study the approach of utilizing techniques from bounded model checking to determine whether the given program is stabilizing.

Keywords: Verification, Stabilization, Model checking.

1 Introduction

One of the successful automated approaches is model checking [2]. Model checking is a technique to automatically verify whether a given model meets a given property. If the program does not meet the given property, the process of model checking typically produces a counterexample.

In this paper, we evaluate the effectiveness of SMT solvers in verifying stabilization with the use of bounded model checking. The process of using bounded model checking stabilization to verify consists of two parts, (1) verification of *closure* and (2) verification of *convergence*. Specifically, the former requires that if the program begins in a legitimate state then it remains in legitimate states. And, the latter requires that if the program starts in a state outside its set of legitimate states then it eventually reaches a legitimate state.

2 Approach for Verifying Stabilization with SMT Solvers

In this section, we present the approach of verifying self-stabilization properties with SMT solvers by utilizing techniques from bounded model checking.

Verification of stabilization consists of two parts: (1) verifying *closure* and (2) verifying *convergence*. In Section 2.1, we identify the formula whose satisfiability can be used to determine whether closure property is satisfied. In Section 2.2, we identify the formula whose satisfiability can be used to determine whether convergence property is satisfed.

A.W. Richa and C. Scheideler (Eds.): SSS 2012, LNCS 7596, pp. 179–182, 2012.
© Springer-Verlag Berlin Heidelberg 2012

2.1   Verifying Closure

Let $\mathcal{P}$ be the given program and let $\mathcal{I}$ be the legitimate state predicate to conclude that $\mathcal{P}$ is stabilizing. Let $\mathcal{T}$ be the predicate that characterizes transitions of $\mathcal{P}$.

Observe that the closure property requires that if (s_0, s_1) is a transition of program $\mathcal{P}$ and state s_0 is a legitimate state then state s_1 is also a legitimate state. Thus, this can be captured by formula $\neg\Psi_l$, where

$$\Psi_l \;=\; (\mathcal{I}(s_0) \wedge \mathcal{T}(s_0, s_1) \wedge \neg\mathcal{I}(s_1))$$

Remark. For compactness, the formula Ψ_l does not explicitly specify the program or the set of legitimate states that are inputs in deciding closure.

Based on whether Ψ_l is satisfiable or not, we have two scenarios, SC_1 and SC_2:

1. SC_1 : if Ψ_l is satisfiable then it proves that it is possible to begin in a legitimate state, execute a program transition and be in a state that is not a legitimate state. This implies that the closure property is not satisfied. Moreover, in this case, assignment to s_0 and s_1 (which in turn includes values of variables of the program in state s_0 and s_1) provides a counterexample.
2. SC_2 : if Ψ_l is unsatisfiable then this implies that the closure property is satisfied.

2.2   Verifying Convergence

We verify convergence by checking that starting from an arbitrary state, the program, say $\mathcal{P}$, reaches a legitimate state (in $\mathcal{I}$) in k steps, where k is a given parameter used in the verification. Observe that the convergence property requires us to consider a sequence of states, $s_0, s_1, \cdots, s_k$ such that each successive transitions are program transitions. Moreover, to verify (negation of) convergence requirement, we require that $\mathcal{I}(s_k)$ should be false. Additionally, in this verification, we can utilize the closure requirement to add additional constraints requiring that $\mathcal{I}(s_j)$, $0 \leq j \leq k$, should be false. Additionally, in bounded model checking, one typically adds constraint about what the initial state should be. Thus, the formula Ψ_v used for verifying convergence is as follows:

$$\begin{aligned}\Psi_v = \;& \mathcal{T}(s_0, s_1) \wedge \mathcal{T}(s_1, s_2) \wedge \cdots \wedge \mathcal{T}(s_{k-1}, s_k) \\ & \neg\mathcal{I}(s_0) \wedge \neg\mathcal{I}(s_1) \wedge \cdots \wedge \neg\mathcal{I}(s_k)\end{aligned}$$

Based on whether Ψ_v is satisfiable or not, we have the following two scenarios:

1. SC_3 : if Ψ_v is satisfiable, convergence cannot be achieved in k steps. In this case, the number of steps needs to be increased. If the state space of the program is finite and k equals the number of states in the program then this implies that the convergence property is not satisfied.
2. SC_4 : if Ψ_v is unsatisfiable, then it proves that even if we begin in an arbitrary state, it is impossible for the program to be in an illegitimate state if it executes for k steps. In other words, the convergence property is satisfied.

3   Study Case: K-State Token Ring Program

In this section, we study Dijkstra's K-state token ring program [1] for illustration purpose. The token ring program is as follows: The program consists of $N + 1$ processes, numbered from 0 to N. Each process $p.i$, $0 \leq i \leq N$, has one variable $x.i$. The domain of $x.i$ is $\{0, 1, \ldots, K - 1\}$. These processes are organized in a unidirectional ring.

The program consists of two types of actions. The first type is for process 0. This action is enabled when $x.0$ equals $x.N$. When $p.0$ executes its action, it increments $x.0$ by 1 in modulo K arithmetic. The second type of action is for process $p.i$, $i \neq 0$. This action is enabled when $x.i$ is not equal to $x.(i-1)$. When $p.i$ executes its action, it copies $x.(i-1)$. Thus, the actions are as follows:

$$K_0:: \quad x.0 = x.N \quad \longrightarrow \quad x.0 = (x.0 + 1) \bmod K;$$
$$K_i:: \quad x.i \neq x.(i-1) \quad \longrightarrow \quad x.i = x.(i-1);$$

Performance Evaluation. We evaluate the performance of the token ring program in Table 1. In particular, Table 1 illustrates the time for verifying the closure and the convergence property.

Table 1. Verification Time for Ψ_v for Token Ring

Number of nodes	state space	Number of steps for convergence	Execution time(s) for convergence	Execution time(s) for closure
3	10^1	4	0.008944	0.005617
4	10^2	14	0.494496	0.005979
5	10^3	25	214.0957	0.013349

4   Conclusion

We find that the effectiveness of SMT solvers in verification of stabilization is mixed. Specifically, compared with existing approaches [3, 4] that utilize BDD based model checkers to verify stabilization, the time for verification is larger with SMT solvers. However, BDD based tools require one to identify the order of program variables in the BDD. An incorrect ordering of variables can increase the verification time by orders of magnitude making it significantly worse than the corresponding verification time with SMT solvers. Also, the results in [3, 4] apply only for verifying finite state programs. By contrast, the results in this paper demonstrate the feasibility of verifying infinite state program.

Acknowledgement. This work is supported by NSF CNS-0914913 and AFOSR Award FA9550-10-1-0178.

References

1. Dijkstra, E.W.: Self stabilizing systems in spite of distributed control. Communications of the ACM 17(11) (1974)
2. Orna, G., Clarke, M.E., Peled, D.A.: Model Checking. The MIT press (2000)
3. Chen, J., Abujarad, F., Kulkarni, S.: Effect of Fairness in Model Checking of Self-stabilizing Programs. In: Lu, C., Masuzawa, T., Mosbah, M. (eds.) OPODIS 2010. LNCS, vol. 6490, pp. 135–138. Springer, Heidelberg (2010)
4. Tsuchiya, T., Nagano, S., Paidi, R.B., Kikuno, T.: Symbolic model checking for self-stabilizing algorithms. IEEE Trans. Parallel Distrib. Syst 12, 81–95 (2001)

Brief Announcement:
MP-State: State-Aware Software Model Checking of Message-Passing Systems

Can Arda Muftuoglu, Péter Bokor, and Neeraj Suri

Technische Universität Darmstadt,
Darmstadt, Germany
{arda,pbokor,suri}@cs.tu-darmstadt.de

Introduction. Software model checking [4] is a useful and practical branch of verification for verifying the implementation of the system. The wide usability comes at a price of low time and space efficiency. In fact, model checking of even simple single-process programs can take several hours using state-of-the-art techniques [6]. Verification complexity gets even worse for concurrent programs that simultaneously execute loosely coupled processes. Verification efficiency can be greatly improved by capturing the state of the program, a technique generally referred to as *stateful* model checking [2]. Intuitively, state capture enables to detect that two states are identical and, therefore, to consider only a representative state for verification. Unfortunately, capturing the state in general software systems can be very hard, even if the entire state of the system resides in the (local) memory. As a result, certain verification approaches (commonly called stateless model checking) do not capture the system's state at all [4]. Stateful model checking is in principle possible for software, however, at a price of considerable overhead. Therefore, stateful model checking is efficient only if the achieved reduction of redundantly explored states compensate for the overhead.

Our focus is on fault-tolerant message-passing protocols, a class of systems that can particularly benefit from formal verification for various mission-critical applications. Although the verification of fault-tolerant message-passing protocols is known to be a hard problem due to concurrency and faults, model checking has proven to be an efficient approach to debug and verify small instances of deployed protocols [5].

In this brief announcement, we propose the state capture algorithm MP-State, which improves software model-checking of general message-passing protocols. MP-State makes use of two techniques that enable time- and space-efficient model checking. The first technique is a *selective hashing* mechanism that captures state information only if this might interfere with the specification. The second technique is a *selective push-on-stack* strategy, which is an optimization that filters the states that are pushed onto the search stack and, hence, are subject to backtracking. Selective push-on-stack is sound because filtered-out states have no unvisited successor states.

Motivating Example. We give the intuition behind the proposed approach through a simple message-passing example with two processes, p_1 and p_2. Process p_1 sends two messages m_1 and m_2 to process p_2. Process p_2 stores in its local state the messages it receives. It is possible for m_2 to arrive later than m_1 at p_2 due to network delays and p_2 can process available messages (m_1 and m_2) in one atomic step. Having received m_1

A.W. Richa and C. Scheideler (Eds.): SSS 2012, LNCS 7596, pp. 183–186, 2012.

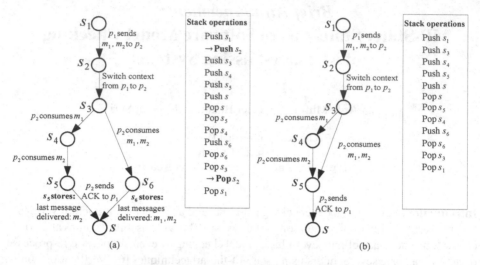

Fig. 1. (a) Naive depth-first search (DFS) and (b) MP-State search

and m_2, p_2 sends an ack message to p_1, informing that it has successfully received the messages sent by p_1.

Figure 1(a) shows the state graph of the protocol as explored by a naive depth-first search (DFS) and the corresponding operations of the search stack. We observe that software model checkers can utilize *auxiliary variables* for the implementation of the model checking process. These variables are not specified by the protocol under test. For example, in Basset and MP-Basset [1], an auxiliary variable stores the messages delivered by a transition that is scheduled for execution. As a result, s_5 and s_6 are different states, with the overhead of storing two states and exploring the successor state s two times. In addition to auxiliary variables, model checkers may have *auxiliary transitions*. Auxiliary transitions are the transitions that are "independent" from the protocol under test. For example, Basset and MP-Basset uses auxiliary transitions for the purpose of switching context between processes, which is related to the model checker, not to the protocol. As a result, states involved in the execution of such transitions (such as s_2 and s_3 in Figure 1) are considered by DFS as any other state.

Selective Hashing. We observe that (a) the transitions of common message-passing protocols depend only on the local states of the processes and pending (undelivered) messages; and (b) the usual properties of these protocols concern only about local states. Therefore, it is sufficient to capture local states and pending messages of each visited state. We refer to this technique as *selective hashing*. In our example, the state graph resulting from selective hashing is shown in Figure 1(b). Note that states s_5 and s_6 collapse into the same state because p_1 and p_2 have the same local states in both states and the set of pending messages is empty. The gain of selective hashing is that (i) different states resulting from differing values of auxiliary variables have to be processed only once by the model checker, e.g., for successor states of s_5 and s_6, which is s, and (ii) it is time efficient because state capture does not need to process the entire state.

Selective Push-on-Stack. We also observe that (c) usually auxiliary transitions are not concurrent with other transitions and (d) auxiliary transitions and states where these transitions are executed do not have to be remembered for counterexamples. Therefore, states with enabled auxiliary transitions do not have to be pushed onto the search stack. We refer to this technique as *selective push-on-stack*. Consider the auxiliary transition t from s_2 to s_3 in our example. Since t is the only transition that can be executed in s_2, no state remains unvisited if s_2 is not backtracked by the search. Also, a path excluding s_2 and t preserves all protocol-specified information. The application of selective push-on-stack to our example leads us to the search stack in Figure 1(b), where s_2 is not involved in any stack operation. Note that selective push-on-stack visits the same states as the naive search but it is more time efficient thanks to fewer stack operations.

MP-State and other Reductions. Broadly-studied and intuitive reductions are partial-order (POR) [3] and symmetry reductions (SR) [7]. Figure 1 demonstrates that MP-State is not a special case of these reductions. Firstly, POR is based on the idea of swapping the order of commutative transitions but the path ($s_1 \rightarrow s_2 \rightarrow s_3 \rightarrow s_6 \rightarrow s$) that is excluded in the reduced state graph in Figure 1(b) cannot be obtained by re-ordering the transitions of another path in the graph. Formally, considering the main-stream POR semantics, Figure 1(b) is not a stubborn/persistent/ample set reduction of (a) because in every state of the reduced state graph the number of enabled transitions is the same as in the unreduced one.

Secondly, SR is based on the symmetrical structure of the state graph but there is no such symmetry in Figure 1(a). Formally speaking, there is no permutation acting over the set of states (the formal notion of symmetry [7]) that would preserve the transition relation. In fact, in order to symmetry reduce Figure 1(a) into (b), a permutation would have to transpose s_5 and s_6 but these two states are not "symmetric" because of s_4.

Our Achieved Reductions Up to 69%. Our evaluation of MP-State with deployed fault tolerant message-passing protocols (Paxos consensus, distributed storage, and atomic broadcast) fortifies our initial claim that despite its overhead, stateful model checking outperforms stateless model checking. Besides, the results of our experiments show that MP-State is highly efficient, achieving a reduction of model checking time and memory by up to 69% over naive (unreduced) stateful model checking with depth-first search. In one of our experiments, we managed to reduce model checking time from 22 hours 19 minutes to 10 hours 22 minutes.

References

1. Bokor, P., Kinder, J., Serafini, M., Suri, N.: Efficient Model Checking of Fault-Tolerant Distributed Protocols. In: Proc. of DSN-DCCS, pp. 73–84 (2011)
2. Clarke, E., Grumberg, O., Peled, D.: Model Checking. MIT Press (2000)
3. Godefroid, P.: Partial-Order Methods for the Verification of Concurrent Systems: An Approach to the State-Explosion Problem. Springer (1996)
4. Godefroid, P.: Model Checking for Programming Languages using VeriSoft. In: Proc. of POPL, pp. 174–186 (1997)

5. Guo, H., Wu, M., Zhou, L., Hu, G., Yang, J., Zhang, L.: Practical Software Model Checking via Dynamic Interface Reduction. In: Proc. of SOSP, pp. 265–278 (2011)
6. Kuznetsov, V., Kinder, J., Bucur, S., Candea, G.: Efficient State Merging in Symbolic Execution. In: Proc. of PLDI, pp. 193–204 (2012)
7. Miller, A., Donaldson, A., Calder, M.: Symmetry in Temporal Logic Model Checking. ACM Computing Surveys 38(3) (2006)

Oblivious Assignment with m Slots

Giuseppe Ateniese[1], Roberto Baldoni[2], Silvia Bonomi[2],
and Giuseppe Antonio Di Luna[2]

[1] Dipartimento di Ingegneria Informatica, Automatica e Gestionale Antonio Ruberti
Università degli Studi di Roma La Sapienza
Via Ariosto, 25 I-00185 Roma, Italy
{baldoni,bonomi,diluna}@dis.uniroma1.it
[2] Dipartimento di Informatica
Università degli Studi di Roma La Sapienza
Via Salaria, 113 I-00198 Roma, Italy
ateniese@di.uniroma1.it

Abstract. Preserving anonymity and privacy of customer actions within
a complex software system, such as a cloud computing system, is one of
the main issues that must be solved in order to boost private computation outsourcing. In this paper, we propose a coordination paradigm,
namely oblivious assignment with m slots of a resource $\mathcal{R}$ (with $m \geq 1$),
allowing processes to compete to get a slot of $\mathcal{R}$ while ensuring, at the
same time, both fairness of resource allocation and obliviousness, that is,
the impossibility for any process to infer which slot of $\mathcal{R}$ is assigned to
any other process. We study oblivious assignment with m slots solvability issues based on the message pattern of the algorithm. We also present
a distributed algorithm solving oblivious assignment with m slots within
a distributed system, assuming the existence of at least two *honest* processes and $m \leq n$ (where n is the number of processes). The algorithm
is based on a rotating token paradigm and employs an adaptation of the
ElGamal encryption scheme to work with multiple parties and to ensure
obliviousness of the assignment. Finally, the correctness of the algorithm
is formally proved.

Keywords: distributed coordination abstractions, secure computations,
mutual exclusion, distributed systems.

1 Introduction

In this paper, we investigate the problem of oblivious assignment with m slots.
Informally, we consider n non-anonymous processes competing for accessing one
of the m slots of a resource $\mathcal{R}$. Each slot can be assigned to at most one process
at a time. When a resource is not needed anymore, it is released and assigned to
another requesting process. Note that, processes are utterly identifiable but we
strive to protect the allocations of resource slots to processes. Thus, *processes are
oblivious and in particular they are unaware of assignments between processes
and resource slots.*

A.W. Richa and C. Scheideler (Eds.): SSS 2012, LNCS 7596, pp. 187–201, 2012.

This problem is particularly interesting because it crystallizes the difficulty in coordinating processes that wish to interact with a resource without being noticed by anyone else. Resource sharing environments, channel assignments in telco systems are examples of domains where this problem can be relevant. As an example, an oblivious assignment scheme can help a group of clients of a cloud provider to hide and protect their allocation of resources within a virtualized environment or across distinct domains. Resources can thus be obliviously allocated to clients. Not even the cloud provider is aware of these various assignments. We target organizations moving to the cloud, or outsourcing their services, that wish to access or allocate virtual resources anonymously. Cryptographic systems, such as fully homomorphic encryption [11], do not solve the oblivious assignment problem. Homomorphic encryption allows clients to perform computation over encrypted data ensuring that sensitive information remain inaccessible to the cloud provider. However, the provider can derive which resources are allocated to which clients. This constitutes a side-channel leak we aspire to prevent. We stress that this type of side-channel has not been considered before in the context of cloud computing.

The paper first defines the *oblivious assignment with m slots* (O-mA) problem. More precisely, if an honest process p_i gets a slot r_j, then no other process is aware of this assignment. We also provide a stronger form of this problem, namely *strong oblivious assignment with m slots* (SO-mA). In this case, given a process p_i, no other process will learn whether any slot was assigned to p_i or not. That is, it is not possible to infer whether a specific process is using a resource slot or not. We study solvability issues of O-mA and SO-mA problems based upon the message pattern generated by distributed algorithms. We will show that SO-mA and O-mA can be implemented via token-based algorithms. We also show that a standard perpetual circulating algorithm is successful only in the presence of $n-1$ honest processes (where n is the number of processes). Then, we introduce a rotating token distributed algorithm solving O-mA where we assume the existence of at least two *honest* processes and with $m \leq n$. The algorithm employs an adaptation of ElGamal encryption scheme to ensure obliviousness of the assignment. Finally, the correctness of the algorithm is formally proved.

The rest of the paper is organized as follows: related work is in Section 2 and the system model is defined in Section 3. Section 4 formalizes the oblivious assignment with m slots problem and provides some solvability conditions, while Section 5 presents a distributed algorithm solving the oblivious assignment problem. Finally, Section 6 concludes the paper. Due to the lack of space some proofs are omitted in the text and can be found in [1].

2 Related Work

Defining distributed algorithms for accessing resources in mutual exclusion has been a mainstream field of research in the eighties [18] and several efficient algorithms have been devised (e.g., [19], [21], [16] just to cite a few). To facilitate fault tolerance without assuming failure detection, the general mutual exclusion problem has been extended to the k-mutual exclusion one [17], where at most k different processes can concurrently access the same resource; general strategies working in a failure-free environment have been adapted to solve this more general problem in an asynchronous message passing system (e.g. [14], [8]).

A different generalization of the mutual exclusion problem, namely k-assignment, has been presented in [9]. In k-assignment there are $k < n$ identical, named resources that may be requested by n processes and the authors shown that the problem can be solved in an asynchronous distributed system, as long as at most $k/2$ processes can fail.

Similarly, in the renaming problem [3], each participating process is initially associated to a unique identifier from a large name space and the final objective is to select unique identifiers from a smaller name space. A more general specification, called k-assignment with m slots, is defined in [4] by combining together renaming and k-exclusion. Informally, such a problem requires that at most k processes access concurrently one of the m distinct available slots. All these existing algorithms do not mask the assignment between slots and competing processes. On the contrary, they exploit their knowledge about assignments to minimize the number of exchanged messages.

Generally, the oblivious assignment problem can be solved using secure multi-party computation [22]. This is a paradigm that allows several parties to evaluate a function $f(x_1, \ldots, x_n)$, or multiple functions, without revealing the inputs $x_1, \ldots, x_n$. That is, every party p_i contributes x_i but at the end of the protocol it will only learn $f(x_1, \ldots x_n)$ and nothing else. Unfortunately, these generic techniques are notoriously very expensive and call for an exorbitant number of messages to be exchanged. However, there exist more efficient alternatives for many functionalities. The one that is more closely related to the oblivious assignment functionality is referred to as *mental poker*. Mental poker algorithms [20] allow people to play card games over networks without any trusted dealer. The basic idea is to assign cards to players such that cards stay private and can be safely shuffled. In addition, it is possible to detect cheaters. While the original scheme [20] represented each card with a large number of bits, more recent work [6] makes card sizes smaller and independent of the number of players.

The oblivious assignment problem does not fit completely within the mental poker framework, however. In our model, we must avoid starvation and ensure liveness and thus allow a process to pick a specific slot of a resource within a fixed amount of time (while this is not possible in mental poker). The release of a resource is also significantly simpler than discarding a card from hand. Indeed, we do not have to preserve the value of the slot (or card) and thus we can just set, obliviously, a boolean flag.

3   System Model

The distributed system is composed of a set of n processes $\Pi = \{p_1, p_2 \ldots, p_n\}$, each one having a unique identifier, that compete for m distinct slots $\{r_1, \ldots, r_m\}$ of a resource $\mathcal{R}$, where $m \leq n$. Each process p_i competes to get exclusive access to a slot of $\mathcal{R}$. At any time, each slot can be assigned to at most one process and allocated slots must be released within a finite period of time. Specifically, when process p_i needs to acquire one of the m slots of $\mathcal{R}$, it invokes a request() operation and waits until a grantResource() event occurs returning the id of the slot r_j assigned to p_i. To release the slot r_j, p_i invokes a release() operation. Note that we operate under the assumption that processes do not crash.

We assume the existence of a coalition $\mathcal{C}$ (with $1 \leq |\mathcal{C}| \leq n - 2$) of *honest-but-curious* processes [12]. Such processes act according to their algorithm but they can collaborate to acquire and share information about others processes. Processes not belonging to the coalition $\mathcal{C}$ are said to be *honest*, i.e., they are correct, behave according to the algorithm and do not attempt to infer other information, except the ones obtained during the algorithm execution.

Processes coordinate their access to slots of $\mathcal{R}$ by exchanging messages. We assume that for any pair of processes $p_i, p_j \in \Pi$, there exists a reliable FIFO point-to-point communication channel connecting them. Messages are delivered *"most of the time"* within δ time units, that is the underlying communication system is synchronous most of the time. However, there could be finite periods of time where the systems behaves as asynchronous. We assume that processes belonging to the coalition $\mathcal{C}$ are powerful enough to know both the communication bound δ and if the system is in a synchronous period or not. Such processes can use this knowledge to infer information about other honest processes.

4   Oblivious Assignment with m Slots

Given a generic resource $\mathcal{R}$, it can be used concurrently by different processes; however, any of its m slots can be used in an exclusive way. We remark that every process can always get at most one slot of $\mathcal{R}$, that is, *the assignment of multiple slots to a single process is not allowed*. At the same time, it must be guaranteed that competing processes will eventually obtain a slot of $\mathcal{R}$. In addition, resource assignment must be kept private.

4.1   Problem Definition

The *Oblivious assignment with m Slots* (O-mA) problem is specified by the following properties:

1. UniqueAssignment : If p_i and p_j access concurrently the resource $\mathcal{R}$, then the slot r_x assigned to p_i is different from the slot r_y assigned to p_j.
2. LockoutAvoidance : If a process p_i requests the access to the resource $\mathcal{R}$, then it eventually gets a slot r_j of $\mathcal{R}$.
3. ObliviousAssignment : if a slot r_j is assigned to an honest process p_i, then no other process is aware of this assignment.

As an example, consider a distributed system composed by two honest processes, p_1 and p_2, and $n - 2$ honest-but-curious processes. Let r_1 and r_2 be two slots of a resource. Suppose that after a run of an oblivious assignment algorithm both processes obtain a single slot, thus only two assignments are possible: (i) $\langle p_1, r_1 \rangle$, $\langle p_2, r_2 \rangle$ or (ii) $\langle p_1, r_2 \rangle$, $\langle p_2, r_1 \rangle$. The ObliviousAssignment property requires that the coalition of $n - 2$ honest-but-curious processes will not be able to determine which is the actual assignment between the two possible options.

4.2 Strong Oblivious Assignment with m Slots (SO-mA)

We consider a stronger variant of the O-mA problem, which is referred to as SO-mA, where it is not possible to determine whether resources are allocated to a specific process. The SO-mA problem can be defined as O-mA by replacing the ObliviousAssignment property with the following one:

StrongObliviousAssignment : For any process p_i, no other process can infer whether p_i owns a slot of a resource $\mathcal{R}$ or not.

In the previous example, the $n - 2$ honest-but-curious processes may not know what was the actual assignment but they can collectively determine that certain slots were assigned to p_1 and p_2. This violates the Strong Oblivious Assignment property.

4.3 Solvability Issues for O-mA and SO-mA Problems

In the following, we will show a necessary condition for an algorithm to solve O-mA and SO-mA. In particular, we will show that there exist constraints on the message pattern that any algorithm must satisfy to solve our problem.

Lemma 1. *Let A be a slot assignment algorithm, ensuring properties 1 and 2. If the message pattern of A expects a process p_i to send a request message m to another process p_j to acquire a slot r_j and $|\mathcal{C}| \geq 1$, then A cannot solve O-mA.*

Proof Let's consider the following protocol run, where p_i is a process in the honest-but-curious coalition $\mathcal{C}$ and p_j needs to access a slot of a resource $\mathcal{R}$. It is possible for p_j to ask for a slot r_j from p_i. As a consequence, p_i will learn that p_j is willing to access the slot r_j. From this time on, p_i declares the assignment $\langle p_j, r_j \rangle$. Considering that A satisfies properties 1 and 2, p_i will eventually access the slot and this violates property 3. $\qquad\square_{Lemma\ 1}$

A a consequence of Lemma 1, assignment algorithms based on explicit permissions for resource allocation cannot solve O-mA and thus neither SO-mA. Examples of such algorithms in the context of distributed mutual exclusion are ([14], [16], [17], [18]). A class of algorithms that satisfies the necessary condition of Lemma 1 is the one based on a rotating coordinator approach (also called perpetual circulating token [5], [15]) as shown in the next section.

5   A Rotating Token Algorithm for Solving O-mA

5.1   Ruling Out Trivial Perpetual Circulating Token Algorithms

Let us consider a standard token-based algorithm, namely *trivial-A*, assigning slots as follows: When a process receives the token, it could select and access a slot of the resource $\mathcal{R}$, without sending out any notification.

Once the token owner releases the slot, the token is forwarded to another process, according to a deterministic order defining a logical ring.

Note that, this algorithm satisfies property 1 and 2 and it is not in the family defined by Lemma 1.

The following Lemmas show that this simple algorithm implements O-mA and SO-mA only if there is at most one honest-but-curious process.

Lemma 2. *Consider an algorithm trivial-A running on the top of the distributed system described in Section 3 and satisfying properties 1 and 2. If $|\mathcal{C}| \geq 2$, then trivial-A cannot ensure SO-mA property.*

Proof Let us consider the following run where two honest-but-curious processes are respectively the predecessor and the successor of an honest process p_i in the ring and the communication delay is bounded by δ (see Section 3). When p_{i-1} sends the token to p_i and it decides to access a slot r_j, if p_i keeps the slot for an interval of time greater than 2δ then p_{i-1} and p_{i+1} can collude to infer deterministically that p_i has acquired a slot. This can be simply accomplished by looking at the timestamps of token messages sent from p_{i-1} to p_i and from p_i to p_{i+1}. This violates the SO-mA property. $\square_{Lemma\ 2}$

The next Lemma follows directly from the previous one:

Lemma 3. *Consider a distributed system with a bound δ on message transfer delay and an algorithm trivial-A running on top of it. If $m = 1$ and $|\mathcal{C}| \geq 2$, trivial-A cannot ensure O-mA property.*

5.2   A Rotating Token Algorithm Resilient to $|\mathcal{C}| \leq n - 2$ Honest-But-Curious Processes

Our algorithm is token-based and works in rounds. As in the trivial algorithm, the token circulates on the top of a logical ring formed by the processes (i.e. each process p_i passes the token to its neighbor $p_{i+1 mod n}$). Each round is characterized by two phases, *allocation phase*, where request() operations are handled and resource slots are allocated to processes, and *release phase*, where each process frees its assigned slot once it has finished with it. Each round is led by a coordinator p_c that takes care of the token creation, encoding, and dissemination for that specific round. A round ends when all allocated slots are released. The next round is coordinated by the process that follows p_c in the logical ring. In the following, we will use the term *ticket* to indicate a numerical representation of a slot. The coordinator will create n tickets (that is, a ticket per process in the system) regardless of the number of actual slots.

Allocation Phase: The coordinator of the current round creates a token, *request_token*, containing a set of tickets $\{tk_1, tk_2, \ldots, tk_n\}$, each one identifying a resource slot. Only m out of n tickets will univocally be associated to actual slots of the resource (i.e. *valid tickets*) while the remaining $n - m$ tickets (i.e. *invalid ticket*) represent dummy slots. Invalid tickets help prevent leakage of information on actual assignments.

At the beginning of each round, the coordinator picks one ticket, encrypts the *request_token* via ElGamal encryption [10], and forwards the token to the next process in the ring. Upon the receipt of the token, a process p_i picks a ticket, re-encrypts the token to make it indistinguishable, and forwards it to the next process in the ring. After getting the ticket, p_i will decrypt it by asking other processes for their ephemeral keys i.e., a temporary key that can be used only to decrypt the current ticket; if the ticket is valid and p_i requested a slot of $\mathcal{R}$, then it will trigger the grantResource event, otherwise it is ready for the release phase.

Release Phase: The release phase starts when the *request_token* returns to the coordinator. The coordinator creates a *release_token*, used to identify the released tickets, and starts to circulate it in the logical ring. A ticket is released by a process p_i in two cases: (i) p_i did not request a slot of $\mathcal{R}$ or, (ii) p_i finished with the slot (i.e., when invoking the release() operation). Every time the *release_token* is passed to the next process, it is re-encrypted to avoid information leakage.

The token *release_token* circulates continuously till the coordinator verifies that the number of released tickets is equal to n. At this point, the round is completed and the next process in the ring becomes the new coordinator for a new round.

5.3   ElGamal Encryption with Multiple Parties

Notation and Assumptions. In the following, we use $y \leftarrow f(x)$ to indicate the assignment to y of the value obtained evaluating a function f over the input x, while we will use $y \xleftarrow{u} S$ to indicate that y is a random element uniformly selected from a set S. We indicate with $\mathbb{Z}_q$ the class of residues modulo q. In the following, we will assume to have a cyclic subgroup G of prime order q and generator g where the Decisional Diffie-Hellman (DDH) assumption [7] holds. Informally, the DDH assumption states that given a triple (g^x, g^y, g^{xy}) with $x, y \xleftarrow{u} \mathbb{Z}_q$ it can be distinguished from a triple in the form (g^x, g^y, g^z), with $z \xleftarrow{u} \mathbb{Z}_q$, by using a probabilistic polynomial time algorithm, with negligible probability. For a concrete instantiation, we consider G to be the set of quadratic residues of $\mathbb{Z}_p^*$ where p is a *safe* prime, i.e., $p = 2q + 1$ with prime q. A generator g of the group G is simply found by selecting $\bar{g} \xleftarrow{u} \mathbb{Z}_p^*$ and setting $g = \bar{g}^2 \bmod p$ whenever $\bar{g} \neq 1$.

ElGamal Encryption. The idea behind ElGamal scheme is to use g^{xy} as a shared secret between sender and recipient. The private key is $y \xleftarrow{u} \mathbb{Z}_q$ while the public key is the value $g^y \in G$.

To encrypt an element $m \in G$, it is enough to randomly select an element $r \xleftarrow{u} \mathbb{Z}_q$ and compute the ciphertext as a pair $(c_1, c_2) = (g^r, mg^{ry}) \in G \times G$. The recipient of the ciphertext (c_1, c_2) recovers m by computing $c_2/c_1^y \in G$.

Note that, under the DDH assumption, ElGamal encryption is semantically secure [7]. Intuitively, a semantically secure scheme does not leak any information about the encrypted message. In particular, given a ciphertext (c_1, c_2) of one of two messages m_0 and m_1, an adversary cannot tell which message was encrypted. This holds even if the adversary chooses both messages, as long as they are both in G.

Adaptation. We adapt the ElGamal crypto-system to work with multiple parties. Each process p_i has a private key $Pr\_key_i \xleftarrow{u} \mathbb{Z}_q$, and the corresponding public key is calculated as $g^{Pr\_key_i}$. In addition, p_i also maintains the *group public key* as the value $g^Y = g^{\sum_{p_i \in \Pi} Pr\_key_i}$.

We use the ElGamal crypto-system to encrypt tickets whose values contain relevant information about slots of the resource $\mathcal{R}$ (e.g. such as network address, memory location, printer ID, etc...). Thus, generic numerical tickets must be mapped into elements of the subgroup G of quadratic residues in $\mathbb{Z}_p^*$.

The standard mapping-then-encrypt procedure works as follows: (i) Consider the ticket t as an element of $\mathbb{Z}_q$, (ii) set $\bar{t} = t + 1$, and (iii) encrypt the value $\bar{t}^2 \bmod p$. The decryption phase is more involved: (i) decrypt and recover the plaintext $\bar{m} = \bar{t}^2 \bmod p$, (ii) compute a square root of $\bar{m}$ as $m = \bar{m}^{(p+1)/4} \bmod p$, and return the ticket $m - 1$ if $m \leq q$, or $p - (m - 1)$ when $m > q$. In the rest of the paper we assume that tickets or any arbitrary messages are in G, either directly or through the mapping described above.

A ticket t is encrypted for the group of precesses as (g^r, tg^{rY}). Each process must contribute to the decryption phase in order to recover the ticket by computing the partial value $g^{rPr\_key_i}$. The product modulo p of these partial values from all processes is equal to g^{rY} which is used to recover t as in standard ElGamal. We define a function *removeLayer* that receives as input a valid ciphertext and *removes* the component $g^{rPr\_key_i}$ from it, effectively allowing other processes to decrypt the message. This function is executed locally by the process p_i.

Notice that, ElGamal ciphertexts can easily be randomized, i.e., given a ciphertext (c_1, c_2) anyone can produce a new ciphertext (c_1', c_2') on the same message without knowing any secret key or learning the message itself. Indeed, given (g^r, tg^{rY}), it is enough to select $r^* \xleftarrow{u} \mathbb{Z}_q$ and compute a new and unlinkable ciphertext $(g^{r+r^*}, tg^{(r+r^*)Y})$. The security of this randomized ElGamal encryption still holds as shown in [13].

5.4 The Algorithm

In this section, we provide the details of the oblivious assignment scheme for our system model. In particular, we first describe the data structures maintained locally by each process p_i, then we provide the details about the coordinator selection and the round phases, i.e., the assignment phase and the release phase.

```
Init:
(01)   round_i ← 1; coordinator_i ← false; state_i ← NCS; releasing_i ← true;
(02)   Pr_key_i ← init_private_key(p_i); Pb_key_i ← init_public_key();
(03)   keys_i ← ∅; ticket_i ← ⊥; resource_i ← ⊥ ;

(04)   when Init or round_i changes
(05)        reset_variables();
(06)        if (i = round_i mod(n))
(07)             then coordinator_i ← true
(08)        endif

(09)   when coordinator_i becomes true
(10)        if (state_i = waiting)
(11)             then resource_i ← select_valid_slot({r_1, r_2, .., r_n})
(12)                  state_i ← CS
(13)                  releasing_i ← false
(14)                  trigger grantResource (resource_i)
(15)             else resource_i ← select_notValid_slot({r_1, r_2, .., r_n})
(16)        endIf
(17)        request_token ← create_request_token({r_1, r_2, .., r_n} \ resource_i)
(18)        send REQUEST (request_token) to p_(i+1)mod n
```

Fig. 1. The rotating leader protocol (code for p_i)

Data structures. Each process p_i maintains locally the following data structures:

- $round_i$: is an integer representing the round p_i is participating in;
- $coordinator_i$: is a boolean variable set to true when p_i is the coordinator for the current round, false otherwise;
- $state_i$: is a variable that can be set to $\{NCS, waiting, CS\}$ and it represents the state of p_i, respectively p_i is not interested in any resources, p_i is waiting for a resource, p_i has obtained a resource;
- $ticket_i$: is a pair $< rd, tk >$ where tk is an encrypted ticket associated to a slot (whether real or not) and rd is a random number used by the encryption algorithm and it is necessary but not sufficient to recover the decrypted value of the ticket;
- Pr_key_i/Pb_key_i: ElGamal private/public keys used to decrypt/encrypt tickets;
- $keys_i$: is a set variable, used in the assignment phase, to store all the temporary keys (i.e. *ephemeral keys*) needed to decrypt the selected ticket.
- $resource_i$: is an integer representing the slot id obtained by p_i;
- $releasing_i$: is a boolean flag. It is set to true when p_i has no assigned slot of $\mathcal{R}$, false otherwise.

In addition, the algorithm also employees two tokens, namely *request_token* and *release_token*. A token is essentially a set containing encrypted tickets and each ticket refers to real or dummy slots.

Round and Coordinator Change. The pseudo-code for the round and coordinator change is shown in Figure 1.

We defined the following functions to simplify the code:

- init_private_key(p_i)/init_public_key(): initialize p_i's private and public keys.
- reset_variables(): reset all variables, except $round_i$, as declared into the Init statement.

```
upon event request()
(01)    state_i ← waiting

(02)    when REQUEST (request_token) is delivered
(03)        if (¬coordinator_i)
(04)            then request_token ← shuffle(request_token)
(05)                request_token ← randomize_token(request_token)
(06)                ticket_i ← select_ticket(request_token)
(07)                send REQUEST (request_token) to p_{(i+1)modn}
(08)                for each p_j ∈ Π do
(09)                    send GET_EPHEMERAL_KEY (i, ticket_i) to p_j
(10)                endfor
(11)            else release_token ← create_release_token()
(12)                release_token ← release_resource(release_token, releasing_i, resource_i)
(13)                send TOKEN_RELEASE (release_token) to p_{(i+1)modn}
(14)        endif

(15)    when GET_EPHEMERAL_KEY(j, tk) is delivered:
(16)        ep_key_i ← generate_ephemeral_key(Pr_key_i, tk);
(17)        send EPHEMERAL_KEY (ep_key_i, i) to p_j

(18)    when EPHEMERAL_KEY(ep_key, j) is delivered:
(19)        keys_i ← keys_i ∪ {< ep_key, j >};

(20)    when (|keys_i| = n)
(21)        resource_i ← decodeElement(ticket_i, (keys_i ∪ {< Pr_key_i, i >}));
(22)        if ((resource_i ∈ valid) ∧ (state_i = waiting))
(23)            then state_i ← CS
(24)                releasing_i ← false
(25)                trigger grantResource (resource_i)
(26)        endif
```

Fig. 2. The request() protocol (code for p_i)

- select_valid_slot($\{r_1, r_2, .., r_n\}$): given the set of (real and dummy) resource slots $\{r_1, r_2, .., r_n\}$, select a real slot.
- select_notValid_slot($\{r_1, r_2, .., r_n\}$): given the set of (real and dummy) resource slots $\{r_1, r_2, .., r_n\}$, select a dummy slot.
- create_request_token($r_1, r_2, \ldots, r_{n-1}$): given the set of (real and dummy) resource slots $\{r_1, r_2, .., r_{n-1}\}$, creates a set of tickets and the corresponding request token.

A new round starts as soon as $round_i$ is updated (line 04 Figure 1, line 19 Figure 3) and this causes all local variable, except $round_i$, to be reset (line 05). Each process p_i checks whether it is a coordinator of the current round. If so, it sets the local $coordinator_i$ variable to true (lines 06 - 08). This triggers a new assignment phase lead by p_i (line 09). The new coordinator checks if it is in the waiting state (line 10) (that is, it is waiting for a slot) and, in that case, it selects a real slot of the resource (lines 11). Otherwise, the coordinator selects a dummy slot (line 15). After the selection, p_i creates and encrypts the request_token (line 17) and sends it to its "neighbor" $p_{i+1mod (n)}$ (line 18).

The request() Operation and the Assignment Phase. The pseudo-code of the request() operation and the assignment phase is shown in Figure 2. The functions in the pseudo-code are defined as follows:

- shuffle(T): given a token T, randomly permute the sequence of tickets
- randomize_token(T): given token T, re-encrypt each ticket in T
- select_ticket(T): return a ticket tk randomly selected and removed from the token T.
- generate_ephemeral_key($Pr\_key_j, ticket_i$): given a private key Pr_key_j and a ticket $ticket_i = < rd, tk_j >$, generates a temporary key (also called *ephemeral*) starting from the number rd included in $ticket_i$, that can be used to decrypt tk_j and get the slot $\hat{r}_j$.
- decodeElement($tk, \{k_1, k_2 \ldots k_j\}$): given a set of keys $\{k_1, k_2 \ldots k_j\}$ and a ticket tk, decrypt tk and return its cleartext value
- create_release_token(): create the *release_token* to collect released tickets.
- release_resource(T, b, r_j): given a token T, a boolean value b, and a slot r_j, process the token T according to the boolean value b. In particular, if b is true then the slot r_j is released otherwise the function does nothing.

When a process p_i needs a slot of $\mathcal{R}$, it invokes the request() operation. The variable $state_i$ is thus set to *waiting* (line 01). When the *request_token* is delivered to p_i, it checks if it is the coordinator for this round (line 02). If p_i is not the coordinator, then it means that the assignment phase for this round is still running and a ticket can be chosen from the token. The selection consists of three steps: token shuffling (line 04) , token re-randomization (line 05) and finally ticket selection (line 06). Once a ticket has been selected, it has to be decrypted to recover the slot id. For this purpose, p_i sends a GET_EPHEMERAL_KEY message to other processes (lines 08 - 10).

If p_i is the coordinator, then all slots have been assigned for the current round and a release phase should start (line 11 - 14). Hence, p_i creates the *release_token* (line 11), and embeds its encrypted $releasing_i$ flag into the token (line 12). Finally, the token is passed to $p_{i+1 \bmod n}$ (line 13).

When a process p_i receives a GET_EPHEMERAL_KEY(j, tk) message, it generates a temporary key that can only be used to decrypt the ticket tk (line 16) and returns it to p_j. When all ephemeral keys are available (line 20), then p_i decrypts the ticket, recovers the slot id (line 21), and use the slot in case is a real one (lines 22 - 25).

The release() Operation and the Release Phase. The pseudo-code of the release() operation and the release phase is shown in Figure 3.

In the pseudo-code, we used release_resource(T, b) and randomize_token(T) defined earlier and we use the following new functions:

- remove_layer(T): given an encrypted release token T, removes the encrypted layer of p_i
- isFree(T): given a token T, check if each slot in the release token T has been released.

A slot is released by calling the release() operation. In this case, the variable $state_i$ is set to NCS and the flag $releasing_i$ is set to true (lines 01 - 02). When p_i receives *release_token*, it checks whether it is the coordinator for the current round. If p_i is not the coordinator, according to its state, it releases or keeps

```
upon event release():
(01)    state_i ← NCS
(02)    releasing_i ← true

(03)    when TOKEN_RELEASE (release_token) is delivered
(04)        if (¬coordinator_i)
(05)            then release_token ← release_resource(release_token, releasing_i, resource_i);
(06)                release_token ← randomize_token(release_token)
(07)                release_token ← remove_layer(release_token)
(08)                send TOKEN_RELEASE (release_token) to p_(i+1)modn
(09)            else if (isFree(release_token))
(10)                then coordinator_i ← false
(11)                    round_i ← round_i + 1;
(12)                    send NEW_ROUND (round_i) to p_(i+1)modn
(13)                else release_token ← create_release_token()
(14)                    release_token ← release_resource(release_token, releasing_i, resource_i)
(15)                    send TOKEN_RELEASE (release_token) to p_(i+1)modn
(16)                endif
(17)        endif

(18)    when NEW_ROUND(rd) is delivered
(19)        if (rd > round_i)
(20)            then round_i ← rd;
(21)        endif
(22)        send NEW_ROUND (rd) to p_(i+1)modn
```

Fig. 3. The release() protocol (code for p_i)

the assigned slot (line 05), it re-randomizes the token (line 06), removes its encryption layer (line 07), and finally passes the token to its neighbor in the logical ring (line 08). If p_i is the coordinator for the current round, then it checks whether all other processes released their assigned slots (lines 09 - 16). If all slots were released, then p_i sends a NEW_ROUND message to its neighbor so that a new round can be started (line 12). Otherwise, the current token is discarded and a new turn of the release phase is started (lines 13 - 16). Finally, when a process p_i receives a NEW_ROUND message, it updates the local variable $round_i$ and forwards the NEW_ROUND message to its neighbor (lines 19 - 22).

Correctness Proofs. Due to lack of space, we provide here only the statements of the main Lemmas. Proof of lemma 6 can be found in [1].

Lemma 4. *Let $\Pi = \{p_1, p_2, \ldots, p_n\}$ be the set of processes of the distributed system and let $\{r_1, r_2, \ldots, r_m\}$ be the set of slots of the resource $\mathcal{R}$. Given the algorithm shown in Figures 1 - 3 and given two processes $p_i, p_j \in \Pi$, if p_i and p_j access concurrently the resource $\mathcal{R}$, then the slot r_x assigned to p_i and the slot r_y assigned to p_j are distinct.*

Lemma 5. *Let $\Pi = \{p_1, p_2, \ldots, p_n\}$ be the set of processes of the distributed system and let $\{r_1, r_2, \ldots, r_m\}$ be the slots of the resource $\mathcal{R}$. Given the algorithm shown in Figures 1 - 3, then any process p_i that invokes the request() operation will eventually obtain a slot r_j of $\mathcal{R}$.*

Lemma 6. *Let $\Pi = \{p_1, p_2 \ldots p_n\}$ be the set of processes of the distributed system and let $\{r_1, r_2, \ldots r_m\}$ be the slots of the resource $\mathcal{R}$. Given the algorithm shown in Figures 1 - 3, if $|\mathcal{C}| \leq n - 2$ then the O-mA property is satisfied.*

5.5   Discussion

Improving Resource Utilization. The algorithm shown in Figures 1 - 3 might suffer in some runs from poor resource utilization, i.e., a competing process may not obtain a valid slot even if there are several available. Indeed, only the coordinator is able to deterministically selects a valid ticket. All other processes pick an encrypted ticket at random. As a consequence, even though fairness is provided (because eventually every process will become a coordinator), resource utilization is quite poor. As an example, consider a process p_i that is m hops away from the coordinator. It may happen that all m slots are assigned to the intermediate processes (i.e., those between the coordinator and p_i) that are not interested in accessing a slot. One way to improve resource utilization could be executing concurrent rounds with multiple coordinators. The idea is to let coordinators start new rounds as soon as slots become available. There could be up to m concurrent rounds in which each slot is managed by a distinct coordinator.

Comparison with an Algorithm Based on a Trusted Third Party. In [1], we considered an algorithm based on a fair Trusted Third Party (TTP) that regulates access to the slots. Each process sends a request to access a slot of $\mathcal{R}$ to the TTP. The TTP assigns one of the m slots, every time that one is available, and sends a reply to the process. We proved a bound on the maximum number of honest-but-curious processes (i.e., $|\mathcal{C}| \leq n - 2$) that can be tolerated to solve O-mA with the TTP-based algorithm. Intuitively, the communication bound δ creates an information leakage that can be exploited by a coalition $\mathcal{C}$ with $|\mathcal{C}| = n - 1$ processes. Processes in $\mathcal{C}$ may collude and issue requests to the TTP exactly at the same time. If a slot is not allocated by the TTP to a honest-but-curious process within the time bound, then it is possible to infer that the honest process has received one slot. Such a slot can also be uniquely identified which implies that O-mA is violated. This bound matches the one found in Lemma 6. Thus our algorithms has the same resiliency to honest-but-curious processes as the one based on a TTP.

Adapting the Algorithm to Satisfy SO-mA. Our basic scheme does not provide the SO-mA property. Indeed, if the round leader belongs to $\mathcal{C}$, it will find out the number of processes that are using any slots of the resource. This is enough to violate, in some runs, the SO-mA property. It is possible to avoid this leakage by modifying the release phase implementing a *secure − or* of the internal states of the processes. In particular, *secure-or* will return 1 if there is at least one process in CS (critical section) state, false otherwise. But the number of processes in CS state is kept private. The *secure-or* can be implemented by simply exploiting the homomorphic property of ElGamal encryption. We will investigate further this idea in future work.

6   Conclusion

This paper introduced the oblivious assignment problem, i.e., a coordination problem, where n processes compete to get exclusive access to one of the m

available slots of a resource $\mathcal{R}$, while still maintaining the obliviousness of the assignment. A rotating token algorithm solving the oblivious assignment problem has been introduced. This algorithm has been proven correct as long as at least two honest processes are in the distributed system. This bound matches the one proved in [1] when considering a centralized TTP that assigns slots to processes. All these results are versatile and take into account the fact that honest-but-curious processes are aware of both when the communication delay is within a certain bound and the value of the bound itself.

We are studying how to strengthen our algorithm to cope with byzantine adversaries that can actively and arbitrarily disrupt the protocol. We believe certain technical tools can be used to convert our scheme for honest-but-curious adversaries into a scheme resilient against byzantine adversaries. For example, it's possible to prevent injection of spurious messages via insubvertible encryption [2], that is, ciphertexts can still be randomized as in our scheme but no adversary can inject ciphertexts not produced by the round leader and no existing ciphertext can be corrupted unless it is a legitimate re-randomization. The correctness of other operations can be performed via standard zero-knowledge proofs. We leave the details of this approach to future work.

References

1. Ateniese, G., Baldoni, R., Bonomi, S., Di Luna, G.A.: Oblivious Assignment with m Slots. Technical report, MIDLAB 2/12 - University of Rome "La Sapienza" (2012), http://www.dis.uniroma1.it/~midlab/publications.php
2. Ateniese, G., Camenisch, J., de Medeiros, B.: Untraceable rfid tags via insubvertible encryption. In: Proceedings of the 12th ACM Conference on Computer and Communications Security, CCS 2005, pp. 92–101. ACM, New York (2005)
3. Attiya, H., Bar-Noy, A., Dolev, D., Peleg, D., Reischuk, R.: Renaming in an asynchronous environment. Journal of the ACM 37, 524–548 (1990)
4. Attiya, H., Welch, J.: Distributed Computing: Fundamentals, Simulations and Advanced Topics, 2nd edn. John Wiley Interscience (March 2004)
5. Baldoni, R., Virgillito, A., Petrassi, R.: A distributed mutual exclusion algorithm for mobile ad-hoc networks. In: IEEE Symposium on Computers and Communications, p. 539 (2002)
6. Barnett, A., Smart, N.P.: Mental Poker Revisited. In: Paterson, K.G. (ed.) Cryptography and Coding 2003. LNCS, vol. 2898, pp. 370–383. Springer, Heidelberg (2003)
7. Boneh, D.: The Decision Diffie-Hellman Problem. In: Buhler, J.P. (ed.) ANTS 1998. LNCS, vol. 1423, pp. 48–63. Springer, Heidelberg (1998)
8. Bulgannawar, S., Vaidya, N.H.: A distributed k-mutual exclusion algorithm. In: International Conference on Distributed Computer Systems, pp. 153–160 (1995)
9. Burns, J.E., Peterson, G.L.: The ambiguity of choosing. In: Proceedings of the Eighth Annual ACM Symposium on Principles of Distributed Computing, Priciple of Distributed Computing 1989, pp. 145–157. ACM, New York (1989)
10. El Gamal, T.: A Public Key Cryptosystem and a Signature Scheme Based on Discrete Logarithms. In: Blakely, G.R., Chaum, D. (eds.) CRYPTO 1984. LNCS, vol. 196, pp. 10–18. Springer, Heidelberg (1985)

11. Gentry, C.: Fully homomorphic encryption using ideal lattices. In: Proceedings of the 41st Annual ACM Symposium on Theory of Computing, pp. 169–178. ACM (2009)
12. Goldreich, O.: Foundations of Cryptography: vol. 2, Basic Applications. Cambridge University Press, New York (2004)
13. Golle, P., Jakobsson, M., Juels, A., Syverson, P.: Universal re-encryption for mixnets. In: Proceedings of the 2004 RSA Conference, pp. 163–178. Springer (2002)
14. Kakugawa, H., Fujita, S., Yamashita, M., Ae, T.: A distributed k-mutual exclusion algorithm using k-coterie. Information Processing Letters 49(4), 213–218 (1994)
15. Le Lann, G.: Distributed systems - towards a formal approach. In: Congress of International Federation for Information Processing, pp. 155–160 (1977)
16. Maekawa, M.: A square root n algorithm for mutual exclusion in decentralized systems. ACM Transaction on Computer System 3(2), 145–159 (1985)
17. Raymond, K.: A distributed algorithm for multiple entries to a critical section. Information Processing Letters 30(4), 189–193 (1989)
18. Raynal, M.: Algorithms for mutual exclusion. MIT Press, Cambridge (1986)
19. Ricart, G., Agrawala, A.K.: An optimal algorithm for mutual exclusion in computer networks. Communincations of the ACM 24(1), 9–17 (1981)
20. Shamir, A., Rivest, R.L., Adleman, L.M.: Mental Poker. Technical Report MIT-LCS-TM-125, Massachusetts Institute of Technology (1979)
21. Suzuki, I., Kasami, T.: A distributed mutual exclusion algorithm. ACM Transaction on Computer System 3(4), 344–349 (1985)
22. Yao, A.C.: Protocols for secure computations. In: 23st Annual IEEE Symposium on Foundations of Computer Science, pp. 160–164. IEEE Computer Society Press (1982)

BLIP: Non-interactive Differentially-Private Similarity Computation on Bloom filters

Mohammad Alaggan[1], Sébastien Gambs[1], and Anne-Marie Kermarrec[2]

[1] Université de Rennes 1 – INRIA/IRISA, Rennes, France
malaggan@irisa.fr, sebastien.gambs@irisa.fr
[2] INRIA Rennes Bretagne-Atlantique, Rennes, France
anne-marie.kermarrec@inria.fr

Abstract. In this paper, we consider the scenario in which the profile of a user is represented in a compact way, as a Bloom filter, and the main objective is to privately compute in a distributed manner the similarity between users by relying only on the Bloom filter representation. In particular, we aim at providing a high level of privacy with respect to the profile even if a potentially unbounded number of similarity computations take place, thus calling for a non-interactive mechanism. To achieve this, we propose a novel non-interactive differentially private mechanism called BLIP (for BLoom-and-flIP) for randomizing Bloom filters. This approach relies on a bit flipping mechanism and offers high privacy guarantees while maintaining a small communication cost. Another advantage of this non-interactive mechanism is that similarity computation can take place even when the user is offline, which is impossible to achieve with interactive mechanisms. Another of our contributions is the definition of a probabilistic inference attack, called the "Profile Reconstruction attack", that can be used to reconstruct the profile of an individual from his Bloom filter representation. More specifically, we provide an analysis of the protection offered by BLIP against this profile reconstruction attack by deriving an upper and lower bound for the required value of the differential privacy parameter ϵ.

1 Introduction

Consider a distributed network in which each node is an individual that has a profile representing his interests. In this context, many distributed applications, like recommender systems or private matching, require computing some kind of pairwise similarity between the profiles of different nodes[1]. Moreover, in a dynamic system, such computation takes place continuously as new nodes join the system. Some of the challenges that such systems would face include privacy and scalability issues. For instance, privacy concerns arise naturally due to the potentially sensitive nature of profiles, and some users may even refuse to participate in the similarity computation if they have no guarantees on the privacy of their profiles.

---

[1] For the sake of simplicity, we consider in the rest of the paper a user per machine, and we refer to it as a node.

A.W. Richa and C. Scheideler (Eds.): SSS 2012, LNCS 7596, pp. 202–216, 2012.
© Springer-Verlag Berlin Heidelberg 2012

Dwork and Naor [12] have proved a strong impossibility result stating that for any privacy mechanism whose output has some utility (measured in terms of min-entropy[2]), there exists a piece of auxiliary information, which if available to an adversary, can cause a privacy breach whose amount of information provided on the original database (that was supposed to be protected) is at least of the same order than the utility. Therefore, Dwork and Naor [12, Section 3] recommended to depart from an *absolute* definition of privacy to a *relative* one such as *differential privacy*, which is the one that we adopt in this paper.

The main privacy guarantee provided by differential privacy is that for any privacy breach the adversary is able to cause with respect to the database, adding or removing a single row from the database will not significantly change the probability of success of causing this privacy breach for an adversary observing the output of the differentially-private mechanism. In general, in the literature the database model considered is such that each row contains the data of a particular individual and therefore the database effectively corresponds to the collection of the individuals' data. In this setting, protecting a row through differential privacy means protecting the privacy of a particular individual (which corresponds to a row). In our setting, the database is actually the profile of an individual, which is composed of the items he has liked, and therefore the guarantees provided by differential privacy protects the items contained in the profile.

One of the usual limits of differential privacy is that each time a differentially private interactive computation takes place, the user loses a little bit of privacy (as measured by the value of some privacy parameter ϵ). Therefore, if this computation takes place too many times, the user may spend all his privacy budget and remains with no privacy left (*i.e.*, the adversary will be able to reconstruct almost entirely the user's profile). However, in a dynamic system as the one we consider, there is no upper bound on the maximum number of similarity computations that can occur (as nodes continuously keep joining the system) and therefore an interactive mechanism would be of limited applicability.

To simultaneously address the privacy and scalability issues, we propose BLIP (for BLoom-then-flIP), a non-interactive differentially private mechanism, which computes a standard *Bloom filter* [7] from the profile of a node, and then perturbs it prior to its public release in order to ensure high privacy guarantees. This randomized Bloom filter can be used an unbounded number of times to compute the similarity of this node with other profile without breaching the privacy of the profiles. Moreover, this approach has exactly the same communication cost as "plain" (*i.e*, non-private) Bloom filters, while offering much higher privacy guarantees, but at the cost of a slight decrease of utility.

In differential privacy, the trade-off between utility and privacy can be set through the privacy parameter ϵ. However, being able to choose an appropriate value for this parameter is still an open research question, which has not really been investigated, with a few exceptions [17,1]. In this paper, we address this issue by proposing an inference attack called the "Profile Reconstruction attack", that can be used to reconstruct the profile of a node from its perturbed Bloom filter representation. More specifically, we provide an analysis of the protection and the utility offered by BLIP against this

---

[2] We refer the interested reader to [1] for a discussion on the min-entropy of the output of a differentially-private mechanism.

attack, by deriving an upper and lower bound for the required value of the differential privacy parameter ϵ. In short, the lower bound gives theoretical guarantees on the resulting approximation error generated by a specific value of the privacy parameter, while the upper bound demonstrates experimentally that the privacy parameter must be below a certain threshold to be able to prevent this attack. Furthermore, we evaluate experimentally the trade-off between privacy and utility that can be reached with BLIP on a semantic clustering task in which nodes are grouped based on the similarity between their profiles.

The paper is organized as follows. First, in Section 2, we present the system model and background on Bloom filters and differential privacy necessary to understand our work. Afterwards, we propose BLIP, a non-interactive differentially private mechanism for randomizing Bloom filters in Section 3 and analyze in details the privacy guarantees it provides. In Section 4, we evaluate the impact of this mechanism on utility, as measured in terms of recall on a semantic clustering task. In Section 5, we describe a novel inference attack, called the profile reconstruction attack, that can reconstruct a profile from its Bloom filter representation and show how BLIP can be used to drastically reduce its impact. Finally, we give an overview of the related work in Section 6 before concluding in Section 7.

2   System Model and Background

2.1   System Model

We consider a distributed system of nodes, in which nodes are characterized by their profile representing the associated user's interests. For example, the profile of a node can be a vector of items that have been tagged using a collaborative platform [2] such as Delicious[3], or queries that have been performed on a search engine or ratings on movies. We denote the profile of a user as c, a set of items, which is a subset of an application domain $\mathcal{I}$. While $\mathcal{I}$ may be infinite (e.g., the set of all possible URLs), a specific profile is always finite.

We assume that the computation of similarity between pairs of nodes takes place on a regular basis as nodes in the network get in contact with new nodes, and try to dynamically maintain a list of the most similar nodes in the network. For instance, in the case of a distributed semantic clustering algorithm [6], nodes need to compute regularly their similarity in order to update their semantic neighborhood. In our constructions, we also assume that a node never releases directly its profile, but rather a Bloom filter representation [7] (cf. Section 2.2) of it. When some node a wants to compute its similarity with another node b, it will do so by using b's public Bloom filter.

The profile is a personal and private information that should be protected, and therefore our main concern is *how to compute the similarity measure while preserving its privacy*. In this context, this means not revealing the contents of the profile and restricting the possibility for an adversary observing the Bloom filter to infer the presence or absence of a particular item in this profile. We consider a computationally-unbounded adversary that can observe the released Bloom filter, but not the internal state of a node

---

[3] http://delicious.com/

while computing the Bloom filter. In particular, the adversary does not have access to the random coins used by the node when computing a perturbed version of the Bloom filter's representation of its profile.

2.2 Bloom Filters

A Bloom filter [7] is a probabilistic data structure composed of an array of m bits along with a set $\mathcal{H}$ of k hash functions. Each hash function maps an item to a uniform random position $\{0, \ldots, m-1\}$ in the Bloom filter. Bloom filters form a compact representation of sets as they can represent any set with just m bits, for a given trade-off between the size of the structure and the false positive probability (*i.e.*, the probability of an item being considered to be in the Bloom filter while it is not). Bloom filters are often used for applications in which the storage space is limited or for protocols for which the communication cost has to be low but some false positives are tolerable.

Bloom filters are associated with two operations: the add operation inserts an item into the Bloom filter while the query operation tests if an item is already present in it (some types of Bloom filters also support the removal of items [23] but we do not consider them in this paper). Both operations start by applying the k hash functions from $\mathcal{H}$ to the item in question to obtain a subset of $\{0, \ldots, m-1\}$ of positions in the Bloom filter. The add operation inserts the item by setting the bits corresponding to those positions to one in the Bloom filter, and does this independently of the previous values of these bits. The query operation checks if an item is included in the Bloom filter by verifying whether or not all those bits are set to one.

In short, the probability of false positive is a function of m, k, and n the number of items inserted in the Bloom filter. In general, the values of m and k are chosen according to a trade-off decision between the space usage and the false positive rate (an upper and lower bound for this trade-off is provided in [9]).

2.3 Similarity Measure

A *similarity measure* sim is a function that takes as input two sets A and B representing the profiles of two nodes and outputs a value in the range between 0 and 1 (*i.e.*, $\text{sim}(A, B) \in [0, 1]$), where 0 indicates that the sets are entirely different (the profiles have no items in common) while 1 means that the sets are identical (the nodes can be considered as sharing exactly the same interests). Recall that in this paper, the profiles are represented as Bloom filters and therefore the similarity is computed directly on the Bloom filters and not on the profiles themselves. As a concrete instance, consider the *cosine similarity* that is commonly used to assess the similarity between two sets [6] and can be seen as a normalized overlap between the sets. The cosine similarity is defined as

$$\text{cos\_sim}(A, B) = \frac{|A \cap B|}{\sqrt{|A| \times |B|}},\tag{1}$$

where $|A|$ and $|B|$ are the sizes of the sets A and B. The *size of the set intersection* between A and B (*i.e.*, $|A \cap B|$) is equivalent to the *scalar product*[4] in the case where the sets are represented as binary vectors (*i.e.*, characteristic function).

2.4   Differential Privacy

In this paper, we are interested in a recent notion of privacy, called *differential privacy* [10]. Differential privacy aims at providing strong privacy guarantees with respect to the input of some computation by randomizing the output of this computation, and this independently of the auxiliary information that the adversary may have gathered. In our setting, the input of the computation is the raw profile of a node and the randomized output will be a perturbed version of the Bloom filter representation of this profile.

Two profiles $\mathbf{x}$ and $\mathbf{x}'$ are said to *differ in at most one element* or said to be *neighbors* if they are equal except for possibly one entry.

Definition 1 (Differential privacy [11]). *A randomized function* $\mathcal{F} : \mathcal{D}^n \to \mathcal{D}^n$ *is* ϵ-*differentially private, if for all neighboring profiles* $\mathbf{x}, \mathbf{x}' \in \mathcal{D}^n$ *and for all* $\mathbf{t} \in \mathcal{D}^n$:

$$\Pr[\mathcal{F}(\mathbf{x}) = \mathbf{t}] \leqslant e^{\epsilon} \cdot \Pr[\mathcal{F}(\mathbf{x}') = \mathbf{t}] .$$

This probability is taken over all the coin tosses of $\mathcal{F}$ *and* e *is the base of the natural logarithm.*

The parameter ϵ is public and may take different values depending on the application (for instance it could be 0.01, 0.1 or even 0.25). The smaller the value of ϵ, the higher the privacy but also, as a result, the higher the impact might be on the utility of the resulting output.

Dwork, McSherry, Nissim and Smith have designed a generic technique, called the *Laplacian mechanism* [11], that achieves ϵ-differential privacy for a function f by adding random noise to the true answer of f before releasing it. Subsequently, McSherry and Talwar have proposed another mechanism, called the *exponential mechanism* [19] that, unlike the Laplacian mechanism that works only for functions with numerical output, provides differential privacy for functions whose output is more structured (*e.g.*, graphs or trees). These mechanisms are *interactive* as they require a two-way communication protocol between the curator (the entity in charge of the database) and the client performing the query. Therefore, during this computation, the curator has to be online in order to receive the query and prepare the associate response to this query.

On the other hand, a *non-interactive* mechanism computes some function from the original database and releases it once and for all, which corresponds to a one-way communication protocol. The output released by the non-interactive mechanism can later by used by anyone to compute the answer to a particular class of queries (usually not just a single specific query), without requiring any further interactions with the curator. It is important to understand that the answer is not computed by the non-interactive mechanism, but rather that the answer can be computed from the output released by

---

[4] The scalar product of two vectors of length l, $a = (a_1, \cdots, a_\ell)$ and $b = (b_1, \cdots, b_\ell)$, is defined as $\sum_{i=1}^{\ell} a_i b_i$.

the non-interactive mechanism, thus after publishing this output the curator can go of-fline. Examples of non-interactive mechanisms for differential privacy include [4,18]. Our proposition of differentially-private Bloom filter is based on the work of Beimel, Nissim and Omri [4] in which the authors address the "binary sum" problem, which deals with the computation of the number of ones in a private binary vector. More pre-cisely, we adapt their non-interactive mechanism to Bloom filters rather than binary vectors, with the goal of computing scalar product between two Bloom filters rather than computing the number of ones.

3 The Bit-Flipping Mechanism

We propose a novel approach relying on bit flipping to achieve differential privacy. The intuition behind our proposed mechanism is simple: before releasing a Bloom filter, each bit is flipped with a given probability so as to ensure differential privacy on the *items* of the profile from which the Bloom filter is derived. In this section, we provide a formal definition of our mechanism and compute the flipping probability that has the least impact on utility while preserving differential privacy. A particular challenging task is to derive how the flipping of bits influences the privacy of the items themselves.

3.1 Bloom-then-flip

More formally, the proposed non-interactive mechanism is a randomized function that for each bit of a Bloom filter, tosses a biased coin and based on the result, either out-puts the original value of the bit or its opposite (*i.e.*, flip it). Since the mechanism *flips* the Bloom filter representation of a profile, we call it BLIP (for *Bloom-then-flip*). For example, the mechanism may take as input the Bloom filter $(0, 1, 1, 0)$ and randomly decides to flip the first two bits with some bias, thus outputting $(1, 0, 1, 0)$. BLIP can be described as a randomized function $\mathcal{F} : \{0, 1\}^n \to \{0, 1\}^n$, where each bit of the output is the opposite as the corresponding bit of the input with probability p (the flip-ping probability), while otherwise it remains the same. Therefore, BLIP consists of (1) generating the Bloom filter representation of the profile first, and then (2) flipping the resulting Bloom filter (which is a binary vector).

The idea of randomizing each bit independently (as opposed to perturbing the final answer itself) is also known as the *randomized response technique* [24], and precedes the notion of differential privacy. The application of randomized response for differen-tial privacy was previously studied [4] but the definition of differential privacy adopted ([4, Definition 2.4]) slightly differs from ours. Indeed, in the model adopted in this pre-vious work [4], each individual bit belongs to and is held by a different node. Therefore, this model is very close to the setting of secure multiparty computation, while in our model all the bits of the Bloom filter belong to the same node. It is worth mentioning that the node owning this Bloom filter will publishes the perturbed version of the Bloom filter *once and for all*. This process may introduce permanent artifacts but the error they induced is bounded by $O(\sqrt{n})$ with constant probability. Due to space constraints, we leave the details of the proof of this bound to the full version of the paper.

The following is the definition for the local model of differential privacy that we also use in the setting of non-interactive differential privacy.

Definition 2 (Differential privacy (local model)). *A randomized function* $\mathcal{F}(\mathbf{x}) = (f(x_1), \ldots, f(x_n))$, *where* $f : \mathcal{D} \to \mathcal{D}$ *and* $\mathbf{x} = (x_1, \ldots, x_n)$, *is ϵ-differentially private, if for all values* $y, y' \in \mathcal{D}$, *and for all output* $t \in \mathcal{D}$:

$$\Pr[f(y) = t] \leqslant e^{\epsilon} \cdot \Pr[f(y') = t] ,$$

where the probability is taken over the randomness of f.

Definition 2 originally introduced in [4] is equivalent to Definition 1 as shown by Lemma 1. In this *local variant* of the definition, the perturbation is applied individually to each row of the database, and then the function is computed on the collection of perturbed rows. In contrast to the original (*i.e.*, global) model of differential privacy in which the function is computed first and then the answer is perturbed before releasing it. Moreover, in the local model if the dataset is split among several nodes, each node can perform the randomization locally before releasing its perturbed part of the data.

Lemma 1 (Equivalence of definitions.). *Definition 1 is equivalent to Definition 2.*

Proof. Let $(\mathbf{x}_{-i}, y)$ denotes the vector resulting from replacing the i-th coordinate the $\mathbf{x}$ with y (*e.g.*, $(x_1, \ldots, y, \ldots, x_n)$). We proceed by first proving that the proposed definition implies Definition 1 along the lines of [4].

Definition 2 $\implies$ *Definition 1.* For any two neighboring vectors $\mathbf{x}$ and $(\mathbf{x}_{-i}, y)$:

$$\frac{\Pr[\mathcal{F}(\mathbf{x}) = \mathbf{t}]}{\Pr[\mathcal{F}(\mathbf{x}_{-i}, y) = \mathbf{t}]} = \frac{\Pr[f(x_i) = t_i]}{\Pr[f(y) = t_i]} \cdot \frac{\prod_{j \neq i} \Pr[f(x_j) = t_j]}{\prod_{j \neq i} \Pr[f(x_j) = t_j]} \leqslant e^{\epsilon} ,$$

where $\mathbf{t} = (t_1, \ldots, t_n)$. In the above formula, the equality is obtained by independence while the inequality results from Definition 2.

Definition 1 $\implies$ *Definition 2.* For all x_i, y:

$$\frac{\Pr[f(x_i) = t_i]}{\Pr[f(y) = t_i]} = \frac{\Pr[f(x_i) = t_i]}{\Pr[f(y) = t_i]} \cdot \frac{\prod_{j \neq i} \Pr[f(x_j) = t_j]}{\prod_{j \neq i} \Pr[f(x_j) = t_j]} = \frac{\Pr[\mathcal{F}(\mathbf{x}) = \mathbf{t}]}{\Pr[\mathcal{F}(\mathbf{x}_{-i}, y) = \mathbf{t}]} \leqslant e^{\epsilon} ,$$

where $\mathbf{t} = (t_1, \ldots, t_n)$. In the above formula, the last equality is obtained by independence while the inequality results from Definition 1. $\square$

Clearly, the result holds only in case $\mathcal{F}$ could be decomposed to applications of a function f to each row independently. One of the consequence of this lemma is that it is possible to analyze only the local perturbation at the level of a single bit of a Bloom filter, while still guaranteeing differential privacy for the entire Bloom filter without requiring to analyze the BLIP mechanism as a whole.

3.2 The Flipping Probability

The bit-flipping function (flip) plays the role of the local function f in Definition 2, while the BLIP mechanism corresponds to $\mathcal{F}$ in this definition. The local perturbation function flip takes a bit x and outputs $1 - x$ with probability $p < 1/2$ and x otherwise. The main challenge is to find the optimal probability p that flip should use in order to maximize utility as a function of the privacy parameter ϵ. With respect to the utility, the smaller p, the more accurate the output and therefore the best utility can be obtained by minimizing p.

It is important to realize that analyzing the flipping of a bit of the Bloom filter *in isolation* is not sufficient to guarantee the privacy of individual *items* of the profile that are encoded in the Bloom filter. Indeed, recall that an item can potentially impact k different bits due to the use of k different hash functions. In particular, differential privacy is guaranteed *for individual items* by the randomized mechanism $\mathcal{F}$ if for each item $i \in \mathcal{I}$ and for each pair of neighboring profiles P_1, P_2 such that $i \notin P_2$ and $P_1 = P_2 \cup \{i\}$, and for all bit strings $t \in \{0,1\}^m$, the following condition holds:

$$\left| \ln \frac{\Pr(\mathcal{F}(\mathcal{B}_1) = t)}{\Pr(\mathcal{F}(\mathcal{B}_2) = t)} \right| \leqslant \epsilon , \tag{2}$$

where $\mathcal{B}_1$ is the Bloom filter of P_1 and $\mathcal{B}_2$ the Bloom filter of P_2.

Theorem 1 (Privacy guarantees for items). *Setting the bit-flipping probability p to $1/(1 + e^{\epsilon/k})$ satisfies condition (2) and thus provides ϵ-differential privacy for items. In other words, flipping the bits of a Bloom filter with this probability guarantees ϵ-differential privacy for the items encoded in this Bloom filter.*

Proof. Given a Bloom filter $\mathcal{B}$ equipped with a set $\mathcal{H}$ of hash functions, and an item i, let $T = \bigcup_{h \in \mathcal{H}} \{h(i)\}$ be the set of positions whose corresponding bits in $\mathcal{B}$ are equal to one if i is in $\mathcal{B}$, and $k = |T|$ be the number of those positions (not counting duplicates). We divide the Bloom filter $\mathcal{B}$ into two partitions: $\mathcal{B}^T$ and $\mathcal{B}^{-T}$, where the former is the restriction to the bits whose positions are in T as defined earlier, and the latter is the restriction to all other bits. A particular partition t^T (respectively t^{-T}) is defined in a similar manner. We denote by $q = 1 - p$, the inverse of the flipping probability (it is always the case that $q > p$).

As the profiles (and therefore the Bloom filters as well) are universally quantified, hence they can be treated as constants and not random variables. As a consequence, they do not affect the independence properties of $\mathcal{F}$, which is itself independent for each bit by definition. The proof proceeds as follows:

$$\left| \ln \frac{\Pr(\mathcal{F}(\mathcal{B}_1) = t)}{\Pr(\mathcal{F}(\mathcal{B}_2) = t)} \right| = \left| \ln \frac{\Pr(\mathcal{F}(\mathcal{B}_1^T) = t^T) \Pr(\mathcal{F}(\mathcal{B}_1^{-T}) = t^{-T})}{\Pr(\mathcal{F}(\mathcal{B}_2^T) = t^T) \Pr(\mathcal{F}(\mathcal{B}_2^{-T}) = t^{-T})} \right| \qquad \text{by independence}$$

$$= \left| \ln \frac{\Pr(\mathcal{F}(\mathcal{B}_1^T) = t^T)}{\Pr(\mathcal{F}(\mathcal{B}_2^T) = t^T)} \right| \qquad \text{because } \mathcal{B}_1^{-T} = \mathcal{B}_2^{-T}$$

$$= \left| \ln \frac{\Pr(\mathcal{F}(\overbrace{1 \ldots 1}^{k}) = t^T)}{\Pr(\mathcal{F}(\mathcal{B}_2^T) = t^T)} \right| \qquad \text{as } i \text{ is in } \mathcal{B}_1$$

$$= \left| \ln \frac{p^z q^{k-z}}{\delta} \right| = \left| \ln \left[\frac{q^k}{\delta} \left(\frac{p}{q} \right)^z \right] \right| ,$$

where $p^k \leqslant \delta \leqslant q^k$ (as $\mathcal{B}_2^T$ is just a fixed bit string) and $0 \leqslant z \leqslant k$ is the number of zero bits in t^T. If $p = 1/(1 + e^{\epsilon/k})$ then $q^x = (1 - p)^x = \exp(\epsilon x/k) p^x$ and

$(p/q)^x = \exp(-\epsilon x/k)$. Therefore $p^k \leqslant \delta \leqslant \exp(\epsilon)p^k$ or $1 \leqslant \delta/p^k \leqslant \exp(\epsilon)$ implying that $1 \geqslant p^k/\delta \geqslant \exp(-\epsilon)$, and hence $0 \geqslant \ln(p^k/\delta) \geqslant -\epsilon$.

$$\left| \ln\left[\frac{q^k}{\delta} \left(\frac{p}{q}\right)^z \right] \right| = \left| \ln\left[\frac{\exp(\epsilon)p^k}{\delta} \exp(-\epsilon z/k) \right] \right| = \left| \ln(p^k/\delta) + \epsilon(k-z)/k \right| .$$

We have for the second term $0 \leqslant \epsilon(k-z)/k \leqslant \epsilon$, from which it follows immediately that the maximum value of $\left| \ln(p^k/\delta) + \epsilon(k-z)/k \right|$ is at most ϵ, thus proving the theorem. Moreover, this maximum is tight showing that this choice of p is tight as well. $\quad\square$

Remark 1 (Optimality of p.). The case $k = 1$ reduces to protecting individual bits. In order to compute the values of p that ensures differential privacy *for a single bit* (in accordance to Definition 2), it is easy to verify that $p = \frac{1}{1+e^\epsilon}$ is the minimum value for which

$$\left| \ln \frac{\Pr(\mathrm{flip}(y) = b)}{\Pr(\mathrm{flip}(y') = b)} \right| \leqslant \epsilon ,$$

holds for all b, y, y' in $\{0, 1\}$. This value coincides with the value obtained by substituting 1 for k in $p = \frac{1}{1+e^{\epsilon/k}}$, thus showing its optimality.

We show how it is possible to address and correct the approximation error resulting from the bit flipping mechanism in the full version of this paper due to space constraints.

4   Utility Evaluation

In this section, we evaluate experimentally how the utility is impacted by the BLIP mechanism by applying it for the computation of a semantic clustering algorithm. More precisely, we consider a semantic clustering protocol whose objective is to provide each node of the system with its c closest nodes, as measured by the similarity based on the scalar product on their Bloom filters. In this setting, we measure the utility in terms of *recall*, which we formally define later [6]. We have used the three following datasets for our experiments from the Delicious and Digg collaborative platforms traces and a news survey conducted in our lab. The survey has been conducted on 120 users who gave their (binary) opinion on 100 news items. The profile of a user in the Digg trace are the items forwarded; in the Delicious trace, the items tagged; and in the survey trace, the news items liked.

	# of users	# of items	average profile size	Bloom filter size (m)	# of hash func. (k)
Delicious	500	51453	135	5000	18
Digg	500	1237	317	5000	18
Survey	120	196	68	5000	18

The experiment is conducted by simulating a clustering protocol, similarly to [6]. In this experiment, each node corresponds to one node from one of the three datasets described previously. In a random manner, each node i divides its profile p_i into two disjoint subsets, the *training* subset t_i and the *search* (or *evaluation*) subset s_i, such that $t_i \cup s_i = p_i$ and $|s_i|/|t_i| \approx 0.9$ (the value 0.9 has been chosen to match the setting of

[6]). The experiment is split into two steps: the clustering (*i.e.*, training) phase and the search phase.

The clustering phase is divided into 20 rounds. At each round, every node i exchanges its Bloom filter with its current neighbors and some other nodes picked at random [15]. Based on the information acquired, the node keeps as new neighbors, the nodes displaying a high similarity (if any). At the end of the clustering phase, each node will have chosen the c most similar nodes met so far as its *neighbors*. Usually after a sufficient number of rounds, the neighbors of a node should converge towards the optimal ones in terms of the recall (as defined in the next paragraph) [6].

Afterwards, the utility is evaluated by checking if each node can find the items contained in its search set s_i in the profiles of its neighbors. The number of the items found is divided by $|s_i|$ (for normalization) and forms the *recall* metric r (for $0 \leqslant r_i \leqslant 1$). Considering a particular clustering, the higher r, the more useful the clustering is. More formally, during the search phase, each node i computes its recall value r_i defined as:

$$r_i = \frac{|s_i \cap (\cup_{j \in n_i} t_j)|}{|s_i|},$$

where n_i is the set of neighbors of the node i once the clustering phase is terminated. The overall recall $r = \text{mean}(r_1, \ldots, r_n)$ simply corresponds to the average of the recalls of all the $n = 500$ (or $n = 120$ for the survey dataset) nodes (*cf.* Figure 1).

We provide in Figure 1 the results of the experiments for the recall versus privacy parameter ϵ (average over 100 runs). On this plot, we use $p = 1/(1 + \exp(\epsilon/k))$ for the flipping probability ($k = 18$). The main plot displays the recall obtained when using the cosine similarity based on the bias-corrected scalar product (which is developed in the full version of the paper). The other lines show the recall obtained for two different cases that act as a baseline: (1) when the similarity is computed on totally random Bloom filters (*i.e.*, Bloom filters whose bits are flipped with probability 0.5) and (2) when the similarity is computed with a plain Bloom filters that have not been flipped at all. Note that the intrinsic value of the recall that can be reached and the gap between the

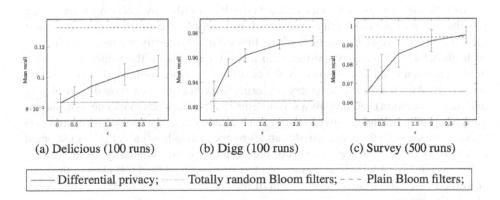

(a) Delicious (100 runs)   (b) Digg (100 runs)   (c) Survey (500 runs)

—— Differential privacy; ········· Totally random Bloom filters; - - - Plain Bloom filters;

Fig. 1. Recall obtained with BLIP. The bars correspond to the standard deviation.

baseline (1) and baseline (2) are directly dependent of the characteristics of the dataset considered.

From these plots, we can observe that the utility remains non-trivial even for values of ϵ that are small, in comparison to the utility obtained with totally randomized Bloom filters (which directly lead to a random neighborhood for each node). In general the utility obtained is far from the non-private solution (for Delicious the value is about 0.261) in which nodes exchange directly their profiles but this is inherent to the fact that the similarity is computed based on the Bloom filters (and not the profiles themselves) and this is not a drawback due to our flipping mechanism. When combined with the results of the experiments described in the next section (resilience to inference attacks), it is possible to observe the trade-off between privacy (*i.e.*, resilience against the profile reconstruction attack) and utility (*i.e.*, recall in the case of the semantic clustering task).

5   Profile Reconstruction Attack

In this section, we try to answer some of the fundamental questions raised by the use of differential privacy such that "How to choose the value of ϵ?" or "What does it mean for ϵ to be equal to 0.5 or 1?" by considering a particular inference attack. In a setting in which each node has its profile represented in the form of a Bloom filter, the main objective of the adversary is to infer the description of the profile of a node from its Bloom filter representation. We assume that in the same manner as other nodes in the network, the adversary (which in fact could simply be one of these nodes) can have easily access to the ϵ-differentially private Bloom filters released by the BLIP mechanism. We describe thereafter an inference attack, called the "profile reconstruction attack", by which the adversary produces as output a guess of the original profile behind a given Bloom filter. In doing so, we aim at empirically computing an upper bound on the privacy parameter that will prevent this attack from being effective.

5.1   Description of the Attack

Remember that we consider a computationally-unbounded adversary. In the *profile reconstruction attack*, the adversary exhausts the Bloom filter by querying it on all the possible items of the application domain. More precisely, the attack works as follows: the adversary is given a Bloom filter whose bits are independently and randomly flipped with probability p to ensure ϵ-differential privacy (we assume the value of p to be a public parameter and to be known by the adversary to avoid some kind of security by obscurity). Afterwards, the adversary performs some computation (possibly during an unbounded duration) and outputs a set of items that corresponds to its guess of the underlying profile behind the given Bloom filter, hence the name "profile reconstruction attack". We measure the success of this attack by measuring how close the reconstructed profile is to the original one in terms of the (squared) cosine similarity. Note that due to the probability of false positives inherent to Bloom filters (and this even in the non-perturbed case), the exact reconstruction of the original profile with 100% confidence may be impossible.

In a nutshell, the implementation of the profile reconstruction attack that we propose works as follows. For each item in the application domain, the adversary checks its corresponding bits in the Bloom filter it observed and sets k_0 to be the number of those bits that were found to be 0 while k_1 is the complementary quantity. Using those two values, the adversary calls a predicate q to determine if an item should be included or not in the reconstructed profile. More precisely, the predicate $q(k_0, k_1) > c$ is defined as $p^{k_1}(1 - p)^{k_0} \binom{k_1+k_0}{k_0} > c$, for $0 < c < 1$ a constant and p the flipping probability applied by the BLIP mechanism. The main intuition behind the use of $q(k_0, k_1)$ is that it represents exactly the probability that k_0 bits were flipped while k_1 bits were not flipped. Note that k_0 (respectively k_1) is the number of bits in the subset of the Bloom filter corresponding to the item currently considered that were set to 0 (respectively 1). We also tried other possible predicates such as the predicate $k_1 > c' \cdot k_0$ for some other appropriate constant c', but the other predicates were always less efficient than the one considered, therefore we disregarded them.

5.2   Experimental Evaluation

In order to assess how the variation of the privacy parameter ϵ affects the success of the attack, we conduct an experiment on the three datasets introduced earlier. The objective of this experiment is to derive empirically an upper bound on ϵ, such that for all c, the success of the adversary in reconstructing the profile through the inference attack is as low as possible. In this experiment, the adversary performs the profile reconstruction attack on each Bloom filter of each user for different values of ϵ and c. Finally, the squared cosine similarity is computed between the reconstructed profile outputted by the adversary and the original profile. All values of c between 0 and 1 in steps of 0.01 have been considered. Then, for each ϵ the adversary success is measured by the maximum mean similarity value over all values of c, where the mean (and standard deviation) is taken over the users.

Figure 2 shows significant diversity between the three considered datasets in the least possible adversarial success. For instance, the smallest squared cosine similarity attained in the Survey dataset is about 0.3 whereas it is 0.002 in the Delicious dataset. This may possibly stem from the difference in the size of item domain among the datasets. Nonetheless, we can conclude that in the worst case BLIP successfully prevents the adversary from producing a reconstructed profile having a cosine similarity with the original one much higher than the baseline (which is different for each dataset) when ϵ is less than 10, for all the considered datasets. As a consequence, we can derived an empirical upper bound on ϵ.

To summarize, the exact value of the similarity threshold above which the profile reconstructed attack is considered successful may depend not only upon the application considered but also upon the privacy preferences of the individual from which the Bloom filter is computed. However, choosing this value to be too conservative (i.e., too low) is likely to decrease dramatically the utility of the output. Therefore, the achievable trade-off between utility and privacy should be set by taking also into account the error bounds discussed in the full version of the paper due to space constraints.

6   Related Work

Non-interactive differential privacy. Most of the previous works studying non-interactive mechanisms in the context of differential privacy [8,18] have considered mechanisms that release a synthetic database that can be used to perform queries instead of the original one. The first work [8] is very inefficient due to its high computational complexity while [18] considers only input databases that have a sparse representation.

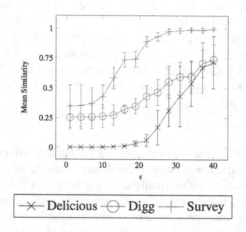

Fig. 2. Profile reconstruction attack. The vertical bars represent the standard deviation. The values on the y-axis are squared cosine similarity between the original profile and the reconstructed profile.

Privacy and Bloom filters. The literature on using Bloom filters for designing privacy-preserving techniques is quite diverse but often assumed a kind of client-server model, in which the owner of the Bloom filter (server) wants to answer some query asked by the client. In this context, some solutions focus on concealing the content of the query from the server, thus ensuring client's privacy (similarly to private information retrieval schemes), while others try to prevent the client from getting more information than the answer to its query, thus ensuring server's privacy (in the spirit of oblivious transfer). The application domains of these techniques include searching document indexes [13,3,5], private information retrieval [21], private matching [22], private publication of search logs [14] and anti-counterfeiting in supply chains [16].

Due to lack of space we do not detailed these methods but for the closest to our work is [14], which provides a probabilistic version of differential privacy (*i.e.*, the privacy guarantee holds for all except a small fraction of items). However, this technique only works for multi-sets and it is not straightforward to apply it on normal sets such as user profiles.

7 Conclusion

In this paper, we have proposed BLIP (for BLoom-then-flIP), a differentially private non-interactive mechanism that releases a randomized version of the Bloom filter representation of a profile. The randomized Bloom filter offers high privacy guarantees (in the sense of differential privacy) while still maintaining a good level of utility. For instance, the differentially private Bloom filter can be used to compute a similarity measure, such as cosine similarity or scalar product, with another Bloom filter in a non-interactive manner. We have demonstrated how the BLIP mechanism affects the privacy of the underlying profile and how to guarantee privacy at the level of items (as opposed to bits of the Bloom filter) by tuning the flipping probability. We have also described an generic inference attack against the flipped Bloom filter, called the profile reconstruction attack, which enables reconstruction of the full original profile (almost) if applied on a plain (*i.e.*, non-randomized) Bloom filter but does not work anymore on the perturbed Bloom filter if the value of the parameter ϵ is chosen wisely (we provide a technique for choosing an upper bound to this parameter).

In the future, we plan to broaden the scope of inference attacks considered in order to evaluate their rate of success on a Bloom filter released by the BLIP mechanism. In particular, we want to design more sophisticated inference attacks in which the adversary has some partial knowledge about the profile of a user or that exploit the correlations between items and assess empirically if the ϵ-differential privacy ensures an efficient protection against these attacks. We also plan to study how the relaxation of the notion of full differential privacy to computational differential privacy [20] and the combination with the compressive mechanism [18] can be used to provide a lower error bound for the same privacy guarantees. Another avenue of research that we will explore is how the difference of expectations in terms of privacy among different users (which could lead to different values of ϵ) affect the privacy guarantees offered globally for different types of users and items.

References

1. Alvim, M.S., Andrés, M.E., Chatzikokolakis, K., Palamidessi, C.: On the Relation between Differential Privacy and Quantitative Information Flow. In: Aceto, L., Henzinger, M., Sgall, J. (eds.) ICALP 2011, Part II. LNCS, vol. 6756, pp. 60–76. Springer, Heidelberg (2011)
2. Amer-Yahia, S., Benedikt, M., Lakshmanan, L.V.S., Stoyanovich, J.: Efficient network aware search in collaborative tagging sites. PVLDB 2008, 1(1) (August 2008)
3. Bawa, M., Bayardo, R.J., Agrawal, R., Vaidya, J.: Privacy-preserving indexing of documents on the network. The VLDB Journal 18(4), 837–856 (2009)
4. Beimel, A., Nissim, K., Omri, E.: Distributed Private Data Analysis: Simultaneously Solving How and What. In: Wagner, D. (ed.) CRYPTO 2008. LNCS, vol. 5157, pp. 451–468. Springer, Heidelberg (2008)
5. Bellovin, S.M., Cheswick, W.R.: Privacy-enhanced searches using encrypted Bloom filters. Tech. rep., Columbia University CUCS-034-07 (2007)
6. Bertier, M., Frey, D., Guerraoui, R., Kermarrec, A.M., Leroy, V.: The Gossple anonymous social network. In: Proceedings of the 11th International Middleware Conference (Middleware 2010), ACM/IFIP/USENIX, Bangalore, India, November 29 - December 3, pp. 191–211 (2010)

7. Bloom, B.H.: Space/time trade-offs in hash coding with allowable errors. Communications of the ACM 13(7), 422–426 (1970)
8. Blum, A., Ligett, K., Roth, A.: A learning theory approach to non-interactive database privacy. In: Dwork, C. (ed.) Proceedings of the 40th Annual ACM Symposium on Theory of Computing (STOC 2008), pp. 609–618. ACM, Victoria (2008)
9. Bose, P., Guo, H., Kranakis, E., Maheshwari, A., Morin, P., Morrison, J., Smid, M., Tang, Y.: On the false-positive rate of Bloom filters. Information Processing Letters 108(4), 210–213 (2008)
10. Dwork, C.: Differential Privacy: A Survey of Results. In: Agrawal, M., Du, D.-Z., Duan, Z., Li, A. (eds.) TAMC 2008. LNCS, vol. 4978, pp. 1–19. Springer, Heidelberg (2008)
11. Dwork, C., McSherry, F., Nissim, K., Smith, A.: Calibrating Noise to Sensitivity in Private Data Analysis. In: Halevi, S., Rabin, T. (eds.) TCC 2006. LNCS, vol. 3876, pp. 265–284. Springer, Heidelberg (2006)
12. Dwork, C., Naor, M.: On the difficulties of disclosure prevention in statistical databases or the case for differential privacy. Journal of Privacy and Confidentiality 2(1), 93–107 (2010)
13. Goh, E.J.: Secure indexes. Tech. rep., Cryptology ePrint Archive 2003/216 (March 16, 2004)
14. Götz, M., Machanavajjhala, A., Wang, G., Xiao, X., Gehrke, J.: Privacy in search logs. CoRR abs/0904.0682 (2009)
15. Jelasity, M., Guerraoui, R., Kermarrec, A.-M., van Steen, M.: The Peer Sampling Service: Experimental Evaluation of Unstructured Gossip-Based Implementations. In: Jacobsen, H.-A. (ed.) Middleware 2004. LNCS, vol. 3231, pp. 79–98. Springer, Heidelberg (2004)
16. Kerschbaum, F.: Public-Key Encrypted Bloom Filters with Applications to Supply Chain Integrity. In: Li, Y. (ed.) DBSec. LNCS, vol. 6818, pp. 60–75. Springer, Heidelberg (2011)
17. Lee, J., Clifton, C.: How Much Is Enough? Choosing ϵ for Differential Privacy. In: Lai, X., Zhou, J., Li, H. (eds.) ISC 2011. LNCS, vol. 7001, pp. 325–340. Springer, Heidelberg (2011)
18. Li, Y.D., Zhang, Z., Winslett, M., Yang, Y.: Compressive mechanism: utilizing sparse representation in differential privacy. CoRR abs/1107.3350 (2011)
19. McSherry, F., Talwar, K.: Mechanism design via differential privacy. In: Proceedings of the 48th Annual IEEE Symposium on Foundations of Computer Science (FOCS 2007), Providence, RI, USA, October 20-23, pp. 94–103 (2007)
20. Mironov, I., Pandey, O., Reingold, O., Vadhan, S.P.: Computational Differential Privacy. In: Halevi, S. (ed.) CRYPTO 2009. LNCS, vol. 5677, pp. 126–142. Springer, Heidelberg (2009)
21. Pon, R.K., Critchlow, T.: Performance-Oriented Privacy-Preserving Data Integration. In: Ludäscher, B., Raschid, L. (eds.) DILS 2005. LNCS (LNBI), vol. 3615, pp. 240–256. Springer, Heidelberg (2005)
22. Shikfa, A., Önen, M., Molva, R.: Broker-Based Private Matching. In: Fischer-Hübner, S., Hopper, N. (eds.) PETS 2011. LNCS, vol. 6794, pp. 264–284. Springer, Heidelberg (2011)
23. Tarkoma, S., Rothenberg, C.E., Lagerspetz, E.: Theory and practice of Bloom filters for distributed systems. IEEE Communications Surveys & Tutorials (99), 1–25 (2011)
24. Warner, S.L.: Randomized response: a survey technique for eliminating evasive answer bias. Journal of the American Statistical Association 60(309), 63–69 (1965)

DQMP: A Decentralized Protocol to Enforce Global Quotas in Cloud Environments*

Johannes Behl[1], Tobias Distler[2], and Rüdiger Kapitza[1]

[1] TU Braunschweig
[2] Friedrich–Alexander University Erlangen–Nuremberg

Abstract. Platform-as-a-Service (PaaS) clouds free companies of building infrastructures dimensioned for peak service demand and allow them to only pay for the resources they actually use. Being a PaaS cloud customer, on the one hand, offers a company the opportunity to provide applications in a dynamically scalable way. On the other hand, this scalability may lead to financial loss due to costly use of vast amounts of resources caused by program errors, attacks, or careless use.

To limit the effects of involuntary resource usage, we present *DQMP*, a decentralized, fault-tolerant, and scalable quota-enforcement protocol. It allows customers to buy a fixed amount of resources (e. g., CPU cycles) that can be used flexibly within the cloud. DQMP utilizes the concept of diffusion to equally balance unused resource quotas over all processes running applications of the same customer. This enables the enforcement of upper bounds while being highly adaptive to all kinds of resource-demand changes. Our evaluation shows that our protocol outperforms a lease-based centralized implementation in a setting with 1,000 processes.

1   Introduction

Cloud computing is considered a fundamental paradigm shift in the delivery architecture of information services, as it allows to move services, computation, and/or data off site to large utility providers. This offers customers substantial cost reduction, as hard- and software infrastructure needs not to be owned and dimensioned for peak service demand. With Platform-as-a-Service (PaaS) clouds like Windows Azure [1] and Google App Engine [2] providing a scalable computing platform, customers are able to directly deploy their service applications in the cloud. In the ideal case, cloud customers only pay for the resources their applications actually use; that is, "... pricing is based on direct storage use and/or the number of CPU cycles expended. It frees service owners from coarser-grained pricing models based on the commitment of whole servers or storage units." [3]

While it is very inviting to have virtually unlimited scalability and pay for it like electricity and water, this freedom poses a serious risk to cloud customers: the use of vast amounts of resources, caused, for example, by program errors,

* The research leading to these results has received funding from the European Union's Seventh Framework Programme (FP7/2007-2013) under grant agreement n°257243 (TClouds project: http://www.tclouds-project.eu/).

A.W. Richa and C. Scheideler (Eds.): SSS 2012, LNCS 7596, pp. 217–231, 2012.

attacks, or careless use, may lead to high financial losses. Imagine an unforeseen input leads to a livelock that consumes massive amounts of CPU cycles. The costs for the resources used unintentionally could be tremendous and may even exceed the estimated profits of running the service.

To address this problem, we propose to employ a quota-enforcement service that allows cloud customers to specify global quotas for the resources (e. g., CPU, memory, network) used by their applications. Such a service can be integrated with the cloud infrastructure in order to ensure that the combined usage of all processes assigned to the same customer does not exceed the upper bound defined for a particular resource.

In domains like grid computing, where application demands are predictable, enforcing global quotas can be done statically during the deployment of an application [4]. However, for user-accessed services in a dedicated utility computing infrastructure [5] like a PaaS cloud, this problem needs to be solved at run time once previously unknown services get dynamically deployed. Further, the quota-enforcement service must not impose any specific usage restrictions: processes must be able to freely allocate resources on demand as long as free quota is available. In this respect, the enforced global quota can be compared to a credit-card limit, which protects the owner from overstepping his financial resources while not making any assumptions on when and how the money is spent. All in all, dealing with a dynamically varying number of processes with unknown resource usage patterns makes quota enforcement a challenging task within clouds.

The straight-forward approach would be to set up a centralized service that manages all quotas of a customer and grants resources to applications on demand. However, as shown in our evaluation, such a service implementation does not scale for applications comprising a large number of processes, which is a common scenario in the context of cloud computing. Moreover, additional mechanisms like, for instance, state-machine replication had to be applied in order to provide a fault-tolerant and highly available solution. Otherwise, the quota-enforcement service would represent a single point of failure.

To avoid the shortcomings of a centralized approach, we devised a decentralized quota-enforcement service including a novel protocol named *Diffusive Quota Management Protocol*, short *DQMP*. DQMP is fault-tolerant and highly scalable by design, two properties that are indispensable for cloud environments. Its basic idea is to use the concept of diffusion to balance information about free quotas across all machines hosting a certain application of a customer. By distributing quota information, the permissions to allocate resources can be granted via local calls. Our service offers a simple and lightweight interface that can be easily integrated to extend existing infrastructures with quota-enforcement support. An evaluation of our prototype with up to 1,000 processes residing on 40 machines shows that DQMP scales well and outperforms a centralized solution.

The remainder of this paper is structured as follows: Section 2 discusses related approaches, Section 3 presents the architectural components of our quota-enforcement service, Section 4 outlines the concept of diffusive quota enforcement and presents the DQMP protocol, Section 5 presents results gained from an experimental evaluation of our prototype, and Section 6 concludes.

2   Related Approaches

Whereas earlier work on diffusion algorithms and distributed averaging addressed various areas such as dynamic load balancing [6,7,8], distributing replicas in unstructured peer-to-peer networks [9], routing in multihop networks [10] and distributed sensor fusion [11], none of them handles quota enforcement. Karmon et al. [12] proposed a quota-enforcement protocol for grid environments that relies on a decentralized mechanism to collect information about free resource quotas as soon as an application issues a demand. In contrast, our protocol proactively balances such information over all machines serving a customer, which allows granting most demands for free quota instantly. Furthermore, this paper goes beyond [12] in extending fault tolerance and in discussing how to integrate with cloud computing. Raghavan et al. [13] proposed an approach targeting distributed rate limiting using a gossip inspired algorithm in cloud-computing environments. They specifically focus on network bandwidth and neglect fault tolerance. Pollack et al. [14] proposed a micro-cash–inspired approach for disk quotas that provides lower overhead and better scalability than centralized quota-tracking services. A quota server acts as a bank that issues resource vouchers to clients. Clients can spend fractions of vouchers to allocate resources on arbitrary nodes of a cluster system. For good resource utilization and to prevent overload of the quota server bank, this requires previous knowledge about the resource demand. Gardfjäll et al. [15] developed the SweGrid accounting system that manages resources via a virtual bank that handles a hierarchical project namespace using branches. Based on an extended name service, each branch can be hosted on a separate node. This approach requires explicit management to be scalable and misses support for fault tolerance. Furthermore, there are distributed lock systems [16,17] that provide fault-tolerant leases based on variants of the Paxos algorithm. Contrary to the presented approach, they are dedicated to manage low volume resources like specific files. As shown by the evaluation, our decentralized protocol scales above such replicated service solutions.

3   Architecture

In this section, we present the key components of our quota-enforcement service which is realized on basis of DQMP and explain how these components interact with existing cloud infrastructures.

3.1   Host Architecture

DQMP uses a decentralized approach to manage the resource quota of customers. It distributes information about free quota units across the machines running applications of the same customer, providing each machine with a *local quota*. Quota enforcement in DQMP spans two levels: (1) At the host level, a *resource controller* guarantees that the local resource usage of an application process does not exceed the local quota. (2) At the global level, a network of *DQMP daemons*

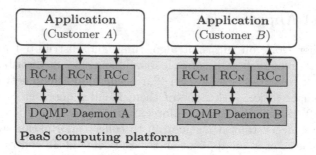

Fig. 1. Basic architecture of a PaaS cloud host running DQMP to enforce resource quotas: quota requests issued by applications of different customers are handled by different DQMP daemons relying on a set of resource controllers (e.g., for memory usage (RC_M), network transfer volume (RC_N), and CPU cycles (RC_C))

enforces a *global quota* by guaranteeing that the sum of all local quotas does not exceed the total quota for a particular resource, as specified by the customer.

Figure 1 shows the basic architecture of a PaaS cloud host that relies on our protocol to enforce quota for two customers A and B. For each of them, a separate DQMP daemon is running on the host. Each DQMP daemon is assigned a set of resource controllers (RC_*) which are responsible for enforcing quotas for different resource types (e.g., memory, network, and CPU).

Resource Controller. In general, PaaS computing platforms provide means to monitor the resource consumption of an application process [18]. For DQMP, we extend these mechanisms with a set of resource controllers, one for each resource type. Each time an application seeks to consume additional resources, the corresponding resource controller issues a resource request to its local DQMP daemon and blocks until the daemon grants the demand.

DQMP Daemon. A cloud host executes a separate DQMP daemon for every customer executing at least one application process on the host; that is, a DQMP daemon serving a certain customer is only executed on a host when there actually runs a process that may demand resource quota. The main task of a DQMP daemon is to fulfill the resource demands of its associated resource controllers. To do so, the daemon is connected to a set of other DQMP daemons (assigned to the same customer) that run on different cloud hosts, forming a peer-to-peer network. For the remainder of this paper, we will refer to daemons connected in a DQMP network as *nodes*. Moreover, the first node that joins the network is called *quota manager*. It serves as a stable access point for the infrastructure, since the composition of a DQMP network is dynamic as nodes join and leave depending on whether their local machines currently host processes for the customer.

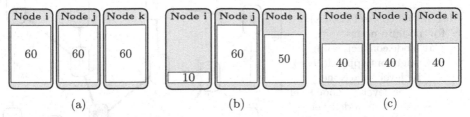

Fig. 2. Example scenario for diffusion-based quota balancing: (a) The local free quotas are balanced across nodes. (b) Processes on nodes i and k demand resources → the diffusion of quota starts. (c) The free quotas have been rebalanced.

3.2 Node Registry

In addition to the DQMP components running on the same hosts as the customer applications, we provide a *node-registry* service that manages information about all nodes (i.e., DQMP daemons) assigned to the same customer. We assume the node registry to be implemented as a fault-tolerant service; for example, by using multiple registry instances. When a new node joins the DQMP network, the registry sets up an entry for it. As each node periodically sends a heartbeat message the registry is able to garbage collect entries of crashed nodes. When a node leaves the DQMP network (e.g., due to the last local application process having been shut down), the node instructs the registry to remove its entry.

4 The DQMP Protocol

This section presents the algorithms used by our decentralized quota-enforcement protocol DQMP to enforce global resource quotas of customers. In addition to a description of the basic protocol, we also discuss extensions for fault tolerance.

4.1 Diffusion-Based Quota Balancing

We give a basic example scenario to outline how the general concept of diffusion is applied to balance free global quota information. In this example, three machines have been selected to host the application of a customer. For simplicity, we examine the diffusive balancing process of a single resource quota.

Each node (i.e., DQMP daemon) in the DQMP network is connected to a set of *neighbor nodes* (or just *"neighbors"*). Quota balancing is done by pairwise balancing the free local quota of neighbors. As neighbor sets of different nodes overlap, a complete coverage is achieved. In our example (see Figure 2), nodes i and j form a pair of neighbors, and nodes j and k form another pair of neighbors. At start-up, the global quota of the customer (180 units in our example) is balanced over all participating nodes (see Figure 2a).

When the application starts executing, the resource controller at node i demands 50 resource units and the resource controller at node k demands 10 units.

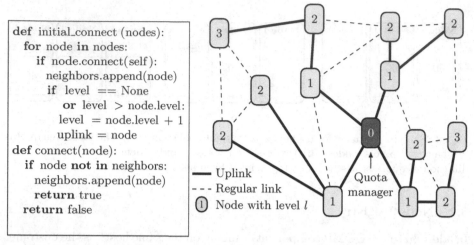

```
def initial_connect (nodes):
  for node in nodes:
    if node.connect(self):
      neighbors.append(node)
      if level == None
        or level > node.level:
        level = node.level + 1
        uplink = node
def connect(node):
  if node not in neighbors:
    neighbors.append(node)
    return true
  return false
```

Fig. 3. Connecting nodes

Fig. 4. Example tree in a DQMP network

Figure 2b shows that nodes i and k react by reducing the amount of locally available free quota q. Thus, both nodes can grant their local resource demands immediately. Changing the amounts of free quota starts the diffusive quota-balancing process and causes nodes i and k to exchange quota information with other nodes; in this case node j. As the free quota of node j exceeds the free quota of node i (i.e., $q_j > q_i$), $\lceil \frac{q_j - q_i}{2} \rceil$ quota units are migrated to i. The same applies to nodes j and k which, again, leads to different amounts of free quota on nodes i and j. As a result, further balancing processes are triggered and balancing continues until equilibrium is reached. The equilibrium (see Figure 2c) enables node i to be well prepared for future resource demands, as its amount of free quota has risen to the global average of 40.

In case a resource controller issues a resource demand that exceeds q, a node obtains the requested quota by successively reducing q after each balancing process. As soon as the node has collected the full amount, it grants the resource demand to the resource controller.

Using discrete quota, there might be an imbalance of one unit between two neighboring nodes if $mod(\sum q, n) \neq 0$ (n is the total number of nodes), causing balancing to never stop. To avoid this, we restrict balancing to differences above one unit. As a result, this introduces a potential system-wide gradient, which we cope with using probabilistic migration [19]. This strategy migrates small amounts of quota with a certain probability, even if the imbalance is not reduced.

4.2 Basic Protocol

This section describes the basic DQMP protocol. We assume a fail-stop behavior of nodes and the reliable detection of node and connection failures.

Connection Process. When a new application is deployed, our quota-enforcement service starts local DQMP daemons on the corresponding hosts and selects one of these nodes to be the quota manager (see Section 3.1). Then, our service

Table 1. Data structures managed by a DQMP daemon

Field	Description
level	Level in the quota tree
neighbors	List of neighbors, where each entry is a triple of **connection**, **counter**, and **level**
quota	Available local resource quota
consumed	Consumed resource quota (see Section 4.3)

supplies all nodes of this first set with the addresses of all other nodes. Next, each node establishes a connection to some of the other nodes, adding them to its neighbor set (see `initial_connect()` in Figure 3 and Table 1).

During this procedure, every node determines its *level* in a tree (see Figure 4) that is formed as a by-product of the connection process. At first, only the quota manager (representing the tree root) is part of the tree and is therefore assigned level zero. Next, all other nodes join the tree using the following algorithm: (1) A node collects the level information of all of its neighbors. (2) It selects the neighbor n that has the lowest level l_n (i. e., the node with the smallest distance to the tree root) to be its parent node in the tree. From now on, we refer to the connection to n as the *uplink*; in Section 4.3, we investigate how the uplink is used to provide fault tolerance. (3) The node sets its own level to $l_n + 1$.

When a node has connected a predefined number of neighbors, it sends an announcement including its contact details and level information to the node registry managing a list of nodes assigned to the customer (see Section 3.2). In case the application of a customer scales up capacity by starting processes on additional hosts, newcomers query the node registry for addresses of nodes in the DQMP network. This information is then used as input for `initial_connect()`.

Quota Balancing. When the set of initial nodes is connected, nodes can be provided with quota by simply initializing the quota manager's local free quota with the amount of globally granted quota. In consequence, the diffusion process starts and every node balances its free quota with all connected neighbors.

Figure 5 outlines the basic balancing process, organized in rounds, each comprising a single call to `do_balancing()`. During a round, for each neighbor, a node d determines the amount of free quota and sends it to the neighbor via `balance()`. This method adjusts the free quota at the neighbor and returns the amount by which to change the local free quota of d. The round ends when d

```
def do_balancing():
    for n in neighbors:
        free = quota
        # ask other node how to change my quota
        quota += n.balance(free)
```

```
def balance(remote_free):
    free = quota
    avg = (free + remote_free) / 2
    quota += avg − free
    return −(avg − free)
```

Fig. 5. Simplified quota balancing process

has balanced quota with each of its neighbors. Note that quota balancing with a neighbor only takes a single message round-trip time.

If the local free quota has changed during a round of balancing, a node immediately starts another round. Otherwise, the next round is triggered when the node receives a demand from a local resource controller or when the quota exchange with another node modifies the local free quota.

4.3 Extension for Fault Tolerance

In this section, we describe how to extend the basic protocol presented in Section 4.2 in order to tolerate node failures.

General Approach. To handle faults, every node maintains a counter for each neighbor link. This link counter represents the net amount of free quota transferred to the neighbor and is updated on each quota exchange via the corresponding link: if a node passes free quota to a neighbor, it increments the

```
def fix_crashedNode(neighbor):
    quota += neighbor.counter
    neighbors.remove(neighbor)
    # check if uplink is concerned
    replace_crashedNode()
```

Fig. 6. Recovery after neighbor crash

```
def do_balancing():
 for n in neighbors:
    free = quota
    if n.level < level:
       # pass the consumed quota
       # up to the root
       n.counter += consumed
       result = n.balance(id, free,
                          consumed)[0]
       consumed = 0
    else:
       # receive consumed quota
       # from lower nodes
       (remote_consumed, result) =
                 n.balance(id, free)
       n.counter -= remote_consumed
       consumed += remote_consumed

    n.counter -= result
    quota += result
```

Fig. 7. Issuing a balancing request

```
def balance(id, remote_free,
                remote_consumed = 0):

    neighbor = neighbors[id]
    free = quota
    avg = (free + remote_free) / 2

    # handle the consumed quota
    if neighbor.level < level:
       remote_consumed = consumed
       neighbor.counter += remote_consumed
       consumed = 0
    else:
       neighbor.counter -= remote_consumed
       consumed += remote_consumed

    # balance the remaining quota
    if remote_free < 0 and free < 0:
       # nothing left on both sides
       return (remote_consumed, 0)
    elif remote_free < 0 or free < 0:
       # take care of negative quotas
       # [...]
    else:  # free quota on both sides
       quota += avg − free
       neighbor.counter −= avg − free
       return (remote_consumed,
              −(avg − free))
```

Fig. 8. Responding to a balancing request

local link counter by the amount transferred; the neighbor decrements its counter by the same amount. A negative counter value indicates that a node has received more free quota over that link than the node has passed to the neighbor.

When a node crashes, all connected neighbors detect the crash: each neighbor removes the crashed node from its neighbor set and adds the counter value of the failed link to its local amount of free quota (see Figure 6). This way, the free quota originally held by the crashed node is reconstructed by all neighbors, requiring no further coordination. Note that such a recovery may temporarily leave single nodes with negative local free quota. However, the DQMP network compensates this by quickly balancing quota among remaining nodes.

Consumed Quota. So far, this approach is only suitable for refundable quota like disk space, since link counters are unaware that non-refundable quota, like CPU cycles, transferred to a node may have been consumed by a local application process. Thus, neighbors would reassign more free quota than the crashed node actually had. To address this, nodes gather and distribute information about consumed quota, and adjust their link counters to prevent its reassignment.

For each resource, a node maintains a **consumed** counter (see Table 1) that is updated whenever a local application process consumes quota. Each node periodically reports the value of its **consumed** counter to its uplink, which in turn passes it to its own uplink, and so on, all up to the quota manager. Having reported the consumed quota, a node increments its uplink link counter by the amount announced; the uplink in turn decrements its link counter by the same value, similar to the modifications triggered during quota balancing. As a result, link counters are adjusted to reflect the reduced global free quota. Figures 7 and 8 show updated listings of the balancing process presented in Figure 5.

Handling Cluster Node Failures. Link counters are an easy and lightweight mean to compensate link crashes and single node failures. They also allow tolerating multiple crashes of directly connected nodes, because adjacent nodes can be seen as one large node with many neighbors. In case a node set is separated from the rest of the network, the node set that is not part of the quota-manager partition eventually runs out of quota, since free quota is always restored in the direction of its origin (i. e., the quota manager). However, after reconnection, the balancing process re-distributes the free quota, enabling the application processes on all nodes to make progress again. To avoid permanent partitions within the network, the protocol makes use of the level information. When a node except the quota manager and its direct neighbors loses the connection to its uplink, it has to select a node with a lower level than its own as new uplink. Preferably, the node uses one of its current neighbors for that purpose; however, it can also query the node registry (see Section 3.2) for possible candidates. If a suitable uplink cannot be found, the node is shut down properly.

Handling Crashes of the Quota Manager. If the quota manager crashes, its neighbors do not consolidate their link counters. If they did, all global quota of a customer would vanish as it has been originally injected via the quota manager.

Instead, all links to the quota manager are marked *initial links* and are therefore ignored during failure handling, allowing the network to proceed execution.

However, we assume a timely recovery of the quota manager as an application cannot be provided with additional quota while this node is down. We therefore assume that its state can be restored (e. g., using a snapshot). Note that the state of the quota manager to be saved is small: it only includes the set of neighbor addresses as well as the `quota`, `consumed`, and `counter` values (see Table 1) for every managed resource, making frequent snapshots and a fast recovery feasible.

At restart, the quota manager reconnects all level-one nodes. In case of one or more of them having crashed in the meantime, it starts the regular failure handling. At this point, we cannot tolerate network partitions between the quota manager and its neighbors, as this would lead to a duplication of free quota.

5   Evaluation

We evaluate DQMP on basis of a prototype implemented in Java. The tests are performed on 40 hosts, all equipped with 2.4 GHz quad-core CPU, 8 GB RAM, and connected over switched Gigabit Ethernet. Each host executes up to three Java virtual machines (JVMs) to support the simulation of larger networks. In this set-up, raw ping times range from 0.2 to 0.5 ms and simple Java RMI method calls take between 0.7 and 1.0 ms. On top of the physical network, two DQMP networks, consisting of 100 and 1,000 nodes, are simulated, with the maximum number of neighbors set to 6. Comparison measurements show, that simulating up to nine nodes within a single JVM has no significant impact on the results.

Test runs are performed as follows: After the DQMP network is built up, a quota amount of 50,000 units per node is injected. When the initial equilibrium is established, all nodes are instructed to begin with the execution of the actual test. After a test has finished, the local results of the nodes are collected. Except time charts, all presented results are the average of at least three test runs.

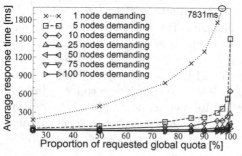
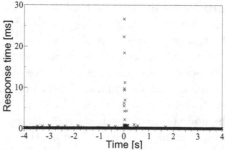

Fig. 9. Response times for single demands of varying amounts from varying parts out of 100 nodes

Fig. 10. Response times of a single test run with 100 constantly requesting nodes and a crash of 25 nodes at $t = 0$

5.1   Response Time Behavior of DQMP

Single Demands. In the first test, we examine the response times of DQMP for single demands within the small network containing 100 nodes. In this scenario, a subset of nodes orders a predefined amount of quota at the same time. The proportion of demanding nodes is raised stepwise from 1% to 100% and the overall amount of quota requested by this proportion is varied between 25% and 100%. This means that in one case, for instance, a single node requests the entire quota available and in another case, each of 100 nodes requests 1% of it.

From the results, as depicted in Figure 9, it can be inferred that the decisive factor for the performance of our protocol is the ratio between the free local quota held by each node and the size of the local demand: the smaller the demand compared to the local quota, the faster it can be satisfied. Since DQMP aims to an even distribution of free quota over all nodes, the demand size can be put into relation to the globally free quota: if demands of single nodes exceed the average size of free quota held by each node to a great extent, it is likely that quota has to be transferred not only from nearer nodes but also from farther ones to satisfy the demand. For instance, if a single node asks for the entire available quota, every quota unit in the network has to reach the same destination. With our settings, this takes about 7.8 seconds and 770 balancing rounds per node. However, this case is not realistic as only such nodes participate in DQMP networks that are actually used by processes demanding quota. If 50 nodes request 95% of the overall quota, the provisioning time already drops below 30 ms. Here, it takes about 45 balancing rounds per node until the request is fulfilled and until the network comes to a rest, that is, until no messages are transmitted anymore. Moreover, if only a small amount of the overall quota is needed or a large demand is split between many nodes, DQMP can provide extremely low response times. When a demand of a node can be fulfilled by its local quota, the DQMP daemon is even able to instantly grant the demanded amount, turning the assignment of global quota within a distributed system into a local operation.

Crashes of Nodes. After this first evaluation, we now examine how our protocol behaves in the presence of node crashes, since fault tolerance was a primary objective for the design of DQMP. As basis for this evaluation, we choose a scenario in which nodes demand and release quota constantly. In detail, each node performs the following in a loop: It adds a randomly chosen delta d, with $-10,000 \leq d \leq +10,000$, to its previous quota demand. It ensures that the new demand does not exceed the upper bound b of $50,000$ units, which limits the demand of all nodes combined to 100% of the overall quota injected into the system. According to the calculated value, the node issues a request either demanding new or releasing already granted quota. Subsequently, it waits until the request is fulfilled. Then it sleeps for a randomly chosen time between 25 and 75 ms to simulate fluctuating resource requirements.

Figure 10 shows the course of response times from a single test run with 100 requesting nodes, issuing a total of approximately 14,000 requests within 8 seconds, and an induced crash of 25 nodes at $t = 0$. The first outcome of this test is, that under the given scenario, which simulates the distribution of a

large demand over all available nodes, almost all quota requests can be fulfilled
locally, leading to a standard response time below 0.2 ms. For the same reason,
the processing of most requests is hardly affected by crashes of neighbors. Quota
releases are inherently not affected at all anyway. Consequently, despite the crash
of 25% of the nodes, there are only 4 requests for which it took between 10 and
30 ms to process them and 8 requests that lie in the range between 1 and 10 ms.
Thus, the balancing process of DQMP is able to compensate node crashes very
quickly by redistributing the quota over all remaining nodes.

5.2   Comparison of Different Architectures

Next, we compare DQMP to other architectures addressing quota enforcement in
distributed systems. For this purpose, we implemented a RMI-based quota server
and a passively replicated variant of it by means of the group communication
framework JGroups[1]. During test runs, the quota server as well as each replica
is executed by a dedicated machine. In the following, the term "node" is not
confined to DQMP daemons; it also denotes clients in the other architectures.[2]

As scenario for the comparison serves an extended variant of the scenario
used for examining the behavior of DQMP in the presence of nodes crashes
(see Section 5.1). Different to the previous scenario, here, a network of 1,000
nodes is used and the proportion p of requesting nodes is varied between 1%
and 100%. Further, the combined demand of all requesting nodes is limited to
75% of the overall injected quota in one case and to 100% in another. This is
achieved by setting the maximum demand of a single node b to $b_{75\%} = \frac{37.500}{p}$
and $b_{100\%} = \frac{50.000}{p}$, respectively. The delta d for every simulated demand change
is randomly chosen between $-0.2b$ and $+0.2b$ quota units.

Single-cluster Network. For a first comparison, all network connections have
similar latencies, just as in the previous tests and just as found within a local
area network, for instance within a single data center of a cloud provider. The
results of this scenario are depicted in Figure 11a. Since response times of the
central quota server and its replicated variant are only dependent on the number
of quota requests that have to be processed, and particularly are independent of
quota amounts, only a single set of results is reported for these architectures.

This test reveals the deficiencies of not completely decentralized systems in
terms of scalability: Due to limited resources such as CPU power, memory and
bandwidth and due to the contention arising from the shared usage of such
resources, these systems have a limited rate they can process requests at. In
our settings, for instance, all quota-server–based systems are able to process the
requests of a smaller number of requesting nodes within less than 2 ms on average.
However, in the presence of 1,000 requesting nodes, a single quota server already

---

[1] http://www.jgroups.org/

[2] We also implemented a quota-enforcement service based on the coordination service
Apache ZooKeeper (http://zookeeper.apache.org/). However, the optimistic lock
approach of ZooKeeper is not suitable for the high number of concurrent writes
needed in such systems, resulting in some orders of magnitude higher response times.

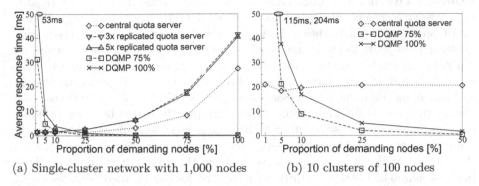

(a) Single-cluster network with 1,000 nodes   (b) 10 clusters of 100 nodes

Fig. 11. DQMP compared to other architectures regarding response times

requires about 28 ms. Using a more reliable replicated server system makes this even worse. The increased communication overhead leads to an average response time of over 40 ms.

In contrary, using DQMP response times decrease when demands are split up between more nodes. DQMP is able to fulfill requests within an average of 1 ms, and is thus faster than the server systems when the proportion of requesting nodes exceeds 25%. Beyond 50% the response time drops constantly below 0.2 ms. Since the total demand was fixed to either 75% or 100% of the globally injected quota, single demands get smaller with an increasing number of requesting nodes, leading to a higher chance that requests can be fulfilled through the local quotas of the nodes. That is the reason why, as shown by our results, DQMP is even able to outperform a non-saturated central quota server in terms of average response times when demands are distributed over multiple nodes.

Clustered Network. Normally, cloud providers do not maintain only a single data center but multiple ones, spread all over the world. These data centers form a clustered network, a network in which groups of well-connected nodes can only communicate among each other over relatively slow connections. To simulate such an environment, respectively wide area networks in general, we assign each out of 1,000 nodes to one of 10 clusters and artificially delay message exchange between nodes from different clusters by 20 ms.

The results, as presented in Figure 11b, suggest the conclusion that a central quota server is not well suited for the scenario described here. The server is located in one of the 10 clusters, which entails that 90% of all nodes experience prolonged delays while communicating with it. Thus, in 90% of all quota requests, demands or releases, the delay of 20 ms is fully added as an offset to the processing time. In case of DQMP, nodes can exchange quota with all of their neighbors in parallel, mitigating the effects of slower connections. Furthermore, all requests that can be fulfilled locally, including all releases, are not affected at all by communication delays. These are the reasons, why DQMP is able to provide better response times than a quota server in this scenario already when only 10% of the nodes demand and release quota.

Protocol Overhead. Concerning the protocol overhead of DQMP regarding network transfers, it can be observed that DQMP has completely different characteristics than a traditional quota server. If a quota server is used, each quota request leads to the exchange of two messages, a request message and its reply. In our implementation, the two messages require about 100 bytes. With DQMP instead, requests have only an indirect influence on the balancing process and hence, on the number of messages transferred. For the unrealistic case (see above) that relatively large demands are infrequently issued by a single node, causing, in the worst case, continuous balancing processes all over the network, the ratio between number of requests and messages transferred is unfavorable. With an increasing number of requests, however, the ratio gets more appropriate. In the scenario of 1,000 constantly requesting nodes our protocol requires about 3 kilobytes per request in average. Although this is still more than needed by the quota-server system, it has to be noted, that DQMP provides fault-tolerant operation while a central quota server does not and that network traffic between hosts of the same data center is usually not billed by cloud providers, hence, using DQMP would not generate additional transfer costs for cloud customers.

6   Conclusion

In this paper, we presented DQMP, a decentralized quota-enforcement protocol that provides the fault tolerance and scalability required by cloud-computing environments. DQMP can help customers of platform services, to prevent themselves from financial losses due to errors, attacks, or careless use causing involuntary resource usage. The utilized diffusion-based balancing of free quota enables customers to enforce global limits on resource usage while retaining flexibility and adaptability regarding the actual local demands within their deployments. Nonetheless, DQMP is not confined to this application. Cloud providers can employ it, for example, to restrict customers of their platform or infrastructure services on a global level by enforcing quota for virtual machines. As the evaluation of our prototype implementation shows, DQMP is able to provide better response times than a centralized service in a setting with 1,000 nodes. Moreover, our protocol is well suited for clustered networks as formed by interconnected data centers. Both is important since traditional, not fully decentralized solutions might soon reach their limit as distributed systems get larger and larger.

References

1. Windows Azure Platform, http://www.microsoft.com/windowsazure/
2. Google App Engine, http://code.google.com/appengine/
3. Creeger, M.: Cloud computing: An overview. ACM Queue 7 (2009)
4. Schopf, J.M.: Ten actions when Grid scheduling: the user as a Grid scheduler. In: Grid Resource Management: State of the Art and Future Trends, pp. 15–23. Kluwer Academic Publishers (2004)
5. Rolia, J., Cherkasova, L., Arlitt, M., Machiraju, V.: Supporting application quality of service in shared resource, pools. Communications of the ACM 49, 55–60 (2006)

6. Cybenko, G.: Dynamic load balancing for distributed memory multiprocessors. Journal of Parallel Distributed Computing 7(2), 279–301 (1989)
7. Boillat, J.E.: Load balancing and Poisson equation in a graph. Concurrency: Practice and Experience 2, 289–313 (1990)
8. Corradi, A., Leonardi, L., Zambonelli, F.: Diffusive load-balancing policies for dynamic applications. IEEE Concurrency 7(1), 22–31 (1999)
9. Uchida, M., Ohnishi, K., Ichikawa, K.: Dynamic storage load balancing with analogy to thermal diffusion for P2P file sharing. In: Proc. of the 2006 Work on Interdisciplinary Systems Approach in Performance Evaluation and Design of Computer & Communications Systems (2006)
10. Tassiulas, L., Ephremides, A.: Stability properties of constrained queueing systems and scheduling policies for maximum throughput in multihop radio networks. In: Proc. of the 29th IEEE Conf. on Decision and Control, pp. 2130–2132 (1990)
11. Xiao, L., Boyd, S., Lall, S.: A scheme for robust distributed sensor fusion based on average consensus. In: Proc. of the 4th Intl. Symp. on Information Processing in Sensor Networks, pp. 63–70 (2005)
12. Karmon, K., Liss, L., Schuster, A.: GWiQ-P: An efficient decentralized grid-wide quota enforcement protocol. SIGOPS OSR 42(1), 111–118 (2008)
13. Raghavan, B., Vishwanath, K., Ramabhadran, S., Yocum, K., Snoeren, A.C.: Cloud control with distributed rate limiting. In: Proc. of the 2007 Conf. on Applications, Technologies, Architectures, and Protocols for Computer Communications, pp. 337–348 (2007)
14. Pollack, K.T., Long, D.D.E., Golding, R.A., Becker-Szendy, R.A., Reed, B.: Quota enforcement for high-performance distributed storage systems. In: Proc. of the 24th Conf. on Mass Storage Systems and Technologies, pp. 72–86 (2007)
15. Gardfjäll, P., Elmrothaell, E., Elmroth, E., Johnsson, L., Mulmo, O., Sandhol, T.: Scalable grid-wide capacity allocation with the SweGrid Accounting System (SGAS). Concurrency and Computation: Practice and Experience 20(18), 2089–2122 (2008)
16. Hupfeld, F., Kolbeck, B., Stender, J., Högqvist, M., Cortes, T., Marti, J., Malo, J.: FaTLease: scalable fault-tolerant lease negotiation with Paxos. In: Proc. of the 17th Intl. Symp. on High Performance Distributed Computing, pp. 1–10 (2008)
17. Burrows, M.: The Chubby lock service for loosely-coupled distributed systems. In: Proc. of the 7th Symp. on Operating Systems Design and Implementation, pp. 335–350 (2006)
18. Weissman, C.D., Bobrowski, S.: The design of the Force.com multitenant Internet application development platform. In: Proc. of the 35th SIGMOD Intl. Conf. on Management of Data, pp. 889–896 (2009)
19. Douglas, S., Harwood, A.: Diffusive load balancing of loosely-synchronous parallel programs over peer-to-peer networks. ArXiv Computer Science e-prints (2004)

Brief Announcement: KARYON: Towards Safety Kernels for Cooperative Vehicular Systems*

António Casimiro[1], Jörg Kaiser[2], Johan Karlsson[3], Elad Michael Schiller[3], Philippas Tsigas[3], Pedro Costa[4], José Parizi[5], Rolf Johansson[6], and Renato Librino[7]

[1] Univ. Lisboa
casim@di.fc.ul.pt
[2] Otto-von-Guericke Univ. Magdeburg
kaiser@ivs.cs.uni-magdeburg.de
[3] Chalmers Univ. Tech.
{johan,elad,tsigas}@chalmers.se
[4] GMVIS SKYSOFT
pedro.costa@gmv.com
[5] EMBRAER SA
parizi@embraer.com.br
[6] SP AB
rolf.johansson@sp.se
[7] 4S SRL
renato.librino@4sgroup.it

KARYON, a kernel-based architecture for safety-critical control, is a European project that proposes a new perspective to improve performance of smart vehicle coordination focusing on Advanced Driver Assistance Systems (ADASs) and Unmanned Aerial Systems (UAS). The key objective is to provide system solutions for predictable and safe coordination of smart vehicles that autonomously cooperate and interact in an open and inherently uncertain environment. Currently, these systems are not allowed to operate on the public roads or in the air space, as the risk of causing severe damage cannot be excluded with sufficient certainty. The impact of the project is two-fold; it will provide improved vehicle density without driver involvement and increased traffic throughput to maintain mobility without a need to build new traffic infrastructures. The results will improve interaction in cooperation scenarios while preserving safety and assessing it according to standards. The prospective project results include self-stabilizing algorithms for vehicle coordination, communication and synchronization. In addition, we aim at showing that the safety kernel can be designed to be a self-stabilizing one.

The key objective of KARYON is to provide system solutions for predictable and safe coordination of smart vehicles that autonomously cooperate and interact in an open and inherently uncertain environment. This is a challenging

---

* This work was partially supported by the EC, through project FP7-STREP-288195, KARYON (Kernel-based ARchitecture for safetY-critical cONtrol).

A.W. Richa and C. Scheideler (Eds.): SSS 2012, LNCS 7596, pp. 232–235, 2012.

objective since the same increasingly complex control components and wireless communication, which would allow improved performance, end up introducing new safety risks, which have to be mitigated or neutralized. Addressing this challenge requires innovative solutions for: (1) A high availability of the complex control system investigating new ways of achieving fault-tolerant distributed control that allow maintaining a high performance level in the presence of uncertainties and failures, and (2) Provision of a safety kernel for constraining system operation in order to avoid hazardous situations.

Thus far, vehicular application safety is typically based on worst-case analysis and pessimistic allocation of resources to achieve the intended functionality. This has a strong impact on the final cost of the solutions. Often, when considering automotive systems, even a slight cost increment is not affordable.

Architectural Support for Safety-Critical Systems.   Safety-critical systems call for predictability, i.e., real-time operation. Traditionally, safety-critical solutions have been based on synchronous system models. These are well understood, both in terms of distributed systems theory and in the design of real-time systems and solutions, in areas such as real-time communication [5,7,2] and real-time scheduling [3,6]. However, when moving to distributed, large-scale, wireless and possibly complex infrastructures, these infrastructures do not provide the timeliness guarantees required. Therefore, designing applications using the synchronous model would cause incorrect system behavior due to assumption violation, and would defeat any safety requirements.

Supporting Services for Sensor-Based Safe Coordination.   Advanced control systems rely on a correct perception of the environment and system state, e.g., consistent view on the system state in the presence of faults and concurrency [8]. Results in this field address synchrony and replication issues but often assume correct information at its origin, and same state replicas. If reliable operation of sensors and actuators are required dealing with the environment perception and actuation on it, these methods have to be extended. Reliable operation has to cope with continuous data where replication is not always possible and redundancy mechanisms have to be different. One can find control models for fault detection of the sensor-to-actuator chain, such as fault detection and isolation (FDI) [4] or analytical redundancy methods [1]. Currently there is no consideration for system impact on largely varying network latencies or dynamically varying sensor information beyond mere statistical effects.

The Technical Approach.   KARYON will define a safety architecture for sensor-based cooperative systems, which is based on a small local safety kernel, that will allow adaptive and dynamic behaviour whilst preventing dangerous behaviour. Because this is a tiny subsystem compared to the overall complex control system, and its design is guided by concepts of fault independence from the rest of the system, possession of it's own resources, highest reliability of operation and autonomy of control decisions, its predictability can be justified. This is essential for guaranteeing overall safety along a set of safety rules. The architecture will be defined in a generic way, like an architectural pattern, without restricting the concrete faults to be considered and the fault-tolerance mechanisms to be deployed. In fact, since KARYON focuses on functional safety, the safety kernel should guarantee that the specified functionality should not fail in a hazardous way. To build a safe product, the integrity of the implementation should be high enough to ensure acceptable risks, where the risks are derived from an analysis of the potential hazards. Therefore, a set of safety rules will have to be derived from each specific application, and will be guarded by the safety kernel. The safety kernel will thus control the adaptive and dynamic behavior of the system, based on information about the integrity of system components and quality of perception (sensor data), and safeguard the system against unsafe control commands, by checking them against the derived set of safety rules. The project will further investigate the relevant fault detection concepts, particularly for the sensor systems, needed to show fulfilment of dependability attributes and argue about safety according to safety standards. At the same time, the idea is to achieve improvements in the reliable and trustworthy environment perception, based on adequate fault models for complex sensor faults, on solutions for increased communication predictability and on environment monitoring components. Simulation and mixed reality techniques will be developed to validate the approach. Furthermore, KARYON will integrate concepts in advanced event dissemination middleware and in improved simulation and fault-injection tools for assessing the behaviour of autonomous, mobile systems under failure conditions and to evaluate safety assurance according to the ISO 26262 safety standard.

Demonstration and Use.   KARYON will explore the elaborated concepts and results in the context of two major use cases from the automotive and avionics areas. Application expertise provided by the respective industrial beneficiaries from the automotive and avionics fields, will ensure that scenarios and evaluation will always be aligned with industrial needs. The automotive use case is related to Advanced Driver Assistance Systems (ADASs) for coordinating vehicles. In particular, KARYON will examine scenarios in which vehicles cooperate while: (1) Going on the road and keeping their distance from other vehicles, (2) Cursing in their lanes and coordinating when lane changes are needed, and (3) Crossing intersections in a coordinated way.

Conclusions.   KARYON opens new perspectives by enabling the use of available technology for safe cooperative systems and for increased efficiency. Global safety predicates are powerful abstractions for describing the intended safe behaviour of systems as a whole. Since that behaviour must be guaranteed at run-time, KARYON will conduct research on the problem of deriving safety monitors from the global safety predicates. We aim at providing a safety kernel and mechanisms for detecting unsafe states and trigger appropriate responses. We expect that KARYON's impact will include benefits of overall increased traffic throughput, safer roads and sustainable transportation.

References

1. Blanke, M., Kinnaert, M., Lunze, J., Staroswiecki, M.: Diagnosis and Fault-Tolerant Control, 2nd edn. Springer (2006)
2. Davis, R.I., Burns, A., Bril, R.J., Lukkien, J.J.: Controller Area Network (CAN) schedulability analysis: Refuted, revisited and revised. Real-Time Systems 35, 239–272
3. Deng, Z., Liu, J.W.-S.: Scheduling real-time applications in an open environment. In: IEEE Real-Time Systems Symposium, pp. 308–319 (1997)
4. Frank, P.M.: Fault diagnosis in dynamic systems using analytical and knowledge-based redundancy- A survey and some new results. Automatica 26, 459–474 (1990)
5. Kopetz, H.: Real-Time Systems. Kluwer Academic (1997)
6. Ramamritham, K., Stankovic, J.: Scheduling algorithms and operating systems support for real-time systems. Proceedings IEEE 82(1), 55–67 (1994)
7. Tindell, K., Burns, A., Wellings, A.J.: Analysis of hard real-time communications. Real-Time Systems 9(2), 147–171 (1995)
8. Verissimo, P., Rodrigues, L.: Distributed Systems for System Architects. Kluwer Academic (2001)

Brief Announcement:
Arbitrators in the Security Infrastructure*

Shlomi Dolev[1], Niv Gilboa[2], and Ofer Hermoni[3]

[1] Department of Computer Sciences
dolev@cs.bgu.ac.il
[2] Department of Communication Systems Engineering
gilboan@bgu.ac.il
[3] Department of Information Systems Engineering
Ben-Gurion University of the Negev, Israel
oferher@bgu.ac.il

Abstract. We introduce the notion of digital arbitration which enables resolving disputes between servers and users with the aid of *arbitrators*. Arbitrators are semi-trusted entities in a social network that facilitate communication or business transactions. The communicating parties, users and servers, agree before a communication transaction on a set of arbitrators that they trust (reputation systems may support their choice). Then, the arbitrators receive digital goods, e.g. a deposit, and a terms of use agreement between participants such that the goods of a participant are returned if and only if the participant acts according to the agreement.

Introduction. The number of transactions in the Internet grows exponentially. The scalability of the Internet is based on the distribution of tasks among the participants. Specifically, peer to peer, machine to machine, clients and servers execute independent transactions with no central controlling entity. A Certificate Authority (CA) is a prominent example of the opposite approach; a centralized entity that is heavily used as part of public key infrastructures or as part of the communication protocol to secure the transactions in the Internet.

We suggest the use of additional semi-trusted entities to relieve the load of tasks handled by a CA. The entities are called *arbitrators*. An arbitrator can be a semi-trusted peer in a social network or an agency (implemented by servers in the system) that gains reputation for being trusted in a distributed reputation system.

* This research has been supported by the Ministry of Science and Technology (MOST), the Institute for Future Defense Technologies Research named for the Medvedi, Shwartzman and Gensler Families, the Israel Internet Association (ISOC-IL), the Lynne and William Frankel Center for Computer Science at Ben-Gurion University, Rita Altura Trust Chair in Computer Science, *Israel Science Foundation* (grant number 428/11), Cabarnit Cyber Security MAGNET Consortium, MAFAT and Deutsche Telekom Labs at BGU. A poster presenting preliminary results of this work was presented in CCS '11 [5].

A.W. Richa and C. Scheideler (Eds.): SSS 2012, LNCS 7596, pp. 236–238, 2012.
© Springer-Verlag Berlin Heidelberg 2012

The number of CAs is very small and the information they have is highly classified. In contrast, the number of arbitrators can be huge (e.g., each peer can act as an arbitrator) and the information given to the arbitrator is limited.

Arbitrators. Arbitrators in the real world are used to resolve disputes between two parties outside the court of law. The parties in a dispute agree that a third party (or parties), generally self-contained, will resolve their dispute. The resolution of the arbitration process is binding for both parties.

We suggest using arbitrators in the digital world that resemble arbitrators in the real world. They are P2P semi-trusted entities that function as a jury in the technology court of law. However, there are naturally a few differences. There is more than one arbitrator, the sanction that takes place in case of violation is set in advance and only a collaboration of enough arbitrators is allowed to carry out the sanction.

Digital Arbitration. Interaction between a user and a server in our setting occurs as follows. At the beginning of the initial phase of the communication between the user and the server, they agree on a contract. The contract contains three parts. A terms of use agreement that defines what is legitimate, namely what the user is allowed to do during the communication; a set of arbitrators; and a resource (digital goods) the server receives in case the user violates the agreement.

Note that the scheme requires a trusted party such as a Certificate Authority (CA) in the initial phase. The CA must vouch for the users' digital resource, otherwise the server cannot be sure that the guaranteed resource is indeed distributed to the arbitrators.

The user then applies to the CA that validates the resource, and sends the user a commitment for the resource. The user then uses a verifiable secret sharing scheme to divide the resource into n shares (n is the number of arbitrators that the user and the server agree on) and submits a share along with the commitment and the user digital signature verification key within each arbitrator. The user also sends the commitment and the user digital signature verification key to the server that verifies with each arbitrator that it has received the share, the commitment and the user digital signature verification key.

During the communication phase the user signs each message sent to the server. If the server believes that the user has violated the agreement, then the server applies to the arbitrators, and if large enough set of arbitrators (more than t, where t is the threshold in the secret sharing scheme) agree that the user actually violated the agreement, they give the server the information that is needed to reconstruct the resource.

Related Work. Some ideas that appear in the literature and are related to our ideas are *revocable privacy, anonymous credential systems, digital money* and *blacklisting*.

Revocable privacy systems (e.g. [4,6,7]) are systems that protect personal information unless a user violates the pre-established terms of service. These systems deal only with the privacy of the user, and the privacy is revoked by a law enforcement entity.

Users in anonymous credential systems (e.g., [3]) communicate anonymously with different servers in an unlinkable fashion. The CA (or open authority as it is called in these systems) issues the credentials to the users and may revoke the anonymity of the users. Our proposed system, on the other hand, separates the entity that issues the credentials (CA) from the entity that revokes the anonymity.

Another group of solutions, is k times anonymous authentication (k-TAA) [8]. These systems provide anonymous authentication k times. Until the k-th time, no one (not even the trusted party) can identify the user, whereas in the $k + 1$ attempt, the anonymity of the user is revoked. Camenisch et al. [2] extend k-TAA to allow k anonymous authentications in a single time period. Namely, after a predefined period of time, the counter is set to zero, and k is recounted.

Solutions such as BLAC [1] and Nymble [9] take a different approach. In these works, the anonymity of a misbehaving user is not revoked. Instead, these systems use blacklists in order to prevent the user from receiving service.

References

1. Au, M.H., Tsang, P.P., Kapadia, A., Susilo, W.: BLACR: TTP-Free Blacklistable Anonymous Credentials with Reputation. Indiana University Technical Report TR695 (May 2011)
2. Camenisch, J., Hohenberger, S., Kohlweiss, M., Lysyanskaya, A., Meyerovich, M.: How to win the clone wars: efficient periodic n-times anonymous authentication. ACM CCS, 201–210 (2006)
3. Camenisch, J., Lysyanskaya, A.: Efficient non-transferable anonymous multi-show credential system with optional anonymity revocation. In: Pfitzmann, B. (ed.) EUROCRYPT 2001. LNCS, vol. 2045, pp. 93–118. Springer (2001)
4. Diaz, C., Preneel, B.: Accountable Anonymous Communication. In: Security, Privacy and Trust in Modern Data Management (2006)
5. Dolev, S., Gilboa, N., Hermoni, O.: Poster: arbitrators in the security infrastructure, supporting positive anonymity. In: CCS 2011, pp. 753–756 (2011)
6. Hoepman, J.H.: Revocable Privacy. ENISA Quarterly Review 5(2), 16–17 (2009)
7. Köpsell, S., Wendolsky, R., Federrath, H.: Revocable Anonymity. In: Müller, G. (ed.) ETRICS 2006. LNCS, vol. 3995, pp. 206–220. Springer, Heidelberg (2006)
8. Teranishi, I., Furukawa, J., Sako, K.: k-Times Anonymous Authentication (Extended Abstract). In: Lee, P.J. (ed.) ASIACRYPT 2004. LNCS, vol. 3329, pp. 308–322. Springer, Heidelberg (2004)
9. Tsang, P.P., Kapadia, A., Cornelius, C., Smith, S.W.: Nymble: Blocking misbehaving users in anonymizing networks. IEEE Trans. Dependable Sec. Comput. 8(2), 256–269 (2011)

Optimization in a Self-stabilizing Service Discovery Framework for Large Scale Systems

Eddy Caron[1], Florent Chuffart[1], Anissa Lamani[2], and Franck Petit[3]

[1] University of Lyon. LIP Laboratory.
UMR CNRS - ENS Lyon - INRIA - UCB Lyon 5668, France
[2] MIS Lab. Université de Picardie Jules Verne, France
[3] LIP6 CNRS UMR 7606 - INRIA - UPMC Sorbonne Universities, France

Abstract. Ability to find and get services is a key requirement in the development of large-scale distributed systems. We consider dynamic and unstable environments, namely Peer-to-Peer (P2P) systems. In previous work, we designed a service discovery solution called Distributed Lexicographic Placement Table (DLPT), based on a hierarchical overlay structure. A self-stabilizing version was given using the Propagation of Information with Feedback (PIF) paradigm. In this paper, we introduce the self-stabilizing CoPIF (for Collaborative PIF) scheme. An algorithm is provided with its correctness proof. We use this approach to improve a distributed P2P framework designed for the services discovery. Significantly efficient experimental results are presented.

1 Introduction

Computing abilities (or *services*) offered by large distributed systems are constantly increasing. Cloud environment grows in this way. Ability to find and get these services (without the need for a centralized server) is a key requirement in the development of such systems. Service discovery facilities in distributed systems led to the development of various overlay structures built over Peer-to-Peer (P2P) systems, *e.g.*, [12,18,26,27]. Some of them rely on spanning tree structures [12,27], mainly to handle range queries, automatic completion of partial search strings, and to extend to multi-attribute queries.

Although fault-tolerance is a mandatory feature of systems targeted for large scale platforms (to avoid data loss and to ensure proper routing), tree-based distributed structures, including tries, offer only a poor robustness in dynamic environment. The crash of one or more nodes may lead to the loss of stored objects, and may split the tree into several subtrees.

The concept of self-stabilization [16] is a general technique to design distributed systems that can handle arbitrary transient faults. A self-stabilizing system, regardless of the initial state of the processes and the initial messages in the links, is guaranteed to converge to the intended behavior in finite time.

In [10], a self-stabilizing message passing protocol to maintain prefix trees over practical P2P networks is introduced. This protocol makes the data structure robust against arbitrary transient faults. The protocol is based on self-stabilizing PIF (*Propagation of*

A.W. Richa and C. Scheideler (Eds.): SSS 2012, LNCS 7596, pp. 239–252, 2012.

Information with Feedback) waves that are used to evaluate the tree maintenance progression. The scheme of PIF can be informally described as follows: a node, called *initiator*, initiates a PIF wave by broadcasting a message *m* into the network. Each non-initiator node acknowledges to the initiator the receipt of *m*. The wave terminates when the root has received an acknowledgment from all other nodes. In arbitrary distributed systems, any node may need to initiate a PIF wave. Thus, any node can be the initiator of a PIF wave and several PIF protocols may run concurrently (in that case, every node maintains locally a data structure per initiator).

Contribution. We first present the scheme of *collaborative* PIF (referred as CoPIF). The main thrust of this scheme is to ensure that different waves may collaborate to improve the overall parallelism of the mechanism of PIF waves. In other words, the waves merge together so that they do not have to visit parts of the network already visited by other waves. Of course, this scheme is interesting in environments were several PIF waves may run concurrently. Next, we provide a self-stabilizing CoPIF protocol with its correctness proof. To the best of our knowledge, it is the first self-stabilizing solution for this problem. Based on the snap-stabilizing PIF algorithm in [8], it merges waves initiated at different points in the network. In the worst case where only one PIF wave runs at a time, our scheme does not slow down the normal progression of the wave. Finally, we present experimental results showing the efficiency of our scheme use in a large scale P2P tree-based overlay designed for the services discovery.

Roadmap. The related works are presented in Section 2. Section 3 provides the conceptual and computational models of our framework. In Section 4, we present our self-stabilizing collaborative protocol—due to the lack of space, the correctness proofs are omitted[1]. In Section 5, experiments show the benefit of the CoPIF approach. Finally, concluding remarks are given in Section 6.

2 Related Work

2.1 Self-stabilizing Propagation of Information

PIF wave algorithms have been extensively proposed in the area of self-stabilization, *e.g.*, [2,5,8,14,30] to quote only a few. Except [5,14,30], all the above solutions assume an underlying self-stabilizing rooted spanning tree construction algorithm. The solutions in [8,14] have the extra desirable property of being snap-stabilizing. A *snap-stabilizing protocol* guarantees that the system always maintains the desirable behavior. This property is very useful for wave algorithms and other algorithms that use PIF waves as the underlying protocols. The basic idea is that, regardless of the initial configuration of the system, when an initiator starts a wave, the messages and the tasks associated with this wave will work as expected in a normal computation. A snap-stabilizing PIF is also used in [11] to propose a snap-stabilizing service discovery tool for P2P systems based on prefix tree.

---

[1] The complete proofs of correctness can be found at
http://hal.inria.fr/hal-00714775.

2.2   Resource Discovery

The resource discovery in P2P environments has been intensively studied [20]. Although DHTs [24,25,28] were designed for very large systems, they only provide rigid mechanisms of search. A great deal of research went into finding ways to improve the retrieval process over structured peer-to-peer networks. Peer-to-peer systems use different technologies to support multi-attribute range queries [6,18,26,27]. Trie-structured approaches outperform others in the sense that logarithmic (or constant if we assume an upper bound on the depth of the trie) latency is achieved by parallelizing the resolution of the query in several branches of the trie.

2.3   Trie-Based Related Work

Among trie-based approaches, Prefix Hash Tree (PHT) [22] dynamically builds a trie of the given key-space (full set of possible identifiers of resources) as an upper layer mapped over any DHT-like network. Fault-tolerance within PHT is delegated to the DHT layer. Skip Graphs, introduced in [3], are similar to tries, and rely on skip lists, using their own probabilistic fault-tolerance guarantees. P Grid is a similar binary trie whose nodes of different sub-parts of the trie are linked by shortcuts like in Kademlia [19]. The fault-tolerance approach used in P-Grid [15] is based on probabilistic replication.

In our approach, the DLPT was initially designed for the purpose of service discovery over dynamic computational grids and aimed at solving some drawbacks of similar previous approaches. An advantage of this technology is its ability to take into account the heterogeneity of the underlying physical network to build a more efficient tree overlay, as detailed in [13].

3   P2P Service Discovery Framework

In this section we present the conceptual model of our P2P service discovery framework and the DLPT data structure on which it is based. Next, we convert our framework into the computational model on which our proof is based.

3.1   Conceptual Model

The two abstraction layers that compose our P2P service discovery framework are organized as follow: (*i*) a *P2P* network which consists of a set of asynchronous peer (physical machines) with distinct identifiers. The peer communicate by exchanging messages. Any peer $P1$ is able to communicate with another peer $P2$ only if $P1$ knows the identifier of $P2$. The system is seen as an undirected graph $G = (V, E)$ where V is the set of peers and E is the set of bidirectional communication link; (*ii*) an overlay that is built on the P2P system, which is considered as an undirected connected labeled tree $G' = (V', E')$ where V' is the set of nodes and E' is the set of links between nodes. Two nodes p and q are said to be neighbors if and only if there is a link (p, q) between the two nodes. To simplify the presentation we refer to the link (p, q) by the label q in the code of p. The overlay can be seen as an indexing system whose nodes are mapped onto the peers of the network. Henceforth, to avoid any confusion, the word *node* refers to a node of the tree overlay, *i.e.*, a logical entity, whereas the word *peer* refers to a physical node part of the *P2P* system.

Reading and writing features of our service discovery framework are ensured as follow. Nodes are indexed with service name and resource locations are stored on nodes. So, client requests are treated by any node, rooted to the targeted service labeled node along the overlay abstraction layer, indexed resource locations are returned to the clients or updated . A more detailed description of the implementation of our framework is given in [9] and briefly reminded in Section 5.1.

The *Distributed Lexicographic Placement Table* (DLPT [12,13]) is the hierarchical data structure that ensures request routing across overlay layer. DLPT belongs to the category of overlays that are distributed prefix trees, *e.g.*, [4,23,1]. Such overlays have the desirable property of efficiently supporting range queries by parallelizing the searches in branches of the tree and exhibit good complexity properties due to the limited depth of the tree. More particularly, DLPT is based on the particular *Proper Greatest Common Prefix Tree* (PGCP tree) overlay structure. *A Proper Greatest Common Prefix* Tree (*a.k.a* radix tree in [21]) is a labeled rooted tree such that the following properties are true for every node of the tree: (*i*) the node label is a proper prefix of any label in its subtree; (*ii*) the greatest common prefix of any pair of labels of children of a given node are the same and equal to the node label.

Designed to evolve in very dynamic systems, the DLPT integrates a self-stabilization mechanisms [10], providing the ability to recover a functioning state after arbitrary transient failures. As such, the truthfulness of information returned to the client needs to be guaranteed. We use the PIF mechanism to check whether DLPT is currently in a recovering phase or not.

3.2 Computational Model

In a first step, we abstract the communication model to ease the reading and the explanation of our solution. We assume that every pair of neighboring nodes communicate in the overlay by direct reading of variables. So, the program of every node consists in a set of shared variables (henceforth referred to as variables) and a finite number of actions. Each node can write in its own variables and read its own variables and those of its neighbors. Each action is constituted as follow: $< Label >::< Guard >\rightarrow< Statement >$. The guard of an action is a Boolean expression involving the variables of p and its neighbors. The statement is an action which updates one or more variables of the node p. Note that an action can be executed only if its guard is true. Each execution is decomposed into steps. Let y be an execution and A an action of p ($p \in V$). A is *enabled* for p in y if and only if the guard of A is satisfied by p in y. Node p is enabled in y if and only if at least one action is enabled at p in y.

The state of a node is defined by the value of its variables. The state of a system is the product of the states of all nodes. The local state refers to the state of a node and the global state to the state of the system. Each step of the execution consists of two sequential phases atomically executed: (*i*) Every node evaluates its guard; (*ii*) One or more enabled nodes execute their enabled actions. When the two phases are done, the next step begins.

Formal description (Section 4.2) and proof of correctness of the proposed collaborative propagate information feedback algorithm will be done using this computational model. Nevertheless, experiments are implemented using the classical message-passing model over an actual peer-to-peer system [7,17].

4   Collaborative Propagation of Information with Feedback Algorithm

In this section, we first present an overview of the proposed Collaborative Propagation of Information with Feedback Algorithm (CoPIF). Next, we provide its formal description.

4.1   Overview of the CoPIF

Before explaining the idea behind CoPIF, let us first recall the well-known PIF wave execution. Starting from a configuration where no message has been broadcast yet, a node, also called *initiator*, initiates the broadcast phase and all its descendant except the leaf participate in this task by sending also the broadcast message to their descendants. Once the broadcast message reaches a leaf node of the network, they notify their ancestors of the end of the broadcast phase by initiating the feedback phase. During both broadcast and feedback steps, it is possible to collect information or perform actions on the entire data structure. Once all the nodes of the structure have been reached and returned the feedback message, the initiator retrieve collected information and executes a special action related to the termination of the PIF-wave. In the sequel, we will refer to this mechanism as *classic*-PIF.

However, the PIF mechanism is a costly broadcast mechanism that involves the whole platform. In this paper, we aim to increase the parallelism of the PIF by making several PIF waves collaborating together. Let us now define some notions that will be used in the description of our solution:

Let an ordered alphabet A be a finite set of letters. Lets define $\prec$ an order on A. A non empty word w over A is a finite sequence of letters $a_1, ... , a_i, ..., a_l$ such as $l > 0$. The concatenation of two words u and v, denoted as uv, is equal to the word $a_1, ..., a_i, ..., a_k, b_1, ..., b_j, ..., b_l$ such that $u = a_1, ..., a_i, ..., a_k$ and $v = b_1, ..., b_j, ..., b_l$. A word u is a prefix (respectively, proper prefix) of a word v if there exists a word w such that $v = uw$ (respectively, $v = uw$ and $u \neq v$). The *Greatest Common Prefix* (respectively, *Proper Greatest Common Prefix*) of w_1 and w_2, denoted $GCP(w_1, w_2)$ (respectively $PGCP(w_1, w_2)$), is the longest prefix u shared by w_1 and w_2 (respectively, such that $\forall i \geq 1, u \neq w_i$).

Let us now describe the outline of the proposed solution through the P2P framework use case.

Use Case. The idea of the algorithm is the following: When a user is looking for a service, it sends a request to the DLPT to check whether the service exists or not. Once the request is on one node of the DLPT, it is routed according to the labelled tree in the following manner: let $l_{request}$ be the label of the service requested by the user and let l_p be the label of the current node u_p. In the case of $PGCP(l_{request}, l_p)$ is true, u_p checks whether there exists a child u_q in the DLPT having a label l_q such that $PGCP(l_{request}, l_q)$ is satisfied. If such a node exists, then u_p forwards the request to its child u_q. Otherwise ($PGCP(l_{request}, l_p)$ is not satisfied), if we keep exploring the sub-tree routed in u_p, the service will not be found. u_p sends in this case the request to its father node in the DLPT. By doing so, either (*i*) the request is sent to one node u_p such that $l_p = l_{request}$, or (*ii*) the request reaches a node u_p such that it cannot be routed anymore. In the former case, the service being found, a message containing the information about the service is sent to the user. In the latter case, the service has not been found and the message "no information about the service" is sent to the user. However, the node has no clue to trust the received information or not. In other words, in the former case, u_p does not know whether it contains the entire service information or if a part of the information is on a node being at a wrong position in the tree due to transient faults. In the latter case, u_p does not know whether the service is really not supported by the system or if the service is missed because it is at a wrong position.

In order to solve this problem, u_p initiates a PIF wave to check the state of all the nodes part of the DLPT. Note that several PIF waves can be initiated concurrently since many requests can be made in different parts of the system. The idea of the solution is to make the different PIF waves collaborating in order to check whether the tree is under construction or not. For instance, assume that two PIF waves, *PIF*1 and *PIF*2, are running concurrently on two different parts of the tree, namely on the subtrees $T1$ and $T2$, respectively. Our idea is to merge *PIF*1 and *PIF*2 so that *PIF*1 (respectively, *PIF*2) do not traverse $T2$ (resp., $T1$) by using data collected by *PIF*2 (resp.*PIF*1). Furthermore, our solution is required to be self-stabilizing.

CoPIF. Basically, the CoPIF scheme is a mechanism enabling the collaboration between different PIF waves. Each node u_p of the DLPT has a state variable S_p that includes three parameters $S_p = (Phase, id_f, id_{PIF})$. Parameter id_{PIF} refers to the identifier of the PIF wave which consists of the couple (id_{peer}, l_{u_i}), where id_{peer} is the identifier of the peer hosting the node u_i that initiated the PIF wave and l_{u_i} is the label of the node u_i. The value id_f refers to the identifier of the neighbor from which u_p received the broadcast. It is set at NULL in the case u_p is the initiator. *Phase* can have four values: C, B, FC and FI. The value C (*Clean*) denotes the initial state of any node before it participates in a PIF wave. The value B (*Broadcast*) or FC (*Feedback correct*) or FI (*Feedback incorrect*) means that the node is part of a PIF wave. Observe that in the case there is just a single PIF wave that is executed on the DLPT, then its execution is similar to the previously introduce *classic*-PIF.

When more than one PIF wave are executed, four cases are possible while the progression of the CoPIF wave. First (*i*), if there is a node u_p in the C state having only one neighboring node q in the B state and no other neighboring node in the FI or FC state, then p changes its state to B. Second (*ii*), if there exists a leaf node u_p in the C state having a neighbor u_q in the B state, then u_p changes its state to FC (resp. FI) if its position in the DLPT is correct (resp. incorrect). Next (*iii*), if there is a node u_p in C-phase having two neighboring nodes u_q and $u_{q'}$ in the B state with different id_{PIF}

then, u_p changes its state to B and sets its id_f to u_q such that the id_{PIF} of u_q is smaller than id_{PIF} of $u_{q'}$. Finally (iv), if there exists a node u_p that is already in the B state such that its id_f is u_q and there exists another neighboring node $u_{q'}$ which is in the B state with a smaller id_{PIF} and a different id_f, then u_p changes its father by setting id_f at $u_{q'}$.

Notice that in the fourth cases, u_q (previously, the id_f of u_p) will have to change its id_f as well since it has now a neighbor u_p in the B state with a smaller id_{peer}. By doing so, the node u_i that initiated a PIF wave with a smaller id will change its id_{peer}. Similarly, notice that u_i is not an initiator anymore. Hence it changes its id_f from NULL to the id of its neighbor with a smallest id_{PIF}. So, only one node will get the answer (the feedback of the COPIF), this node being the one with the smallest id_{PIF}. Therefore, when an initiator sets its id_f to a value different from NULL (as u_i previously), it sends a message to the new considered initiator (can be deduced from id_{PIF}) to subscribe to the answer. So, when an initiator node receives the feedback that indicates the state of the tree, it notifies all its subscribers of the answer.

4.2   Formal Description

In the following we first define the data and variables that are used for the description of our algorithm. We then present the formal description in Algorithm 1.

- Predicates
    - $Request_{PIF}$: Set at true when the peer wants to initiate a PIF wave (There is a *Service - Request* which could not find the desired service).
- Variables
    - $S_p = (A, q, q')$: refers to the state of the node p such that: A corresponds to the phase of the PIF wave p is in. $A \in \{B, FI, FC, C\}$ for respectively Broadcast, Feedback State-Incorrect, Feedback State-Correct, Clean. q refers to the identity of the peer that initiates the PIF wave. q' refers to the identity of the neighboring node of p in the DLPT from which p got the Broadcast.
    - N_p: refers to the set of the identities of the nodes that are neighbor to p
    - $State_{DLPT}$: refers to the state of the DLPT
    - min_p: $q \in N_p, S_q = (B, id_q, z) \wedge z \neq p \wedge id_p = min\{id_{q'}, q' \in N_p, S_{q'} = (B, id_{q'}, z') \wedge z' \neq p\}$.
- Functions
    - Send(@dest, @source, Msg): @source sends the message *Msg* to @dest.
    - Add(Mylist, item): Add to my list the subject *item*.

Character ' - ' in the algorithm means *any value*.

Correctness Proof. We first show that starting from any arbitrary configuration, the system eventually contains no abnormal sequence, *i.e.*, incorrect process states due to the unpredictable initial configurations and transient errors. Next, we show that each node is able to generate a *PIF* wave in finite time. Furthermore, all the nodes of the system are visited by the COPIF wave. Thus, all of them acknowledge the receipt of the question (whether the tree overlay is in a correct state or not) and give an answer to the latter. Finally, one node p of the system receives the answer ($S_p = (B, id, NULL)$). Hence, the following statement holds:

Theorem 1. *Algorithm 1 is a self-Stabilizing* COPIF *algorithm.*

5   Evaluation

In order to evaluate qualitatively and quantitatively the efficiency of CoPIF, we drive a set of experiments. As mentioned before, the DLPT approach and its different features have been validated through analysis and simulation [29]. The scalability and performance of its implementation, SBAM (Spades BAsed Middleware) has ever been improved in [9]. Our goal is now to show the efficiency of the previously described

---

Algorithm 1. CoPIF

- **PIF Initiation**
  - **R1:** $Request_{PIF} \wedge S_p = (C,-,-) \wedge \forall q \in N_p, S_q \neq (-,-,p) \rightarrow S_p = (B,(id_{peer},l_p),NULL), State_{DLPT} = Unknown$
  - **R2:** $Request_{PIF} \wedge S_p = (B,id,q) \wedge q \neq NULL \rightarrow Send(@id,id_{peer},Interested), State_{DLPT} = Unknown$

- **Broadcast propagation**
  - **R3:** $S_p = (C,-,-) \wedge \neg Request_{PIF} \wedge \exists q \in N_p, (S_q = (B,k,-) \wedge q = min_p \wedge \neg \exists q' \in N_p, q \neq q', S_{q'} = (B,k,-)) \wedge \forall q'' \in N_p, S_{q''} \neq (FI \vee FC,-,p) \rightarrow S_p = (B,k,q)$

- **Father-Switch**
  - **R4:** $\exists q \in N_p, S_p = (B,id,q) \wedge \exists q' \in N_p, (q \neq q' \wedge S_{q'} = (B,id',?) \wedge id' < id \wedge q = min_p) \rightarrow S_p = (B,id',q')$

- **initiator resignation**
  - **R5:** $S_p = (B,id,NULL) \wedge \exists q \in N_p, S_q = (B,id',?) \wedge id' < id \wedge q = min_p) \rightarrow S_p = (B,id',q), Send(@id,id'peer,Interested)$

- **Feedback initiation**
  - **R6:** $|N_p| = 1 \wedge State = Correct \wedge \exists q \in N_p, S_q = (B,id,?) \rightarrow S_p = (FC,id,q)$
  - **R7:** $|N_p| = 1 \wedge State = Incorrect \wedge \exists q \in N_p, S_q = (B,id,?) \rightarrow S_p = (FI,id,q)$

- **Feedback propagation**
  - **R8:** $\exists q \in N_p, S_q = (B,id,-) \wedge S_p = (B,-,q) \wedge \forall q' \in N_p/\{q\}, S'_q = (FC,-,p) \rightarrow S_p = (FC,id,q)$
  - **R9:** $\exists q \in N_p, S_q = (B,id,-) \wedge S_p = (B,-,q) \wedge \forall q' \in N_p/\{q\}, S'_q = (FI \vee FC,-,p) \wedge \exists q'' \in N_p/\{q\} S'_q = (FI,?,p) \rightarrow S_p = (FI,id,q)$

- **Cleaning phase initiation**
  - **R10:** $\forall q \in N_p, S_q = (FC,id',p) \wedge S_p = (B,id,NULL) \wedge id = (id_{peer},l_p) \rightarrow State_{DLPT} = Correct, Request_{PIF} = false, S_p = (C,NULL,NULL), Send(@ListToContact, 'DLPT Correct'), State_{DLPT} = Unknown$
  - **R11:** $\forall q \in N_p, S_q = (FI \vee FC,id',p) \wedge S_p = (B,id,NULL) \wedge id = (id_{peer},l_p) \wedge \exists q'' \in N_p/\{q\} S'_q = (FI,-,p) \rightarrow State_{DLPT} = Incorrect, Request_{PIF} = false, S_p = (C,NULL,NULL), Send(@ListToContact, 'DLPT Incorrect'), State_{DLPT} = Unknown$

- **Cleaning phase propagation**
  - **R12:** $\exists q \in N_p, S_p = (FI \vee FC,id,q) \wedge (S_q = (C,-,-) \vee q = NULL) \rightarrow S_p = (C,NULL,NULL)$

- **Correction Rules**
  - **R13:** $S_p = (B,id,NULL) \wedge id \neq (id_{peer},l_p) \rightarrow S_p = (C,NULL,NULL)$
  - **R14:** $\exists q \in N_p S_p = (FI \vee FC,id,q) \wedge \exists q' \in N_p, q \neq q' \wedge S_{q'} \neq (FI \vee FC,-,-) \rightarrow S_p = (C,NULL,NULL)$
  - **R15:** $S_p = (B,id,q) \wedge (S_q \neq (B,-,-) \vee [S_q \neq (B,id',-) \wedge id' > id]) \rightarrow S_p = (C,NULL,NULL)$
  - **R16:** $S_p = (B,-,q) \wedge S_q = (FI \vee FC,-,-) \rightarrow S_p = (C,NULL,NULL)$
  - **R17:** $\exists q \in N_p, S_p = (B,id,q) \wedge S_q = (B,id,p) \rightarrow S_p(C,NULL,NULL)$
  - **R18:** $\exists q,q' \in N_p, S_p = (B,id,q) \wedge q \neq q' \wedge S_{q'} = (B,id,z) \wedge z \neq p \rightarrow S_p = (F,id,q)$
  - **R19:** $\exists q,q' \in N_p, S_p = (C,NULL,NULL) \wedge S_q = (B,id,z) \wedge z \neq p \wedge S_{q'} = (B,id,z') \wedge z' \neq p \rightarrow S_p = (F,id,q)$
  - **R20:** $\exists q,q' \in N_p, S_p = (B,id,q) \wedge S_q = (B,id',z) \wedge z \neq p \wedge id' < id \wedge S_{q'} = (B,id'',z') \wedge z' \neq p \wedge id' < id'' \rightarrow S_p = (B,id',q)$

- **Event: Message reception**
  - Message 'idpeer,Interested': $Add(ListToContact,idpeer)$
  - Message 'Contact id for an answer': $Send(@id,idpeer,Interested)$
  - Message 'DLPT Correct': $State_{DLPT} = Correct$
  - Message 'DLPT Incorrect': $State_{DLPT} = Incorrect$

QoS algorithm (Section 4). We will focus on the size of the tree, and number of PIF that collaborate simultaneously. We will observe the behavior not only from the number of exchanged messages point of view but also in term of duration needed to performs CoPIFs.

5.1 SBAM

We use the term *peer* to refer to a physical machine that is available on the network. In our case, a peer is an instantiated Java Virtual Machine connected to other peers through the communication bus. We call *nodes* the vertices of the prefix tree.

SBAM is the Java implementation of the DLPT. SBAM proposes 2-abstraction layers in order to support the distributed data structure: the *peer*-layer and the *agent*-layer. The *peer*-layer is the closest to the hardware layer. It relies on the Ibis Portability Layer (IPL) [17] that enables the P2P communication. We instantiate one JVM per machine, also called peer. JVM communicate all together as a P2P fashion using the IPL communication bus. The *agent*-layer supports the data structure. Each node of the DLPT is instantiated as a SBAM agent. Agents are uniformly distributed over peers and communicate together in a transparent way using a proxy interface. Since we want to guarantee truthfulness of information exchanged between SBAM-agents, the implementation of an efficient mechanism ensuring quality of large scale service discovery is quite challenging. In the state model described in the section 3.2 a node has to read the state and the variables of its neighbors. In SBAM, the feature is implemented using synchronous message exchange between agents. Indeed, when a node has to read its neighbor states, it sends a message to each and wait all responses. Despite the fact that this kind of implementation is expensive, especially on a large distributed data structure, experiment (Section 5.6) shown that our model implementation stays efficient, even on a huge prefix tree.

5.2 Experimental Platform

Experiments were run on the Grid'5000 platform[2] [7], more precisely on a dedicated cluster *HP Proliant DL165 G7* 17 units, each of them equipped with 2 *AMD Opteron 6164 HE* (1.7GHz) processors, each processor gathering 12 cores, thus offering a 264-cores platform for these experiments. Each unit consists of 48 GB of memory. Units are connected through two Gigabit Ethernet cards. For each experiment, we deployed one peer per unit.

5.3 Scenario of Experiments

The initialization of an experiment works in three phases: (*i*) the communication bus is started on a computing unit (Section 5.2), (*ii*) 16 peers are launched and connected together through the communication bus, and (*iii*) a pilot is elected using the elect feature of the communication bus.

---

[2] http://www.grid5000.fr/

After the initialization, the pilot drives the experiment. It consists in two sequential steps. First, it sends n insertion requests to the distributed tree structure. An insertion request leads to the addition of a new entry in the DLPT tree (Section 3). The insertion requests are sent to a random node of the tree and routed following the lexicographic pattern to the targeted node. Doing so, the node sharing the greatest common prefix with the service name is reached. If the targeted label does not exist, a new node is created on a randomly chosen peer and linked to the existing tree.

In the final step, the pilot selects a set of nodes to initiate *classic*-PIFs and CoPIFs (Section 4). In order to observe distributions, 10 replications of this basic scenario are executed.

5.4 Failures

At this level of description we can distinguish two kind of failure: (*i*) failures in the DLPT data structure, when the prefix tree data structure is corrupted; (*ii*) failures in the CoPIF state variables, when state variable dedicated to CoPIF feature are corrupted.

In our experiments, we consider that the DLPT data structure is not corrupt. It corresponds to the worst case in term of CoPIF truthfulness check. Indeed, if the entire DLPT data structure is correct, the CoPIF has to explore the entire DLPT data structure to check it.

Next, remind that the objective of our experiment is to evaluate the efficiency of CoPIF compared to *classic*-PIF. So, we consider that the CoPIF state variables are not corrupted and we measure the number of messages and the duration of CoPIF when the self-stabilization CoPIF has converged, it means after the clean part of the CoPIF state variables.

5.5 Parameters and Indicators

The experiments conducted are influenced by two main parameters. First, n denotes the number of inserted services in the tree. Second, k refers to the number of PIF waves that are collaborating together.

In these experiments, three trees were created with n in the set $\{2500, 10000, 40000\}$. The number of PIF that collaborate (k) was taken from the set $\{1, 2, 4, 8, 16, 32, 64\}$. For each couple (n, k), 10 replications are performed. Thus, 210 experiments were conducted.

Strings used to label the nodes of the trees were randomly generated with an alphabet of 2 digits and a maximum length of 18 (in a set of 524287 key).

For each experiment we observe two indicators: (*i*) the *total number of exchanged messages* observed and (*ii*) the *time required* to perform k *classic*-PIFs or CoPIFs over distributed data structure, *i.e.*, the time between the issue of the PIFs and the receipt of the response on all nodes that initiate PIFs.

For each indicator we obtain 21 sets of 10 values. We present evolution of the *median*-value of the 10-replication according to k, the number of PIFs (Figures 1(a) and 1(b)). The comparison of these indicators for *classic*-PIFs and CoPIFs provides us a **qualitative** overview of the gain obtain using CoPIF.

In order to **quantitatively** evaluate the efficiency of the CoPIF strategy, for an indicator (I) and for a given number of PIFs k, we compute the **efficiency criterion** with the following formula:

$$E_{I,k} = \frac{I_{\text{ind},k}}{k \times I_{\text{coll},k}},$$

where $I_{\text{classic},k}$ (resp. $I_{\text{CoPIF},k}$) is the value of the indicator I for a given k and in an *classic*-PIF (resp. CoPIF) context. The evolution of this efficiency criterion are shown in Figures 2(a) and 2(b).

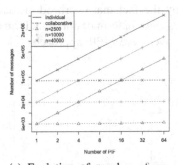 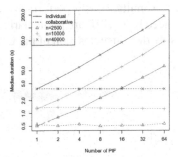

(a) Evolution of number of exchanged messages.

(b) Evolution of duration.

Fig. 1. CoPIF behavior

5.6   Results

Figure 1(a) (resp. 1(b)) presents the evolution of the number of messages (resp. duration) needs to execute PIFs according to number of PIFs (k) that are simultaneously performed and the size of the data structure on which PIFs are performed. The y-axis represents the number of exchanged messages (resp. the duration). On these figures, *classic*-PIFs and CoPIFs strategies are compared. On both curve, the x-axis represents the number of PIF (k) that are simultaneously performed. On these figures, we present 2 curve triplets. Solid (resp. dashed) curves triplet describes indicator in an *classic*-PIF (resp. CoPIF) context. For each triplet, *red-triangle*-curve (resp. *green-+-*curve and *blue-x-*curve) describes behavior of indicator for $n = 2500$ (resp. $n = 10000$ and $n = 40000$).

When the indicators explode in for *classic*-PIF strategy, they stay stable for CoPIF strategy. It **qualitatively** demonstrates gain of the CoPIF strategy over *classic*-PIF approach. Notice that *log*-scale on Figure 1(b) figure out a time overhead associated with the CoPIFs approach for a single wave ($= 1$). This time overhead decreases when n increases. We more detail this observation in the quantitative part of this analysis. The introduction of the *efficiency criterion* in Section 5.5 allows us to measure quantitatively this gain, this overhead and their behaviors.

Figure 2(a) and 2(b) present the efficiency of CoPIF according to the number of exchanged messages and the duration. On these figures we want to observe the impact of the size of the data structure on the efficiency of CoPIF. Figure 2(a) reveals us that, in term of number exchanged messages, on small data structure, the collaborative mechanism is less efficient than on huge one. This result was expected because on small data structure the number of messages due to collision between collaborative PIFs (overhead) represents a more important part of the entire number of exchanged messages. So, the bigger the data structure, the more efficient CoPIF.

More interesting is the analyze of the Figure 2(b). Indeed we can observe the same tendency in term of duration but the efficiency decrease faster with the number of PIFs that are simultaneously performed. It is explain by the fact that overhead messages introduced by CoPIF are particularly expensive messages in term of duration. It **quantitatively** demonstrates gain of the CoPIF strategy over *classic*-PIF approach.

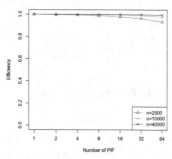

(a) Efficiency according to the number of exchanged messages.

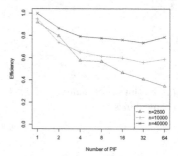

(b) Efficiency according to the duration.

Fig. 2. CoPIF Efficiency

6   Conclusion and Future Work

In this paper we provide a self-stabilized collaborative algorithm called CoPIF allowing to check the truthfulness of a distributed prefix tree. CoPIF implementation in a P2P service discovery framework is experimentally validate, in *qualitative* and in *quantitative* terms. Experiment demonstrates the efficiency of CoPIF w.r.t. *classic*-PIF. CoPIF overhead represents a small part of the number of exchange messages and of the time spend, specially on huge data structures.

We conjecture that the stabilization time is in $O(h^2)$ rounds and the worst case time to merge several classic-PIF waves is in $O(h)$ rounds, h being the height of the tree. We plan to experimentally validate this two complexities. Indeed, experiment were driven considering no corrupted CoPIF variables. In order to do that, we need to define a model of failure, implement or reuse a fault injector and couple it with SBAM before driving a new experiment campaign.

Acknowledgment. This research is funded by french National Research Agency (08-ANR-SEGI-025). Details of the project on http://graal.ens-lyon.fr/SPADES. Experiments presented in this paper were carried out using the Grid'5000 experimental testbed, being developed under the INRIA ALADDIN development action with support from CNRS, RENATER and several Universities as well as other funding bodies (see https://www.grid5000.fr).

References

1. Aberer, K., Cudré-Mauroux, P., Datta, A., Despotovic, Z., Hauswirth, M., Punceva, M., Schmidt, R.: P-grid: a self-organizing structured P2P system. SIGMOD Record 32(3), 29–33 (2003)
2. Arora, A., Gouda, M.G.: Distributed reset. IEEE Transactions on Computers 43, 1026–1038 (1994)
3. Aspnes, J., Shah, G.: Skip Graphs. In: Fourteenth Annual ACM-SIAM Symposium on Discrete Algorithms (January 2003)
4. Aspnes, J., Shah, G.: Skip graphs. ACM Transactions on Algorithms 3(4) (2007)
5. Awerbuch, B., Kutten, S., Mansour, Y., Patt-Shamir, B., Varghese, G.: Time optimal self-stabilizing synchronization. In: STOC 1993: Proceedings of the 25th Annual ACM Symposium on Theory of Computing, pp. 652–661 (1993)
6. Bharambe, A., Agrawal, M., Seshan, S.: Mercury: Supporting Scalable Multi-Attribute Range Queries. In: Proceedings of the SIGCOMM Symposium (August 2004)
7. Bolze, R., Cappello, F., Caron, E., Daydé, M., Desprez, F., Jeannot, E., Jégou, Y., Lanteri, S., Leduc, J., Melab, N., Mornet, G., Namyst, R., Primet, P., Quetier, B., Richard, O., Talbi, E.-G., Irena, T.: Grid'5000: a large scale and highly reconfigurable experimental grid testbed. International Journal of High Performance Computing Applications 20(4), 481–494 (2006)
8. Bui, A., Datta, A.K., Petit, F., Villain, V.: Snap-stabilization and PIF in tree networks. Distributed Computing 20(1), 3–19 (2007)
9. Caron, E., Chuffart, F., He, H., Tedeschi, C.: Implementation and evaluation of a P2P service discovery system. In: Proceedings of the the 11th IEEE International Conference on Computer and Information Technology, pp. 41–46 (2011)
10. Caron, E., Datta, A.K., Petit, F., Tedeschi, C.: Self-Stabilization in Tree-Structured Peer-to-Peer Service Discovery Systems. In: Proc. of the 27th Int. Symposium on Reliable Distributed Systems (SRDS 2008), Napoli, Italy (October 2008)
11. Caron, E., Desprez, F., Petit, F., Tedeschi, C.: Snap-stabilizing prefix tree for peer-to-peer systems. Parallel Processing Letters 20(1), 15–30 (2010)
12. Caron, E., Desprez, F., Tedeschi, C.: A Dynamic Prefix Tree for Service Discovery Within Large Scale Grids. In: Proc. of the 6th Int. Conference on Peer-to-Peer Computing (P2P 2006), Cambridge, UK, pp. 106–113 (September 2006)
13. Caron, E., Desprez, F., Tedeschi, C.: Efficiency of Tree-Structured Peer-to-Peer Service Discovery Systems. In: Proc. of the 5th Int. Workshop on Hot Topics in Peer-to-Peer Systems (Hot-P2P 2008), Miami, USA (April 2008)
14. Cournier, A., Datta, A.K., Petit, F., Villain, V.: Snap-stabilizing PIF algorithm in arbitrary networks. In: 22rd International Conference on Distributed Computing Systems (ICDCS 2002), pp. 199–206. IEEE Computer Society, Vienna (2002)
15. Datta, A., Hauswirth, M., John, R., Schmidt, R., Aberer, K.: Range Queries in Trie-Structured Overlays. In: The Fifth IEEE International Conference on Peer-to-Peer Computing (2005)
16. Dolev, S.: Self-Stabilization. The MIT Press (2000)

17. Drost, N., van Nieuwpoort, R.V., Maassen, J., Seinstra, F., Bal, H.E.: JEL: Unified Resource Tracking for Parallel and Distributed Applications. Concurrency and Computation: Practice and Experience (2010)
18. Cai, M., Frank, M., Chen, J., Szekely, P.: Maan: A multi-attribute addressable network for grid information services. Journal of Grid Computing 2(1), 3–14 (2004)
19. Maymounkov, P., Mazières, D.: Kademlia: A Peer-to-Peer Information System Based on the XOR Metric. In: Druschel, P., Kaashoek, M.F., Rowstron, A. (eds.) IPTPS 2002. LNCS, vol. 2429, pp. 53–65. Springer, Heidelberg (2002)
20. Meshkova, E., Riihijärvi, J., Petrova, M., Mähönen, P.: A survey on resource discovery mechanisms, peer-to-peer and service discovery frameworks. Comput. Netw. 52(11), 2097–2128 (2008)
21. Morrison, D.R.: PATRICIA–Practical Algorithm To Retrieve Information Coded in Alphanumeric. J. ACM 15, 514–534 (1968)
22. Ramabhadran, S., Ratnasamy, S., Hellerstein, J.M., Shenker, S.: Prefix Hash Tree: an Indexing Data Structure over Distributed Hash Tables. In: Proceedings of the 23rd ACM Symposium on Principles of Distributed Computing (2004)
23. Ramabhadran, S., Ratnasamy, S., Hellerstein, J., Shenker, S.: Prefix hash tree: an indexing data structure over distributed hash table. In: Proc. of the 23rd ACM Symposium on Principles of Distributed Computing (PODC 2004), July 2004, p. 368. St John's, Canada (2004)
24. Ratnasamy, S., Francis, P., Handley, M., Karp, R., Shenker, S.: A Scalable Content-Adressable Network. In: ACM SIGCOMM (2001)
25. Rowstron, A., Druschel, P.: Pastry: Scalable, Decentralized Object Location, and Routing for Large-Scale Peer-to-Peer Systems. In: Guerraoui, R. (ed.) Middleware 2001. LNCS, vol. 2218, pp. 329–350. Springer, Heidelberg (2001)
26. Schmidt, C., Parashar, M.: Enabling Flexible Queries with Guarantees in P2P Systems. IEEE Internet Computing 8(3), 19–26 (2004)
27. Shu, Y., Ooi, B.C., Tan, K., Zhou, A.: Supporting Multi-Dimensional Range Queries in Peer-to-Peer Systems. In: Peer-to-Peer Computing, pp. 173–180 (2005)
28. Stoica, I., Morris, R., Karger, D., Kaashoek, M., Balakrishnan, H.: Chord: A Scalable Peer-to-Peer Lookup service for Internet Applications. In: ACM SIGCOMM, pp. 149–160 (2001)
29. Tedeschi, C.: Peer-to-Peer Prefix Tree for Large Scale Service Discovery. PhD thesis, École normale supérieure de Lyon (October 2008)
30. Varghese, G.: Self-stabilization by counter flushing. In: PODC 1994 Proceedings of the Thirteenth Annual ACM Symposium on Principles of Distributed Computing, pp. 244–253 (1994)

Scalable Byzantine Agreement with a Random Beacon*

Olumuyiwa Oluwasanmi and Jared Saia

Department of Computer Science, University of New Mexico, Albuquerque, NM 87131-1386
{muyiwa,saia}@cs.unm.edu

Abstract. We present two Monte Carlo algorithms for efficiently computing Byzantine agreement in the partially synchronous communication model. The algorithms assume the existence of a Random Beacon, which is a stream of random bits, known to all the processors. Both algorithms terminate in $O(1)$ expected time. The first algorithm sends $O(M + n \log^2 n)$ messages in total, where M is the maximum number of messages sent by the bad processors in any round and n is the number of processors. It ensures all processors reach agreement. The second algorithm sends $\tilde{O}(1)$ messages per processor, and is thus load-balanced, and ensures all but a $o(1)$ fraction of the processors reach agreement. Both algorithms succeed with probability $1 - O(1/n^k)$, even against an adaptive adversary that takes over up to a $1/3 - \epsilon$ fraction of the processors for any $\epsilon > 0$. We prove the correctness of both algorithms and provide empirical evidence that they require significantly less bandwidth than previous algorithms for networks of size greater than 4,000 processors. Our algorithms work in the full-information model and thus make no cryptographic assumptions.

1 Introduction

As the size and complexity of the Internet and other large scale networks has grown, so also has the frequency of malicious attacks. These attacks have grown in their scope and severity as well as their economic impact which is on the order of about a hundred billion dollars or more [1,2]. There is thus a growing need to design distributed algorithms that are robust to attack. The growing size of networks also demands that communication costs of any algorithms to be small enough to scale to large n.

A critical problem in reliable distributed computing is *Byzantine agreement*. Byzantine agreement is defined as follows. There are n processors some of which are good and some of which are bad. Good processors follow the protocol and bad processors can deviate in an arbitrary way. The goal is to ensure all good processors output the same bit and that this bit equals the input bit of some good processor. Intuitively, a solution to Byzantine agreement allows us to build a reliable system from unreliable components.

In this paper, we show how to dramatically reduce the cost of Byzantine Agreement algorithms by using a Random Beacon. A Random Beacon is a random stream of bits available to all the processors. It was first defined by Rabin in [3] where it was used to build a contract signing protocol. Maurer et al. in [4,5,6,7] describe a computation model called the Memory Limited or Limited Storage space Model, which uses the existence of a Random Beacon, to build a secure communication system based on private keys.

---

* This research was partially supported by NSF CAREER Award 0644058, NSF CCR-0313160, and an AFOSR MURI grant.

A.W. Richa and C. Scheideler (Eds.): SSS 2012, LNCS 7596, pp. 253–265, 2012.

1.1 Model

Our algorithms assume communication via message passing from processor to processor and the ID's of the other processors in the network are known to each processor. Our communication model is partially synchronous: In particular, we assume a known upper bound on the time it takes to receive a message. Our algorithms work in the full-information model, meaning that all messages being sent are public and can be seen by the adversarial processors and so no cryptographic assumptions are required. We assume t processors are controlled by an adaptive adversary where $t \leq (1/3 - \epsilon)n$ for some $0 < \epsilon \leq 1/3$ and n is the total number of processors. The adversary is adaptive in the sense that: An adaptive adversary can take over processors at any point in the protocol up taking over t processors and once processors are corrupted, they stay corrupted [8]. We also assume that the bits from the Random Beacon are only available at the beginning of a round.

1.2 Our Results

Our algorithms terminate in $O(1)$ expected time. The first algorithm sends $O(M + n \log^2 n)$ messages in total, where M is the maximum number of messages sent by the bad processors in any round. It ensures all processors reach agreement. The second algorithm sends $O(\log^3 n)$ messages per processor, and is thus load-balanced and ensures all but a $o(1)$ fraction of the processors reach agreement. Our algorithms are Monte Carlo, in the sense that they succeed with probability $1 - O(1/n^k)$, even if an adaptive adversary that takes over up to a $1/3 - \epsilon$ fraction of the processors for any $0 < \epsilon \leq 1/3$.

1.3 Related Work

The Byzantine agreement problem was first proposed by Lamport et al. [9] as a way to model basic fault-tolerant distributed computing. It was proved by Lamport, Shostak and Pease proved in [9] that Byzantine agreement is only possible when less than $n/3$ of the processors are bad. Fischer, Lynch and Paterson in [10] also proved that a single Byzantine fault in the asynchronous model of communication renders Byzantine agreement impossible for a deterministic algorithm.

Dolev in [11] showed that if $\Theta(n)$ processors are bad, $\Omega(n^2)$ messages must be sent to ensure Byzantine agreement with probability 1. Dolev and Reishuck in [12] show that even with the assumption of the existence of a digital signature scheme (computationally bounded adversary), there is a lower bound of $\Omega(n + t^2)$ messages to ensure Byzantine agreement with probability 1.

Rabin in [13] solved a randomized version of the Byzantine agreement problem using the notion of a *common coin* (we also refer to this as a Random Beacon). A common coin is a value that is only available to all the processors at the beginning of each round of computation. It is 0 with probability $1/2$ and 1 with probability $1/2$. Rabin's algorithm [13] takes $O(1)$ expected rounds and requires $\Theta(n^2)$ messages. Rabin's algorithm works in the asynchronous, full information model and is correct with probability 1.

Several results allow for solving Byzantine agreement with randomized algorithms even without a global coin. In [14] Karlin and Yao prove a $n - t > 2n/3$ lower bound for randomized Byzantine agreement. Feldman and Micali [15] give a randomized algorithm that has $O(1)$ expected latency and tolerates $t < n/3$ adversarial faults. Their algorithm works in the synchronous model of communication with private channels and makes standard cryptographic assumptions. Their algorithm is correct with probability 1. Recently, King and Saia in [16] describe a Byzantine agreement algorithm that works in the presence of an adaptive adversary but sends $\tilde{O}(n^{3/2})$ messages. Also the series of papers by King, Saia et al. [17,18] describe practical algorithms that send less than $O(n^{3/3})$ messages in the presence of a non-adaptive adversary. Some Byzantine agreement algorithms result in having almost-everywhere agreement which was defined by Dwork et al. in [19]. Almost-everywhere Byzantine agreement results in an $0 < \epsilon < 1$ fraction of the good processors not knowing the value of the bit.

In the empirical section of this chapter, we compare the resource costs of our algorithm with the Byzantine agreement algorithm proposed by Cachin, Kursawe and Shoup [20]. Cachin, Kursawe and Shoup give an algorithm that withstands up to $n/3$ bad processors, runs in constant expected time, and sends $\Theta(n^2)$ messages. However, unlike our algorithm, their algorithm requires a trusted dealer to distribute cryptographic keys initially in order to set up a public key infrastructure. We emphasize that our algorithm does *not* require the establishment of a public key infrastructure. As mentioned earlier, the algorithm we describe in this paper is partially synchronous, while the algorithm of Cachin, Kursawe and Shoup is asynchronous.

Lee, Clark et al. showed in [21,22] how to build a Random Beacon using publicly available information on the Internet, specifically using information from the Dow Jones Industrial Average (DJIA) or from other financial data. Eastlake in [23,24] also describes how to build a selection protocol out of a Random Beacon.

A concern is the actual amount of randomness present in implementations of a Random Beacon from publicly available information, this could be a problem if the publicly available data could be manipulated in some way and hence introducing some bias into the Random Beacon bits. In particular, Clark and Hengartner in [22] determined via experiments the entropy of the stock components of the Dow Jones Industrial Average (DJIA) and show that the Shannon entropy for a single stock in the DJIA per day is between 6.83 and 9.45. They create a Random Beacon from the DJIA and show a Shannon entropy of 218 bits for their Random Beacon.

We further note that there can be hardware implementations of a Random Beacon. For example, a trusted node in a massively parallel computer, a wired node in a sensor network, or a satellite broadcasting random bits may be useful in a broad range of domains.

2 Algorithms and Their Description

We now describe our algorithms.

2.1 RBQUERY

The first algorithm RBQUERY is presented as Algorithm 2.1 (RBQUERY). In section 3.1, we prove the following theorem about this algorithm.

Theorem 1. *For any positive k, there exists sufficiently large C (in the algorithm), such that Algorithm 2.1 has the following properties with probability at least $1 - 1/n^k$:*

- *The algorithm is correct, that is each good processor terminates with the same value and this value equals the input bit of some good processor; and*
- *All good processors terminate in $O(\log n)$ rounds; and*
- *All good processors terminate in $O(1)$ rounds in expectation; and*
- *If all bad processor send no more than M messages per round then the total number of bits sent by all good processors is $O(M + n \log n)$ in expectation.*

We now describe the algorithm RBQUERY. In each round, each processor has a vote which is the bit held by that processor at the start of the round. Also in each round, a processor selects $\Theta(\ln n)$ processors uniformly at random with replacement to query for their votes. Each processor sends its vote to the processors that queried it, while it receives votes from the processors that it queried. After each round, the fraction of votes received that are for the majority bit is computed. If the fraction of processors that vote for the majority bit is $\geq (1 - \epsilon_0)(2/3 + \epsilon/2)$ for some ϵ_0 to be determined later, then the processor sets its vote to the majority bit. Otherwise the processor just sets its bit to the value from the Random Beacon. A processor terminates after it has 1) computed a fraction value at least $\geq (1 - \epsilon_0)(2/3 + \epsilon/2)$ with a majority bit value b, and 2) the global coin value equals b twice.

Initialize:

1. $vote \leftarrow b_i$
2. $Match \leftarrow FALSE$

Repeat until termination:

1. Select $C \ln n$ processors uniformly at random with replacement. Set In $-$ Neighbors to these processors. Send request messages to all processors in In $-$ Neighbors
2. Receive all request messages. Set Out $-$ Neighbors to all processors from which request messages were received
3. Send vote to all processors in Out $-$ Neighbors
4. Collect votes from all processors in In $-$ Neighbors
5. $coin \leftarrow$ next output of random beacon
6. If $Match$ then
   (a) If $coin = vote$ then commit to value $vote$ and **terminate**
7. Else
   (a) $maj \leftarrow$ majority bit among Out $-$ Neighbors
   (b) fraction $\leftarrow$ fraction of votes received for maj
   (c) If $fraction \geq (1 - \epsilon_0)(2/3 + \epsilon/2)$ then
       i. $vote \leftarrow maj$
       ii. If $coin = vote$ then $Match \leftarrow TRUE$
   (d) else
       i. If $coin =$ "heads", then $vote \leftarrow 1$, else $vote \leftarrow 0$;

Algorithm 2.1. RBQUERY

Note that if all processors simply commit to the Beacon, then we would not be able to solve Byzantine agreement as the bit from the Random Beacon may not be the input bit of any good processor. Secondly, it may not be the bit held by a large fraction of the good processors. These scenarios violate the conditions for Byzantine agreement.

We will analyze the correctness of the algorithm in Section 3.1.

2.2 RBSAMPLER

We now describe the algorithm RBSAMPLER. The main difference in this algorithm, compared to RBQUERY, is that we make use of a sampler in determining the communication graph among the processors. RBSAMPLER is thus non-uniform in the sense that there is a different version of the algorithm for each value of n. Also, the neighbors of each processor are fixed and do not change between rounds unlike RBQUERY. Also, unlike the RBQUERY, RBSAMPLER only achieves almost-everywhere agreement.

The algorithm makes the following assumptions: Bad nodes can send any number of messages per round and we have a full information communication model. In section 3.2, we prove the following theorem about RBSAMPLER.

Theorem 2. *For any positive k, there exists sufficiently large C (in the algorithm), such that Algorithm 2.2 (RBSAMPLER) has the following properties with probability at least $1 - 1/n^k$ for almost all processors i.e. all but $O(\log^{d-1} n)$*

Initialize:

1. $vote \leftarrow b_i$
2. $Match \leftarrow FALSE$
3. Set In $-$ Neighbors (resp. Out $-$ Neighbors) to all processors that have in-edges (resp. out-edges) to this processor in the sampler.

Repeat until termination:

1. Send vote to all processors in Out $-$ Neighbors
2. Collect votes from all processors in In $-$ Neighbors
3. $coin \leftarrow$ next output of random beacon
4. If $Match$ then
    (a) If $coin = vote$ then commit to value $vote$ and **terminate**
5. Else
    (a) $maj \leftarrow$ majority bit among Out $-$ Neighbors
    (b) fraction $\leftarrow$ fraction of votes received for maj
    (c) $fraction \leftarrow$ fraction of votes received for maj
    (d) If $fraction \geq (1 - \epsilon_0)(2/3 + \epsilon/2)$ then
        i. $vote \leftarrow maj$
        ii. If $coin = vote$ then $Match \leftarrow TRUE$
    (e) else
        i. If $coin =$ "heads", then $vote \leftarrow 1$, else $vote \leftarrow 0$;

Algorithm 2.2. RBSAMPLER

- *The algorithm is correct: almost all processors terminate with the same value and this value equals the input bit of some good processor; and*
- *Almost all processors terminate in $O(\log n)$ rounds; and*
- *Almost all processors terminate in $O(1)$ rounds in expectation; and*
- *Almost all processors send polylog(n) bits.*

3 Analysis and Proofs

3.1 Analysis and Proofs for RBQUERY

For a fixed round, let $b' \in \{0, 1\}$ be the bit that the majority of good processors vote for in that round. Let S' be the set of good processors that will vote for b' and let $f' = |S'|/n$. Let $0 \leq \epsilon_0 \leq 1$ be a fixed constant to be determined later. We call a processor *informed* for the round if the fraction value for that processor obeys the following inequalities:

$$(1 - \epsilon_0)f' \leq fraction \leq (1 + \epsilon_0)(f' + 1/3 - \epsilon)$$

Lemma 1. *For any positive integers C' and k, there exists a sufficiently large C in Algorithm 2.1 (RBQUERY) above, such that all good processors are informed for the first k rounds with probability at least $1 - 2k/n^{C'}$.*

Proof. Fix a round r. Let G be a bipartite multigraph induced by the In − Neighbors and Out − Neighbors selection process defined in the algorithm for round r. Note that G is constructed as follows. There are n nodes on the left hand side and copies of all these nodes on the right hand side. The adversary chooses a subset of $1/3 - \epsilon$ of the nodes on the left that are bad and each good node on the right chooses $C \log n$ neighbors on the left uniformly at random with replacement. Fix a round r and the set S'. We know that S' is of size at least $(1/3 + \epsilon/2)n$ since at least half of the good processors must vote for the majority bit. Let $f' = |S'|/n$.

Fix a good node, p, on the right hand side of the graph. Note that In − Neighbors is chosen independently of the set S'. Let X be the number of edges from p into the set S'. Note that $E(X) = f'C \ln n$. Moreover, each edge from p falls into some processor in S' independently with probability f'. Thus, we can apply Chernoff bounds to say that for any positive ϵ_0,

$$Pr(X < (1 - \epsilon_0)E[X]) < e^{-E[X]\epsilon_1^2/2} = e^{-(f'C\epsilon_0^2/4)\ln n}.$$

Similarly, we can use Chernoff bounds to say that

$$Pr(Y > (1 + \epsilon_0)E[Y]) < e^{-E[Y]\epsilon_1^2/3} = e^{-(f'C\epsilon_1^2/6)\ln n}.$$

Hence the probability that either of these bounds is violated is no greater than the sum of these two probabilities, or less than $2/n^{C_1}$ for any constant C_1, where $C = 18C_1/\epsilon_0^2$. Let $\xi_{p,r}$ be the event that either of these bounds is violated for fixed processor p in some fixed round r. Further let ξ be the even that either of these bounds is violated for any good processor p in any of the first k rounds. Then by a union bound, we have that

$$Pr(\xi) = \sum_{p,r} Pr(\xi_{p,r})$$
$$\leq (nk)2/n^{C_1}$$
$$\leq (2k)/n^{C_1-1}$$

Where the last equation holds provided that C is sufficiently large, but depending only on ϵ_0.

In the following lemmas, we assume all good processors are informed in all rounds.

Lemma 2. *Assume all good processors have vote value equal to b at the beginning of some round r. Then all good processors will have vote value equal to b in all remaining rounds.*

Proof. If all good processors have vote value equal to b at the beginning of round r, it means that $f' = |S'|/n = 2/3 + \epsilon$. Since all processors are informed in round r, it means that for each processor, $fraction \geq (1 - \epsilon_0)f' \geq (1 - \epsilon_0)(2/3 + \epsilon)$. Thus, each processor in round r will set its vote to the majority value, which equals b. The same argument holds for all remaining round in which all good processors are informed.

Lemma 3. *For any round r, let S_f be the set of good processors in round r that have $fraction \geq (1 - \epsilon_0)(2/3 + \epsilon/2)$. Then, at the end of round r, all processors in S_f will have the same vote value*

Proof. We show this by contradiction. Assume there are two processors, x and y, where $fraction_x$ ($fraction_y$) are the fraction values of x (y, resp.), such that both $fraction_x$ and $fraction_y$ are greater than or equal to $(1 - \epsilon_0)(2/3 + \epsilon/2)$, and x sets its vote to 0 at the end of the round, while y sets its vote to 1. Let f_0' (f_1') be the fraction of good processors that vote for 0 (1) during the round. Then we have that $fraction_x \geq (1 - \epsilon_0)(2/3 + \epsilon/2)$. By the definition of informed, we also know that $fraction_x \leq (1 + \epsilon_0)(f_0' + 1/3 - \epsilon)$. This implies that

$$(1 - \epsilon_0)(2/3 + \epsilon/2) \leq (1 + \epsilon_0)(f_0' + 1/3 - \epsilon).$$

Isolating f_0' in this inequality, we get that

$$f_0' \geq \frac{1/3 + (3/2)\epsilon - \epsilon_0 + (1/2)\epsilon\epsilon_0}{1 + \epsilon_0}.$$

A similar analysis for $fraction_y$ implies that

$$f_1' \geq \frac{1/3 + (3/2)\epsilon - \epsilon_0 + (1/2)\epsilon\epsilon_0}{1 + \epsilon_0}.$$

But then we have that,

$$f_0' + f_1' \geq \frac{2/3 + 3\epsilon - 2\epsilon_0 + \epsilon\epsilon_0}{1 + \epsilon_0}$$
$$> 2/3 + \epsilon$$

where the last line is clearly a contradiction that holds provided that $\epsilon_0 < (3/4)\epsilon$.

Lemma 4. *Assume the first round in which some good processor commits to a value is round r, and assume that some processor commits to value b in that round. Then all good processors that commit in rounds r or later will commit to the value b.*

Proof. Consider a processor p that commits to bit value b in round r. Then processor p's $Match$ value must be equal to true in round r. This means there must have been some previous round, r', in which p's $Match$ value was first set to true. Among processors that commit to values in round r, let p be a processor with the smallest such r' value. Note that at the point that $Match$ was set to true in round r', p's vote value must have been b, since a processor's vote value can not change after its $Match$ value is set to true.

Let S_f be the set of good processors in round r' that have $fraction \geq (1-\epsilon_0)(2/3+ \epsilon/2)$. By Lemma 3, all processors in S_f set their vote value to b at the end of the round. Now since processor p set $Match$ to true in round r', it must be the case that the outcome of the global coin in that round was equal to b. This means at the end of round r', all good processors set their vote values to b. But then, by Lemma 2, for all rounds subsequent to round r', all processors will have vote values equal to b and so if they commit to any value, it will be the value b.

Lemma 5. *In any round r, with probability at least $1/2$, at the end of that round, all good processors will have the same vote value.*

Proof. Let S_f be the set of good processors in round r that have $fraction \geq (1 - \epsilon_0)(2/3 + \epsilon/2)$. By Lemma 3, all processors in S_f will set their vote value to the same value, call it b, at the end of the round. But with probability $1/2$, the global coin in round r will have value b, and all the remaining good processors will set their vote value to b.

Lemma 6. *Consider any round r in which all processors have the same vote value at the beginning of the round. Then the expected number of remaining rounds before all processors terminate is no more than 4.*

Proof. By Lemma 2, in all remaining rounds, all good processors will have the same value, and so all good processors will have $fraction \geq (1-\epsilon_0)(2/3+\epsilon/2)$. Thus, there are at most two events that must occur before any good processor terminates: the global coin must match the processor's vote value twice. The expected number of rounds until these two events occur is 4.

We now prove Theorem 1 below.

Proof. By Lemmas 5, 6, 2 and 1, all processors terminate in $O(\log n)$ rounds with probability at least $1-1/n^k$ for any fixed positive k and all processors terminate in $O(1)$ rounds in expectation. Since the bad processors each send at most $O(\log n)$ messages per round, it follows that the total number of bits sent by all processors is $O(n \log n)$ in expectation. Finally, the fact that the algorithm is correct with probability at least $1 - 1/n^k$ follows from Lemmas 1, 2 and 4.

3.2 Analysis and Proofs for RBSAMPLER

For a fixed round, let $b' \in \{0, 1\}$ be the bit that the majority of good processors vote for in that round. Let S' be the set of good processors that will vote for b' and let

$f' = |S'|/n$. Let $0 \leq \epsilon_0 \leq$ be a fixed constant to be determined later. We call a processor *informed* for the round if the processor is good and the fraction value for that processor obeys the following inequalities:

$$(1 - \epsilon_0)f' \leq fraction \leq (1 + \epsilon_0)(f' + 1/3 - \epsilon)$$

The proof of the following lemma is equivalent to that in King and Saia [16].

Lemma 7 (Graph existence). *For any positive k and positive constants ϵ_0 and d, there exists a directed multigraph G on k vertices with maximum out-degree no more than $C_3 \log^d n$, where C_3 depends only on ϵ_0 and d, such that if this communication graph is used in Algorithm 2.2 (RBSAMPLER), then in every round all but a $1/\log^d n$ fraction of the good processors are informed.*

The following simple corollary follows by summing up the number of processors that are not informed in every round.

Corollary 1. *Let C' be an positive integer. If the conditions of Lemma 1 are met then all but a $C'/\log^{d-1} n$ fraction of the good processors are informed in every one of the first $C' \log n$ rounds.*

We will say that a processor is *always informed* if it is informed for every round from the start of Algorithm 2.2 (RBQUERY), to the round in which the processor terminates.

The proof of the following lemma is identical to the proof of Lemma 4 in the previous section.

Lemma 8. *For any round r, let S_f be the set of informed processors in round r that have $fraction \geq (1 - \epsilon_0)(2/3 + \epsilon/2)$. Then, at the end of round r, all processors in S_f will have the same vote value.*

The proof of the following lemmas are the same as in the previous section.

Lemma 9. *Assume the first round in which some always informed processor commits to a value is round r, and assume that some always informed processor commits to value b in that round. Then all always informed processors that commit in rounds r or later will commit to the value b.*

Lemma 10. *Assume all always informed processors have vote value equal to b at the beginning of some round r. Then all always informed processors will have vote value equal to b in all their remaining rounds.*

Lemma 11. *In any round r, with probability at least $1/2$, at the end of that round, all informed processors will have the same vote value.*

Lemma 12. *Consider any round r in which all always informed processors have the same vote value at the beginning of the round. Then the expected number of remaining rounds before all always informed processors terminate is no more than 4.*

We now prove Theorem 2.

Proof. By Lemmas 11, 12, 10 and 7, almost all processors terminate in $O(\log n)$ rounds with probability at least $1 - 1/n^k$ for any fixed positive k and all processors terminate in $O(1)$ rounds in expectation. Since the bad processors each send at most $O(\log n)$ messages per round, it follows that the total number of bits sent by all processors is $O(n \log n)$ in expectation. Finally, the fact that the algorithm is correct with probability at least $1 - 1/n^k$ follows from Lemmas 7, 10 and 9.

4   Experimental Results

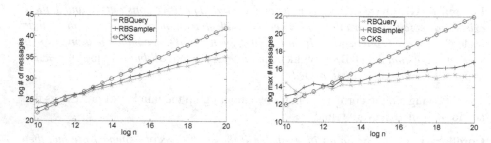

Fig. 1. Left: Log of number of nodes vs. number of messages sent; Right: Log of number of nodes vs max messages sent by a node

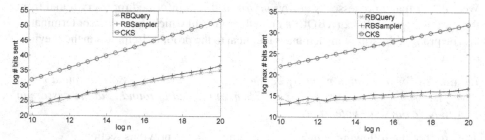

Fig. 2. Left: Log of number of nodes vs. number of bits sent; Right: Log of number of nodes vs max bits sent by a node

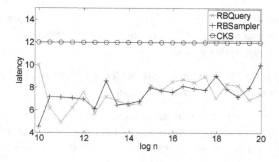

Fig. 3. Algorithm Latency

4.1 Experimental Setup

We used the OpenMP compiler directives in conjunction with the C++11 multi-threading primitives to speed up the simulation on a machine with 128G of memory and 48 cores. Because of the computational resources used by the machine we tracked only the total messages sent and the maximum number of messages sent by any processor. The size of the network simulated was between 1,000 and 1,024,000 processors.

For our simulations of RBQUERY, we selected a value of the constants as dictated by our analysis in section 3.1, $\epsilon_0 = 1/8$, $\epsilon > 1/6$, $C = 40$, we also made the size of the neighbors of a node in the algorithm to be $C \ln^2 n$. Increasing by a factor of $\ln n$ allows us to use a smaller C.

For our simulations of RBQUERY, we selected a value of the constants as dictated by our analysis in 3.2, $\epsilon_0 = 1/8$, $\epsilon > 1/6$, $C = 6$, $d = 3$, which implies that the size of the neighbors of a node in the algorithm is $C \ln^3 n$.

We compare our algorithms with the CKS algorithm from the paper [20] which has $O(1)$ latency but uses cryptography. Our results are averaged over 30 trials.

We make the assumption that the latencies of our algorithms are dominated by the time it takes to send a message and we can use this as the unit cost of an operation. We cite the following paper by Bhatele and Kale [25] which provides information via benchmarks about what these numbers might mean in real world applications. In [25] the values for message latencies are between 5 and 16 milliseconds for the largest message size in the paper (1MB). The benchmarks in the paper consider models that assume the existence or lack thereof, of resource contention. Throughout this paper, we use this assumption in our measurement of the latencies of our algorithms.

4.2 Results

Figure 1 (left) shows the logarithm of the total messages sent, We can see that our two algorithms RBQUERY and RBSAMPLER send less messages than the other algorithms when the network size is larger than 5,000 processors. In particular, RBQUERY sends less messages than the other algorithms for network sizes greater than 2,000 processors. Note that the RBQUERY algorithm sends slightly fewer messages than RBSAMPLER. The slope of the RBQUERY and RBSAMPLER graph is about 3.5 while that of the CKS is about 4.2.

Figure 1 (right) show the maximum messages sent by a processor. RBQUERY and RBSAMPLER, have a maximum number of messages sent that is less than the other algorithms. The crossover point at which RBQUERY and RBSAMPLER is better load-balanced is when the network size is greater than 4,000 processors. RBQUERY is slightly better load-balanced than RBSAMPLER. The slope of the CKS graph is about 1.0, while that of the RBQUERY and RBSAMPLER algorithms is about 0.1 .

Figure 2 (left) shows the total bits sent. Again RBQUERY and RBSAMPLER send less bits than all the other algorithms for all network sizes we consider. The number of bits sent is dramatically less than that of the CKS algorithm since the size of a message in the CKS algorithm is about the same size as an RSA signature. Again the RBQUERY algorithm has a slight edge over the RBSAMPLER. The slope of the graph for the CKS algorithm is about 2.2, while the RBQUERY and RBSAMPLER algorithms have a slope of about 1.3 .

Figure 2 (right) shows the maximum bits sent by a processor. RBQUERY and RB-SAMPLER again perform better than the CKS algorithm for all the network sizes we consider. RBQUERY algorithm sends less bits than RBSAMPLER. The slope of the graph for the CKS algorithm is about 1.0, while the slope for the RBQUERY and RB-SAMPLER algorithms is about 0.4 .

Figure 3 shows the latency of the algorithms. The latency of our algorithms RB-QUERY and RBSAMPLER, seem to be constant and about the same. The RBQUERY and RBSAMPLER algorithms seem to have slightly smaller latency than CKS. Although the latencies for both the RBQUERY and RBSAMPLER vary since the latencies are random variables.

5   Conclusion

We have shown in this paper that with the Random Beacon assumption as a source of global randomness that we can design efficient algorithms for Byzantine agreement.

Our algorithms bring up several interesting questions for future research:

- What is the effect of the Random Beacon not being completely random? How does this affect our ability to perform Byzantine agreement? How much randomness is really required to compute Byzantine agreement sending $\tilde{O}(1)$ messages per processor?
- Lower bounds: If less than a linear fraction of the processors are controlled by an adversary, can we perform Byzantine agreement more efficiently (sending less messages per processor)? Can we perform Byzantine agreement more efficiently when the adversary is non-adaptive?
- Our algorithms work in the partially synchronous model of communication, is it possible to modify our algorithms so that they work in the asynchronous model.

References

1. Lesk, M.: Cybersecurity and economics. IEEE Security Privacy 9(6), 76–79 (2011)
2. (GAO), U.G.A.O.: Cybercrime: Public and private entities face challenges in addressing cyber threats (June 2007)
3. Rabin, M.O.: Transaction protection by beacons. Journal of Computer and System Sciences 27, 256–267 (1983)
4. Maurer, U.M.: Conditionally-perfect secrecy and a provably-secure randomized cipher. Journal of Cryptology 5, 53–66 (1992)
5. Cachin, C., Maurer, U.M.: Unconditional Security against Memory-Bounded Adversaries. In: Kaliski Jr., B.S. (ed.) CRYPTO 1997. LNCS, vol. 1294, pp. 292–306. Springer, Heidelberg (1997)
6. Aumann, Y., Rabin, M.O.: Information Theoretically Secure Communication in the Limited Storage Space Model. In: Wiener, M. (ed.) CRYPTO 1999. LNCS, vol. 1666, pp. 65–79. Springer, Heidelberg (1999)
7. Dziembowski, S., Maurer, U.: Tight security proofs for the bounded-storage model. In: Proceedings of the Thiry-Fourth Annual ACM Symposium on Theory of Computing, STOC 2002, pp. 341–350. ACM, New York (2002)

8. Lysyanskaya, A.: Efficient threshold and proactive cryptography secure against the adaptive adversary (extended abstract)
9. Lamport, L., Shostak, R., Pease, M.: The byzantine generals problem. ACM Trans. Program. Lang. Syst. 4(3), 382–401 (1982)
10. Fischer, M.J., Lynch, N.A., Paterson, M.S.: Impossibility of distributed consensus with one faulty process. J. ACM 32(2), 374–382 (1985)
11. Dolev, D.: The byzantine generals strike again. J. Algorithms 3(1), 14–30 (1982)
12. Dolev, D., Reischuk, R.: Bounds on information exchange for byzantine agreement. J. ACM 32(1), 191–204 (1985)
13. Rabin, M.: Randomized Byzantine generals. In: Proc. Symposium on Foundations of Computer Science, pp. 403–409 (1983)
14. Karlin, A., Yao., A.C.C.: Probabilistic lower bounds for byzantine agreement. Manuscript (1986)
15. Feldman, P., Micali, S.: An optimal probabilistic protocol for synchronous byzantine agreement. SIAM J. Comput. 26(4), 873–933 (1997)
16. King, V., Saia, J.: Breaking the $O(n^2)$ bit barrier: scalable byzantine agreement with an adaptive adversary. In: PODC, pp. 420–429. ACM (2010)
17. King, V., Saia, J.: From almost everywhere to everywhere: Byzantine agreement with $\tilde{O}(n^{3/2})$ bits. In: To appear in Proceedings of DISC 2009: 23rd International Symposium on Distributed Computing, Elche/Elx, Spain, September 23-25 (2009)
18. Oluwasanmi, O., Saia, J., King, V.: An empirical study of a scalable byzantine agreement algorithm. In: 2010 IEEE International Symposium on Parallel Distributed Processing, Workshops and Phd Forum (IPDPSW), pp. 1–13 (April 2010)
19. Dwork, C., Peleg, D., Pippenger, N., Upfal, E.: Fault tolerance in networks of bounded degree. In: STOC 1986: Proceedings of the Eighteenth Annual ACM Symposium on Theory of Computing, pp. 370–379. ACM Press, New York (1986)
20. Cachin, C., Kursawe, K., Shoup, V.: Random oracles in constantipole: practical asynchronous byzantine agreement using cryptography (extended abstract). In: PODC 2000: Proceedings of the Nineteenth Annual ACM Symposium on Principles of Distributed Computing, pp. 123–132. ACM Press, New York (2000)
21. Lee, H.H., Chang, E.-c., Chan, M.C.: Pervasive Random Beacon in the Internet for Covert Coordination. In: Barni, M., Herrera-Joancomartí, J., Katzenbeisser, S., Pérez-González, F. (eds.) IH 2005. LNCS, vol. 3727, pp. 53–61. Springer, Heidelberg (2005)
22. Clark, J., Hengartner, U.: On the use of financial data as a random beacon. In: Proceedings of the 2010 International Conference on Electronic Voting Technology/Workshop on Trustworthy Elections, EVT/WOTE 2010, pp. 1–8. USENIX Association, Berkeley (2010)
23. Eastlake 3rd, D.: Publicly Verifiable Nomcom Random Selection. RFC 2777 (Informational) (February 2000), Obsoleted by RFC 3797
24. Eastlake 3rd, D.: Publicly Verifiable Nominations Committee (NomCom) Random Selection. RFC 3797 (Informational) (June 2004)
25. Bhatele, A., Laxmikant, V.: An evaluative study on the effect of contention on message latencies in large supercomputers. In: Proceedings of the 2009 IEEE International Symposium on Parallel&Distributed Processing, pp. 1–8. IEEE Computer Society Press, Washington, DC (2009)

On Finding Better Friends in Social Networks

Philipp Brandes[1] and Roger Wattenhofer[2]

[1] ETH Zurich
Computer Engineering and Networks Lab (TIK), Switzerland
pbrandes@ethz.ch
[2] ETH Zurich
Computer Engineering and Networks Lab (TIK), Switzerland
wattenhofer@ethz.ch

Abstract. We study the dynamics of a social network. Each node has to decide locally which other node it wants to befriend, i.e., to which other node it wants to create a connection in order to maximize its welfare, which is defined as the sum of the weights of incident edges. This allows us to model the cooperation between nodes where every node tries to do as well as possible. With the limitation that each node can only have a constant number of friends, we show that every local algorithm is arbitrarily worse than a globally optimal solution. Furthermore, we show that there cannot be a best local algorithm, i.e., for every local algorithm exists a social network in which the algorithm performs arbitrarily worse than some other local algorithm. However, one can combine a number of local algorithms in order to be competitive with the best of them. We also investigate a slightly different valuation variant. Nodes include another node's friends for their valuation. There are scenarios in which this does not converge to a stable state, i.e., the nodes switch friends indefinitely.

Keywords: distributed algorithms, social networks, dynamic networks, local algorithms, stable states.

1 Introduction

Psychologists claim that you have a limit of how many friends you can handle [8]. Consequently, you should assess your current friends, and drop those that are unsatisfactory, to make room for new ones! In this paper we study the computational side of finding friends in social networks. We assume that people can only choose new friends among their current social environment, i.e., one can only become friends with friends of friends, or more generally with acquaintances in the ℓ-hop neighborhood of the current friendship graph. If people constantly improve on their friendships with this *local* strategy, will this eventually lead to a social optimum, or at least an approximate solution? What is the best strategy to find new friends? Should one just greedily pick the best available friends? Or should one rather try to be friends with a diverse set of people, in order to profit from a larger set of possible new friends?

Not so surprisingly, we show that any local friend-finding strategy will only converge to a solution that is arbitrarily worse than a global optimum. More surprisingly however, there is no best local strategy. No matter what the strategy is, there is always

A.W. Richa and C. Scheideler (Eds.): SSS 2012, LNCS 7596, pp. 266–278, 2012.

a possible input scenario where other local strategies are much better. In addition we study mixing strategies, i.e., we allow everyone to use several strategies to find their friends. Additionally, we investigate slightly changed valuation models. We show that judging a friend not on his own, but also by his friends, can lead to unstable states, i.e., nodes switch friends indefinitely. We also analyze a valuation model in which breaking up a friendship reduces the valuation of the friendship permanently.

1.1 Related Work

An early ancestor of our work is the stable marriage problem, introduced by Gale and Shapley [6] in 1962: We are given n nodes, partitioned into two sets commonly denoted as men and women. Each woman has a strictly ordered preference list over all men and vice versa. They now want to create a stable matching. A matching is called stable if there is no pair of man and woman such that, instead of being matched to their current partner, they would prefer to be matched to each other. The roommate problem [6] is another related research area, where the nodes are not partitioned into two disjoint sets. Each node again has a complete, strictly ordered preference list. In this basic setting there might not be a stable matching. The problem is further investigated in [1,7], stating restrictions to allow and find stable matchings. An overview on stable marriage can be found in e.g., [11] and a more detailed analysis of matchings in bipartite graphs in [20]. Stable marriage has also been studied as an online problem where the preferences of the men are revealed one at a time [17]. In this setting there are $\Omega(n^2)$ initially unstable marriages in the worst case.

Much research has been done in the stable marriage area on preference lists with ties [9,16], i.e., when the constraint of strictly ordered preference lists is lifted. In our model we assume locality of information, i.e., nodes do not know their complete preference list. Furthermore, we do not require the nodes to have a strict ordering. Finding a maximum matching for stable marriage with these extensions, ties and incomplete preference lists, is known to be $\mathcal{NP}$-hard [14,19]. It can be approximated within a factor of 2 [19]. It can also be approximated within a factor which depends on the number of ties in the preference lists [12].

There have been several approaches to solve stable marriage in a distributed way. In [10] the nodes can only try to be matched to a fixed set of adjacent nodes.

Generally related to our work are network formation games from the field of economics. The nodes create links, as a one shot game or dynamically, to generate welfare which depends on the created links. This welfare is allocated to the players according to some specific rules. These games include models of so called market sharing agreements, in which companies can agree not to sell goods on each others markets to increase their profits [4], and labor markets, where workers get jobs offered and pass the offer to one of their friends if they are already employed [5]. Another example is the model of a general buyer and seller market in which a link represents a potential transaction [18]. A survey on this area is in [15].

So far, the possible matching edges were a fixed set of edges. In [3], the nodes are partitioned into two sets, workers and firms. There are static connections between some workers which indicate friendship. The workers are matched using a local variant of the Gale-Shapley algorithm, but only to firms which are known to their friends. This introduces a dynamic set of matching partners. If a worker changes his company, this can change the set of possible matching partners for his friends. The model used by Martin Hoefer generalizes this [13]. The set of nodes is not partitioned and nodes can possibly have more than one matching partner. In his paper, Hoefer studies the convergence time of matching edges in a social network, with a limited lookahead ℓ. For $\ell = 2$ this means that the nodes only know the neighbors of their neighbors. In general, nodes can only create a connection to nodes which are in a distance of at most ℓ hops. Hoefer's model distinguishes between social links and matching links. Social links are static edges which already exist in the initial graph, and keep existing throughout the execution of the algorithm. Matching links on the other hand are created and possibly removed by the algorithm. In this paper, we drop this difference, and only use one kind of (dynamic) edges. If needed, we can easily emulate social (static) links by adding edges with maximal quality, which will not be removed at any point of the algorithm. Whereas Hoefer's focus was primarily on runtime, we primarily investigate the achieved welfare. Since our model is used to describe cooperation between different players or actual friendship, we also assume that both partners value a potential relationship identically.

1.2   Our Contributions and Paper Structure

We explain our model and our assumptions in Section 2. We describe local algorithms in the context of social networks which try to maximize the welfare of the participants. This means that they try to find good partners for every node, i.e., edges of high quality. The distributed algorithms executed on every node try selfishly to maximize the sum of the qualities of incident edges. We prove in Section 3 that there cannot be an optimal, local algorithm. We do this in two steps. First, in Subsection 3.1, we show that no local algorithm can compete with a global, optimal algorithm, i.e., any local algorithm will be arbitrarily worse in certain scenarios. Afterwards, in Subsection 3.2, in the spirit of [2], we compare local algorithms with other local algorithms. We prove that there is no best local algorithm, i.e., one which is always at least as good as every other local algorithm. For every local algorithm there exists a scenario where it is arbitrarily worse than another local algorithm. This includes randomized algorithms. In Subsection 3.3 we let the nodes execute several algorithms in parallel. Although every local algorithm can be arbitrarily worse than a global optimum, we show that the nodes can achieve a factor 2 approximation in comparison to the best applied strategy.

Furthermore, in Subsection 3.4 we study a slightly modified model, where friends of potential friends also matter for the valuation. We show that there exist scenarios in which a simple algorithm no longer achieves a stable state. In Subsection 3.5 we assume that ending a friendship permanently damages the quality of a friendship. Assuming a breakup reduces the quality of the friendship by a constant, the runtime of any algorithm is limited.

2   Model

We model a social network with a set V of nodes (human beings), $n = |V|$. Between any two nodes $u, v \in V$ there is a quality function $q(u, v) \in [0, 1]$, representing the quality of the friendship, a larger value means better quality. We do not consider negative edge qualities since no node has an incentive to create an edge which reduces its welfare. The quality is symmetric, i.e., $q(u, v) = q(v, u)$. Without symmetry we can create the same cycling as in the roommate problem [6] and thus not reach a stable state. Initially, the nodes are connected by an arbitrary graph $G = (V, E)$, representing the initial knowledge graph. In other words, if two nodes are neighbors in G, they are initially friends. Nodes might decide to create new friendships (edges), and friendships can also be ended. We refrain from changing the friendship graph externally by changing the quality of an edge during the execution of the algorithm, since we want to analyze local algorithms. The set of edges E is as such highly dynamic.

A node's welfare (happiness) depends on the quality of its friendships. Formally, the welfare of a node v is defined as $\sum_{u \in N(v)} q(u, v)$, where $N(v)$ denotes the set of neighbors (current friends) of v. Nodes try to maximize their personal welfare by finding new friends with high quality values.

In reality, one cannot be friends with everybody. However, since our edge qualities are non-negative, nodes could just accumulate more and more friends, until G is a clique. We do not want this effect in our study; as such each node v has a maximum number of possible friends k_v, an individual constant parameter. If a node v already has k_v friends, and fancies a new friend, it must drop an old friend instead.

Nodes cannot choose friends arbitrarily. Instead, they can only choose friends that are already within their visibility. More formally, we define the constant parameter ℓ which we call lookahead. A node can only get a friend within ℓ hops of graph G. For example, if $\ell = 2$, apart from its friends (neighbors in G) a node can only see its 2-hop neighbors (friends of friends); new friends can only be found among these 2-hop neighbors. As such we deal with so-called ℓ-local algorithms. A node has all the information in its ℓ-hop neighborhood. In particular it knows about all the friendships and all the qualities in the ℓ-hop neighborhood.

Nodes run ℓ-local algorithm in order to optimize their friendship graph. Since friendships are a serious business with lots of potential for conflicts of interest, one needs to be careful about the issue which node can propose friendships to which other node at what time. There are various meaningful models here. Indeed, our proofs are relatively robust and work in different kinds of algorithmic models.

For the sake of concreteness, we suggest the *round-robin* model. In this model, all nodes take turns in a round-robin fashion. Whenever it is the turn of a node v, v can propose friendship to different nodes in its ℓ-hop neighborhood. The order in which it asks these nodes is completely up to v; this order is basically the friend-finding algorithm. If v has already k_v friends, it only proposes to nodes whose friendship is more valuable (edge quality is higher) than that of v's worst friend, i.e., to better friends. A node u that is asked by v evaluates the proposed friendship. If u still has room for a new friend, or if v's proposed friendship is better than the worst of u's current friendships, u will accept the edge (and drop its worst friendship if necessary). In other words, a new edge is only added to the graph if both nodes u, v adjacent to edge (u, v) want the edge. If a node gets rejected from a potential new friend, it continues to ask other candidates according to the ordering.

If a node does not find any better friend, the round-robin model asks the next node to find a friend. The procedure ends if no new friendships can be discovered, i.e., if a whole round-robin loop does not change the friendship graph anymore. We call this a stable state.

Note that the initial friendship graph G constrains the final outcome. If two nodes are in different components of the initial graph G, then they can never become friends as they cannot learn about each other. Also, components may partition into smaller components during the execution of the algorithm. For the sake of simplicity, we assume that the initial friendship graph G is connected; however, alternatively, just think of our analysis to take place in one of the original components.

We can imagine various ways to increase the power of the nodes. In particular, nodes might have additional, constant size memory. Memory allows nodes to remember special former partners, e.g., the best ones they dropped, nodes for which the creation of the corresponding edge had some specific properties, or any other mechanism imaginable. Nodes stored in the memory can be added to the list of candidates which will be asked by the algorithm. An algorithm might try to combine several algorithms into one by executing them in parallel. This can be done by performing one round of each algorithm alternately and using the memory to remember the states of the other algorithms. Note that due to the constant memory, only a constant number of algorithms can be combined in this way.

3   On Welfare

In this section we compare different algorithms. As a measurement we use the welfare in the stable states. We compare the globally achieved welfares, i.e., the sum of welfare achieved by all nodes. Algorithm A is said to be arbitrarily worse than algorithm B if the welfare in the stable state of A is $\mathcal{O}(n \cdot \varepsilon)$ whereas it is $\Omega(n)$ in the stable state of algorithm B. Note that ε can be arbitrarily small, e.g., as small as any function in n such as $\varepsilon = 2^{-n}$.

In the model section we have described algorithms which only choose beneficial partners. Let us justify why we focus on this class of algorithms. We show that temporarily accepting worse friends results only in a constant increase in the lookahead.

Lemma 1. *If all nodes are allowed to temporarily choose c worse neighbors, the length of shortest path between two nodes u, v can only decrease by at most a constant factor of ℓ^c.*

Proof. The proof is omitted due to space limitations.

Hence, if nodes are allowed to temporarily choose worse partners, all the proofs still hold by increasing the distances from ℓ to ℓ^c. Thus, we will not treat this separately but mention it briefly in the proofs.

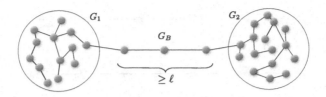

Fig. 1. Two subgraphs G_1, G_2 which are never in contact with each other because they are separated by a bridge G_B with a diameter of at least ℓ

3.1 Local vs Global Algorithms

After having introduced the basic idea of local algorithms, let us now analyze how they perform against a global optimum, i.e., a graph which maximizes the sum of welfare achieved by all nodes.

Theorem 2. *For nodes with a constant lookahead ℓ and a constant size memory there exist scenarios for every local algorithm such that its reached welfare is arbitrarily worse than a global optimum.*

Proof. Consider a scenario as depicted in Figure 1. The initial graph consists of three subgraphs G_1, G_2 and G_B. The two larger subgraphs G_1, G_2 are connected through a bridge G_B which has a diameter of at least ℓ and each node v in the bridge has already k_v friends. The valuations are such that for every pair $(u, v) \in G_1 \times G_2$ the quality is 1, for every pair $(u, v) \in G_i \times G_i$ with $i \in \{1, 2\}$, we have $q(u, v) = \varepsilon$. Furthermore, for every $(u, v) \in G_i \times G_B$ with $i \in \{1, 2\}$, $q(u, v) = \varepsilon/2$. Thus, we only need to specify the valuations within G_B. Every node $v \in G_B$ values other nodes $u \in G_B$ with 2ε if the edge exists in the initial friendship graph and 0 otherwise.

Hence, the nodes in the bridge already have their best possible friends and therefore will not change their friends. These valuations represent an initial friendship graph in which no node really likes his friends but does not know any better candidates.

But this setting is a stable state, hence no local algorithm will create an edge between any node from G_1 with any node from G_2 because of the sheer distance between those subgraphs. This holds due to Lemma 1 even if the nodes are allowed to choose non-beneficial partners. Furthermore, the connecting nodes are not appealing for any node and thus remain isolated. Therefore, the best achievable stable state is $\mathcal{O}(n \cdot \varepsilon)$. In the optimal solution the nodes from the sets G_1, G_2 are connected to each other to achieve a stable state with value $\Theta(n - |G_B|) = \Theta(n)$. $\qquad\square$

Note that this result relies on the fact that any reasonable, local algorithm is only willing to create connections to beneficial partners or is only willing to accept a worse partner a constant number of times. Let us further remark that the initial friendship graph and any stable state reached by a local algorithm is not necessarily Pareto efficient. This means that there are scenarios where we can easily improve the welfare of some nodes without lowering the welfare of other nodes, e.g., by moving one node v from G_1 to G_2. Now v can connect to nodes which it valuates higher. This increases v's welfare (and the welfare of the nodes which are connected to v) but does not lower the welfare of any node.

Fig. 2. A track going from left to right. The dashed, gray edges are created by the execution of a local algorithm, the black edges are given in the initial friendship graph.

3.2   Local vs. Local Algorithms

We now show that there cannot even be a best local algorithm, i.e., an algorithm which can achieve a stable state whose welfare is at least as good as the welfare of any other local algorithm. We prove that for every local algorithm there exist scenarios in which it is arbitrarily worse than another, local algorithm. But first, we need a few more terms.

Proposition 3. *A* track *consists of two disjoint sets, each with j nodes. The nodes of each set are initially arranged in a line as shown in Figure 2 (connected to each other with the edges colored in black). The length of the track is j. The dashed, gray edges have a strictly monotonic increasing quality from left to right. The black edges from the initial friendship graph have a quality of $\mathcal{O}(\varepsilon)$. The remaining edges have a quality of 0 and are therefore never used. Every node v of a track has $k_v \geq 4$. After the initial edge e is created, any algorithm in our model will create the dashed, gray edges, starting with e_1, one by one from left to right, i.e., in increasing order regarding their quality. The creation of one dashed, gray edge allows the creation of the next dashed, gray edge since those nodes are now within ℓ hops of each other. We call the creation of the edges* exploring a track.

Proposition 4. *A* successful track *generates a welfare of $\Omega(n)$ if the initial edge e is created. Without this initial edge the track has only a welfare of $\mathcal{O}(n \cdot \varepsilon)$. A track of length $\Omega(n)$ can have these properties. In such a track we can set the quality of the edges in the initial friendship graph to $\mathcal{O}(\varepsilon)$ and the edge quality of the selected edges connecting those two sets, i.e., the dashed, gray edges in Figure 2 to a constant.*

Upon creating the initial edge e on the left, the track can be explored. After every dashed, gray edge is created, the welfare is $\Omega(n)$; without the initial edge the welfare is generated only by the edges of the initial friendship graph and thus $\mathcal{O}(n \cdot \varepsilon)$.

Proposition 5. *A track T is said to be* blocked *if, during the exploration, no further edge is created because at least ℓ consecutive nodes v have already k_v edges which are better than those of the track T. This stops the exploration since the nodes have no incentive to continue to explore the track.*

Similarly, a track T_2 blocks another track T_1 if the edges of T_2 are part of the reason why T_1 is blocked. An example of this can be seen in Figure 3.

Theorem 6. *For nodes with a constant lookahead ℓ and a constant size memory there exist scenarios for every deterministic, local algorithm such that its reached welfare is arbitrarily worse than that of another deterministic, local algorithm.*

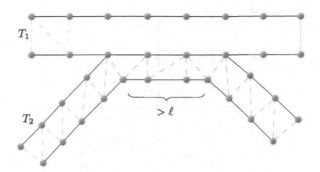

Fig. 3. Two tracks T_1 and T_2 interacting. T_1 is blocked by T_2 since the shared nodes of both tracks have no incentive to create the edges of T_1 since they are content with the edges of T_2.

Proof. Consider two concatenated tracks T_1, T_2 each of length at least ℓ. On top of each of the ℓ nodes of the first track T_1 are four nodes in a line, i.e., each node u_i is connected to a different intermediate node v_i' which is connected to node v_i. This subgraph of the initial friendship graph is depicted in Figure 4. We define $k_{v_i} = 2$ and $k_{u_i} = 4$ for all nodes u_i, v_i with $i \in \{1, \ldots, \ell\}$, i.e., every node u_i can create a connection to exactly one more node whereas v_i must sever an edge to create a new edge. Let v_i' be v_i's worst friend. The qualities are such that $q(u_i, v_i) > q(u_i, x_i)$ holds. Let the edges from the initial friendship graph have a quality larger than $q(u_i, v_i)$ for all $i \in \{1, \ldots, \ell\}$.

We assume that node v_i has two options. It can either create a connection to node u_i or to node w_i; all other nodes are valued with 0. If all nodes v_i decide to create a connection with u_i, T_1 is blocked. Let us explain this in more detail. Since $q(u_i, v_i) > q(u_i, x_i)$ and the quality of every edge of the initial friendship graph is also larger than $q(u_i, x_i)$, node u_i has no incentive to create the edge (u_i, x_i) or any other edge. Thus, the track T_1 is not explored and the initial edge e of T_2 is not created. But if all nodes v_i choose to create a connection with w_i, track T_1 and subsequently track T_2 are explored. Note that it is unimportant if the nodes v_i may have the option to temporarily revise their decision by using their constant memory. It only matters whether the track T_2 is explored at some point execution of the algorithm.

Since the nodes can only see the graph and a part of the track, they have to make a decision with only a subset of the information available. Hence, they have to base their decision on insufficient information because they cannot know whether the exploration of the track T_2 is necessary in order to create partnerships between most of the nodes. This can occur if the track T_2 turns out to be a successful track. But it might also happen that this track blocks a successful track and should therefore not be explored. The latter scenario is shown in Figure 3. In this scenario the chosen track prevents the exploring of the other track. Since these scenarios are indistinguishable for any algorithm, the remainder of the graph can be such that its choice is wrong. It is easy to see that there is another local algorithm which decides correctly for this particular scenario. Limiting the quality of the edges in the subgraph to $\mathcal{O}(\varepsilon)$ yields the theorem. ☐

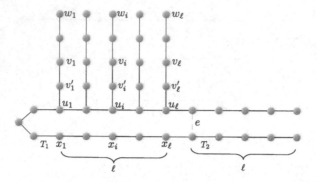

Fig. 4. A subgraph of size $\mathcal{O}(1)$ with outgoing track. Node v_i must now decide if it wants to create a connection to node w_i or to node u_i. If all the connections to u_i are made, the track cannot be explored. Note that edge e is not part of the initial friendship graph.

We can prove a similar result for algorithms which try to execute a constant number of different algorithms in parallel to avoid the aforementioned problem. This allows them to emulate algorithms where one might explore a track whereas another might not.

Corollary 7. *For nodes with a constant lookahead ℓ and a constant size memory there exist scenarios for every local algorithm, which executes several algorithms in parallel, such that its reached welfare is arbitrarily worse than that of another local algorithm.*

Proof. We concatenate tracks such that every executed algorithm fails at least once. The complete proof is omitted due to space limitations.

Theorem 8. *For nodes with a constant lookahead ℓ and a constant size memory there exist scenarios for every randomized, local algorithm such that its reached welfare is arbitrarily worse than that of another deterministic, local algorithm.*

Proof. We concatenate $\Omega(\log n)$ tracks such that the executed algorithm fails with probability at least $1 - n^{-\alpha}$ for a fixed $\alpha > 0$. The complete proof is omitted due to space limitations.

3.3 Executing Local Algorithms in Parallel

We have seen that the welfare in the stable states that different algorithms reach differs significantly. Although, as seen in Corollary 7, none of them may produce an optimal solution, we try to salvage as much as possible by selecting a constant number of algorithms and trying to be as close as possible to the best achieved solution. If we execute several algorithms in parallel, we obtain more than one solution. Due to the fact that the nodes only have a local view, they cannot know which of their connections is part of the best achieved solution. With their limited knowledge, the obvious strategy for the nodes is to simply try to choose the best available connection if still available. This does not yield the best solution as shown in the easy example depicted in Figure 5. But we get a factor 2 approximation compared to the welfare achieved by any of the executed algorithms. To be able to pick edges greedily at the end, we need to show an upper bound on the runtime which allows the nodes to know when any algorithm has terminated.

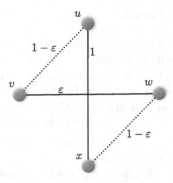

Fig. 5. The best solution consists of the edges $\{u, v\}$ and $\{w, x\}$ whereas our greedily picked solution consists of $\{u, x\}$ and $\{v, w\}$ and is thus a factor of 2 worse than the best solution

Lemma 9. *The runtime of any local algorithm that only chooses higher quality edges is $\mathcal{O}\left(2^{n^2}\right)$.*

Proof. We use a potential function to prove this. Consider a bitstring of length n^2. The i-th bit represents the edge with the i-th largest quality. There is a 1 at position i if the corresponding edge with the i largest quality exists in the graph. The bitstring can be regarded as a counter. Since we only allow beneficial changes, this potential function increases with every change. This limits the total runtime of any algorithm of this type to 2^{n^2}. □

Note that the nodes cannot know when exactly the execution has terminated because of their limited view, but only know the rather weak upper bound of 2^{n^2}. Hence, the greedily selecting of the edges will be started after 2^{n^2} rounds. Since at least one edge is picked every round, this allows the nodes to output a valid solution after $\mathcal{O}\left(2^{n^2} + n^2\right)$ rounds.

Theorem 10. *By running several algorithms in parallel and greedily selecting the best edges at the end, we obtain a factor 2 approximation compared to the best of the executed algorithms.*

Proof. This proof is similar to the proof that any maximal matching is a factor 2 approximation of a maximum matching. Consider the union of edges of all solutions. Whenever two nodes mutually agree to pick an edge, this edge can either be part of the best solution in which case the choice is good. Otherwise, our choice might make it impossible to pick at most two edges from the best solution since both are connected to one of the vertices. But both must have a lower quality than our choice. Hence, our solution is at least half as good as the union of all solutions and therefore at least half as good as the best solution. Continuing this inductively yields the claim. □

3.4 Valuing Friends of My Friends

In a real social network it might not be sufficient to simply evaluate a friend by himself. In order to evaluate a friendship, it is sometimes necessary to also consider the friends of a friend. Thus, we want to introduce another friendship valuation variant. An edge continues to represent an existing friendship, but the new edge quality is a weighted, combined value of the node and its neighbors. More formally this can be expressed as $Q(u, v) := q(u, v) + c \sum_{x \in N(v) \setminus \{u\}} q(u, x)$ where q denotes the quality function as defined before and c is some constant. In this model every edge quality $Q(\cdot, \cdot)$ is directed, i.e., $Q(u, v) \neq Q(v, u)$ is possible.

   In this slightly advanced model, there may not be a stable state. This is due to the asymmetric valuations of the nodes which can be used to create valuations similar as in the roommate problem in [6].

Theorem 11. *If we include the neighbors of a node in the valuation function, there are scenarios in which a local algorithm does not reach a stable state.*

Proof. It is sufficient to consider the nodes a, b, c, d, e and their friends with the following valuation for each other: $q(a, b) = q(a, c) = q(b, c) > q(a, d) = q(b, d) = q(c, d)$. This means the three nodes a, b, c prefer each other over node d. The valuations of node e are such that it has no incentive to choose another friend. Now we can set the edge qualities of the friends of each node such that the final edge qualities are $Q((a, b)) > Q((a, c)) > Q((a, d))$. Node a prefers the friends of b over those of node c and so on. Furthermore, we require $Q(b, c) > Q(b, a) > Q(b, d)$ and $Q(c, a) > Q(c, b) > Q(c, d)$. The evaluations of node d do not matter. A brief technical remark has to be made. In order to achieve this, the friends of each node have to be content with being paired up with their respective partners. Furthermore, neither node must be willing to initiate a connection with any other node than a, b, c or d. For the nodes to be able to know each other all the time, the fifth node e can be connected to a, b, c, d but without any incentive to change its connections. This scenario is depicted in Figure 6.

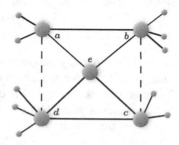

Fig. 6. The edges $\{a, b\}, \{c, d\}$ exist. In this setting b prefers to be paired up with c and c would be happier with that matching. Afterwards a would match with c and thus b with d. In the next round, the cycle would start anew.

This enables us to create a cycle. No matter which node is matched with node d, it wants to change to another node which is willing to do so. Hence, no stable state can be reached.   □

Clearly, neither a statement about the convergence time nor about the globally achieved welfare is possible in this setting.

3.5 Breaking Up a Friendship Is Expensive

In a real social network, breaking up friendships is hardly without consequences to that friendship. To model this we assume that the edge quality decreases every time the corresponding edge is removed. There are two natural choices to reduce the quality of an edge: Either reduce it by a constant term, or by a constant factor.

Theorem 12. *If the edge quality $q(e)$ gets reduced by a constant term every time the edge e is removed, the runtime of any local algorithm is $\mathcal{O}\left(n^2\right)$.*

Proof. The proof is omitted due to space limitations.

4 Conclusion and Outlook

We showed that any local algorithm for finding better friends that has constant memory and constant lookahead is arbitrarily worse than the global optimum. We also compared local algorithms to each other: For every local algorithm there exists a scenario in which it performs arbitrarily worse than another local algorithm.

This was shown for some specific initial friendship graphs. An interesting open problem is how to characterize graph classes where a best local algorithm exists. Are there also some general graph classes where the welfare of a local algorithm is only a constant factor worse than the global optimum? Another open question is whether our results can be generalized. Which problems cannot be solved well by a local algorithm; neither in comparison to other local algorithms nor compared to the optimal solution?

References

1. Abraham, D.J., Levavi, A., Manlove, D.M., O'Malley, G.: The Stable Roommates Problem with Globally-Ranked Pairs. In: Deng, X., Graham, F.C. (eds.) WINE 2007. LNCS, vol. 4858, pp. 431–444. Springer, Heidelberg (2007)
2. Ajtai, M., Aspnes, J., Dwork, C., Waarts, O.: A theory of competitive analysis for distributed algorithms. In: 1994 Proceedings of the 35th Annual Symposium on Foundations of Computer Science, pp. 401–411. IEEE (1994)
3. Arcaute, E., Vassilvitskii, S.: Social Networks and Stable Matchings in the Job Market. In: Leonardi, S. (ed.) WINE 2009. LNCS, vol. 5929, pp. 220–231. Springer, Heidelberg (2009)
4. Belleflamme, P., Bloch, F.: Market Sharing Agreements and Collusive Networks. International Economic Review 45(2), 387–411 (2004)
5. Calvó-Armengol, A., Jackson, M.O.: Networks in labor markets: Wage and employment dynamics and inequality. Journal of Economic Theory 132(1), 27–46 (2007)

6. Gale, D., Shapley, L.S.: College Admission and the Stability of Marriage. American Mathematical Monthly 69(1), 9–15 (1962)
7. Diamantoudi, E., Miyagawa, E., Xue, L.: Random paths to stability in the roommate problem. Games and Economic Behavior 48(1), 18–28 (2004)
8. Dunbar, R.: How Many Friends Does One Person Need?: Dunbar's Number and Other Evolutionary Quirks. Harvard University Press (2010)
9. Echenique, F., Oviedo, J.: A theory of stability in many-to-many matching markets. Theoretical Economics 1(2), 233–273 (2006)
10. Floréen, P., Kaski, P., Polishchuk, V., Suomela, J.: Almost Stable Matchings by Truncating the Gale-Shapley Algorithm. Algorithmica 58(1), 102–118 (2010)
11. Gusfield, D., Irving, R.W.: The Stable marriage problem - structure and algorithms. Foundations of computing series. MIT Press (1989)
12. Halldórsson, M.M., Irving, R.W., Iwama, K., Manlove, D.F., Miyazaki, S., Morita, Y., Scott, S.: Approximability results for stable marriage problems with ties. Theoretical Computer Science 306(1-3), 431–447 (2003)
13. Hoefer, M.: Local Matching Dynamics in Social Networks. Automata Languages and Programming, 113–124 (2011)
14. Iwama, K., Miyazaki, S., Manlove, D., Morita, Y.: Stable Marriage with Incomplete Lists and Ties. In: Wiedermann, J., Van Emde Boas, P., Nielsen, M. (eds.) ICALP 1999. LNCS, vol. 1644, pp. 443–452. Springer, Heidelberg (1999)
15. Jackson, M.O.: A Survey of Models of Network Formation: Stability and Efficiency, pp. 1–62. Cambridge University Press (2005)
16. Kelso, A.S., Crawford, V.P.: Job Matching, Coalition Formation, and Gross Substitutes. Econometrica 50(6), 1483–1504 (1982)
17. Khuller, S., Mitchell, S.G., Vazirani, V.V.: On-line algorithms for weighted bipartite matching and stable marriages. Theoretical Computer Science 127, 255–267 (1994)
18. Kranton, R.E., Minehart, D.F.: A theory of buyer-seller networks. American Economic Review 91(3), 485–508 (2001)
19. Manlove, D.F., Irving, R.W., Iwama, K., Miyazaki, S., Morita, Y.: Hard variants of stable marriage. Theoretical Computer Science 276(1-2), 261–279 (2002)
20. Roth, A.E., Sotomayor, M.: Two-sided matching. Handbook of Game Theory vol 1 78(2), 75–95 (1990)

Brief Announcement: Detecting Users' Connectivity on Online Social Networks

Na Li[1], Sajal K. Das[1], and Nan Zhang[2]

[1] University of Texas at Arlington, Computer Science and Engineering Department
na.li@mavs.uta.edu, das@uta.edu
[2] George Washington University, Computer Science Department
nzhang10@gwu.edu

Abstract. We present a heuristic algorithm which leverages the topological properties of social networks to efficiently detect a small subgraph on an OSN which connects a group of target users, particularly from the perspective of a third-party analyst.

1 Introduction and Motivation

As Online Social Networks (OSNs) grow in popularity, more and more people are surfing the Internet to network with others. These social sites have been collecting a huge amount of data from their users' online activities, part of which are visible on the sites. For example, we can see a user's friend list on his profile page on Facebook which indicates his friendships with other users.

This brief announcement focuses on how to detect a small subgraph connecting a given group of users on the relationship network derived from users' relationship information on the OSN. Particularly, we intend to cope with this problem from the perspective of a third-party analyst, which leads to challenges as the information a third-party analyst can glean is limited. Specifically, one web access, namely one query, only provides the list of direct friends of a user on the Facebook, which we therefore call *local view*. To picture the entire relationship network, the third-party analyst may crawl the site by accessing all users' profile pages; however, the time for the brute force crawling is non-trivial. Furthermore, intensively accessing the OSN will cause the overload of its server, which is the main reason why nowadays many online social sites limit the number of web accesses to them from one (or a group of) IP address(es).

Therefore, our goal is not only to detect a desirable subgraph with a small size but also find it with a small number of web queries. Technically, we apply the well-known topological properties of social networks, including small-world, scale-free and the well-connectivity of high degree vertices in [7], to directing query procedure aimed to efficiently discover target users's connectivity on OSNs.

2 System Model and Problem Definition

We model an OSN by an undirected graph, $G(V, E)$, in which each vertex in V represents a user and each edge in E denotes a relationship between two

A.W. Richa and C. Scheideler (Eds.): SSS 2012, LNCS 7596, pp. 279–281, 2012.

users, such as friendship. Then querying a user's profile page returns the list of the user's neighboring nodes in the graph. Under this model, detecting the connectivity of a group of target users is based on the interactions with the OSN by a sequence of queries. We keep track of not only vertices already queried but also vertex candidates to be queried, where a *candidate* is referred to as a vertex which has not been queried while has been seen by querying other vertices. As more vertices are queried, the third-party analyst's view on the OSN graph becomes larger.

Problem 1. *Local-view based Minimum Subgraph Detection (LMSD): Given a set of target vertices S_0 in the graph of an OSN $G(V, E)$ the topology of which is unknown initially, find the minimum number of vertices from $V \setminus S_0$ to connect all target vertices by the minimum number of queries for the local-view discovery.*

Under the system model, we define our problem as Local-view based Minimum Subgraph Detection in Problem 1. Note the LMSD problem requires both the size of detected subgraph and the number of queries be minimized, which is hard to achieve at the same time. Therefore, we heuristically handle them sequentially. We first look for a subgraph connecting all target vertices through a small number of queries, from which we detect an even smaller one linking all of the target users. The rationale behind this is if the number of queried vertices is small, the size of the finally detected subgraph should not be that large. We can prove that even given the entire graph detecting the minimum subgraph covering a group of nodes is an NP-hard problem by a polynomial reduction from Minimum Steiner Tree problem which is a class NP-complete problem. Therefore, solving LMSD is challenging.

3   Our Search Technique

Our technique starts with querying all target vertices on the OSN graph. Each target vertex and its corresponding neighboring nodes returned form a subgraph. Initially, these subgraphs are most likely disjoint due to the sparse topology of social network graphs. Each of the subgraphs has its own set of vertex candidates which have been seen while have not been queried yet, and they will grow as their vertex candidates are queried. Now our LMSD problem becomes how to select vertices to query so that the subgraphs of all target vertices can be merged into one connected piece quickly.

Inspired by the critical role of high-degree vertices in searching on social network graphs in [1,2], we also prioritize vertex candidates of high degrees to query. However, as the real degree of a vertex candidate is unknown until we query it, we define *current degree* for each vertex candidate - *the number of the discovered edges of the vertex upon searching*. Moreover, we define *subgraph degree* - the maximum degree of queried vertices in the subgraph. Our search technique runs the following three steps: (1) query all target vertices on the OSN graph and form individual subgraphs; (2) select the subgraph with minimum subgraph degree as the *target subgraph* and (3) pick up a vertex of the highest current degree from the candidate set of the target subgraph to query (break tie arbitrarily). Steps 2 and 3 will be repeated until the subgraphs of all target vertices are connected together.

If querying a vertex causes any subgraphs to overlap, they will be merged. Their vertex candidate sets will be combined and the current degrees of their vertices will be updated. Note that after querying a vertex, the subgraph degree will be updated if the newly queried vertex has a degree higher than the current degree of that subgraph. One can see that the degree of the target subgraph may be increased as the search goes on, so that when it becomes greater than the minimum subgraph degree among all subgraphs, the target subgraph will be reassigned. In our technique, the target subgraph is dynamically changed to take care of low-degree subgraphs, therefore, we call this technique Balanced Multiple-Subgraph searching (BMS). Given the subgraph finally merged in the above search, we apply a classic approximate Steiner Tree algorithm in [3] to detecting a even smaller subgraph connecting all target users.

4   Findings and Conclusion

Through the experiments over the large-scale real-world data sets from Facebook [6], Epinion [5], and Slashdot [4], we evaluated the effectiveness and efficiency of our search technique with the size of detected subgraph and the number of queries, respectively. We found that the size of detected subgraph by our technique is comparable to the size of the subgraph discovered by [3] even given the entire graph. Furthermore, the size of our detected subgraph is similar to the number of queries conducted in BMS, which indicates the effectiveness of using topological properties of social network graphs in design of our search. We believe that an OSN graph is so different from a random graph that designing search techniques based on its unique topological features will enhance search efficiency. We will further investigate on this topic in our future work.

References

1. Adamic, L., Adar, E.: How to search a social network. Social Networks 27(3), 187–203 (2005)
2. Adamic, L.A., Lukose, R.M., Puniyani, A.R., Huberman, B.A.: Search in power-law networks. Physical Review E 64(4) (2001)
3. Kou, L., Markowsky, G., Berman, L.: A fast algorithm for steiner trees. Acta Informatica 15(2), 141–145 (1981)
4. Leskovec, J., Lang, K., Dasgupta, A., Mahoney, M.: Community structure in large networks: Natural cluster sizes and the absence of large well-defined clusters. Internet Mathematics 6(1), 29–123 (2009)
5. Richardson, M., Agrawal, R., Domingos, P.: Trust Management for the Semantic Web. In: Fensel, D., Sycara, K., Mylopoulos, J. (eds.) ISWC 2003. LNCS, vol. 2870, pp. 351–368. Springer, Heidelberg (2003)
6. Viswanath, B., Mislove, A., Cha, M., Gummadi, K.P.: On the evolution of user interaction in facebook. In: Proceedings of WOSN (August 2009)
7. Wilson, C., Boe, B., Sala, A., Puttaswamy, K.P., Zhao, B.Y.: User interactions in social networks and their implications. In: Proceedings of EuroSys (2009)

Brief Announcement:
Discovering and Assessing Fine-Grained Metrics in Robot Networks Protocols

François Bonnet[1,*], Xavier Défago[1,**], Franck Petit[2,***],
Maria Gradinariu Potop-Butucaru[2,***], and Sébastien Tixeuil[2,3,***]

[1] School of Information Science, JAIST
[2] UPMC Sorbone Universités, LIP6 CNRS
[3] Institut Universitaire de France

Motivation. In discrete anonymous environments, robot algorithms consist in a list of rules, where each rule takes a configuration of the system as input and outputs the set of robots that are required to move when the system is in this configuration. Based on these rules and on the robots' activations by the scheduler, the system globally evolves and, when the algorithm is correct, it solves the targeted problem.

Such algorithms (*i.e.* sets of rules) are usually defined for a specific topology and restricted to a certain number of robots. As example, we consider the exclusive perpetual exploration problem (all robots must visit all nodes infinitely often) studied in [1] for partial grids with sense of direction, in [2] for uniform rings without sense of direction, and [3] for grids without sense of direction. While each of these works was handcrafted, general conditions on the number of robots and the network size had to be assumed for the generic solution to be valid. The case of small instances typically requires ad hoc protocols that are specifically designed. Moreover some cases are left open, *e.g.*, the case of $n <= 10$ for more than $k = 3$ robots in [2]. Such a manual treatment is problematic both for the sake of completeness and for the sake of correctness.

Proving that no protocol instance can work in a particular network requires checking that every possible protocol leads to a contraction, which is highly error-prone if humanly managed. The case of possibility is also tricky, since it is relatively easy to find protocols for perpetual exclusive exploration in rings of size 10 with 3, 4, 6, or 7 robots, but unlikely to find one with 5 robots. For the same reasons, it is also difficult to prove analytically the optimality of a given algorithm.

Contribution. We propose a tool that can automatically answers this kind of questions by generating exhaustively all possible algorithms for a given number of robots and a given network topology. We target anonymous systems and

* Supported by the JSPS Postdoctoral Fellowship for Foreign Researchers and by MEXT KAKENHI No. 22-00720.
** Supported by MEXT Grant-in-Aid for Scientific Research (C) No. 23500060.
*** Supported by the French ANR Projects R-DISCOVER and SHAMAN.

A.W. Richa and C. Scheideler (Eds.): SSS 2012, LNCS 7596, pp. 282–284, 2012.
© Springer-Verlag Berlin Heidelberg 2012

therefor we suppose that all robots and nodes are respectively indistinguishable. This constraint implies that an algorithm cannot distinguish isomorphic configurations. The current work consider only *rigid* configurations (*i.e.*, asymmetrical and aperiodic) in ring and torus topologies but could be extended to include other types of configurations and topologies.

In a few words, our approach can be decomposed in a 4-step process: (1) the generation of all different configurations, (2) the generation of all possible robots' moves for each configuration and the corresponding evolution on the global configuration, (3) the generation of all algorithms, and (4) the analysis of the generated data. The two initial steps allow the creation of the *graph of configurations* that describes all the possible evolutions of the considered system; the key point lies in the bijection between the set of possible perpetual algorithms and the set of simple cycles of this graph.

Application to the Perpetual Exploration Problem. As a matter of illustration, we represent on Figure 1 the set of all rigid configurations for the 10-node ring topology with 5 robots, and on Figure 2 the corresponding graph of configurations.

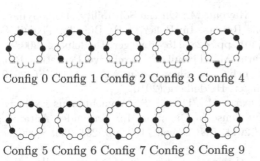

Config 0 Config 1 Config 2 Config 3 Config 4

Config 5 Config 6 Config 7 Config 8 Config 9

Fig. 1. List of all non-isomorphic rigid configurations of 5 robots in the 10-node ring

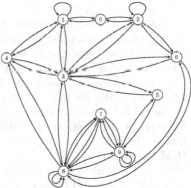

Fig. 2. Graph of configurations

After analysis, it appears (and it is a new result/proof) that it is impossible to solve the perpetual exploration problem under these assumptions; 5 robots in a 10-node ring, even if one can choose the initial configuration to avoid complex initial symmetry breaking. However we found 72 different algorithms that solve a weaker version of the problem, namely, all nodes must be visited infinitely often, but not necessarily by all robots. Among these algorithms, we can find optimal ones with respect to some properties. For example, we discover the algorithm proposed on Figure 3 that uses the minimum number of 2 different configurations and solves the exploration problem in a partitioned way; each node is visited infinitively often, but always by the same robot[1].

---

[1] The animation does (obviously) not appear on the printed version. Moreover it requires the use of the official Adobe Reader to read it on a computer.

Fig. 3. Exploration algorithm (click on the figure to start animation)

Extension. We believe our modeling (and automatic protocol generator) could prove useful for various other problems that were investigated in the context of mobile anonymous and oblivious robots evolving on graphs, such as *gathering* [4] (all robots are requested to reach a single node, not known beforehand), and *exploration with stop* [5] (all nodes must be visited by at least one robot, and eventually all robots must stop moving).

References

1. Baldoni, R., Bonnet, F., Milani, A., Raynal, M.: On the Solvability of Anonymous Partial Grids Exploration by Mobile Robots. In: Baker, T.P., Bui, A., Tixeuil, S. (eds.) OPODIS 2008. LNCS, vol. 5401, pp. 428–445. Springer, Heidelberg (2008)
2. Blin, L., Milani, A., Potop-Butucaru, M., Tixeuil, S.: Exclusive Perpetual Ring Exploration without Chirality. In: Lynch, N.A., Shvartsman, A.A. (eds.) DISC 2010. LNCS, vol. 6343, pp. 312–327. Springer, Heidelberg (2010)
3. Bonnet, F., Milani, A., Potop-Butucaru, M., Tixeuil, S.: Asynchronous Exclusive Perpetual Grid Exploration without Sense of Direction. In: Fernàndez Anta, A., Lipari, G., Roy, M. (eds.) OPODIS 2011. LNCS, vol. 7109, pp. 251–265. Springer, Heidelberg (2011)
4. Klasing, R., Markou, E., Pelc, A.: Gathering asynchronous oblivious mobile robots in a ring. Theoretical Computer Science 390(1), 27–39 (2008)
5. Flocchini, P., Ilcinkas, D., Pelc, A., Santoro, N.: Computing Without Communicating: Ring Exploration by Asynchronous Oblivious Robots. In: Tovar, E., Tsigas, P., Fouchal, H. (eds.) OPODIS 2007. LNCS, vol. 4878, pp. 105–118. Springer, Heidelberg (2007)

All-to-All Gradecast Using Coding
with Byzantine Failures

John F. Bridgman III* and Vijay K. Garg**

Parallel and Distributed Systems Lab
Electrical and Computer Engineering
The University of Texas at Austin
Austin, TX USA
johnfbiii@utexas.edu, garg@ece.utexas.edu

Abstract. This paper presents a method that uses forward error correction codes to minimize the message bit complexity when acquiring consistent global information in the presence of faulty processes. We show a modification to the gradecast algorithm that implements our method. Gradecast, first proposed by Feldman and Micali, is a broadcast algorithm for distributed systems that can handle Byzantine failures. It can be used as a basic building block to solve many important problems in distributed computing in the presence of Byzantine failures, such as agreement, clock synchronization, and approximate agreement. Many of these problems require a step where all processes need to send information to all other processes. We refer to the version of gradecast where all processes broadcast to all other processes as all-to-all gradecast. In a distributed system with n processes, n instances of the original gradecast algorithm to perform all-to-all gradecast has a message bit complexity of $O(mn^3)$, where m is the length of the message. In this paper, we present an all-to-all gradecast algorithm that takes $O(mtn^2)$ message bits, where t is the maximum number of faulty processes. This is a significant reduction in message bit complexity in real systems where $t << n$. Our all-to-all gradecast algorithm uses coding theory to mask Byzantine failures and has wide applicability in distributed systems. For example, by replacing the original gradecast in the byzantine agreement algorithm proposed by Ben-Or, Dolev and Hoch with $O(mtn^3)$ message bit complexity, we get a new byzantine agreement algorithm with $O(mt^2n^2)$ message bit complexity. Also, this algorithm can be used with their approximate agreement algorithm to get $O(kn^2t)$ instead of $O(kn^3)$ message bit complexity.

1   Introduction

Many distributed algorithms require a step in which every participating process needs a value from every other process. For example, in a clock synchronization

---

* This research was supported in part by the Virginia and Ernest Cockrel, Jr. Fellowship in Engineering.

** This research was supported in part by the NSF Grants CNS-0718990, CNS-1115808, Cullen Trust for Higher Education Endowed Professorship.

A.W. Richa and C. Scheideler (Eds.): SSS 2012, LNCS 7596, pp. 285–298, 2012.

algorithm, every process may collect the values of clocks of all other processes. In a sensor network, a group of sensors may collect values from each other to compute the average value, or some other global function such as the minimum, the maximum or the sum of all the values. In a system that requires a uniform action, the processes may collect proposals from all other processes to determine an action. This paper addresses these problems in the presence of Byzantine failures. Many fault tolerant algorithms need to have information about what other processes know about other processes. We call this second-order information. In order to perform a fault tolerant broadcast, second-order knowledge is required. The usual method to acquire second-order information is for every process to broadcast the information that they have; then, every process rebroadcasts what they receive. But, rebroadcasting the information is inefficient when it is known that the number of faulty processes is bounded. The technique described in this paper uses a forward error correction (FEC) code to minimize the size of the messages that are rebroadcast. As an example, we apply the technique to gradecast. Gradecast can be used as a basic building block for many distributed algorithms that handle Byzantine failures.

The gradecast algorithm, first proposed by Feldman and Micali[1], is a broadcast algorithm that gives the receivers a confidence level in the value received. Let $value_j[k]$ be the value that process P_j outputs for process P_k, $confidence_j[k]$ be the confidence value process P_j outputs for process P_k, and v_k be the initial input value to the algorithm for process P_k. The confidence level returned is from the set $\{0, 1, 2\}$ and the confidence value gives information about the state of the other processes. The gradecast algorithm provides three main properties of the confidence level that allow a process to reason about the knowledge of other processes.

1. For all non-faulty process P_i, and non-faulty process P_j, and any process P_k, if $confidence_j[k] > 0$ and $confidence_i[k] > 0$; then, $value_j[k] = value_i[k]$.
2. For any non-faulty process P_i, and non-faulty process P_j, and any process P_k, $|confidence_i[k] - confidence_j[k]| \leq 1$.
3. If P_k is non-faulty, then for all non-faulty processes P_i, $confidence_i[k] = 2$ and $value_i[k] = v_k$.

The original one-to-all gradecast algorithm broadcasts a value from one process to all the other processes. We define message bit complexity as the total number of bits sent by all non-faulty processes in one invocation of the algorithm. The one-to-all gradecast algorithm has a message bit complexity of $O(mn^2)$, where m is the length of the message and n is the number of processes. The properties of gradecast make it a useful primitive in distributed systems.

Consider the case where all processes wish to broadcast a value to all other processes using gradecast. We call this all-to-all gradecast and it is used in many applications such as Byzantine agreement, approximate agreement, and multiconsensus[2]. The standard implementation of all-to-all gradecast, where n instances of the one-to-all gradecast algorithm are used, has $O(mn^3)$ message bit complexity. We show a method, using coding, that gives an all-to-all gradecast algorithm with only $O(mtn^2)$ message bit complexity, where t is the specified maximum number of faulty processes. This is a significant reduction in message bit complexity when t is much smaller than n, which is usually the case. Gradecast requires $t < n/3$ for correctness.

Our all-to-all gradecast algorithm uses error correction codes[3] to mask Byzantine failures and has wide applicability in distributed systems. For example, by replacing the original gradecast in the byzantine agreement algorithm proposed by Ben-Or, Dolev and Hoch[2] with $O(mtn^3)$ message bit complexity, a new byzantine agreement algorithm with $O(mt^2n^2)$ message bit complexity results. If the number of actual failures is $f \leq t$, then, the algorithm by Ben-Or, Dolev and Hoch will take $\min(f+2, t+1)$ rounds. This property is often referred to as early stopping. The bit complexity of approximate agreement algorithm [4,5,2] is reduced from $O(kn^3)$ to $O(kn^2t)$, where k is the number of rounds used in the approximate algorithm. Algorithms that have better message bit complexity exist; but, they sacrifice round complexity or reduce the maximum number of faulty processes tolerated. The example byzantine agreement algorithms in this paper are given because of the simplicity of their implementation on top of an all-to-all gradecast algorithm. There exist algorithms with better message bit complexity. For example, the algorithm by Coan and Welch[6] has message bit complexity of $O(t^2 + nt)$ to agree on a single bit. This algorithm does not posses an early stopping property.

Error correction codes can be viewed as a projection from a smaller space to a larger space with good separation. Because the points in the larger space are separated, small perturbations in the point in the larger space are still close to the original mapped point and the point in the original smaller space can be recovered. Generally, the spaces are high dimensional vector spaces over finite fields and the measure of distance between two elements of the space is the number of coordinates that have a different value. *Systematic* codes can be constructed that encode a vector as the original vector concatenated with an error correction vector. Our method relies on the observation that every process is sending a value to every other process and only the faulty processes will send conflicting data. So, the vector built at each process will differ in at most t locations. This can be viewed as transmitting the vector and each process receiving a corrupted version. Then, only the error correction part of the encoded vector can be sent between processes to correct these "errors". The original vector is not actually transmitted. In a traditional application of error correction codes, an input block is encoded and then the whole output codeword is transmitted. We are not transmitting the whole codeword. Only a portion of the codeword is transmitted. A proper selection of the code allows an error correction vector that can correct t errors to be no longer than $2t + 1$.

This method of using coding is also applicable to other types of broadcast algorithms. Srikanth and Toueg[7] give a broadcast algorithm to simulate authenticated broadcasts that has the important properties of authenticated messages. These are as follows: If a correct process P_i broadcasts a message; then, all other correct processes receive that message and if a correct process P_i does not broadcast a message; then, no correct process receives a message from P_i. The message bit complexity of a consistent broadcast is $O(mn^2)$ and therefore, the message bit complexity of all-to-all consistent broadcast is $O(mn^3)$. By using our method, the bit complexity of all-to-all consistent broadcast can be reduced to $O(mtn^2)$.

All-to-all gradecast can also be used to implement an interactive consistency algorithm. Interactive consistency[8,9] is the problem in which each process has a vector with an entry that needs to be filled from every other process and all vectors should be the same at the end of the algorithm. Interactive consistency is at least as difficult as Byzantine agreement.

There are earlier works that use error correcting codes for Byzantine broadcast algorithms. Liang and Vaidya[10] give an algorithm that achieves communication complexity of $O(mn)$ bits for broadcast with Byzantine failures if $m = \Omega(n^6)$. This is quite useful in situations where the message being broadcast is a very long stream of bits. An example of such messages is all the samples from a sensor in a long running system. However, for small message size, m, the communication complexity is $O(nm + n^4 m^{1/2} + n^6)$. Our work is useful when every process is doing a broadcast and the message size may not be large. Friedman, Mostéfaoui, Rajsbaum and Raynal [11] show a mapping from a distributed agreement problem to a coding problem. Our approach is to use coding to reduce the size of the messages being sent. The work by Krol[12] gives a set of algorithms that use coding to perform Byzantine consensus. Essentially, Krol[12] replaces broadcast with encoding, and decision making with decoding. These algorithms are based on the original algorithm by Pease, Shostak and Lamport[13] and have exponential message complexity.

The remainder of this paper is organized in the following manner. First, an overview of the original algorithm is given in section 2. The algorithm is described in section 3. Next, proofs of its correctness are in section 4. Then, in section 5, applications of an all-to-all gradecast algorithm are discussed. Concluding remarks are in section 6.

Table 1. Notation

n	number of processes
t	maximum number of faulty processes
i, j, k	process IDs
u, v, w, x, y, z	scalar values
U, V, W, X, Y, Z	non-scalar values
$confidence_i[j]$	confidence value P_i has in P_j's value
$value_i[j]$	value process P_i received from process P_j
G	set of all non-faulty processes

2   One-to-All Gradecast

2.1   Execution Model

The execution model used in this paper is the standard reliable synchronous message passing model. Processes can only communicate by passing messages. Processes are assumed to be fully connected. Message passing is assumed to be such that a process knows the identity of who sent the message. Only deterministic algorithms are considered. The algorithm assumes that only t out of the n processes in the system may fail; but, they may be Byzantine, that is to say, faulty in arbitrary ways. For algorithm correctness, we require that $n - 2t > t$ which simplifies to $t < n/3$. This bound is optimal because a Byzantine agreement algorithm can be build on top of gradecast that has the same requirements on t as the underlying gradecast algorithm. It has been proven that no Byzantine agreement algorithm exists for $t \geq n/3$. This model assumes that authenticated messages are not available; otherwise, the broadcast problem becomes trivial. Authenticated messages allow a process to verify the message's contents and source.

2.2   Overview of Original One-to-All Gradecast

This section gives a quick overview of the original algorithm presented by Feldman and Micali[1]. This algorithm broadcasts a value from one process to all other processes. This can be modified to an all-to-all gradecast algorithm by vectorizing. Pseudo-code for the algorithm is in Fig. 1. It assumes that the values n, t, and h are common knowledge to all processes, where n is the number of processes, t is the maximum number of faulty processes, and h is the broadcasting process. The algorithm proceeds in four steps. In the first step, the broadcaster h sends out its value to all processes. After this step, the algorithm is symmetric. In the second step, all process rebroadcast the value received from h to all other processes. Then, in the third step, each process looks at the values received from Step 2. If there is a common value that has been received at least $n - t$ times; then, it broadcasts that value. Otherwise, the process broadcasts no value. Finally, in Step 4, the received values from Step 3 are examined. Let x be the value that appears the most in Z_i. If there is a tie between two values, some common agreed upon tie breaking strategy must be performed. For example, if values are real numbers, we can always take the minimum. If x appears at least $2t + 1$ times; then, P_i outputs x with confidence 2. If x appears less than $2t + 1$ and more than t times; then, P_i outputs x with confidence 1. Otherwise, P_i outputs $\perp$ with confidence 0.

This algorithm has message bit complexity $O(mn^2)$ and when replicated to perform all-to-all gradecast, will have $O(mn^3)$ message bit complexity. The next section gives a vectorized modification to this algorithm that reduces the all-to-all gradecast message bit complexity to $O(mtn^2)$.

```
Pᵢ::
    Inputs to Pₕ:
        vₕ : input value for broadcaster
    Common Knowledge:
        n : number of processes
        t : maximum number of faulty processes
        h : broadcaster
    Variables:
        uᵢ : value process Pᵢ receives in Step 2
        Xᵢ[1..n] : vector of values received in Step 3
        Zᵢ[1..n] : vector of values received in Step 4

    // Step 1
    if i = h then
        for j : 1 to n do Pᵢ.send(Pⱼ, vₕ); end
    end
    // Step 2
    uᵢ = Pᵢ.receive(Pₕ);
    for j : 1 to n do Pᵢ.send(Pⱼ, uᵢ); end
    // Step 3
    for j : 1 to n do Xᵢ[j] = Pᵢ.receive(Pⱼ); end
    if ∃x such that |{k : Xᵢ[k] = x}| ≥ n − t then
        for j : 1 to n do Pᵢ.send(Pⱼ, x); end
    end
    // Step 4
    for j : 1 to n do
        if Pⱼ sent a message then
            Zᵢ[j] = Pᵢ.receive(Pⱼ);
        else Zᵢ[i] =⊥; end
    end
    if maxₓ |{k : Zᵢ[k] = x}| ≥ 2t + 1 then
        valueᵢ = arg maxₓ |{k : Zᵢ[k] = x}|;
        confidenceᵢ = 2;
    elseif maxₓ |{k : Zᵢ[k] = x}| > t then
        valueᵢ = arg maxₓ |{k : Zᵢ[k] = x}|;
        confidenceᵢ = 1;
    else
        valueᵢ =⊥; confidenceᵢ = 0;
    end
    Output valueᵢ and confidenceᵢ.
```

Fig. 1. Original one-to-all gradecast algorithm

3   Algorithm for All-To-All Gradecast

This section gives our all-to-all gradecast algorithm that has $O(mtn^2)$ message bit complexity. This algorithm is based on vectorizing the gradecast algorithm presented by Feldman and Micali[1]. As before, each process P_i has an input value v_i and the algorithm produces two vectors $value_i$ and $confidence_i$ which are the received values and the confidence level respectively. The algorithm assumes that the set of all messages can be encoded as members of a finite field, with one field member reserved to represent "no message" which we will denote as $\bot$. This assumption only requires that there exists a mapping between the messages and the field elements such that every message has a unique field element assigned to it with at least one field element unassigned.

There is a standard technique, called interleaving, to apply a small code to larger blocks without increasing the code length. The tool Parity Archive Volume Set[14] uses this technique. Our usage of this technique relies on the fact that only t blocks may be corrupt. It is very similar to breaking up the message to be transmitted into blocks and running each block through the code, except it is broken into interleaved blocks. What this means for the problem here, is that, if a code that uses octets as the basic unit and one message is ten octets; then, the first block will be the first octet from each message in the vector of messages, the second block will be the second octet from each message, and so on. Note, for the purposes here, the blocks are only interleaved in this manner for the encoding and decoding process. For example, if the vector to encode is $[[a, b], [c, d], [e, f]]$; then, $[a, c, e]$ would be run through the encoder to produce $[a, c, e, g, h]$ and $[b, d, f]$ to produce $[b, d, f, i, j]$ and the final output of the encoder is then $[[a, b], [c, d], [e, f], [g, i], [h, j]]$, which is then used in our algorithm. With this method, messages longer than the field size can be used.

Pseudo-code for the algorithm is provided in Fig. 2. This algorithm proceeds in four steps. The following description is from the point of view of process P_i, because the algorithm is symmetric. First, in Step 1, P_i broadcasts its value to every other process. Step 2 starts to differ from the original gradecast algorithm. The original algorithm rebroadcasts the values received from Step 1. Because of the messaging system reliability, $\forall P_i, P_j, P_k \in G : V_i[k] = V_j[k]$, where G is the set of all non-faulty processes. This implies that $\forall P_i, P_j \in G : |\{k : V_i[k] \neq V_j[k]\}| \leq t$. This means that at least $n - t$ values between non-faulty processes are identical; so, sending the whole vector, V_i, is inefficient. Therefore, our algorithm uses coding techniques to send at most $2t + 1$ values, which can be used in conjunction with the knowledge that the receiving process possesses to recover everything the sender knows. To finish Step 2, P_i sends the error correction vector of V_i.

In Step 3, P_i receives the encoded message from all other processes and uses its current knowledge to construct matrix X_i of all the values that every process claims that every other process possesses as their input value. The value $X_i[j][k]$ is the value that j claims k sent to it. The reliability of the messaging system and how the coding process works implies that $\forall P_i, P_j \in G, \forall k : X_i[j][k] = V_j[k]$. Now an array Y_i is constructed from X_i in the following manner. For each P_j, if there is a value that appears at least $n - t$ times in the column $X_i[\cdot][j]$; then, set $Y_i[j]$ to that value, otherwise, set $Y_i[j]$ to $\bot$. Then, an encoding of Y_i is sent to all processes.

Finally, in Step 4, Z_i is constructed in the same manner as X_i in Step 3. P_i uses its knowledge of Y_i and the encoded value sent to it from each other process j to recover Y_j and then places that value in the row $Z_i[j][\cdot]$. That gives the property $\forall P_i, P_j \in G, \forall k : Z_i[j][k] = Y_j[k]$. Then, P_i looks at columns of $Z_i[\cdot][j]$ for each P_j to decide its output. If $\max_x |\{k : Z_i[k][j] = x\}| \geq 2t + 1$; then, P_i sets $value_i[j] = x$ and $confidence_i[j] = 2$. If $2t + 1 > \max_x |\{k : Z_i[k][j] = x\}| > t$; then, P_i sets $value_i[j] = x$ and $confidence_i[j] = 1$. Otherwise, P_i sets $value_i[j] = \perp$ and $confidence_i[j] = 0$. Notice that the reduction in message bit complexity comes from taking advantage of the knowledge that is known to be common across processes, because of the constraint that at most t processes can be faulty. The processes also do not know which of the t values are not common. This is why they must exchange information in Step 2 and 3. But, coding is used to ensure that the amount of information exchanged is small.

3.1 Example

The following example shows how the algorithm works. For this example, $n = 4$ and $t = 1$. The possible messages are the non-zero values over the finite field $GF(2^8)$ and the zero value is reserved to represent no message. Let P_4 be the faulty process and let the initial value for the non-faulty processes be $\{241, 86, 35\}$. For the encoder, we will use a Reed Solomon[15] code with a code length of 2^8 that can correct one error. The error correction terms are calculated by taking the remainder of the values to encode as a polynomial with the generator polynomial $102 + 164x + x^2$ over the finite field $GF(2^8)$. For example, $[241, 86, 35, 35]$ is encoded as the polynomial $35x^{251} + 35x^{252} + 86x^{253} + 241x^{254}$. The remainder is taken, which gives us the polynomial $78 + 39x$, which corresponds to the values $[39, 78]$. Note that all the arithmetic operations are done over the finite field $GF(2^8)$. Decoding is much more involved and we recommend the reader consult the literature on the subject[3,15]. The Schifra[16] library was used to compute these values.

For Step 1, all processes send their values to all other processes. For this example, the received values for each process are:

$$V_1 = [241, 86, 35, 35]$$
$$V_2 = [241, 86, 35, 35] \tag{1}$$
$$V_3 = [241, 86, 35, 40]$$

Encoding these we get:

$$[V_1, Vecc_1] = [241, 86, 35, 35, 39, 78]$$
$$[V_2, Vecc_2] = [241, 86, 35, 35, 39, 78] \tag{2}$$
$$[V_3, Vecc_3] = [241, 86, 35, 40, 82, 30]$$

Then, each process sends the $Vecc_i$ values which are of length two.

Next, for Step 3, all processes receive the values sent in Step 2. Since P_4 is faulty, it will send $[22, 77]$ to P_1, $[0, 136]$ to P_2 and $[121, 159]$ to P_3. For this example, the processes then receive:

P_i::

Inputs:

   v_i : Input value for P_i

Common knowledge:

   n : The number of processes

   t : Maximum number of faulty processes

Variables:

   $V_i[1..n]$: Vector received in Step 2, initially $\perp$

   $Vecc_i[1..2t+1]$: error correction vector for V_i

   $X_i[1..n][1..n]$: Matrix of decoded values in Step 3

   $Y_i[1..n]$: Vector of values computed in Step 3

   $Yecc_i[1..2t+1]$: Error correction vector for Y_i

   $Z_i[1..n][1..n]$: Matrix of decoded values in Step 4

   $value_i[1..n]$: Vector of output values

   $confidence_i[1..n]$: Vector of confidence levels

// Step 1

for $j : 1$ to n **do** $P_i.send(P_j, v_i)$; **end**

// Step 2

for $j : 1$ to n **do** $V_i[j] = P_i.receive(P_j)$; **end**

$Vecc_i = encode(V_i)$;

for $j : 1$ to n **do** $P_i.send(P_j, Vecc_i)$; **end**

// Step 3

for $j : 1$ to n **do** $X_i[j] = decode(V_i, P_i.receive(P_j))$; **end**

$\forall j$ let $Y_i[j] = x$ if $\exists x$ s.t. $|\{k : X_i[k][j] = x\}| \geq n - t$ otherwise $Y_i[j] = \perp$

$Yecc_i = encode(Y_i)$;

for $j : 1$ to n **do** $P_i.send(P_j, Yecc_i)$; **end**

// Step 4

for $j : 1$ to n **do** $Z_i[j] = decode(Y_i, P_i.receive(P_j))$; **end**

for $j : 1$ to n **do**

   if $\max_x |\{k : Z_i[k][j] = x\}| \geq 2t+1$ **then**

      $value_i[j] = \arg\max_x |\{k : Z_i[k][j] = x\}|$;

      $confidence_i[j] = 2$;

   elseif $\max_x |\{k : Z_i[k][j] = x\}| > t$ **then**

      $value_i[j] = \arg\max_x |\{k : Z_i[k][j] = x\}|$;

      $confidence_i[j] = 1$;

   else $value_i[j] = \perp$; $confidence_i[j] = 0$;

   end

end

Output $value_i$ and $confidence_i$.

Fig. 2. All-to-all gradecast algorithm

$$P_1.receive(P_1) = [39, 78]$$
$$P_1.receive(P_2) = [39, 78]$$
$$P_1.receive(P_3) = [82, 30]$$
$$P_1.receive(P_4) = [22, 77]$$

(3)

$$P_2.receive(P_1) = [39, 78]$$
$$P_2.receive(P_2) = [39, 78]$$
$$P_2.receive(P_3) = [82, 30]$$
$$P_2.receive(P_4) = [0, 136]$$
(4)

$$P_3.receive(P_1) = [39, 78]$$
$$P_3.receive(P_2) = [39, 78]$$
$$P_3.receive(P_3) = [82, 30]$$
$$P_3.receive(P_4) = [121, 159]$$
(5)

Each process concatenates the received value to the end of its V_i vector and runs this through the decoder to get:

$$X_1 = \begin{bmatrix} 241, 86, 35, 35 \\ 241, 86, 35, 35 \\ 241, 86, 35, 40 \\ 241, 49, 35, 35 \end{bmatrix}$$
(6)

$$X_2 = \begin{bmatrix} 241, 86, 35, 35 \\ 241, 86, 35, 35 \\ 241, 86, 35, 40 \\ 241, 86, 129, 35 \end{bmatrix}$$
(7)

$$X_3 = \begin{bmatrix} 241, 86, 35, 35 \\ 241, 86, 35, 35 \\ 241, 86, 35, 40 \\ 157, 86, 35, 40 \end{bmatrix}$$
(8)

Following the instructions for building Y_i in Step 3 we get:

$$Y_1 = [241, 86, 35, 35]$$
$$Y_2 = [241, 86, 35, 35]$$
$$Y_3 = [241, 86, 35, 0]$$
(9)

Then building $Yecc_i$ gets:

$$[Y_1, Yecc_1] = [241, 86, 35, 35, 39, 78]$$
$$[Y_2, Yecc_2] = [241, 86, 35, 35, 39, 78]$$
$$[Y_3, Yecc_3] = [241, 86, 35, 0, 8, 182]$$
(10)

Each process i then sends its $Yecc_i$. Let P_4 send $[87, 77]$ to process 1 and 2 and $[123, 149]$ to process 3.

Finally, in Step 4, each process constructs the Z_i matrix in the same way it constructed the X_i matrix. Then, we have:

$$Z_1 = Z_2 = \begin{bmatrix} 241, 86, 35, 35 \\ 241, 86, 35, 35 \\ 241, 86, 35, 0 \\ 241, 86, 0, 35 \end{bmatrix}$$
(11)

$$Z_3 = \begin{bmatrix} 241, 86, 35, 35 \\ 241, 86, 35, 35 \\ 241, 86, 35, 0 \\ 241, 86, 35, 82 \end{bmatrix} \tag{12}$$

Finally, the algorithm will output for each process:

$$
\begin{aligned}
value_1 &= & [241, 86, 35, 35] \\
confidence_1 &= [2, 2, 2, 2] \\
value_2 &= & [241, 86, 35, 35] \\
confidence_2 &= [2, 2, 2, 2] \\
value_3 &= & [241, 86, 35, 35] \\
confidence_3 &= [2, 2, 2, 1]
\end{aligned}
\tag{13}
$$

4   Proof of Correctness

In this section, we show the correctness of our algorithm. The first lemma shows a crucial property of Y in Step 3 of Fig. 2.

Lemma 1. *Assume P_i and P_j are non-faulty processes. In Step 3 of Fig. 2, if P_i sets $Y_i[k]$ to $x \neq \perp$ and P_j sets $Y_j[k]$ to $y \neq \perp$; then, $x = y$. Formally, $\forall P_i, P_j \in G, \forall k : Y_i[k] \neq \perp \wedge Y_j[k] \neq \perp \Longrightarrow Y_i[k] = Y_j[k]$.*

Proof. If P_i sets $x \neq \perp$ to $Y_i[k]$, then the kth column of X_i contained at least $n - t$ copies of x. Only t rows can correspond to faulty processes, so at least $n - 2t$ of the rows that contain x in column k come from non-faulty processes. This means that those $n - 2t$ non-faulty processes also sent vectors to P_j which set x to the kth column for those processes. Suppose $y \neq x$ and $y \neq \perp$. This means that there must be $n - 2t$ values which are $\perp$ in the kth column of X_j at process P_j. But, $n - 2t > t$ so P_j will set $Y_j[k]$ to $\perp$, which contradicts that $y \neq \perp$ and $y \neq x$.

Theorem 1 (Property (1)). *All non-faulty processes with positive confidence about process k have identical value$[k]$. Formally,*

$$\forall P_i, P_j \in G, \forall k : confidence_i[k] > 0 \wedge confidence_j[k] > 0$$

implies

$$value_i[k] = value_j[k].$$

Proof. First note that the Z_i matrix will contain the Y_j vectors from Step 3 of Fig. 2 for all P_j. By Lemma 1, if there is a majority of a value that is not $\perp$ in the kth column of Z_i; then, all values in that column that are not the majority and not $\perp$ are from a faulty process. This implies that if any non-faulty process P_j sets $confidence_i[k] \geq 1$; then, all other non-faulty processes P_j that set $confidence_j[k] \geq 1$ also set $value_j[k] = value_i[k]$.

Theorem 2 (Property (2)). *For any two non-faulty processes, the difference in their confidence levels for any process P_k can differ by at most 1. Formally,* $\forall P_i, P_j \in G, \forall k : |confidence_i[k] - confidence_j[k]| \leq 1.$

Proof. Assume some non-faulty process P_i sets $confidence_i[k] = \delta$ and $value_i[k] = x$. Process P_i setting $confidence_i[k] = \delta$ implies that a set R of processes sent x to P_i in Step 3 of Fig. 2. Let $R_e \subseteq R$ be the faulty processes that sent x to P_i. By problem setup, $|R_e| \leq t$. This means that the number of processes that also sent x to any other process can differ by at most t. Let P_j be the process that receive the most messages in support of x. Then, all other processes receive at least $|R| - t$ messages in support of x. Step 4 of the algorithm in Fig. 2 compares the support of x to $2t + 1$ and t to select the confidence level. By the above reasoning, the support of x differs by at most t between any non-faulty process. Therefore, the difference in confidence level between any non-faulty processes is at most 1.

Theorem 3 (Property (3)). *If P_k is non-faulty, then, all non-faulty processes P_i have the value sent by process P_k and their confidence level on this value is 2. Formally,* $\forall P_i, P_k \in G : (confidence_i[k] = 2) \wedge (value_i[k] = v_k).$

Proof. If P_i is a non-faulty process, then, all processes will receive v_i from P_i in Step 2 of Fig. 2. Next, all non-faulty processes will also claim that P_i sent v_i for Step 3. Let G be the set of all non-faulty processes, by the assumptions of our problem $|G| \geq n - t$ and all non-faulty processes will distribute error correction vectors with v_i in the ith entry in Step 3. So, every non-faulty process P_j will set $confidence_j[i] = 2$ and $value_j[i] = v_i$ in Step 4.

Theorem 4. *The algorithms in Fig. 2 has bit message complexity of $O(mtn^2)$.*

Proof. In Step 1, every process sends its value to every other process taking mn^2 message bits. In Step 2, each process computes $Vecc_i$ which contains at most $2t + 1$ values of length m bits. Every process then sends its $Vecc_i$ to every other process resulting in at most $m(2t + 1)n^2$ message bits. In Step 3, the same number of message bits are sent as Step 2. This results in a total of at most $mn^2 + 2m(2t + 1)n^2$ message bits being sent by this algorithm. This is $O(mtn^2)$.

5   Application

The all-to-all gradecast algorithm can be used to create an exceptionally simple byzantine agreement algorithm. Ben-Or, Dolev and Hoch[2] give a simple algorithm for Byzantine agreement and approximate agreement based on the gradecast algorithm. A modification to the gradecast algorithm is needed for their Byzantine agreement algorithm. The modification is to make the algorithm take a set of known faulty processes that the algorithm will ignore and set all values for processes in the faulty set to $\bot$. This has the effect of making that process in the faulty set disappear as if they had crashed. The Byzantine consensus algorithm is symmetric, can agree upon an arbitrary value (as long as there is some method of resolving a tie), and has an early stopping property. They define early stopping to mean if there are $f \leq t$ actual failures; then, the algorithm terminates in $\min(f + 2, t + 1)$ rounds. The message bit complexity with our all-to-all gradecast algorithm is $O(mt^2n^2)$.

The algorithm starts off with a faulty set which is initially empty. Then, for each round r up to $t + 1$ rounds the algorithm performs as follows: The algorithm performs an all-to-all gradecast of the current value ignoring all processes in the faulty set. The algorithm then adds up how often each value was received which had a confidence greater than or equal to one. Next, it sets the current value to the value that has the largest count. If there is more than one with the same count; then, use some tie breaking scheme, such as always choosing the smaller value. The algorithm adds all processes that have confidence one or less to the faulty set. Next, the algorithm counts the number of processes that sent the current value with confidence 2. If this count is greater than $n - t$, the algorithm performs one more iteration of the loop and then exits the loop prematurely. To finish, the algorithm returns the current value.

The approximate agreement algorithm presented by Ben-Or, Dolev and Hoch is very similar to the byzantine agreement algorithm described above. The all-to-all gradecast algorithm we describe can be plugged into their algorithm without changing any of the properties of the original algorithm.

6 Conclusion

Many algorithms have a step where every process broadcasts a value. Gradecast is a broadcast algorithm that gives a confidence level to each receiving process. This confidence level gives information about the state of other processes. We have presented an all-to-all gradecast with message bit complexity $O(mtn^2)$. The original gradecast algorithm presented by Feldman and Micali[1] is a one to all broadcast protocol. Using the original gradecast algorithm to produce all-to-all gives $O(mn^3)$ message bit complexity. Our algorithm can be used in place of the original gradecast algorithm when an all-to-all broadcasts is used. The algorithm presented uses coding to reduce the amount of redundant information being transmitted. We presented proofs that our modified algorithm maintains the important properties of the original gradecast. Having an all-to-all gradecast algorithm that is efficient in message bit complexity admits a simple symmetric arbitrary valued Byzantine agreement with early stopping property that only takes $O(mt^2n^2)$ message bit complexity. Other algorithms may also benefit from using coding in the fashion presented here.

References

1. Feldman, P., Micali, S.: Optimal algorithms for byzantine agreement. In: Proceedings of the Twentieth Annual ACM Symposium on Theory of Computing, Ser. STOC 1988, pp. 148–161. ACM, New York (1988),
   http://doi.acm.org/10.1145/62212.62225

2. Ben-Or, M., Dolev, D., Hoch, E.N.: Simple gradecast based algorithms (September 2010), http://arxiv.org/abs/1007.1049
3. Roth, R.M.: Introduction to coding theory. Cambridge University Press (2006)
4. Dolev, D., Lynch, N.A., Pinter, S.S., Stark, E.W., Weihl, W.E.: Reaching approximate agreement in the presence of faults. Journal of the ACM 33, 499–516 (1986)
5. Fekete, A.D.: Asymptotically optimal algorithms for approximate agreement. In: Proceedings of the Fifth Annual ACM Symposium on Principles of Distributed Computing, ser. PODC 1986, pp. 73–87. ACM, New York (1986), http://doi.acm.org/10.1145/10590.10597
6. Coan, B.A., Welch, J.L.: Modular construction of a byzantine agreement protocol with optimal message bit complexity. Information and Computation, 97(1), 61–85 (1992), http://www.sciencedirect.com/science/article/pii/089054019290004Y
7. Srikanth, T.K., Toueg, S.: Simulating authenticated broadcasts to derive simple fault-tolerant algorithms. Distributed Computing, 2, 80–94 (1987), http://dx.doi.org/10.1007/BF01667080
8. Hélary, J.-M., Hurfin, M., Mostéfaoui, A., Raynal, M., Tronel, F.: Computing global functions in asynchronous distributed systems prone to process crashes. In: International Conference on Distributed Computing Systems, pp. 584–591 (2000)
9. Pease, M., Shostak, R., Lamport, L.: Reaching agreement in the presence of faults. J. ACM 27, 228–234 (1980), http://doi.acm.org/10.1145/322186.322188
10. Liang, G., Vaidya, N.H.: Error-free multi-valued consensus with byzantine failures. CoRR, vol. abs/1101.3520 (2011)
11. Friedman, R., Mostéfaoui, A., Rajsbaum, S., Raynal, M.: Asynchronous agreement and its relation with error-correcting codes. IEEE Trans. Computers 56(7), 865–875 (2007)
12. Krol, T.: Interactive consistency algorithms based on voting and error-correcting codes. In: Twenty Fifth International Symposium on Fault-Tolerant Computing, Digest of Papers, FTCS-25 Silver Jubilee, pp. 89–98. IEEE Computer Society Press, Los Alamitos (1995)
13. Lamport, L., Shostak, R., Pease, M.: The byzantine generals problem. ACM Trans. Program. Lang. Syst. 4, 382–401 (1982), http://doi.acm.org/10.1145/357172.357176
14. Parchive: Parity archive tool, http://parchive.sourceforge.net/
15. Reed, I.S., Solomon, G.: Polynomial codes over certain finite fields. Society for Industrial and Applied Mathematics 8(2), 300–304 (1960)
16. Partow, A.: Schifra reed-solomon error correcting code library, http://www.schifra.com/

Fault-Tolerant Exploration of an Unknown Dangerous Graph by Scattered Agents

Paola Flocchini[1], Matthew Kellett[2], Peter C. Mason[2], and Nicola Santoro[3]

[1] School of Electrical Engineering and Computer Science, University of Ottawa
[2] Defence R&D Canada – Ottawa, Government of Canada
[3] School of Computer Science, Carleton University

Abstract. Black hole search (BHS) is the problem of mapping or exploring a network where there are dangerous sites (black holes) that eliminate any incoming searcher without leaving a discernible trace. Dangerous graph exploration (DGE) extends the BHS problem to include dangerous links (black links). In the literature, both problems have only been studied under the assumption that no faults occur in the network during the exploration. In this paper, we examine the impact that link failures can have on the exploration of dangerous graphs. We study the DGE problem under the following conditions: there are multiple black holes and black links, the network topology is unknown, the searchers are initially scattered in arbitrary locations, and the system is totally asynchronous. In this difficult setting, we assume that links can fail during the computation. We present an algorithm that solves the DGE in the presence of such dynamic link failures. Our solution to the problem works with an optimum number of searchers in a polynomial number of moves. This is the first result dealing with fault-tolerant computations in dangerous graphs.

1 Introduction

Network mapping is an important problem that goes all the way back to Claude Shannon's building of a physical maze solving machine [20]. Mapping and its associated problem of exploration, the visiting of every node in a network or the crossing of every edge, has been a significant focus of research in the mobile agent model of distributed computing. In the last decade, a significant portion of that work has focussed on exploration and mapping when the network is not safe for the agents.

A particular kind of danger is the presence in the network of *black holes*, network sites that eliminate agents arriving at them without leaving a discernible trace. The *black hole search* (BHS) problem is the problem of locating such harmful sites. In order to solve the problem, a team of agents must work together to find the black holes because some agents must be eliminated in order for it be detected. The *dangerous graph exploration* (DGE) problem extends the BHS problem to include *black links*, network links that act in the same way as black holes, destroying any agent traversing them without leaving a discernible

A.W. Richa and C. Scheideler (Eds.): SSS 2012, LNCS 7596, pp. 299–313, 2012.

trace. In both the BHS and DGE problems, there are three basic requirements for solvability and for termination: the *safe* portion of the network (i.e., the remaining network once the black links, as well as the black holes and their incident links are removed) has to be connected; the number k of agents must be greater that the size f of the *frontier* (i.e., the links from the safe nodes to the unsafe portion of the network); information about the number n_s of safe nodes or the size of the frontier must be known. We assume that such requirements are met.

The BHS problem was introduced by Dobrev et al. in [10], which focuses on finding a single black hole in an asynchronous ring network, and there has been extensive research since then [1–3, 5–9, 11, 13–19, 21]. The DGE problem was first investigated by Chalopin, Das, and Santoro in [4], where agents scattered in an anonymous network of unknown topology solved the DGE problem as a consequence of solving the mobile agent rendezvous problem. The same problem when the unknown network is not anonymous is examined in [12]. The solution presented there works in $O(nm)$ agent moves, where n is the number of nodes and m is the number of links, a cost which is proven to be optimal in [19].

In all existing investigations of the BHS and DGE problems, it is assumed that the environment is fault-free—that is, the computation is dangerous by nature, due to the presence of black holes and black links. What happens if the network topology is not static or if links could go down while the computation takes place? None of the existing solutions addresses these questions and none would tolerate even a single link failure.

The goal of this paper is to start examining the problem of *fault-tolerant* exploration of dangerous graphs. In particular, we focus on solving the DGE problem in presence of *dynamic link failures*. Dealing with link failures is a first step towards algorithms for fully dynamic networks, which would also have to deal with link insertions, node failures or departures, and node insertions. Link failures are of particular concern because if an adversary can take control of a link or links in a network—either physically in a wired network or through attacks such as the wormhole attack in wireless networks—a well-timed link failure could wreak havoc.

Main Contributions: We consider a rather difficult setting: a network of arbitrary topology with a multiplicity of black holes and black links. The agents initially scattered in arbitrary safe locations are unaware of the network topology, start at arbitrary times, and are totally asynchronous (that is, all their actions take a finite but arbitrary amount of time). The initial location of the agents and the timing and duration of their actions are arbitrary, as determined by an adversary.

In this already difficult setting, we allow network links to fail by disappearing during the computation; the timing, choice, and number of link failures is arbitrary, as determined by an adversary. We assume however that any such failure occurs only when no agent is traversing that link, and that the failures do not disconnect the safe part of the network (otherwise the DGE problem is clearly unsolvable).

The main contribution of this paper is the proof that it is still possible to solve the DGE problem in spite of such dynamic link failures. Interestingly, this can be done with the same optimal number $f + 1$ of agents as in the fault-free case. The proof is constructive. We present a protocol that using $f + 1$ agents solves this new DGE with link deletions (DGE-LD) problem. Not surprisingly, the protocol, based on the fault-free algorithm from [12], is rather complex; interestingly, its cost is $O(nm^2)$ moves, showing that the price of *fault-tolerance* is at most a factor $O(m)$ from the optimal cost without faults.

This is the first result about fault-tolerant computations in dangerous graphs.

The rest of the paper is structured as follows. We describe the model and introduce the terminology in Section 2. We describe the algorithm in detail in Section 3. Finally, we prove the correctness and analyze the complexity of the algorithm in Section 4. Some proofs are omitted due to space limitations.

2   Model

We model the network as a simple undirected graph $G = (V, E)$ with $n = |V|$ vertices or nodes and $m = |E|$ edges or links. The edges incident at a node are locally labeled with distinct values (port numbers). There is a set A of $k = |A|$ agents working in G. They all follow the same protocol or algorithm. Each has a distinct id, its own memory, and can move from node to neighbouring node. They start scattered in the network at arbitrary times. They move and compute asynchronously, meaning that all their actions take a finite but unpredictable amount of time. The initial locations of the agents as well as the timing of their actions are determined by an adversary.

The agents communicate with each other using shared memory in the form of whiteboards located at each node. Each node's whiteboard can be accessed in fair mutual exclusion by the agents resident on that node. The mutual exclusion property allows the agents to operate as if the links are first in, first out (FIFO) and as if the nodes have unique ids. Without loss of generality, we assume that the links and nodes have these properties.

In the network are sets of black holes and black links, nodes and links that eliminate agents arriving at or traversing them without leaving a discernible trace. Let $V_B \subset V$ be the set of black holes and $E_B \subseteq E$ be the set of black links. All other nodes and links are said to be safe. Let $E_I = \{[u, v] \in E : u, v \in V_B\}$ be the set of inaccessible links, black or safe, connecting pairs of black holes. Let $F_B = \{[u, v] \in E : u \in V \setminus V_B \wedge v \in V_B\}$ be the set of frontier links, black or safe, connecting safe nodes to black holes. We can now define the safe portion of the network as $G_S = (V_S, E_S)$, where $V_S = V \setminus V_B$ is the set of safe nodes and $E_S = E \setminus (E_B \cup E_I \cup F_B)$ is the set of safe links. The choice of the sets V_B and E_B is made by an adversary; however, the safe portion of the graph is connected (the problem is otherwise unsolvable). The value $n_S = |V_S|$ is known to the agents (otherwise termination is impossible). Additionally, since at least one agent must survive, the number of agents must be greater than the number f of links incident on a safe node exploring which an agent will die: $f = |F_B| + 2|E_B \setminus (E_I \cup F_B)|$; thus we assume that there are $k \geq f + 1$ agents.

In this setting, we allow network links to fail by disappearing during the computation. An edge failure is locally detectable at an incident node only in the sense that, if information about that edge (identified by its port number) is written on the whiteboard, an agent can notice the absence of an edge with such a port number; if no information is written, it is like the edge never existed. The timing, choice, and number of link failures is arbitrary, as determined by an adversary. However, any such failure occurs only when no agent is traversing that link, and the failures do not disconnect the safe part of the network (otherwise, the DGE problem is clearly unsolvable). Note that allowing failures during the execution of the algorithm is not equivalent to removing the links that will fail before the algorithm starts. Any solution to exploration in a dangerous graph requires the team of agents to coordinate their search. A link failure during the execution can severely disrupt this coordination.

The dangerous graph exploration with link deletions (DGE-LD) problem is for a team of agents to visit every accessible link in a network and, within finite time, to mark locally all frontier links F_B and accessible black links $E_B \setminus E_I$ as dangerous. During the execution of the algorithm, an adversary can delete any link as long as no agents are traversing it. We say that the problem is solved if, within finite time, at least one agent survives, all accessible links have been visited, all frontier links and accessible black links are marked locally as such, and all surviving agents enter a terminal state.

3   The Algorithm

We present an algorithm, *ExploreDG-LD*, that solves the DGE-LD problem. We start by describing the basic work activities of exploring, verifying, and merging. We then describe how an agent deals with deletions during its work.

3.1   Overview

In general, algorithm *ExploreDG-LD* works as follows. The agents build spanning trees of the safe area starting from their homebases in the *exploration* process. The root of each tree contains coordinating information for the agents working on the same tree. The *cautious walk* technique is used during exploration to ensure that only one agent is eliminated per frontier link and at most two agents are eliminated per black link. The *verification* process is used to detect when a newly explored link connects two trees. When two trees are found to be adjacent, they are merged in the *merging* process. An agent terminates the algorithm when the current tree contains n_S nodes and there is no verification or exploration work left. In the absence of link deletions, algorithm *ExploreDG-LD* is very similar in structure to the algorithm presented in [12] and solves the traditional fault-free DGE problem.

Link deletions obviously complicate the entire process, in particular the processes of building the trees and connecting them together. Some deletions—such as the deletion of an unexplored link or an inaccessible link between two black holes—have no effect on the execution of the algorithm. On the other hand, the deletion of a tree link can have a significant effect. The trees that the agents build out from their homebases provide safe paths through the safe portion of the network, G_S. By eliminating a tree link, the adversary can cut an agent or agents off from access to the coordinating information at the root of the tree in which they are working.

In the following, we describe the algorithm from the point of view of an agent and with the help of Figures 1–7, which show the movement of the agent from the time it starts on a single work task until it finishes that task. The square numbers in each of the diagrams refer to the cases where no deletion is encountered. The circled letters in subsequent diagrams refer to cases where a deletion is encountered.

3.2 Operations without Deletions

In the absence of link deletions, algorithm *ExploreDG-LD* solves the traditional fault-free DGE problem using a logical structure similar to the algorithm presented in [12], which is however not fault-tolerant. Let us discuss the structure.

When an agent a first wakes up, it enters the *initialization* phase. It accesses the whiteboard of its homebase to see if the node has a root marker. If there is no root marker then agent a creates one. The *root marker* contains a map of the tree rooted at the node, as well as all the information needed to find verification and exploration work in the tree. In fact, every node visited by an agent has the root marker for the subtree of which it is the root, even if that subtree is only the node itself. We say that a root marker is *active* if its node has no parent; otherwise, we say that a root marker is *passive*. Only active root markers are used to coordinate work and, as we will see, a passive root marker only becomes active because of the deletion of the link to its parent in the tree.

After initialization, the agent enters the *main loop* of the algorithm and continues until the termination conditions are met. Each round, the agent looks for work in the active root marker. If the current node does not have an active root marker then the agent "grabs" the active root marker by following the parent pointers at each node until the agent finds it. The agent first looks to see if there is any verification work in the root marker. If there is no verification work then it looks for exploration work. Finally, if there no exploration work then it waits until work arrives, following the active root marker if it moves because of a merger. We describe the work of the agent starting first with exploration, then verification, and then merging.

Exploration is the work of exploring every accessible link in the network using cautious walk. Agent a in tree T with root r, as shown in Figure 1, chooses a link $[u, v]$ for exploration and takes the tree path from r to u. The agent updates all the passive root markers along the path noting that $[u, v]$ is being explored. It then uses the *cautious walk* technique to test if $[u, v]$ is safe. It marks as *dangerous* the port on u leading to $[u, v]$ and then traverses $[u, v]$ to v. If $[u, v]$ is a black link or v is a black hole then the agent is eliminated as shown in case $\boxed{1}$ in Figure 1. The port on u remains marked as dangerous and no other agent can enter it to be eliminated.

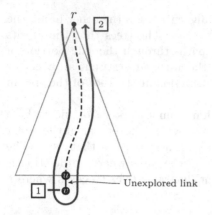
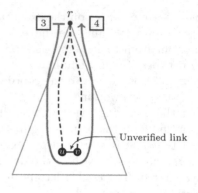

Fig. 1. Exploration of unexplored link $[u, v]$ with no deletions. Cases include encountering a black hole or black link (1), and successful return to its own root (2) (possible movement of r due to mergers is not shown).

Fig. 2. Verification of internal link $[u, v]$ with no deletions. Cases include the successful verification of the link (3, 4).

If the agent is not eliminated then it checks to see if v has been previously visited. If v has not been previously visited then a marks it as visited on its whiteboard, creates a parent pointer pointing towards u, and creates a root marker for the subtree rooted at v. It completes the cautious walk by returning to u and marking the port to $[u, v]$ as *explored*. It returns from u to r (or wherever the active root marker is) by grabbing the root marker, adding v to all the passive root markers along the way, marking $[u, v]$ for verification, and marking v's other links for exploration. If v has been previously visited then a completes the cautious walk and returns to r marking $[u, v]$ for verification in all the root markers along the way.

A safe return to r is shown as case 2 in Figure 1. Note that because of merging, which we describe below, the active root marker may have moved. In this case, the agent continues following the parent pointers up the tree, adding the information about v to each root marker it passes, until it reaches the active root marker. Its exploration is then done.

Verification is the work of determining whether every safely explored link is internal or external to the tree in which the agent is working. If an external link is found then the agent may try to merge the two trees connected by the link.

We look first at the verification of internal links as shown in Figure 2. Agent a working in tree T with root r chooses link $[u, v]$ for verification. By construction, $[u, v]$ can only be marked for verification if $u \in T$ and $[u, v]$ has already been explored. The agent needs to determine if $v \in T$ or $v \notin T$. If v is in the map of T's active root marker at r then the agent knows that $[u, v]$ is internal and it does not even have to leave r to complete the verification, which is shown as case $\boxed{3}$ in Figure 2. Case $\boxed{3}$ always occurs for tree links that have been marked for verification.

If v is not in the map, it could be because $v \notin T$ or the agent from T that explored v has not yet returned to the active root marker. For an internal link, it must be the latter case. Agent a traverses to the root of v's tree T' with root r' to determine if $T \subseteq T'$ (since r may have been merged with r' during the agent's traversal). The agent traverses from r to u, across $[u, v]$, and then from v to r'. Since we can assume that the links are FIFO and we are looking at internal link verification, we know that the agent that explored v must reach the active root marker before a reaches it and a marks the link as internal on its return, which is shown as case $\boxed{4}$ in Figure 2. Agent a's verification of $[u, v]$ is finished.

Unlike during exploration, agent a does not mark $[u, v]$ as being verified on all the passive root markers on its traversal from r to u and v to r', where $T \subseteq T'$. Instead, the agent checks to see if v is in the map of the subtree rooted at each passive root marker it passes on the path from v to r'. If it is then a marks the link as internal to that subtree. Otherwise, a does nothing. Note that all the root markers from r to u already had $[u, v]$ marked for verification by the agent that explored $[u, v]$ and the same is true for the link $[v, u]$ on the path from r' to v. As a result, if a deletion were to create a new tree below the point where both u and v are in the same subtree, the link would already be marked for verification again in the new active root marker.

We now look at the verification of external links as show in Figure 3. Agent u working in tree T with root r chooses link $[u, v]$ for verification. In the external case, node v belongs to some tree T' with root r', where $T \not\subseteq T'$. The agent traverses from r to u, across $[u, v]$, and from v to r' using parent pointers to find the active root marker in T', which is shown as case $\boxed{5}$ in Figure 3. Along the way it marks $[v, u]$ for verification in every root marker, if it is not already there. The agent must now decide whether to merge T' with T. If $\mathrm{id}(r') > \mathrm{id}(r)$, where $\mathrm{id}()$ is a function that returns the id of a node's root marker, it picks up the active root marker to perform a merger. If $\mathrm{id}(r') < \mathrm{id}(r)$, it adds $[v, u]$ to the links in need of verification, if it is not already there, and begins working in tree T'. In either case, agent a's verification of $[u, v]$ is finished.

Merging is the work of adding one tree to another. Agent a has picked up the active root marker in tree T' with root r' and it traverses from r' to v. Along the way, it reverses the parent pointer to point towards the tree's new root and adjusts the maps of the passive root markers along the way to reflect the branch of the subtree lost by the reversal. It then adds $[v, u]$ as a tree link and traverses from u to the active root marker, on r or elsewhere due to mergers, adding T' and its work information to the root markers along the way, including the active root marker. The merger is then finished as shown in case $\boxed{6}$ in Figure 3.

A reader familiar with the technique used in [12] would note two crucial differences: unlike [12], in *ExploreDG-LD* every node visited by an agent has a root marker, and there are no restrictions on the number of verifying agents for the same tree. Precisely these two factors enable the agents to cope with link failures and in particular to avoid deadlocks.

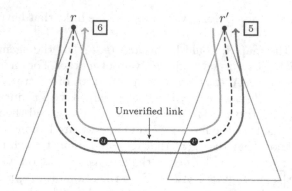

Fig. 3. Verification of external link $[u, v]$ and merging across link $[v, u]$ with no deletions. Cases include successfully verifying the link is external ($\boxed{5}$), and successfully merging the two trees ($\boxed{6}$) (possible movement of r or r' due to mergers is not shown).

3.3   Operations with Deletions

There are certain types of deletion that an agent never encounters or which have very little effect on the agent. For instance, the deletion of an inaccessible link or the deletion of a link between two unvisited nodes would have no effect on the agent's execution of the algorithm. The deletion of a known non-tree link is worth noting in the agent's map if it passes by it, but it does not have an effect on the actions taken by the agent. As a result, we are only concerned with the deletion of a tree link or of a link being explored or verified. When we discover such a deletion, we work around it while taking steps to repair the damage. The actions taken often depend more on what was deleted than on the work being performed by the agents, so many of the deletion handling cases overlap. We look at the actions taken by the agent in each case and note any task specific differences.

As a consequence of how we have defined work—the exploration or verification of a link or the merging of one root marker with another—it is only possible for an agent to encounter two deletions during a single piece of work. It can encounter a single deletion either on its way away or back towards the root of its own tree. It can only encounter two deletions if it encounters one on the way away from the root of its own tree and another on the way back. If an agent is unable to return to its own root, it simply starts working wherever it is. The cases presented below take into account both possibilities, one deletion or two, where necessary. In each case, we describe what the agent does when its work is "interrupted" by a deletion.

The cases cover the following work. Let r, r', and r'' be the roots of trees T, T', and T'', respectively. For exploration, an agent a is exploring link $[u, v]$, where $u \in T$. For internal verification, an agent a is verifying link $[u, v]$, where $u \in T$, $v \in T'$, and $T \subseteq T'$. For external verification, an agent a is verifying link $[u, v]$, where $u \in T$, $v \in T'$, and $T \neq T'$. For merging, an agent a is merging

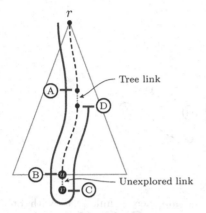

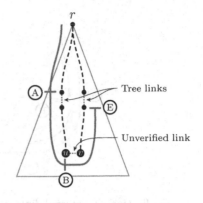

Fig. 4. Exploration of unexplored link $[u, v]$ with one deletion. Cases include the deletion of a tree link (Ⓐ, Ⓓ) and the deletion of the unexplored link, (Ⓑ, Ⓒ).

Fig. 5. Verification of internal link $[u, v]$ with one deletion. Cases include the deletion of a tree link (Ⓐ, Ⓓ, Ⓔ)), and the deletion of the unverified link (Ⓑ).

across link $[v, u]$, where $v \in T'$ or $v \in T''$ depending on the number of deletions, $u \in T$, $T'' \subset T'$, and $T \neq T'$. Let $[x, y]$ be a tree link on the path from the root to the link being worked on, where x is closest to the root and y is closest to the link.

Case Ⓐ in Figures 4 to 6 applies to an exploring or verifying agent that finds a tree link $[x, y]$ deleted on the path from r to u. The agent returns from x to the active root marker deleting the subtree rooted in x from the map of every root marker along the way. The agent then looks for new work.

Case Ⓑ in Figures 4 to 6 applies to an exploring or verifying agent that finds that the link $[u, v]$ it is meant to explore or verify has been deleted. The agent returns from u to the active root marker marking the deletion on the map of every root marker along the way. The agent then looks for new work.

Case Ⓒ in Figure 4 applies to an exploring agent that finds that $[u, v]$ has been deleted after it has traversed it during the first step of its cautious walk. If v is a new node, the agent creates a root marker and begins working in the new tree rooted at v. If v has already been visited, the agent traverses from v to the active root marker in v's tree. The agent then looks for new work.

Case Ⓓ in Figures 4 and 7 applies to an exploring agent that finds a tree link $[y, x]$ deleted on the path to r. The agent starts working for the new active root marker at y.

Case Ⓔ in Figures 5 and 6 applies to a verifying agent that finds a tree link $[y, x]$ deleted on the path from v to the root of v's tree. If $\text{id}(y) > \text{id}(r)$ then the agent picks up y's root marker and merges it. If $\text{id}(y) < \text{id}(r)$ then the agent adds $[v, u]$ to the links to be verified, if it is not already there, and starts working for the new active root marker at y.

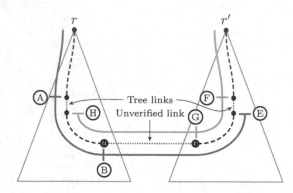

Fig. 6. Verification of external link $[u, v]$ and merging across link $[v, u]$ with one deletion. Cases for verifying (Ⓐ, Ⓑ, Ⓔ) and merging (Ⓕ, Ⓖ, Ⓗ) include the deletion of a tree link (Ⓐ, Ⓔ, Ⓕ, Ⓗ) and deletion of the unverified link, (Ⓑ, Ⓖ).

Case Ⓕ in Figures 6 and 7 applies to a merging agent that finds a tree link $[x, y]$ deleted on the path to v. The agent deletes the subtree rooted in y from the now active root marker on x and starts working there.

Case Ⓖ in Figures 6 and 7 applies to a merging agent that finds the link $[v, u]$ deleted. The agent starts working for the active root marker at v.

Case Ⓗ in Figures 6 and 7 applies to a merging agent that finds a tree link $[y, x]$ deleted on the path from u to r. The agent starts working for the new active root marker at y.

4   Correctness and Complexity

4.1   Absence of Failures

We first prove that, in absence of failures, algorithm *ExploreDG-LD* is a correct solution to the DGE problem. The proof follows a series of lemmas.

Lemma 1. *In the absence of deletions, an agent that is verifying will finish verifying within finite time.*

Lemma 2. *In the absence of deletions, an agent that is exploring will finish exploring within finite time.*

From Lemmas 1 and 2 it follows that:

Lemma 3. *In the absence of deletions, at any time, there is at least one agent alive that is not waiting.*

Lemma 4. *In the absence of deletions, every link in $E \backslash E_I$ is eventually explored and those in G_S are also verified.*

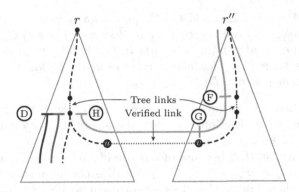

Fig. 7. Agent encounters second deletion during exploration, verification, or merging. Cases include, for returning exploring and verifying agents, the deletion of a tree link (ⓓ), and, for merging agents, the deletion of tree links (ⓕ, ⓗ) and the deletion of the verified link (ⓖ).

Lemma 5. *In the absence of deletions, the tree of a verifying agent that becomes an exploring agent is merged within finite time.*

Proof. When a verifying agent verifies an external link and finds the tree on the other side has a lower id than its own tree, it starts working for that tree. Let a_2 be the verifying agent from tree T_2 with root r_2 that is verifying edge $[v_2, u_1]$ between T_2 and T_1 and has arrived on root r_1. Let $id(r_1) < id(r_2)$. Since T_1 has a lower id root marker, a_2 marks the edge it was verifying, but in the opposite direction, $[u_1, v_2]$, for verification in T_1's root marker, and then starts working there. Without loss of generality, assume that all other agents are currently working on exploration and there are no other links to be verified. Agent a_2 immediately chooses to verify $[u_1, v_2]$ and returns to r_2. Since T_2 has a higher id root marker, agent a_2 picks it up and returns to r_1 to merge T_2's root marker with T_1's. Hence the lemma follows.

While it is possible that other agents are already trying to merge the two trees, we know that the mergers are only performed by agents from lower id trees, so we still have a finite number of mergers that can take place and no cycle of mergers can emerge.

We can now prove the following.

Theorem 1. *Algorithm* ExploreDG-LD *correctly solves the* DGE *problem in the absence of failures.*

4.2 Dynamic Link Failures

We now prove that algorithm *ExploreDG-LD* is also a correct solution to the DGE-LD problem. That is

Theorem 2. *Algorithm* ExploreDG-LD *correctly and within finite time solves the* DGE-LD *problem by constructing a rooted spanning tree of G_S, marking all safe edges as such, and marking all ports in G_S leading to a black hole or to a black edge as dangerous. The total number of moves by the agents is at most $O(k^2 \cdot n_S + n_S \cdot m + k \cdot n_S \cdot D)$.*

To prove the theorem, we prove the correctness of algorithm *ExploreDG-LD* by showing that, while deletions can slow the algorithm, they cannot stop the algorithm from making progress.

We start by noting that because of our use of cautious walk, a team size of $k = f + 1$, where $f = |F_B| + 2|E_B \setminus (E_I \cup F_B)|$ is the number of links incident on safe nodes whose traversal will cause an agent to be teliminated, and the assumption that deletions do not eliminate agents, we can say that at any time, there is always one agent alive.

We next look at work that is aborted as the result of deletion. We say that a work task—exploration, verification, or merging—is *aborted* if the agent is unable to reach the link being explored, verified, or merged over, respectively.

Lemma 6. *Within finite time, an agent completes aborted work.*

Note that in the case of exploration and verification, the active root marker may have moved farther away due to a merger or closer due to a deletion.

We now show that there is always at least one edge leading out of any tree or subtree explored by the agents that cannot be deleted by the adversary.

Let G_E be the explored portion of the graph. Let $G_{SD} = (V_{SD}, E_{SD})$ be the safe portion of the graph G_S after the adversary has performed all its deletions. Let $T = (V_T, E_T)$ be any tree or portion thereof, where $V_T \neq \emptyset$, built by the agents during the algorithm. We define a tree *border* edge as any safe edge connecting two safe nodes where one end is in the tree and one is not in the tree. Let the set of tree border edges be $E_{TF} = \{e \in E_S : e = [u, v] \wedge u \in V_T \wedge v \notin V_T\}$. For any such tree or subtree thereof that covers less than all the nodes, we show that there is a tree border edge that cannot be deleted.

Lemma 7. *For any tree or subtree $T \subseteq G_E$, where $V_T \subset V_S$, there is a safe edge $e \in E_{TF}$ such that $e \in E_{SD}$.*

Proof. By contradiction, assume that no such edge $e \in E_{TF} \cap E_{SD}$ exists. Since we have assumed that no edge is in E_{TF} and E_{SD}, the adversary deletes the all edges in E_{TF}. Since $V_T \subset V_S$, T cannot span the entire safe portion of the graph. As a result, the deletions of all the edges in E_{TF} disconnects T from the rest of the graph, contradicting our assumption that deletions do not disconnect the safe portion of the graph.

We now focus on work in the trees created by the agents. Each tree has an active root marker. We show that, with one exception, all tree border edges are marked for work in the tree's active root marker, being worked on, or become internal within finite time. The one exception comes as the result of the deletion of a tree link. For the links that become internal, we assume that there is an agent available to do the work that leads to this outcome. We show later that such an agent eventually becomes available.

When the adversary deletes a tree link, it creates a subtree in the tree where the deletion takes place, even if that subtree is only a single node. We call a subtree created in this way a *deletion subtree* and the tree to which the deleted edge currently belongs the *original tree.*

Let T_O be the original tree and T_S be the deletion subtree created by the deletion of tree edge e_D. Let E_{OS} be the tree border edges, if any, that connect T_O to T_S and E_{SO} be the same edges in the opposite direction. Let $E_{OS} = E_{SO} = \emptyset$, if the tree is not an original tree or a deletion subtree, respectively.

Lemma 8. *For any tree $T \subseteq G_E$ with an active root marker, where $V_T \subset V_S$, all edges $e \in E_{TF} \setminus E_{OS}$ are marked for work in T's active root marker, being worked on, or are marked as internal within finite time.*

We now consider what happens to the links in E_{OS}. The reason that they are not marked for work is because they are marked internal to T_O even though they are now external due to the deletion of e_D. By contrast, the links of E_{SO}, which are the same links as E_{OS} but in the opposite direction, are automatically marked for verification in T_S's active root marker. By construction, when an agent verifies an internal link, it only marks the link as internal in the passive root markers on its path if both ends are in the subtree rooted in the passive root marker; otherwise, the link remains marked for verification. The set E_{SO} are exactly those links in T_S that are internal to T_O before the deletion but were marked for verification in T_S's passive root marker when it became active.

We now prove that the links in E_{OS} are guaranteed to be marked for work in T_O's active root marker if there is previously reported work in T_S, there is an agent working in T_O, and there are no other connections to T_S; otherwise, there is no guarantee they are marked for work.

Lemma 9. *Let $e_W \in T_S \setminus E_{SO}$ be marked for work in T_S and let T_S have no agents working for it. Let an agent a in T_O choose to work on e_W. Within finite time, the links in E_{OS} are marked for work in the active root marker of T_O.*

This result suggests that there is two circumstances when a deletion subtree is never detected: the subtree contains no agents and no work except for the links in E_{SO}, or the subtree contains agents exploring frontier or black links and no other work except for the links in E_{SO}. We say such a deletion subtree is *empty.*

Lemma 10. *The links E_{OS} leading to an empty deletion subtree are never marked for work.*

These *empty* trees do not affect the correctness of the algorithm.

Lemma 11. *The failure to detect a deletion subtree with no other work than E_{SO} does not affect the correctness of the algorithm.*

The same is true of the deletion of non-tree links, although they can and do affect the complexity of the algorithm.

Lemma 12. *The deletion of a non-tree link does not stop the agent from completing its current work.*

We now need to deal with the assumption in Lemma 9 that there must be an agent in T_O that chooses to work on $e_W \in T_S$ in order to guarantee that the links in E_{OS} are marked for work and in Lemma 8 that there is an agent available to verify $[v, u]$ in the deletion subtree T_i, where $i \geq 1$. We show that before termination there must always be an agent working in the network and because that agent must eventually work on edges that cannot be deleted, every tree is eventually worked on.

Lemma 13. *At any time before termination, at least one agent is performing work.*

Corollary 1. *An agent is eventually available to do the work in T_O described in Lemma 9 and in deletion subtree T_i, where $i \geq 1$, described in Lemma 8.*

We can now prove the correctness of the algorithm.

Lemma 14. *Within finite time, all accessible links have been visited and all surviving agents terminate.*

Lemma 15. *After at most $O(k^2 \cdot n_S + n_S \cdot m + k \cdot n_S \cdot D)$ moves, all agents that are still alive terminate.*

The proof of the main result, Theorem 2, now follows.

References

[1] Balamohan, B., Flocchini, P., Miri, A., Santoro, N.: Time Optimal Algorithms for Black Hole Search in Rings. In: Wu, W., Daescu, O. (eds.) COCOA 2010, Part II. LNCS, vol. 6509, pp. 58–71. Springer, Heidelberg (2010)

[2] Balamohan, B., Flocchini, P., Miri, A., Santoro, N.: Improving the Optimal Bounds for Black Hole Search in Rings. In: Kosowski, A., Yamashita, M. (eds.) SIROCCO 2011. LNCS, vol. 6796, pp. 198–209. Springer, Heidelberg (2011)

[3] Chalopin, J., Das, S., Labourel, A., Markou, E.: Tight Bounds for Scattered Black Hole Search in a Ring. In: Kosowski, A., Yamashita, M. (eds.) SIROCCO 2011. LNCS, vol. 6796, pp. 186–197. Springer, Heidelberg (2011)

[4] Chalopin, J., Das, S., Santoro, N.: Rendezvous of Mobile Agents in Unknown Graphs with Faulty Links. In: Pelc, A. (ed.) DISC 2007. LNCS, vol. 4731, pp. 108–122. Springer, Heidelberg (2007)

[5] Cooper, C., Klasing, R., Radzik, T.: Searching for Black-Hole Faults in a Network Using Multiple Agents. In: Shvartsman, M.M.A.A. (ed.) OPODIS 2006. LNCS, vol. 4305, pp. 320–332. Springer, Heidelberg (2006)

[6] Czyzowicz, J., Dobrev, S., Královič, R., Miklík, S., Pardubská, D.: Black Hole Search in Directed Graphs. In: Kutten, S., Žerovnik, J. (eds.) SIROCCO 2009. LNCS, vol. 5869, pp. 182–194. Springer, Heidelberg (2010)

[7] Czyzowicz, J., Kowalski, D., Markou, E., Pelc, A.: Complexity of searching for a black hole. Fund. Inform. 71(2,3), 229–242 (2006)

[8] Dobrev, S., Flocchini, P., Královič, R., Ružička, P., Prencipe, G., Santoro, N.: Black hole search in common interconnection networks. Networks 47(2), 61–71 (2006)

[9] Dobrev, S., Flocchini, P., Prencipe, G., Santoro, N.: Searching for a black hole in arbitrary networks: Optimal mobile agents protocols. Distrib. Comput. 19(1), 1–19 (2006)

[10] Dobrev, S., Flocchini, P., Prencipe, G., Santoro, N.: Mobile search for a black hole in an anonymous ring. Algorithmica 48(1), 67–90 (2007)

[11] Flocchini, P., Ilcinkas, D., Santoro, N.: Ping pong in dangerous graphs: Optimal black hole search with pebbles. Algorithmica 62(3–4), 1006–1033 (2012)

[12] Flocchini, P., Kellett, M., Mason, P.C., Santoro, N.: Map construction and exploration by mobile agents scattered in a dangerous network. In: Proceedings of IPDPS (2009)

[13] Flocchini, P., Kellett, M., Mason, P.C., Santoro, N.: Searching for black holes in subways. Theory Comput. 50(1), 158–184 (2012)

[14] Glaus, P.: Locating a Black Hole without the Knowledge of Incoming Link. In: Dolev, S. (ed.) ALGOSENSORS 2009. LNCS, vol. 5804, pp. 128–138. Springer, Heidelberg (2009)

[15] Klasing, R., Markou, E., Radzik, T., Sarracco, F.: Hardness and approximation results for black hole search in arbitrary networks. Comput. Sci. 384(2-3), 201–221 (2007)

[16] Klasing, R., Markou, E., Radzik, T., Sarracco, F.: Approximation bounds for black hole search problems. Networks 52(4), 216–226 (2008)

[17] Kosowski, A., Navarra, A., Pinotti, C.M.: Synchronous black hole search in directed graphs. Theor. Comput. Sci. 412(41), 5752–5759 (2011)

[18] Královič, R., Miklík, S.: Periodic Data Retrieval Problem in Rings Containing a Malicious Host. In: Patt-Shamir, B., Ekim, T. (eds.) SIROCCO 2010. LNCS, vol. 6058, pp. 157–167. Springer, Heidelberg (2010)

[19] Miklík, S.: Exploration in faulty networks. Ph.d. thesis, Faculty of Mathematics, Physics, and Informatics, Comenius University, Bratislava, Slovakia (2010)

[20] Shannon, C.: Presentation of a maze-solving machine. In: Proceedings of the 8th Conference of the Josiah Macy Jr. Foundation (Cybernetics), pp. 173–180 (1951)

[21] Shi, W.: Black Hole Search with Tokens in Interconnected Networks. In: Guerraoui, R., Petit, F. (eds.) SSS 2009. LNCS, vol. 5873, pp. 670–682. Springer, Heidelberg (2009)

A Theory of Fault Recovery
for Component-Based Models*

Borzoo Bonakdarpour[1], Marius Bozga[2], and Gregor Gössler[3]

[1] School of Computer Science, University of Waterloo
borzoo@cs.uwaterloo.ca
[2] VERIMAG/CNRS, Gieres, France
marius.bozga@imag.fr
[3] INRIA-Grenoble, Montbonnot, France
gregor.goessler@inria.fr

Abstract. This paper introduces a theory of *fault recovery* for component-based models. We specify a model in terms of a set of atomic components incrementally composed and synchronized by a set of glue operators. We define what it means for such models to provide a recovery mechanism, so that the model converges to its normal behavior in the presence of faults (e.g., in self-stabilizing systems). We identify *corrector* components whose presence in a model is essential to guarantee recovery after the occurrence of faults. We also formalize component-based models that effectively *separate* recovery from functional concerns. We also show that any model that provides fault recovery can be transformed into an equivalent model, where functional and recovery tasks are modularized in different components.

Keywords: Fault-tolerance, Transformation, Separation of concerns, BIP.

1 Introduction

Fault-tolerance has always been an active line of research in design and implementation of *dependable* systems. Intuitively, tolerating faults involves providing a system with the means to handle unexpected defects, so that the system meets its specification even in the presence of faults. In this context, the notion of specification may vary depending upon the guarantees that the system must deliver in the presence of faults. Such guarantees can be broadly characterized by *safety* and *liveness* properties. For instance, dependable mission-critical systems often employ monitoring or control techniques to ensure safety properties in the presence of faults, and, provide a *recovery* mechanism to meet liveness properties, if the system reaches an unexpected state. *Self-stabilization* is a special type of fault-tolerance (largely concerned with liveness only), where a system always reaches a correct state no matter what state it is initialized with.

---

* This work is partially sponsored by Canada NSERC Discovery Grant 418396-2012.

A.W. Richa and C. Scheideler (Eds.): SSS 2012, LNCS 7596, pp. 314–328, 2012.
© Springer-Verlag Berlin Heidelberg 2012

The concept of fault-tolerance as described above addresses the overall behavior of the system and is independent of the structure the system. In order to associate fault-tolerance properties with the structure of a system and study their interdependence, one has to focus on a specific methodology. The *component-based* approach is a popular divide-and-conquer technique for designing and implementing large systems as well as for reasoning about their correctness. Ideally, in this approach, a system is designed incrementally by composing smaller components, each responsible for delivering a certain set of tasks to separate different concerns. Thus, component-based design and analysis of fault-tolerant systems is highly desirable in order to achieve systematic modularization of such systems.

We believe that we currently lack a formal approach that rigorously relates a component-based methodology with fault-tolerance/self-stabilization concerns. With this motivation, in this paper, we propose a novel formal framework for component-based design and analysis of *non-masking* models [2], where recovery and, hence, liveness is guaranteed in the presence of faults. We use the semantics of the BIP (Behavior, Interaction, Priority) framework [12] to specify components and their composition. In BIP, the *behavior* of an atomic component is specified by a labelled transition system. A model (i.e., a composite component) is represented as the composition of a set of atomic components by using two types of operators: *interactions* describing synchronization constraints between components, and *priorities* to specify scheduling constraints. Given a BIP model, the tool chain can automatically generate a stand-alone, distributed, real-time, multi-threaded, or synchronous C++ implementation that is correct-by-construction (i.e., by preserving functional semantics of the original model) [1,4,5,8]. Thus, our results in this paper can be applied in model-based design an analysis of component-based fault recovery for a wide range of settings such as in distributed systems.

Contributions. Our contributions in this paper are the following:

- We formally define non-masking fault-tolerance for atomic and composite components based on their observational behavior. This is different from the approach in [2], where fault-tolerance is defined based on reachability of predicates.
- We present a sufficient condition for *incrementally constructing* non-masking composite components by starting from a set of non-masking atomic components.
- Inspired by the work in [3], we define *corrector* components that establish a desirable observational behavior and show that the necessary condition for a composite component to be non-masking is to contain atomic or composite correctors. We also introduce the notion of *pure correctors* that only exhibit recovery behavior and do not participate in functional tasks of a composite component. We show that models containing pure correctors can effectively separate functional from recovery concerns and, hence, can be compositionally verified.

– Leveraging the separation of concerns supported by pure components, we provide an automated transformation of a component-based model into an equivalent model consisting of pure components whose behaviors are orthogonal: when a normal execution phase is interrupted by the occurrence of faults, control is transferred from the impacted functional components to corrector components in charge of fault handling and recovery, and handed back to the functional components once normal behavior is reestablished.

Organization. In Section 2, we present the preliminary concepts. Section 3 is dedicated to describe our fault model and the notion of fault recovery while Section 4 introduces our theory of component-based recovery. Then, in Section 5, we describe separation of recovery and functional concerns. Related work is discussed in Section 6. Finally, we make concluding remarks in Section 7.

2   Basic Semantic Models of BIP

Atomic Components. We define an *atomic component* as a transition system with a set of ports labeling individual transitions. These ports are used for communication between different components.

Definition 1. *An* atomic component B *is a labelled transition system represented by a tuple* $(Q, P, \rightarrow, q^0)$ *where*

– Q *is a set of* states,
– P *is a set of* communication ports,
– $\rightarrow \subseteq Q \times (P \cup \{\tau\}) \times Q$ *is a set of* transitions *including (1) observable transitions labelled by ports, and* unobservable τ *transitions, and*
– $q^0 \in Q$ *is the initial state.*

For any pair of states $q, q' \in Q$ and a port $p \in P \cup \{\tau\}$, we write $q \xrightarrow{p} q'$, iff $(q, p, q') \in \rightarrow$. When the label is irrelevant, we simply write $q \rightarrow q'$. Similarly, $q \xrightarrow{p}$ means that there exists $q' \in Q$, such that $q \xrightarrow{p} q'$. In this case, we say that p is *enabled* in state q. Figure 1(a) shows an atomic component B, where $Q = \{s, t\}$, $q^0 = s$, $P = \{p, q, r\}$, and $\rightarrow = \{(s, p, t), (t, q, s), (t, r, t)\}$.

A *trace* of a component $B = (Q, P, \rightarrow, q^0)$ is a finite or infinite sequence of ports $\pi = p_0 p_1 p_2 \cdots$, such that for all $i \geq 0$:

1. $p_i \in P \cup \{\tau\}$,
2. there exists state sequence $q_0 q_1 \cdots$, such that:
   – $q_0 = q^0$ (i.e., q_0 is the initial state), and
   – $q_0 \xrightarrow{p_0} q_1 \xrightarrow{p_1} q_2 \cdots$

For a trace $\pi = p_1 \cdots p_n$, by $q \xrightarrow{\pi} q'$, we denote $\exists q_1 \cdots q_{n-1} : q \xrightarrow{p_1} q_1 \xrightarrow{p_2} \cdots \xrightarrow{p_{n-1}} q_{n-1} \xrightarrow{p_n} q'$. The same concept applies for unobservable transitions (e.g., $q \xrightarrow{\tau^* \pi} q'$ is a trace that includes a prefix of τ-transitions and then suffix π).

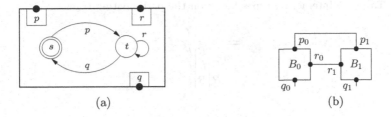

Fig. 1. A BIP atomic and composite component

Interaction For a given system built from a set of m atomic components $\{B_i = (Q_i, P_i, \rightarrow_i, q_i^0)\}_{i=1}^m$, we assume that their respective sets of ports are pairwise disjoint, i.e., for any two $i \neq j$ from $\{1..m\}$, we have $P_i \cap P_j = \emptyset$. We can therefore define the set $P = \bigcup_{i=1}^m P_i$ of all ports in the system. An *interaction* is a set $a \subseteq P$ of ports. When we write $a = \{p_i\}_{i \in I}$, we suppose that for $i \in I$, $p_i \in P_i$, where $I \subseteq \{1..m\}$.

Definition 2. *A* composite component *(or simply* model*) is defined by a composition operator parameterized by a set of interactions* $\gamma \subseteq 2^P$. $B \overset{def}{=} \gamma(B_1 \ldots B_m)$, *is a transition system* $(Q, \gamma, \rightarrow, q^0)$, *where* $Q = \bigotimes_{i=1}^m Q_i$, $q^0 = (q_1^0 \ldots q_m^0)$, *and* $\rightarrow$ *is the least set of transitions satisfying the rule*

$$\frac{a = \{p_i\}_{i \in I} \in \gamma \qquad \forall i \in I: \ q_i \overset{p_i}{\rightarrow}_i q_i' \qquad \forall i \notin I.\ q_i = q_i'}{(q_1, \ldots, q_m) \overset{a}{\rightarrow} (q_1', \ldots, q_m')}$$

In a composite component, τ-*transitions do not synchronize but execute in an interleaving fashion.*

The inference rule in Definition 2 says that a composite component $B = \gamma(B_1, \ldots, B_m)$ can execute an interaction $a \in \gamma$, iff for each port $p_i \in a$, the corresponding atomic component B_i can execute a transition labelled with p_i; the states of components that do not participate in the interaction stay unchanged.

In general, one can view a model $\gamma(\mathcal{B}_1, \mathcal{B}_2)$, where $\mathcal{B}_1$ and $\mathcal{B}_2$ are two sets of atomic components, as one component whose set of transitions is γ. Thus, $\gamma(\mathcal{B}_1, \mathcal{B}_2)$ denotes the composite component glued by γ, and, γ denotes the set of interactions of this composite component. In practice, atomic components are extended with variables. Transitions and interactions are associated with guards on variables. Also, interactions can transfer data.

Figure 1(b) illustrates a composite component $\gamma(B_0, B_1)$, where both B_0 and B_1 are identical to the component in Figure 1(a) and $\gamma = \{\{p_0, p_1\}, \{r_0, r_1\}, \{q_0\}, \{q_1\}\}$.

Similar to traces of an atomic component, a trace of a composite component $B = \gamma(B_1, \ldots, B_n)$ is a finite or infinite sequence of interactions $a_0 a_1 a_2 \cdots$, such that for all $i \geq 0$ (1) a_i is an interaction of γ, and (2) there exists states $q_0 q_1 \cdots$ of B, such that $q_0 = q^0$ and $q_0 \overset{a_0}{\rightarrow} q_1 \overset{a_1}{\rightarrow} q_2 \cdots$.

Table 1. Interaction types based on the participating transitions

$$
\begin{array}{c||c|c|c}
 & n & r & f \\
\hline\hline
n & N & R & F \\
f & F & F & F \\
r & R & R & F
\end{array}
$$

3   Fault Model and Fault Recovery

3.1   Fault Model

Let $B = (Q, P, \rightarrow, q^0)$ be an atomic component. We classify the observable transitions in $\rightarrow$ into the following three pairwise disjoint sets:

- A set $\rightarrow_n$ of observable *normal* transitions that embodies the normal execution of the component.
- A set $\rightarrow_f$ of observable *fault* transitions that expresses the faulty behavior of the component.
- A set $\rightarrow_r$ of observable *recovery* transitions that restore the normal behavior of the component or help other components to restore their normal behavior through participating in cross-component interactions.

Finally, $\rightarrow_\tau$ (i.e., τ-transitions of B) is the set of *unobservable fault* transitions and expresses the local faulty behavior of B. Intuitively, a component normally executes transitions in $\rightarrow_n$. However, faults in $\rightarrow_{f,\tau}$ may perturb the state of B to a state that may or may not be reachable by other transitions and in particular, $\rightarrow_n$.

Notation. Let $B = (Q, P, \rightarrow, q^0)$ be an atomic component. By $\rightarrow_x$, we denote the union of transitions of the types in x, where $x \in 2^{\{n,f,\tau,r\}}$. By B_x, we mean the component $(Q, P, \rightarrow_x, q^0)$ induced by transitions in x only.

Definition 3. *We say that $B = (Q, P, \rightarrow, q^0)$ is a* faulty component *if $\rightarrow_{f,\tau}$ is nonempty.*

Now, let $B = \gamma(B_1, \ldots, B_m)$ be a composite component. Observe that in an interaction $a = \{p_i\}_{i \in I}$ in γ, for any two $j \neq k$ in $\{1..m\}$, transitions $\xrightarrow{p_k}_k$ and $\xrightarrow{p_j}_j$ may belong to any of the above classes of transitions of their respective components. Thus, we define the type of interactions of a composite component as follows (see Table 1):

- Following Definition 2, an unobservable fault does not participate in an interaction; i.e., the corresponding component only takes a silent move from one state to another without synchronizing with other components.
- If an interaction consists of transitions of the same type, then the interaction type is equivalent to the type of participating transitions.

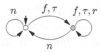

Fig. 2. Non-masking atomic component; the gray state models unstable period

- Otherwise, the type of the interaction is determined by the greatest type of the participating transitions in the total order $n < r < f$.

Thus, we partition interactions of $B = \gamma(B_1, \ldots, B_n)$ into γ_N, γ_R, and γ_F.

3.2 Fault Recovery

Arora and Gouda [2] formally define the *levels of fault-tolerance* based on combinations of meeting safety and liveness in the presence of faults. In this paper, our focus is on *non-masking* fault-tolerance. Non-masking systems are only concerned with ensuring liveness in the presence of faults by guaranteeing deadlock- and livelock-freedom through providing a finite-step *recovery* mechanism; i.e., the system always eventually reaches a good state even in the presence of faults. However, in such a system, when faults occur, safety may be temporarily violated during recovery, but not after the system reaches a good state.

Non-masking Atomic Components. We characterize fault recovery of an atomic component by ω-regular expressions based on the behavior of transition types identified in Subsection 3.1. For example, the ω-regular expression $f^* r n^\omega$ is the set of infinite traces of an atomic component where a finite number of observable fault transitions is followed by one recovery transition and an infinite sequence of normal transitions.

Definition 4. *We say that $B = (Q, P, \rightarrow, q^0)$ is a non-masking atomic component iff its set of traces satisfies the ω-regular expression $[n^*((f + \tau)r^*)^*n]^\omega$.*

The intuitive description of Definition 4 is the following (see Figure 2). If no faults occur, the program executes only normal transitions (i.e., the left state in Figure 2). If fault(s) occur, the component reaches a state from where execution of normal transitions is not possible (the gray state in Figure 2). In this case, we say that the component enters a finite *unstable* period (i.e., sub-trace $(f + \tau)r^*$). After a finite number of steps, the component recovers and only executes normal transitions again. Also, note that according to Definition 4 the number of occurrences of faults in each unstable period is finite. Observe that a non-masking component does not exhibit deadlock or livelock in the absence or presence of faults. Also, a non-masking component can use any recovery transition, be it safe or unsafe, to converge to its normal behavior.

Non-masking Composite Components. We characterize fault recovery of a composite component based on observational behavior of interaction types identified earlier; i.e., γ_N, γ_F, and γ_R. There is, however, an important difference between non-masking atomic and composite components. In a composite component, if a fault occurs in an atomic component, the fault may force a set of components to execute transitions other than their normal transitions, while a set of other atomic components can resume their normal operation. Thus, unlike non-masking atomic components, non-masking composite component may as well exhibit normal interactions in their unstable period.

Definition 5. *We say that $B = \gamma(B_0 \cdots B_m)$ is a non-masking composite component iff:*

1. *Its set of traces satisfies the following ω-regular expression:*
$$(N^*(F + R + N)^*N)^\omega .$$

2. *If a trace prefix of B ends with NR, then there exists an atomic component B_i, $0 \leq i \leq m$, such that projection of the prefix on B_i results in a local prefix that ends with $n\tau^+$.*

Intuitively, in Definition 5, traces of a non-masking composite component behave similarly to those of non-masking atomic components, except that normal interactions can also occur during the unstable period. Moreover, in a non-masking composite component if a recovery interaction occurs immediately after a normal interaction, then we require the existence of an atomic component in which an unobservable fault causes the execution of the recovery interaction. Notice that in Definition 5, we do not require that atomic components of a non-masking composite component should be non-masking as well. This is because we would like our definition to cover cases where an atomic component is not subject to faults locally, but it participates in recovery interactions in the composite component that contains other faulty atomic components.

3.3   Example

Figure 3 illustrates a component-based non-masking communication protocol. The behavior of the model is as follows. The component Sender sends a packet

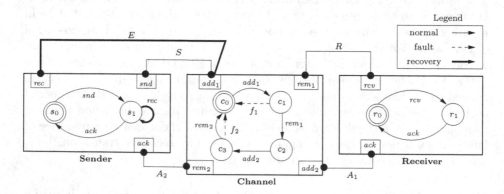

Fig. 3. A simple non-masking communication protocol

via port snd and receives the corresponding acknowledgement through port ack. Likewise, Receiver receives the sent packet through port rcv and sends an acknowledgement through port ack. By each transmission, component Channel adds an item to its single-space buffer (through ports add_1 and add_2) and by each delivery, the item is removed (via ports rem_1 and rem_2). Our channel is lossy and faults cause loss of the sent packet (i.e., transition f_1) or the acknowledgement (i.e., transition f_2). Both faults are unobservable faults (i.e., f_1 and f_2 are τ-transitions). Recovery involves re-transmitting the packet through the rec port in Sender. Thus, the classification of transitions is as follows:

- Sender: $\rightarrow_n = \{s_0 \xrightarrow{snd} s_1, s_1 \xrightarrow{ack} s_0\}$, $\rightarrow_f = \rightarrow_\tau = \emptyset$, $\rightarrow_r = \{s_1 \xrightarrow{rec} s_1\}$.
- Receiver: $\rightarrow_n = \{r_0 \xrightarrow{rcv} r_1, r_1 \xrightarrow{ack} r_0\}$, $\rightarrow_f = \rightarrow_\tau = \rightarrow_r = \emptyset$.
- Channel: $\rightarrow_n = \{c_0 \xrightarrow{add_1} c_1, c_1 \xrightarrow{rem_1} c_2, c_2 \xrightarrow{add_2} c_3, c_3 \xrightarrow{rem_2} c_0\}$,
  $\rightarrow_f = \rightarrow_r = \emptyset$, $\rightarrow_\tau = \{c_1 \longrightarrow c_0, c_3 \longrightarrow c_0\}$.

In the composite component $\gamma(\text{Sender}, \text{Channel}, \text{Receiver})$, interactions $\gamma = \{S, R, E, A_1, A_2\}$ synchronize the atomic components as follows. A transmission by Sender or Receiver is synchronized with adding the item to the buffer of Channel (i.e., interactions S and A_1, respectively). Likewise, delivery of the item to Sender or Receiver is synchronized with its removal by Channel (i.e., interactions A_2 and R, respectively). The recovery interaction E ensures re-transmission of the message if a fault occurs. Thus, we have: $\gamma_N = \{S, R, A_1, A_2\}$, $\gamma_R = \{E\}$, and $\gamma_F = \emptyset$. In the absence of faults the set of traces of the composite component satisfies expression: $(SRA_1A_2)^\omega$. In the presence of faults, one possible characterization of the model is the set of traces: $(SE^*RA_1(E^+RA_1)^*A_2)^\omega$.

Notice that recovery interaction E occurs after normal interactions S or A_1 only if a fault occurs in Channel. Also, although the model is non-masking, atomic component Sender is not non-masking, as it has traces with prefix $(snd.ack)^*.snd.rec$; i.e., Sender exhibits a recovery transition although no local fault has occurred. Another interesting observation in this example is that although all faults occur in component Channel, this component does not contain any recovery transitions. In fact, the only way for Channel to recover after the occurrence of a fault is by getting assistance from component Sender.

4   Correctors and Component-Based Recovery

4.1   Correctors

The concept of correctors is inspired by the work in [3, 7]. The definition of correctors in [3, 7] is based on correction of an invariant predicate, no matter how it is reached. Our definition of correctors in this paper is based on observation of recovery and normal transitions/interactions in atomic/composite components. In other words, our notion of correctors is tailored for component-based models.

Roughly speaking, a corrector is concerned with two types of transitions: recovery and normal. A corrector component ensures two properties: (1) once a fault occurs, the component somehow recovers and eventually exhibits normal behavior (i.e., recovery results in restoring the normal behavior), and (2) execution of normal transitions eventually stabilizes (i.e., once normal behavior is restored the component behaves normally unless another fault occurs).

Definition 6. *Let $B = (Q, P, \rightarrow, q^0)$ be an atomic component. We say that B is a corrector for the set $\rightarrow_n$ of normal transitions, if there exists the set $\rightarrow_r$ of recovery transitions, such that $\rightarrow_n \cap \rightarrow_r = \emptyset$ and any trace $\pi = p_0 p_1 \cdots$, where $p_i \in P$, satisfies the following two conditions:*

1. *(Progress) If there exists $i \geq 0$, such that transition $q_i \xrightarrow{p_i} q_{i+1}$ is not in $\rightarrow_{r,n}$, then there exists $j \geq i + 1$, such that $q_j \xrightarrow{p_j} q_{j+1}$ is in $\rightarrow_n$.*
2. *(Weak Stability) For all $i \geq 0$, if $q_i \xrightarrow{p_i} q_{i+1}$ is in $\rightarrow_n$, then $q_{i+1} \xrightarrow{p_{i+1}} q_{i+2}$ is either (1) in $\rightarrow_n$, or (2) not in $\rightarrow_{r,n}$.*

A *composite corrector component* is defined in the same fashion for interactions of types R and N. A composite component may be a corrector for a set of transitions local to one of its atomic components. Such correctors are of interest where a faulty component achieves recovery to its normal behavior by the help of a set of other components. The model presented in Subsection 3.3 is an example of such correctors.

Formally, let $B = \gamma(B_0 \cdots B_m)$ be a composite component and $B_i = (Q_i, P_i, \rightarrow_i, q_i^0)$, $0 \leq i \leq m$, be an atomic component. We say that B is a corrector for the set $\rightarrow_{i_n}$ of normal transitions of B_i if and only if by projecting any trace $\pi = a_0 a_1 \cdots$, where $a_j \in \gamma$ for all j, on component B_i and obtaining trace π', there exists recovery transitions $\rightarrow_{i_r}$, such that $\rightarrow_{i_r}$ and $\rightarrow_{i_n}$ satisfy Progress and Weak Stability.

In our example in Figure 3, component Channel is faulty and if fault f_1 or f_2 occurs the whole model (without recovery interactions) deadlocks. Component Sender provides the recovery mechanism, when a fault occurs. It is straightforward to observe that the composite component γ(Channel, Sender) acts as a corrector in the model for normal interactions of $\gamma_N(Sender, Channel)$ (γ is the set of interactions identified in Subsection 3.3), where $\gamma_R(Sender, Channel) = \{E\}$. Observe that our model allows delivery of duplicate messages, which may be considered as violation of safety. However, this is not an issue, since by definition, a non-masking model allows temporary violation of safety while recovering in the presence of faults. Observe that when the model recovers to its normal behavior, each packet is delivered only once.

4.2   Containment of Correctors in Non-masking Models

In this subsection, we show that the necessary condition for a model to be non-masking is to contain a subset of components that act a corrector for each components that is subject to faults. Recall that in Definition 5, we allowed components that do not interact with a faulty component to continue their normal behavior, while interacting components with the faulty component recover. We note that in our model, fault propagation is possible in the sense that components that do not interact with a faulty component may get involved in achieving recovery as well. In order to ensure that recovery makes progress in non-masking models, we assume that composite components are *weakly fair*.

Assumption 1. *Let $B = \gamma(B_0 \cdots B_m)$ be a composite component. We assume that if an interaction $\alpha \in \gamma$ is continuously enabled in a trace $\pi = a_0 a_1 \cdots$, then there exists $i \geq 0$, such that $a_i = \alpha$.*

Assumption 1 is necessary to show containment of correctors in non-masking models. The containment theorem is the following.

Theorem 1. *Let $B = \gamma(B_0 \cdots B_m)$ be a non-masking composite component. For each faulty atomic component $B_l = (Q_l, P_l, \rightarrow_l, q_l^0)$, where $0 \leq l \leq m$, there exists a set C of atomic components, such that $C \subseteq \{B_0 \cdots B_m\}$ and $\gamma(B_l, C)$ is a corrector for $\gamma_N(B_l, C)$.*

For example, in Figure 3, one obtains the composite corrector γ(Channel, Sender).

5   Separation of Functional and Recovery Concerns

In Subsection 5.1, we formally define the concept of pure correctors and discuss their role in a model that contains them. In Subsection 5.2, we show that any non-masking model can be transformed into another model that is observationally equivalent to the initial model and only contains pure components and, hence, separates functional from recovery concerns.

5.1   Pure Components and Their Role in Models

Roughly speaking, a *purely functional component* is one that is responsible for performing normal computational tasks of the containing composite component. Such a component may be subject to faults, but is not concerned with achieving fault recovery. On the contrary, a *pure corrector* is a component that only helps a system restoring the normal behavior through achieving recovery and it does not perform any functional tasks.

Definition 7. *Let $B = (Q, P, \rightarrow, q^0)$ be an atomic component. We say that B is* purely functional *iff its set of traces satisfies the ω-regular expression:*

$$((n + \tau)^*(f + r)n)^\omega.$$

Intuitively, in a purely functional component a sequence of normal and unobservable fault transitions may occur (see also the left automaton in Figure 4). Then, the component executes one fault or recovery transition (normally in order to synchronize with a corrector) and reach normal behavior. Obviously, if no fault occurs, a purely functional component continues executing normal transitions.

Fig. 4. Pure functional component (left) and corrector (right)

Definition 8. *Let $B = (Q, P, \rightarrow, q^0)$ be an atomic component. We say that B is a* pure corrector *for the set $\rightarrow_n$ of normal transitions, iff*

1. *B is a corrector for $\rightarrow_n$.*
2. *(Strong Stability) For any trace $\pi = p_0 p_1 \cdots$ of component B, for all $i \geq 0$, if $q_i \xrightarrow{p_i} q_{i+1}$ is in $\rightarrow_n$, then $q_{i+1} \xrightarrow{p_{i+1}} q_{i+2}$ is not in $\rightarrow_{n,r}$.*

Notice that in a pure corrector when a normal transition is executed, it does not execute any more normal transitions (see also the right automaton in Figure 4). This intuitively means that this normal transition marks the completion of recovery and the pure corrector stops working unless another fault occurs. Thus, we require that this normal transition synchronizes with some normal or recovery transition (normally a purely functional component) in the composite component. The left state of the functional component models periods of normal behavior or where no fault has been detected yet; the right state models a failure state where the pure functional component is inactive. Symmetrically, the left state of the pure corrector models a period of normal behavior where the corrector is inactive, and the right-hand side stands for an unstable period.

Theorem 2. *Let $B = \gamma(B_0 \cdots B_m)$ be a composite component and B_i, $0 \leq i \leq m$, be the one and only pure corrector in B. The set of traces of $\gamma_N(B_0 \cdots B_m)$ and $\gamma(B_{0_n} \cdots B_{i-1_n}, B_{i+1_n} \cdots B_{m_n})$ are equal.*

A trivial but important consequence of Theorem 2 is that pure correctors do not *interfere* with pure functional components.

Corollary 1. *Let $B = \gamma(B_0 \cdots B_m)$ be a composite component and $B_i = (Q_i, P_i, \rightarrow_i, q_i^0)$, $0 \leq i \leq m$, be the one and only pure corrector in B. Let $\pi = a_0 a_1 \cdots$ be a trace of B. If for all $j \geq 0$, $a_j \in \gamma_N$, then no interaction in π involves a port in P_i.*

The other side of the coin is that when a fault occurs in a purely functional faulty component, it stops working until recovery from the fault is complete.

Theorem 3. *Let $B = \gamma(B_0 \cdots B_m)$ be a composite component and B_i, $0 \leq i \leq m$, be the one and only purely functional atomic component in B. The set of traces of $\gamma_R(B_0 \cdots B_m)$ and $\gamma(B_{0_r} \cdots B_{i-1_r}, B_{i+1_r} \cdots B_{m_r})$ are equal.*

An immediate application of Corollary 1 and Theorem 3 is in compositional analysis of fault-tolerant systems. For instance, in order to verify the correctness of functional (respectively, recovery) properties of a non-masking composite component, one can simply remove pure correctors (respectively, functional components) from the model and verify the remaining composite component with respect to functional (respectively, recovery) properties. Such decomposition clearly assists in reducing the size of state space in the context of model checking.

5.2 Transforming a Non-masking Model to One That only Contains Pure Components

The goal of this section is to show that any non-masking model can be transformed into another model that behaves *equivalently*, but ensures separation of concerns by only containing pure components. To this end, we provide an algorithm that automatically transforms a non-masking component $B = \gamma(B_1, ..., B_n)$ into a non-masking component $B' = \gamma'(f(B_1), ...f(B_n), c(B_1), ..., c(B_n))$, such that all $f(B_i)$ (resp. $c(B_i)$) are purely functional (resp. pure corrector) components, and the behaviors of B and B' are related by a form of *bisimulation*. defined next.

Definition 9 ($\simeq$). *Let $B_i = (Q_i, \gamma_i, \rightarrow_i, q_i^0)$ with $\gamma_i \subseteq 2^{P_i}$, $i - 1, 2$. We define $\simeq \subseteq Q_1 \times Q_2$ as the largest relation such that*

1. *if $q_1 \simeq q_2$ and $q_1 \xrightarrow{\alpha_1}_1 q_1'$, then $\exists q_2' \in Q_2 \; \exists \alpha_2 \in \gamma_2 : q_2 \xrightarrow{\alpha_2}_2 q_2' \wedge q_1' \simeq q_2' \wedge \alpha_1 \cap P_2 = \alpha_2 \cap P_1$; and*
2. *if $q_1 \simeq q_2$ and $q_2 \xrightarrow{\alpha_2}_2 q_2'$, then $\exists q_1' \in Q_1 \; \exists \alpha_1 \in \gamma_1 : q_1 \xrightarrow{\alpha_1}_1 q_1' \wedge q_1' \simeq q_2' \wedge \alpha_1 \cap P_2 = \alpha_2 \cap P_1$.*

B_1 *and* B_2 *are* equivalent, *written* $B_1 \simeq B_2$, *if* $q_1^0 \simeq q_2^0$.

Intuitively, the transformation $\mathcal{T}r$ decomposes the behavior of each atomic component B_i into its normal sub-behavior and its unstable sub-behavior. A pure functional component $f(B_i)$ is then obtained by replacing the unstable behavior by a single state q^{T} that is reached by the first fault or recovery transition after a normal execution phase, and left again by the first normal transition after the unstable phase, as in Figure 4 (left). Similarly, a pure corrector $c(B_i)$ is obtained by replacing the normal behavior of B_i with a single state q^{N}, such that the obtained behavior refines Figure 4 (right). Both $f(B_i)$ and $c(B_i)$ interact on the transitions from and to q^{T} and q^{N} in such a way that the control is handed from $f(B_i)$ to $c(B_i)$ at the beginning of an unstable phase, and back to $f(B_i)$ again at the first normal transition.

Theorem 4. *If B is an atomic component, then $\gamma_B(f(B), c(B)) \simeq B$. If B is a composite component, then $\mathcal{T}r(B) \simeq B$.*

An immediate implication of Theorem 4 is that the output of our transformation results in a non-masking model.

Corollary 2. *If B is non-masking, then $\mathcal{T}r(B)$ is non-masking as well.*

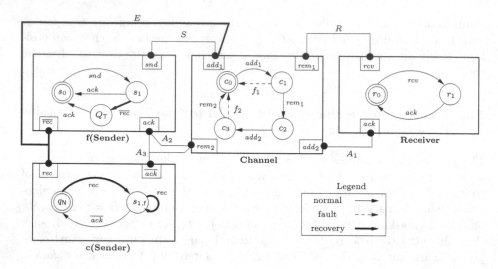

Fig. 5. Transformation applied to the communication protocol in Figure 3

Example 1. Applied to the communication protocol of Figure 3, we obtain the transformed protocol shown in Figure 5. In $f(Sender)$, q^T represents the unstable part of the behavior during which $c(Sender)$ has control. Conversely, during normal behavior $c(Sender)$ is in state q^N and inactive until the recovery interaction $\{rec, \overline{rec}, add_1\}$ is enabled. Maximal progress ensures that interaction $\{ack, rem_2\}$ is disabled whenever interaction $\{ack, \overline{ack}, rem_2\}$ is enabled.

In Figure 5, $f(Sender)$ is a purely functional component and $c(Sender)$ is a pure corrector. Since the original protocol is non-masking, the transformed protocol is non-masking by construction.

6   Related Work

Component-based analysis of fault-tolerant untimed models was first studied by Arora and Kulkarni [3]. They show that a fault-tolerant program that satisfies safety and liveness properties in the presence of faults can be decomposed into a fault-intolerant program and a set of components called detectors and correctors. Detectors ensure satisfaction of safety and correctors guarantee satisfaction of liveness properties in the presence of faults. In their work, a program is represented as a set of guarded commands in the shared memory model. Moreover, a detector (resp. corrector) component is defined based on state predicate detection (resp. correction) properties that a set of computations meets. In other words, unlike the results in this paper, the notion of a component in [3] does not resemble normal software modules, each having their own state space, behavior, and interface. The work in [3] is extended to the context of real-time systems by Bonakdarpour, Kulkarni, and Arora [7] and is enriched by introducing non-interference rules for compositional model checking in [6].

In [10], the authors propose a formal component model that incorporates the notion of a *safety* interface. This work is fundamentally different from our work in that we focus on recovery which implies guaranteeing liveness in the presence of faults. Lui and Joseph [15, 16] introduce a uniform framework for specifying, refining, and transforming programs that provide fault-tolerance and schedulability using the Temporal Logic of Actions [13]. Our work is different from [16] in that we focus on the structure and analysis of *component-based* programs that provide fault recovery. In particular, our transformation is fundamentally different in that we propose a method to separate fault recovery from functional properties. A survey of similar methods on monolithic systems is presented in [11]. Leal and Arora [14] describe a compositional approach to ensure stabilization. The approach relies on an acyclic dependency relation between components, which is a more high-level (less fine-grained) approach compared to ours. Finally, the approach proposed by Brukman and Dolev [9] is also more high-level than ours, where they introduce a generic proof scheme for recovery-oriented programming.

7 Conclusion

In this paper, we proposed a generic formal framework for specifying and reasoning about fault recovery (also called *non-masking* fault-tolerance) for component-based models. We characterized component-based models based on the BIP (Behavior, Interaction, Priority) framework [12]. However, our method is not limited to BIP. Unlike the approaches in [3, 7, 13, 15, 16] where a monolithic model is analyzed or components are defined in terms of properties of sets of computations, our method is based on observational behavior of a model in the presence of faults. Also, we use explicit components, each having its own private state space and behavior. We defined what it means for a component to be a *corrector* and showed that non-masking models must contain corrector components. These components correct the observational behavior of a faulty model and we illustrated they can be constructed as stand-alone components interacting with components that provide functional tasks. We described the application of this result in compositional model checking. Moreover, we illustrated that any non-masking model can be transformed into an equivalent model, where functional and recovery tasks are modularized in different components.

We plan to incorporate the results in this paper in our work on automated derivation of distributed implementation from BIP models [5], where fault-tolerance plays an important role. An interesting future research direction is developing methods that transform an arbitrary non-masking model into a well-structured model, where all atomic components are non-masking.

References

1. Abdellatif, T., Combaz, J., Sifakis, J.: Model-based implementation of real-time applications. In: ACM International Conference on Embedded Software (EMSOFT), pp. 229–238 (2010)

2. Arora, A., Gouda, M.G.: Closure and convergence: A foundation of fault-tolerant computing. IEEE Transactions on Software Engineering 19(11), 1015–1027 (1993)
3. Arora, A., Kulkarni, S.S.: Detectors and correctors: A theory of fault-tolerance components. In: International Conference on Distributed Computing Systems (ICDCS), pp. 436–443 (1998)
4. Basu, A., Bonakdarpour, B., Bozga, M., Sifakis, J.: Systematic Correct Construction of Self-stabilizing Systems: A Case Study. In: Dolev, S., Cobb, J., Fischer, M., Yung, M. (eds.) SSS 2010. LNCS, vol. 6366, pp. 4–18. Springer, Heidelberg (2010)
5. Bonakdarpour, B., Bozga, M., Jaber, M., Quilbeuf, J., Sifakis, J.: A framework for automated distributed implementation of component-based models. Springer Journal on Distributed Computing, DC (to appear, 2012)
6. Bonakdarpour, B., Kulkarni, S.S.: Compositional verification of real-time fault-tolerant programs. In: ACM International Conference on Embedded Software (EMSOFT), pp. 29–38 (2009)
7. Bonakdarpour, B., Kulkarni, S.S., Arora, A.: Disassembling real-time fault-tolerant programs. In: ACM International Conference on Embedded Software (EMSOFT), pp. 169–178 (2008)
8. Bozga, M., Sfyrla, V., Sifakis, J.: Modeling synchronous systems in BIP. In: ACM International Conference on Embedded Software (EMSOFT), pp. 77–86 (2009)
9. Brukman, O., Dolev, S.: Recovery oriented programming: runtime monitoring of safety and liveness. Springer Journal on Software Tools for Technology Transfer (STTT) 13(4), 377–395 (2011)
10. Elmqvist, J., Nadjm-Tehrani, S., Minea, M.: Safety Interfaces for Component-Based Systems. In: Winther, R., Gran, B.A., Dahll, G. (eds.) SAFECOMP 2005. LNCS, vol. 3688, pp. 246–260. Springer, Heidelberg (2005)
11. Gärtner, F.C.: Transformational approaches to the specification and verification of fault-tolerant systems: Formal background and classification. Journal of Universal Computer Science 5(10), 668–692 (1999)
12. Gössler, G., Sifakis, J.: Composition for component-based modeling. Sci. Comput. Program. 55(1-3), 161–183 (2005)
13. Lamport, L.: The temporal logic of actions. ACM Transactions on Programming Languages and Systems (TOPLAS) 16, 872–923 (1994)
14. Leal, W., Arora, A.: Scalable self-stabilization via composition. In: Distributed Computing Systems (ICDCS), pp. 12–21 (2004)
15. Liu, Z., Joseph, M.: Transformation of programs for fault-tolerance. Formal Aspects of Computing 4(5), 442–469 (1992)
16. Liu, Z., Joseph, M.: Specification and verification of fault-tolerance, timing, and scheduling. ACM Transactions on Programming Languages and Systems (TOPLAS) 21(1), 46–89 (1999)

Author Index